EMMET DALTON

EMMET DALTON

Somme Soldier, Irish General, Film Pioneer

SEAN BOYNE

MERRION
PRESS

First published in 2015 by Merrion Press
an imprint of Irish Academic Press
8 Chapel Lane
Sallins
Co. Kildare

British Library Cataloguing in Publication Data
An entry can be found on request

978-1-78537-074-8 (paper)
978-1-908928-96-2 (PDF)
978-1-908928-70-2 (mobi)

Library of Congress Cataloging in Publication Data
An entry can be found on request

Inside design by www.jminfotechindia.com

Cover design by www.phoenix-graphicdesign.com

Cover front: Emmet Dalton, taken outside 10 Downing Street, London, on the
morning of the first meeting between the Irish and British delegations, Anglo-Irish
Treaty talks, 11 October 1921. Photograph courtesy of Mercier Archives.

Cover back: Emmet Dalton (front row, right) at funeral of Michael Collins, with
General Richard Mulcahy (left) and Adjutant General Gearóid O'Sullivan (centre),
1922. Photograph courtesy of Audrey Dalton Simenz.

Printed and bound in Great Britain by TJ International Ltd, Padstow

Contents

Acknowledgements

I would like to thank all those who gave assistance with this book. In particular I would like to thank Emmet Dalton's daughter, Audrey Dalton Simenz, and his son, Richard F. Dalton for their invaluable help. I am also grateful to Robin Dalton for sharing memories of Emmet, her late father-in-law. (I should make it clear that while I had cooperation from members of the Dalton family, this is not an authorized biography, so any errors are my responsibility alone.)

My thanks to historian John Borgonovo for his editing work on the book.

I am most grateful to Louis O'Connell for giving me a lengthy interview and for access to important documents and photographs in his collection. Louis is the son of Sean O'Connell who, along with Emmet Dalton, comforted a dying Michael Collins after he was shot in an ambush at Bealnablath on 22 August 1922. The writer Ulick O'Connor, who knew Dalton well, was also most helpful. I made use of material and/or background information from people whom I interviewed in the past for other projects – one was the late Lieutenant Colonel Sean Clancy, who as a young officer knew Michael Collins and marched in the cortege at his funeral.

I would like to thank staff at the Irish Military Archives at Cathal Brugha Barracks, Dublin; staff at the National Library of Ireland and Seamus Helferty and his staff at the archives department at University College Dublin for facilitating my research and for their courtesy. I am grateful also to the National Library for permission to reproduce images. My thanks to staff at the National Archives in Kew for locating and forwarding the Dublin Castle file on Emmet Dalton. I wish to thank staff at the Dublin City Library, Pearse Street, and at my local library in Terenure, Dublin. My thanks also to Lar Joye, Alex Ward and Lisa O'Halpin of the National Museum of Ireland.

I would like to thank my friend and neighbour John Cooney for loaning rare books from his own extensive library, and for inviting me to speak on the subject of Emmet Dalton at the Humbert Summer School of which he is director. I am grateful for access to the archives of Hermitage Golf Club – I would like to thank Eddie Farrell, manager of Hermitage and Gerry Hogan, the club archivist and, of course, Liam Murray for his invaluable advice. In regard to the Hermitage research, my thanks also to Maurice Murray and Paddy McCrory.

Among others whom I would like to thank for their courtesy and assistance are Martin Brennan, Maurice Byrne, Vincent Caprani, Brian Chambers, Noel Coghlan, Ronnie Daly, Róisín de Buitléar, Jude Flynn, Godfrey Graham, Barry McGovern, Eithne McKeon, Michael Mulkerrin, John O'Connor, Kate O'Shea, Gerry Rowley, Philip Taubman, William Taubman and Dayna Woerner.

List of Abbreviations

AODB	Association of the Old Dublin Brigade
BMH	Bureau of Military History
CAB	Cabinet [Papers]
C-in-C	Commander-in-Chief
CLO	Chief Liaison Officer
Comdt	Commandant
CGS	Chief of General Staff
CS or C/S	Chief of Staff
DoD	Department of Defence
D/T	Director of Training
FJ	*Freeman's Journal*
GHQ	General Headquarters
GOC	General Officer Commanding
IE/MA	Ireland, Military Archives
IRA	Irish Republican Army
IRAO	IRA Organisation
IRB	Irish Republican Brotherhood
LE	Liaison & Evacuation [Papers]
MC	Military Cross
MP	Mulcahy Papers
MSPC	Military Service Pension Collection
NLI	National Library of Ireland
OC or O/C	Officer Commanding
OSS	Office of Strategic Services
RIC	Royal Irish Constabulary
SOE	Special Operations Executive
TNA	The National Archives (United Kingdom)
TD	Teachta Dála (deputy, Dáil Éireann)
UCDA	University College Dublin Archives
WO	War Office
WS	Witness Statement
W/T	Wireless/Telegraph

List of Plates

1. Emmet Dalton in his youth. Image courtesy of Audrey Dalton Simenz.

2. Emmet Dalton in British Army uniform with unidentified young man – possibly his half-brother Martin. Image courtesy of Audrey Dalton Simenz.

3. Members of D Coy 2nd Leinsters decorated for bravery, front row from left, Emmet Dalton MC, Sgt O'Neill VC, Capt Moran MC and Pte Moffat VC. At right, Lt Dorgan. Dhunn, Germany 9 Jan 1919. Image courtesy of Audrey Dalton Simenz.

4. Emmet Dalton and Michael Collins in London in 1921 during the Anglo-Irish Treaty talks. Image courtesy of Private Collection/Bridgeman Images.

5. Emmet and Charles Dalton in National Army uniform with their parents, James F. and Katherine Dalton and other siblings, from left, Nuala, Deirdre, Dermot and Brendan. Image courtesy of Audrey Dalton Simenz.

6. Shelling of Four Courts, Dublin, 1922 with artillery under command of Major General Emmet Dalton. Image courtesy of the National Library of Ireland.

7. Michael Collins, Commander-in-Chief, National Army (second from left) with Major General Emmet Dalton (third left) at Curragh Camp, August 1922. Also in photo, from left, Colonel Dunphy, Comdt. General Peadar MacMahon and Comdt. General Diarmuid O'Hegarty. Image courtesy of Getty Images.

8. Major General Emmet Dalton (left) with General Tom Ennis, and ship's officers, aboard one of the ships deployed for the Passage West landings. Image courtesy of the National Library of Ireland.

9. Emmet Dalton (front row, right) at funeral of Michael Collins, with General Richard Mulcahy (left) and Adjutant General Gearóid O'Sullivan (centre). Image courtesy of the National Library of Ireland.

10. Wedding of Major General Emmet Dalton and Alice Shannon at Imperial Hotel, Cork, 9 October 1922. Image courtesy of the National Library of Ireland.

11. Emmet Dalton and bride Alice on their wedding day. Image courtesy of the National Library of Ireland.

12. Emmet Dalton and children, from left, Richard, Nuala and Audrey, in the back garden of their home at Iona Road, Dublin. Image courtesy of Audrey Dalton Simenz.

13. Emmet Dalton, smoking a cigarette as he finishes a golf swing. Image courtesy of Audrey Dalton Simenz.

14. Dermot Dalton, in US Army uniform, with brothers Charles and Emmet at Leopardstown races, October 1945. Image courtesy of Audrey Dalton Simenz.

15. Emmet and Alice Dalton and family, 1945/46, in front row Nuala and Richard, at back from left, Sybil, Emmet Michael and Audrey. Image courtesy of Audrey Dalton Simenz.

16. Emmet and Alice Dalton at a film premiere in London. Image courtesy of Audrey Dalton Simenz.

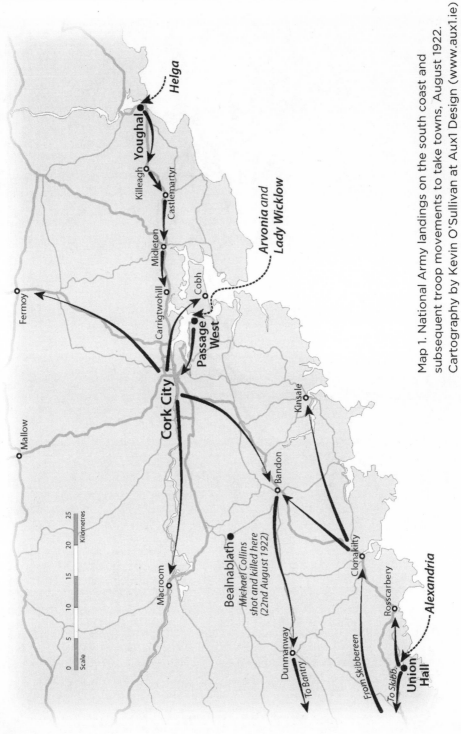

Map 1. National Army landings on the south coast and subsequent troop movements to take towns, August 1922. Cartography by Kevin O'Sullivan at Aux1 Design (www.aux1.ie)

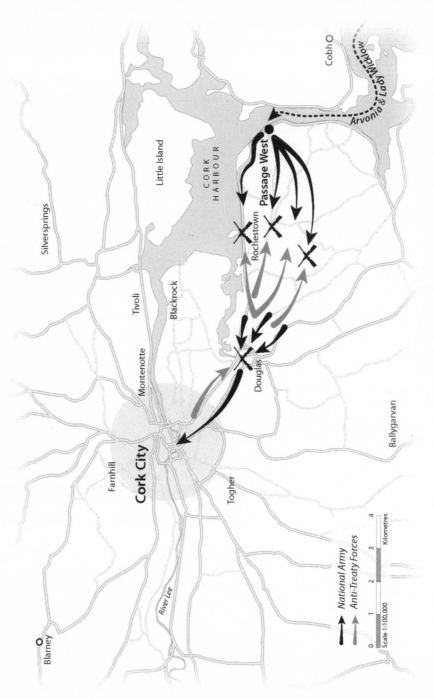

Map 2. National Army advances from Passage West towards
Cork, August 1922, opposed by anti-Treaty IRA forces.
Cartography by Kevin O'Sullivan at Aux1 Design (www.aux1.ie)

Introduction

My fascination with the story of Emmet Dalton goes back to my boyhood in 1950s Dublin. It was a drab, grey era, and it seemed to me that Dalton brought a touch of glamour and much-needed excitement to the austere Irish scene by founding Ardmore film studios near Bray, County Wicklow. My parents were great newspaper readers, we were also great cinema-goers, and I read exciting stories about Dalton's Ardmore venture attracting well-known film stars like James Cagney to Ireland to make movies. Dalton's own teenaged daughter, Audrey, had become a film star in Hollywood, and in the Irish media this was a great success story. It meant that 'one of our own' was appearing in films with some of the biggest names in the movie business.

It emerged that Emmet Dalton was a man with an intriguing military past. Sometimes the newspapers referred to him deferentially as Major General Dalton. I cannot recall when I learned that he had won an award for bravery while serving as a junior officer with the British Army in the First World War. The 1950s was an era when official nationalist Ireland seemed reluctant to acknowledge the role of the countless thousands of Irishmen who had fought in British uniform 'for the rights of small nations' during that conflict. But I do remember being utterly spellbound reading an interview with Dalton about an exploit during the subsequent Anglo-Irish War when he had thrown in his lot with the IRA. He told how he had bluffed his way into Mountjoy Prison in a hi-jacked armoured car in a vain attempt to rescue a notable IRA leader. The article was accompanied by a large photograph of Dalton, a handsome man with a neatly-clipped, military-style moustache. I thought that something of his calm air of authority and his qualities of leadership came through in that picture.

When the Irish republican movement split on the issue of the Anglo-Irish Treaty, Dalton stayed loyal to his friend, the charismatic pro-Treaty leader Michael Collins, known as the Big Fellow, whom he hero-worshipped. Collins, clearly impressed by Dalton's raw courage and his military experience, had brought him to London as an adviser during the difficult Treaty talks with the British. Back in the 1950s I was unaware that Michael Collins had died in his arms in an ambush at a remote valley near a place called Bealnablath during the Irish Civil War.

I eventually discovered that Dalton had been a student of the Christian Brothers at O'Connell School in Dublin where I was educated myself. Two of the older Brothers living at O'Connell's during my era had known Dalton well, I would later

1

discover – one was Brother William Allen. The ethos in the school was strongly nationalist and we were told much about Irish history, especially the 1916 rebellion and the depredations of the Black and Tans. A former teacher at the school, a quiet-spoken man called Joseph Tallon, was brought in by our teacher, An Bráthair Ó Flaitile, to tell us of his own role in the 1916 Rising. (Sadly, I can only remember one quote: 'We had all been to Confession, and we were all prepared to die.') So why were we not told about the exciting military adventures of this very distinguished past pupil, Emmet Dalton? I believe it was to do with the Irish Civil War – it was a taboo subject. This was understandable. When I first attended O'Connell's, it was only thirty years after the end of the 'brother against brother' conflict. Despite some reconciliation that had taken place, memories were still strong and emotional wounds were still raw. Former school friends at O'Connell's had fought on different sides and there was personal bitterness. I was astonished to learn that one of Dalton's former schoolmates had put him on a 'death list' during the war, to be shot at sight. In my ten years at O'Connell's, I don't believe I heard the words 'Irish Civil War' mentioned even once. As a result, it was only in later years that I began to learn about the remarkable story of Emmet Dalton.

As I talked to people who knew him and delved into the archives, a picture of a rather complex man emerged. He was a tough-minded soldier who in times of war could be a relentless fighter and was capable of making very hard decisions; he wanted to protect his men and he wanted his side to win. He was endowed with physical and moral courage, and at least one person talked of the element of 'steel' in his character. He had fine human qualities – he could be sensitive, kind and compassionate, was loyal to comrades and friends, and wrote poetry. He also had a forceful personality, exuded a sense of authority, and had the calm, self-assured air of a natural leader of men. He had a low tolerance for what he regarded as nonsense or subterfuge, and had a reputation for being stubborn. On the other hand, he had great charm and was a pleasant, congenial companion; people liked to be in his company, he was a great raconteur and he was noted for his dry sense of humour. It has been said that old-fashioned patriotism was one of the motives behind his efforts to establish an Irish film industry.

He was a believing Catholic all his life and in his final years took much consolation from his faith. However, some in the church may not have entirely approved of his sideline as a semi-professional gambler, betting heavily on the horses. For a period as a young man he drank heavily, before showing his usual self-discipline by giving up alcohol totally. Apart from some early marital difficulties due to his 'taking to the drink', he had a very happy marriage, and was much loved by his children and grandchildren. He loved sport, played soccer in his youth, and was a gifted golfer.

In addition to his other accomplishments, Dalton was one of the founding fathers of the Irish Defence Forces. It could be argued that he was one of the first members of the Volunteer force, that evolved into the Irish Army, to use an armoured car in an operation – albeit an armoured car hi-jacked from the British, as outlined above. He played a key role in procuring the first aircraft and recruiting the first two pilots for the unit that would develop into the Irish Air Corps. He oversaw the takeover from the British of military bases, some of which are in use by our Defence Forces to this day, and played an important role in training and recruitment as the new National Army took shape. He procured the first field guns for that force, and commanded the first artillery bombardment at the start of the Civil War. When he led a daring seaborne invasion of the south coast, pushing the anti-Treaty forces out of their bases in Cork city and county, one of the ships he deployed was a vessel that would later form the basis of a future Irish naval service. It was the most significant amphibious operation of the Civil War, an Irish mini-version of the D-Day landings, and it played a crucial role in turning the tide of war against the republicans. When he accomplished all this the 'boy general' of the Free Staters was only twenty-four years old. The more I discovered about this past pupil of O'Connell's the more interested I became. This biography is the result of that long-standing fascination with the life and times of Major General James Emmet Dalton (1898–1978).

CHAPTER ONE

Early Days

Emmet Dalton was born in the United States on 4 March 1898 to Irish-American parents who lived in Fall River, Massachusetts, a relatively prosperous mill town. Emmet's father, James Francis Dalton, was feisty and personable, and enthusiastically threw himself into work, business and politics. There were strong Irish connections in the family. James Francis's own father, James senior, was born in Galmoy, County Kilkenny in 1839, just a few years before the Great Famine that forced many Irish to seek refuge in America. James senior took the emigrant ship also, marrying another Irish immigrant, Laois-born Elizabeth Walsh, after settling in Rhode Island. Possibly influenced by the folk memory of the Famine, James F. was a fervent Irish nationalist, convinced that the Irish had suffered many wrongs inflicted by their English overlords. He was an enthusiastic supporter of Irish causes and would become immersed in the campaign for Home Rule.

Like other men of Irish background in the state of Massachusetts, James F. became active in the Democratic Party, and in the 1890s was a state committee man.[1] One of his contemporaries in the party was a man of similar background, John Francis Fitzgerald, known as 'Honey Fitz', whose parents were also Irish-born. Both men loved sport, especially baseball, and James F. was a director of the Fall River Baseball Association. Fitzgerald would go on to become the Mayor of Boston and an extremely powerful figure in Boston politics – his grandson, John Fitzgerald Kennedy, would become President of the United States. With his energy, drive and affability, James F. might also have carved out a career for himself in Massachusetts politics but he was destined to take a different path in life.

When he was in his late twenties, James F. decided on a great adventure – he would leave America, and return with his family to the land of his ancestors. By now, James F. had been married twice, and had two sons. His first wife was Bridget Heffernon, and they had a son, Martin Joseph. After Bridget died, apparently in childbirth, James F. at age 28, married again, this time his bride being Katherine

Lee Riley (20), who was born in Somerset, Massachusetts where her family were farmers. The marriage register lists James F. as a manager by profession, while his bride is described as a stenographer.[2] Katherine was also of Irish-American background: her mother's maiden name was Margaret Cronin; her father's name was Charley Riley. Both parents had been born in Ireland.

The couple were married in Somerset on 2 June 1897 by a Catholic priest, and their son James Emmet Dalton, was born the following year.[3] According to the city birth register, the family then lived in Fall River. The boy was called after the Irish patriot, Robert Emmet, who had the same birthday, 4 March. Robert Emmet, born in 1778, was executed in Dublin in 1803 after an abortive rebellion against British rule. By coincidence, there happened to be an infamous individual with a similar name who was in the news during the 1890s. This was Emmett Dalton, an outlaw in the American Old West who became notorious as an armed robber and member of the Dalton Gang. However, there is little doubt that the baby was called after the patriot rather than the bandit, even though the entry in the Fall River birth register is rendered as 'James E. Dalton', thus giving less emphasis to the 'Emmet' element in the name. The father's occupation is given as 'salesman'.

James F. moved to Dublin, Ireland around 1900, where he went into business. It is unclear if he tried to seek out relations in County Kilkenny. When he had settled in, he sent for his wife Katherine, who set off for Ireland with their infant son Emmet and James's son Martin J. from his first marriage.[4] Arriving in Dublin, they soon moved into the new house that James F. Dalton had acquired for his family. It was in a new housing estate at Drumcondra, with green fields nearby, in an area that was then on the edge of the city. It was a time when Dublin was in the throes of preparations for a visit by Queen Victoria to the city, in April 1900. Young Emmet was most impressed by the colourful uniforms of the soldiers, and this would form one of his earliest memories.

Over the years James F. Dalton would pursue various business projects. He ran a fashionable laundry for a period, the Central Laundry at 60 South William Street, in a genteel area of the south city. He later went into the insurance business, and became an importer and manufacturer's agent, with an office at 15 Wicklow Street. After settling in Dublin, the family quickly expanded. The 1911 census returns show that the family resided at 8 St Columba's Road Upper, Drumcondra. The redbrick two-storey terraced house, with a small front garden, on a quiet residential street, just off Iona Road, is still there. James F. Dalton (42) is described as 'Head of Family', and the manager of a laundry company. His wife is listed as Katherine L. Dalton (34). The census returns record they were both born in the United States and married for 14 years. The family's religion is given as 'Roman Catholic'. Details are provided of four sons and a daughter. The eldest son, Martin J. Dalton, is described as a student at the National University. He is listed as being able to speak Irish and English, the result, no doubt, of an Irish education. Also listed as having been born in the United States, and able to speak Irish and English, is J. Emmet Dalton (13). The remaining children were born in Dublin city. Charles Francis, eight years old at the time, was born in 1903, and no doubt named after his mother's father Charles Riley. Eileen, aged six, was born in 1906 – she would pass away at age nine. The baby in the family at the time of the census was Brendan Ignatius, aged one.

The family was prosperous enough to have a live-in servant, as many of the better-off middle-class Dublin families had in that era – she is listed in the census returns as Mary A. Coughlan (21), a native of Dublin. The couple went on to have other children: Nuala was born in 1913 and became a nun; Deirdre was born in 1916 and Dermot Patrick arrived in 1919. The parents had an obvious preference for traditional Irish names. In all, James F. Dalton fathered eight children, the most famous being Emmet. With his natural air of authority, James was given a nickname within the family – he was known as 'The Sir'.

Drumcondra, like its neighbouring area Glasnevin, enjoyed the seclusion and amenities of a genteel suburb on the edge of Dublin, but was close to the city centre, with its theatres and other amusements. The trams ran along nearby Drumcondra Road, where the Catholic Archbishop of Dublin ruled from an imposing palace behind high walls. There were fields nearby earmarked for housing, and the open countryside was within walking distance. At Finglas Bridge, on the edge of the cemetery lands, boys could swim during the summer in the shallow waters of the Tolka. Dublin's notorious slums and infamous 'Monto' red light district did not impinge on the tranquility of life in Drumcondra.

For a boy interested in sport, the Dalton home was ideally located. In one direction, a few minutes' walk away, there was Croke Park, premier stadium of the Gaelic Athletic Association (GAA), and scene of the All-Ireland senior football and hurling finals every year. In another direction, again within walking distance of the Dalton home, there was located in Phibsboro the stadium known as Dalymount Park, home of Bohemians soccer club, popularly known as 'Bohs'. In that era, on a quiet evening when a match was in progress, locals living within a few miles radius of the stadium could hear the 'Dalymount Roar' as the assembled Dubs cheered a goal or a save. Emmet Dalton would become a regular at Dalymount, both as a player and later as a spectator.

As a devoutly Catholic family, the Daltons would have appreciated the reassuring proximity of the Church of Saint Columba, a grey, granite edifice in Romanesque style, completed in 1905. The church would cater for the spiritual needs of the residents of the new suburbs of Drumcondra and Glasnevin. For the Daltons, daily Mass and Communion, and the nightly Rosary, formed part of their routine. Not too far away from their home, on the other side of the Royal Canal, was the grim outline of the Victorian-era Mountjoy Prison, behind grey, stone walls. From some of the cell windows facing east, one could see St. Columba's church. The prison would also figure in the story of Emmet Dalton.

The family men who lived in this middle-class Drumcondra/Glasnevin suburb of redbrick houses included businessmen, civil servants and clerical workers. Living almost around the corner, at 7 Iona Drive, were the Malleys. They lived in a grander house than the Daltons. Luke Malley was a civil servant, a clerk in the Law Department of the Congested Districts Board (which had a poverty relief role). He and his wife Marion had a large family. One of their sons, Ernie, aged 13 at the time of the census, just like his neighbour Emmet Dalton, would later take the more Gaelic, more romantic version of the surname, O'Malley.[5] He would also figure prominently in the story of Emmet Dalton.

O'Connell School

Emmet was first sent for schooling to the Holy Faith nuns at Glasnevin. Then he went on to O'Connell School (also known as Scoil Uí Chonaill), located on North Richmond Street, just off the North Circular Road. Emmet's brother Charlie would also be educated there, as would Ernie O'Malley, starting in 1907. O'Malley described O'Connell's as 'a fairly good school where we rubbed shoulders with all classes and conditions'.[6] O'Connell School was the most historic of the Christian Brother establishments in Dublin. The foundation stone of the school was laid in June 1828 by Daniel O'Connell, the charismatic leader of the movement for Catholic Emancipation. Apart from inculcating a strong Catholic religious faith, the Brothers were also noted for promoting Irish nationalism and culture, with a particular emphasis on the Irish language.

It has been estimated that about 130 past pupils of O'Connell's took part in the 1916 Easter Rising. One of them, Seán T. O'Kelly, later became President of Ireland. Three of the executed leaders of the Rising were former students of the school – Sean Heuston, Eamonn Ceannt and Con Colbert. Former O'Connell School boys fought in the War of Independence and they were to be found on opposite sides in the Irish Civil War which followed. The writer and theatre critic Gabriel Fallon has recorded that among his 'close companions' at O'Connell's were Emmet Dalton, Noel Lemass and Ernie O'Malley.[7] They were all around the same age. Noel's brother Sean, later to become Taoiseach, was also at O'Connell's around this time, and Emmet knew the Lemass brothers well. O'Malley was close enough to Emmet's younger brother Charlie to entrust him with his books when, in March 1918, he took a break from his medical studies to leave home and organize for the Irish Volunteers in the 1918 election.[8] One of the teachers at O'Connell's who knew Dalton well was Brother William Allen, who would later be noted for his unique collection of rare historical documents, books and artifacts, including arms from Ireland's revolutionary period donated by former pupils.

James F. Dalton, Activist and Organizer

After setting up home in Dublin, Emmet's father, James F. Dalton, threw himself into the political and business life of his adopted city. He became active in nationalist organizations such as the United Irish League and the Ancient Order of Hibernians. He demonstrated his devotion to Irish history by picking shamrock from the tomb of Daniel O'Connell in Glasnevin Cemetery and sending it back to his home town of Fall River. Close on a half century later shamrock based on that original plant was still being grown in Fall River, in a munici-pal greenhouse.[9] Politically, James was a constitutional nationalist, supporting the Irish Parliamentary Party (IPP) led by John Redmond, which was campaigning for Home Rule and which had made some progress towards that goal through its activities in the parliament at Westminster. Yet it was still under the cloud of its spectacular split in 1890–91 following the marriage of party leader Charles Stewart Parnell to a divorcee. But party unity was re-established in 1900 under John Redmond, who came from a noted County Wexford family of Catholic gentry.

James F. Dalton kept a large picture of party leader John Redmond over the mantelpiece in the sitting room of his Drumcondra home. As an extremely hardworking activist for the IPP, James F. made a considerable impact in nationalist circles in Dublin. Perhaps because of his experiences with the Democratic Party in America, he took an active part in committees and fund-raising work linked to the nationalist cause. He proved an extremely good events organizer. Likeable and energetic, he had the ability to win friends. He became friendly with luminaries of the party such as the Belfast-born MP Joe Devlin, a noted orator and skilled political organizer; Willie Redmond MP, a brother of the party leader; and Tom Kettle, poet, journalist, barrister and academic, who had served as an MP up to 1910. Devlin and Kettle would visit the Dalton home to socialize and sometimes play cards. While still a schoolboy, Emmet came to know some of the prominent people in the Home Rule movement.

James F. Dalton was held in such high esteem by those involved in the Home Rule movement that he was the guest of honour at a banquet given for him at the Gresham Hotel on 21 December 1911. The dinner sold out, and senior figures in the IPP were present, including Willie Redmond and Tom Kettle. Though Joe Devlin was unwell, he still made sure to turn up at the Gresham to pay tribute to his friend. Dalton was presented with an illuminated address by an Irish Party activist, Lawrence Wickham, a member of Blackrock Urban Council, in recognition of his work for the 'National Cause'. The address referred to the 'sacrifices' made by Dalton, his 'unselfish patriotism' and the 'great personal regard in which he is held'. The address also referred to his 'almost unique faculty of attracting universal friendship'.

During his address, Tom Kettle said that the most brilliant student that he knew in their Dublin College was a son – Martin J. Dalton – of their guest that night. Joe Devlin said of James F. Dalton, that 'no more loyal friend, no more affectionate comrade' had ever appeared in Ireland. Touched by the occasion, James F. warmly thanked the attendees. 'It has often been told to you by our leaders and others who have visited this great Republic of the West, of the love that is borne not only by the exiles, but also by the children of the exiles, for Ireland. I am proud to say, as the son of an exile, that I intensely love this dear old land...'

It was not surprising that Martin Dalton had come to the notice of Tom Kettle. Apart from being a 'brilliant student' at UCD, Martin was also active in the college's renowned debating society, the Literary and Historical Society, known as the L&H. Kettle had once held the prestigious position of auditor of the society. Martin helped Arthur Cox secure election for auditor in 1913 over the future Taoiseach, John A. Costello. Cox later became a prominent solicitor and ultimately a Catholic priest. He recalled that Martin 'learned much of his politics from his father, organizer of the Irish Parliamentary Party', and 'steered me to victory'.[10]

James F. Dalton helped to organize a massive Home Rule rally held in Dublin on 31 March 1912, with son Martin coordinating the attendance of university students.[11] Dalton senior also played a key role in organizing the elaborate welcome given by the IPP to British Prime Minister Herbert Asquith when he visited Dublin in July 1912 to support Home Rule. The Liberal leader was shepherding a Home Rule Bill through Parliament, and was given a rapturous reception in Dublin, driving through the city in an open-topped carriage with John Redmond. As Organizing Secretary of the Reception Committee, James F. attended a reception for Asquith in the Gresham Hotel. Through his father's activities, Emmet would have gained some understanding of the Home Rule politics of the day.

As he became a citizen of some prominence in Dublin, James F. Dalton became a Justice of the Peace (JP), and went into the insurance business. In 1913 he helped launch the Catholic and General Assurance Association Limited, becoming a director along with luminaries such as the Earl of Orkney.[12] An office was set up at 22 Westmoreland Street and Dalton was on a very good salary of £500 a year. Unfortunately this arrangement ended in acrimony. In early 1916 he launched a legal action in the Dublin courts against his former employer for unfair dismissal, though in April the company settled the case.[13]

Cistercian College, Roscrea

After primary education at O'Connell's, it might have been expected that young Emmet would continue his secondary education at the school. However, in 1912, he was sent away to a boarding school run by monks in County Tipperary. In his retirement, Brother Allen told a story to a friend about the background to Emmet's change of school.[14] The Brothers had installed a new instrument at O'Connell's – a telephone. The Superior of the community, Brother John A. O'Mahony, a man in his sixties, wanted to test the instrument and decided to make a telephone call. One of the few families he knew with a telephone was Emmet Dalton's family. He called the Dalton home in nearby Drumcondra and Mrs Dalton answered. He introduced himself and said he was sorry to hear that influenza had invaded her home. There was a pause, and Mrs Dalton asked, 'Do you have the right family, Brother? There is no influenza in my house. Both Emmet and Charlie went to school this morning.' It was now the Brother's turn to be taken aback. He said only one boy, Charlie arrived at school and this boy apologized for Emmet's absence due to influenza. Alarmed by this information, Emmet's parents carried out inquiries. It emerged that Emmet had been regularly indulging in truancy from school, or 'mitching' as he described it himself in later life, using a traditional Dublin expression.[15] As a result, his parents decided to send him away to boarding school. Looking back on his school days, he said he was not a brilliant student, but was able to pass examinations. He was mainly inclined towards sport and athletics, implying that he was not enormously interested in academic subjects. Referring to his 'mitching', he reckoned he was a 'difficult pupil'.

Emmet was sent for secondary education to the Cistercian College, Roscrea, set in countryside more than 80 miles from Dublin. It was a more exclusive

establishment than O'Connell's, and perhaps more exotic as well. The college had
been set up a few years earlier, in 1905. Travel to the school entailed a lengthy train
journey from Dublin. The extra expense involved in sending 14-year-old Emmet
to such a school would suggest a certain affluence on the part of his father at this
period. The boarding school, which is still in operation, is run by the monks of
Mount St. Joseph Abbey. They belong to the contemplative Order of Cistercians
of the Strict Observance (OCSO). The school, located in an imposing, grey stone
building set in green, wooded countryside, provided a striking contrast to the
urban environment which Dalton had hitherto experienced. In later life, Dalton
talked with affection of his days at O'Connell's, where he said he had received
'brilliant' teaching. But he was also taken with Roscrea, where he felt inspired by
the Cistercian monks he encountered. In old age, he would talk of the many happy
days he had at Roscrea, and his pride at being associated with the various people he
met there, and the example set by the monks' life of 'unselfish devotion'.[16]

Irish Volunteers

With his nationalist background, it was not surprising that Emmet was among the
4,000 who joined the Irish Volunteers, at the inaugural meeting in the Rotunda
Rink in Dublin in November 1913.[17] James F. Dalton became heavily involved in
the movement, as did his friend Tom Kettle. The organization had been founded by
Gaelic scholar Eoin MacNeill, in response to the formation of the Ulster Volunteer
Force by Ulster Unionists opposed to Irish Home Rule. The bill to enact this
legislative autonomy for Ireland was then working its way through the House of
Commons. Many nationalists were not yet ready to accept the idea that the Ulster
Protestants might be regarded as a separate people entitled to self-determination.

In April 1914 the UVF raised the level of tension on the island of Ireland
by landing 25,000 rifles at Larne, Bangor and Donaghadee. On 26 July a small
consignment of about 900 Mauser rifles was landed by the Irish Volunteers very
publicly at Howth, County Dublin from the yacht Asgard skippered by the writer
Erskine Childers. Authorities attempted to capture the rifles landed at Howth; a
small number seized by the police were returned later as they had been confiscated
illegally. Soldiers from a detachment of the King's Own Scottish Borderers had
been involved in an unsuccessful attempt to seize the rifles. When they were jeered
by a crowd at Bachelor's Walk in Dublin city centre some soldiers lost control and
opened fire, killing three civilians and wounding dozens. The deployment of the
military that led to the shooting aroused considerable outrage throughout Ireland.
James F. Dalton attended a meeting of Dublin City magistrates who protested at the
military being called out.[18]

In June, James F. Dalton was one of twenty-seven nominees submitted by
John Redmond to join the ruling Provisional Committee of the Irish Volunteers.
However, the outbreak of the Great War in August 1914 quickly split the Volunteer
movement. To avoid a civil war, the British government placed Home Rule on the
statute book, but postponed its implementation until the end of the war. On 20
September IPP leader John Redmond made a historic speech in Woodenbridge,

County Wicklow, where he declared it was in Ireland's interest for the Volunteers to enlist in the British forces and fight in the war in defence 'of right, of freedom, and religion'. He reasoned that Irish nationalists by fighting in the war alongside Ulster Unionists, would ensure Irish unity when Home Rule was enacted. He also envisaged that the Volunteers who joined the British forces would form the nucleus of a future Irish army that would secure the unity of Ireland. Militant nationalists opposed participating in the war effort, and this split the Irish Volunteer movement. The anti-Redmond element were in a minority and continued to be known as the Irish Volunteers, led by Eoin MacNeill. The vast majority, however, followed Redmond and became known as the National Volunteers. By this time the revolutionary Irish Republican Brotherhood had secretly manoeuvred itself into key controlling positions within the Irish Volunteers and was seeking to capitalize on England's difficulty by using the Irish Volunteers in an uprising against British rule.

James F. Dalton served on the national committee of the new National Volunteers as the militia raised funds, built its organization and armed its members. At a meeting in Dublin City Hall on 30 September 1914, James seconded the motion making Willie Redmond MP (younger brother of John Redmond) one of the Honorary Treasurers.[19] Willie Redmond would later die in British uniform during the Great War. Among the others on hand that night was James's friend, Tom Kettle. Kettle had been in Belgium to procure arms for the Volunteer movement when the war broke out. Like Willie Redmond, he also died in the war. He would be comforted in his dying moments at the Somme by James's son, Emmet.

James F. Dalton had helped supply arms to the Volunteer movement. Patrick Moylett, a businessman from County Mayo, later described how he bought rifles from James Dalton during an arms-buying trip to Dublin in 1914. The arms were to equip local Volunteers in his home town of Ballyhaunis. Probably acting on behalf of the Volunteers, Dalton provided six Mausers of the 1896 Spanish model pattern, and one 1877 Mauser for a total of £25.[20] The transaction seems to have occurred after the outbreak of the Great War in August, possibly before the split in the movement, which would explain Dalton's dealing with Moylett, who affiliated himself to the militant Irish Volunteer group.

Although only about sixteen years old, Emmet Dalton was given the task by his father of delivering the rifles across Ireland to County Mayo. Emmet later recalled the delivery of the heavy parcel, wrapped in sack cloth, to his family home.[21] James Dalton saw his son off on the train at Kingsbridge station for the journey to Ballyhaunis. For a youth of such tender years, it was a challenging assignment. The police could become suspicious and, besides, Emmet could barely lift the heavy parcel. Emmet was wearing his Christian Brothers school cap and this may have helped convey an image of innocence that allayed any suspicions. Dalton senior helped his son heave the package onto the luggage rack of the train.

Moylett stated that a week after he paid for the weapons, Emmet arrived at his business premises in Ballyhaunis with the six rifles, but no ammunition. Moylett had managed to get some ammunition from Belfast from another unlikely source – an Orangeman – but it was only about 25 rounds. 'I took Emmet Dalton and my foreman, Pat Kennedy, who was in the Volunteers, to the police rifle range and we did our practice openly.'[22] Clearly, even as a schoolboy, Emmet knew how to fire a rifle – a useful accomplishment in light of his later military career. Moylett recalled that Emmet told him that he was 18 years of age [sic] and that John Redmond was getting him a commission in the British Army. 'His statement made me sad because it cut straight across what he was doing. I tried to persuade him not to join, but I was not successful.' Moylett became a senior figure in the Irish Republican Brotherhood during the War of Independence, though he took no part in the Civil War.

Emmet Dalton Joins the British Army

In late 1915, Emmet Dalton, aged 17, joined the British Army. He showed considerable independence of spirit and sense of adventure by doing so without consulting his parents. He was said to have been a student of 'great ability' at the college in Roscrea, and he reportedly gained a scholarship to the Royal College of Science but abandoned it to go into the British forces.[23] He was following the call of his father's great idol, John Redmond, who had encouraged the Volunteer movement and Irishmen generally to fight for Britain in the Great War. Dalton later reminisced that the overwhelming majority of the Irish people at this time supported the action being taken by John Redmond and his followers in the National Volunteers. He was imbued with the same feeling of patriotism that existed all around. There was also the glamour of going to war: 'I mean, at eighteen years of age, what do you know?'[24]

His enlistment was assisted by his father's friend, Joe Devlin MP. Devlin gave him a letter of introduction to a man who was in charge of recruiting and who had an office on Grafton Street, Dublin. So far as Dalton could recall, the man's name was Macartney Filgate.[25] Dalton called to the recruiting office, and applied for a temporary commission in the British Army. Dalton lied about his age, claiming to be 18 years old.[26] He received a letter dated 29 December 1915 from the War Office, London appointing him a to a 'temporary Second-Lieutenancy in the New Army (on probation)', posted to the 7th Service Battalion, Royal Dublin Fusiliers. He was required to attend a class of instruction at Cork, and was to present himself, without fail, to the Commandant, School of Instruction, Garrison Office, Cork in one week. He was instructed to report in uniform, but if his uniform was not ready, to report in plain clothes. In a rather parsimonious tone, the letter added: 'Expenses incurred in travelling to join on first appointment must be paid by yourself.'[27]

During the interviews for a 1978 RTÉ TV documentary, Cathal O'Shannon asked Dalton if in joining the British Army he felt he was fighting for Britain, or fighting for Ireland, or for little Belgium? Dalton replied that he was fighting for all three. The 'Irish Brigade' subscribed to the idea of fighting for small countries. They all felt sympathetic to Belgium. Dalton also agreed that in joining the army he was motivated partly by a sense of adventure.[28]

Dalton's father was utterly dismayed when Emmet turned up at the family home in British Army uniform. As an avid supporter of John Redmond, James Dalton probably backed Redmond's call on the Volunteers to join the British Army. At the very least, he had not distanced himself publicly from Redmond's policy. But he was still shocked when he saw his son in the uniform of the King's forces, and his basic Irish nationalist emotions came into play. Emmet's mother was also upset. Emmet managed to calm them down and they came to accept their son's decision. Emmet duly set off for Cork and underwent a course for young trainee officers for about a month at the city's Victoria Barracks. He received further training in Kilworth camp, near Fermoy, County Cork.

Military commissions were formally announced in the British government journal *London Gazette*. The supplement for the edition of 8 January 1916 recorded that, on the first of the month, James Emmet Dalton, had been appointed temporary Second Lieutenant (on probation) with the Royal Dublin Fusiliers (RDF). He was one of many young men from his north Dublin neighbourhood who joined the RDF early in the Great War. One was Frank Malley, older brother of Dalton's school contemporary, Ernie O'Malley. Frank later served with the King's African Rifles, and died in what is now Tanzania.[29]

While Emmet was still undergoing training in Cork, a momentous event took place in Dublin. On Easter Monday 1916, the more militant element of the Irish Volunteers staged the Rising, which utterly transformed the Irish political situation for generations. Organized by members of the Irish Republican Brotherhood, the 1916 Rising was the most significant insurrection against British rule since the 1798 rebellion. The fighting was mainly confined to Dublin where the Irish Volunteers and members of the smaller socialist organization, the Irish Citizen Army seized a number of key buildings, the most iconic being the General Post Office (GPO). Fighting continued for the next six days.

As soon as he learned of the rebellion, James F. Dalton's practical instincts came into play. He instructed his wife to lay in provisions and to buy two hundredweight (101.6 kg) of flour as nobody knew how long the trouble would last. Knowing instinctively that his 13-year-old son Charlie would want to go into town and see what was happening, James F. forbade the boy to go anywhere near the fighting. All Charlie's sympathies were with the rebels and as he recalled later, he would have loved to help with the fight. He was disgusted to see women coming out of their homes to give jugs of tea to British soldiers.[30]

Many Irishmen serving in the British Army were still in Ireland when the rebellion broke out. They must have found themselves in a dilemma, as they had joined to fight for the rights of small nations – not to fight their fellow Irishmen. Many families also found themselves in an equivocal situation – having one son in the British Army and another son involved with or sympathetic to the rebel forces. Charlie Dalton stated that during Easter Week, before going to bed, the family gathered as usual to say the Rosary and to 'pray for the Volunteers'.[31] At the same time it is clear that despite their nationalist proclivities, the Daltons would have remained steadfastly loyal to Charlie's brother Emmet who was now with the Royal Dublin Fusiliers.

A few days after the start of the rebellion, Charlie was talking to his mother when the windows of the house shook with the sound of a deafening explosion – they later discovered that the British gunboat *Helga* had sailed up the River Liffey to shell buildings which were believed to be occupied by rebels. Towards the end of a week of fighting, Charlie was upstairs with his family saying the Rosary, when he saw a red glow in the sky in the direction of the city centre.[32] A man passing by the house the following day said the GPO had caught fire and that the Volunteers had surrendered – he had seen them lined up on the street. Charlie was greatly disappointed at the news. Among the many captured insurgents was an extroverted young man from County Cork, named Michael Collins. All prisoners were released by June 1917.

After the fighting ended, Charlie went into Dublin city centre and walked amid the ruins. He later explained that in his patriotic fervor he wanted to make contact with others who felt the same as he did. He went to one of the Requiem Masses for the dead at the Church of St Mary of the Angels on Church Street, run by the Capuchin Franciscans. He found there what he was looking for. Outside the church he saw an older schoolmate from O'Connell's, Ernie O'Malley, singing rebel songs.[33] Like the Daltons, the O'Malleys had a foot in both camps – Ernie O'Malley had fought with the rebels in the Rising and would later become a prominent IRA leader, while, as previously indicated, his brother Frank was in the British Army. Charlie Dalton recalled that 'we were horrified' at the news of the execution of the Rising leaders.[34] The shooting by firing squad of men such as Pádraig Pearse, his brother Willie and James Connolly, engendered great sympathy for the rebel cause. This accelerated the rise of the separatist Sinn Fein movement and helped to sound the death knell for John Redmond's Irish Parliamentary Party.

Emmet Dalton said in his RTÉ interview with Cathal O'Shannon that when he heard of the Rising his reaction was the same as most of the recruits who were with him in Kilworth Camp, he was surprised, annoyed, and thought it was madness. He felt the rebels represented only a 'tiny minority' at that time, 'and we were the overwhelming majority represented by our people in Parliament...' However, he made it clear that if he had been asked to oppose the rebels in arms, that would be a 'different situation', implying that he would not fight against his fellow-countrymen. In Dublin, Irish troops were among the British soldiers deployed against the rebels, and a number of Dublin Fusiliers were killed. There is no record of any mutiny among them when they were were sent in to suppress the rebellion.

It has been suggested that Emmet Dalton was one of the army cadets who formed part of the British forces that were mobilized for security duties in County Wexford at the time of the rebellion. Because of a shortage of garrison troops, trainee officers, part of the Young Officers Corps at Fermoy, were given rifles and full service kit. They were then sent to County Wexford to guard a munitions factory and other strategic points, and to round up suspects.[35] Fortunately none of them was required to open fire on the insurgents. The Wexford Rising was, in fact, a rather 'gentle' rebellion; although a large number of Volunteers turned out, there was no fighting and nobody was killed. Colonel French, the local commander of the British forces, took a 'softly softly' approach and this helped to resolve the situation without bloodshed. A young man, Francis Carty (a future editor of the *Sunday Press*), lived in Wexford town at the time of the Rising. He later fought with the IRA in the War of Independence and Civil War. He remembered the arrival of a force of cadets in Wexford with a larger number of British troops. He added in his statement to the BMH: 'I think that Emmet Dalton was one of these cadets.'[36]

Richard Mulcahy, IRA Chief of Staff during the War of Independence, claimed that Dalton took the rebel surrender at Enniscorthy in 1916. Mulcahy made the claim in 1927 at an election rally, as a way of praising Dalton for his transformation from a British Army officer who once confronted Irish rebels to a rebel hero of the War of Independence.[37] However, Mulcahy's account raises the question – would a cadet or trainee junior officer be the person deployed to take the surrender of a rebel leader? The leader of the Wexford insurgents, Robert Brennan, told the Bureau of Military History that he surrendered to the British commander, Colonel French.[38]

While brave and idealistic, the insurgents of 1916 did not have an electoral mandate. The party that Irish nationalists voted for in overwhelming numbers was John Redmond's Irish Parliamentary Party. As a result, Dalton and others who followed Redmond's call to join the British Army in the First World War believed that in doing so they were expressing the will of the Irish people. The execution of the leaders of the rebellion helped to swing public sympathy towards the Volunteers' separatist cause, and to divert support away from the Redmondites. In a 1977 interview, Dalton reflected that the general attitude of the Irish people at that time was changed by 'the execution of the leaders perpetrated by the British for no valid reason'.[39]

Referring to the Rising itself, he considered the insurrection a hopeless gamble because it had no hope of success. He could not envision the leaders had ever believed in achieving military victory. He told how his contemporaries at the time looked askance at the Rising. 'They did not see it the way one sees it now...' Nevertheless, Dalton appeared to harbour a suspicion that the measure of independence Ireland ultimately achieved with the 1921 Anglo-Irish Treaty could have been secured peacefully had the 1916 Rising not occurred. In a telling quote, he remarked: 'I think it [the Rising] should never have happened. I think if it had not happened the Home Rule Bill ... could have been achieved, and I don't see that there was a whale of a difference between the Home Rule Bill at that time and the Treaty as it was subsequently accepted.'[40]

Dalton also recognized the galvanizing effect of the British government's attempt to introduce conscription in Ireland in 1918. That move was widely opposed by all elements of nationalist Ireland, including the Irish Parliamentary Party, and was later abandoned. Dalton told RTÉ interviewer Pádraig Ó Raghallaigh that he believed the move to impose conscription had an 'extraordinary effect'. He said the Irish people stood solid against conscription, and he recalled the petition signatures and protests outside the churches on Sundays.[41]

Despite Dalton's doubts and misgivings about the 1916 rebellion, he was destined to serve with the IRA in the War of Independence and, after the Truce, to be a member of Michael Collins's entourage during the talks in late 1921 that resulted in the Anglo-Irish Treaty, but in the meantime he would undergo the horror of the trenches as a young British Army officer in the Great War.

CHAPTER TWO

The Great War

In the high summer of 1916, the Battle of the Somme was raging in France. This great Allied offensive against the German lines was set to become the bloodiest encounter ever experienced by the British Army in its long history. The fighting at the Somme had been in progress for a couple of weeks when, back in Ireland, on 15 July, 18-year-old Emmet Dalton passed his military examinations. He was judged to be an officer who was qualified for active service with the 7th Battalion of the Royal Dublin Fusiliers (RDF). The following month 2nd Lieutenant Dalton was sent to France. The scale of the carnage meant that the British war machine required a constant supply of young men like Dalton to be hurled into the maelstrom. Soon, the teenaged officer would find himself in the firing line in a major offensive. Having lied about his age on joining up, it appears he continued with the subterfuge. In the official booklet given to each officer, the Officer's Record of Services, his date of birth is given as 4 March 1896, instead of 1898 – adding two years to his real age.[1]

In early September Dalton was transferred to the 9th Battalion, RDF, attached to the 48th Irish Brigade. The 48th brigade was part of the 16th (Irish) Division, commanded by Major General W.B. Hickie. Many of the officers and men in the Division were Redmondites, supporters of Home Rule. Like Dalton, there were those who had been shocked and horrified at the news of the Easter Rising in Dublin. The men of the Division were up against a formidable German foe who had already killed many of their comrades, and it seemed to some of them that the rebels back in Dublin had thrown in their lot with this enemy.

For a young man far from home in a dangerous, challenging environment, it can be very reassuring to encounter a familiar, friendly face. Dalton was delighted to meet, among the officers of the 9th, his father's friend Tom Kettle. The former Irish Party MP had forsaken his post as Professor of National Economy for the rather more dangerous role of a company commander with the Royal Dublin Fusiliers. Noted for his eloquence and his scholarship, he had achieved considerable prominence in the Nationalist movement and his father was a co-founder of the Land League.

The 9th Battalion was about to take part in a major offensive to capture what remained of the town of Ginchy. In the few days they were to have together in the advance trenches before the Ginchy operation, Emmet Dalton and Tom Kettle became firm friends, despite the age gap between them. Kettle was 36 years old – twice Dalton's age. Dalton found Kettle to be a 'very charming and delightful man'. Dalton recalled sitting with him just before the movement up to the front line for the offensive. 'He recited to me a poem that he had written to his daughter, and he had it written down in a field notebook.' Dalton said it was a 'delightful little poem'.[2] *To My Daughter Betty, The Gift of God* would become one of the most memorable poems to emerge from the Great War.

Kettle could have avoided the assault on Ginchy in which he was to die but he chose to stay with his men. On the night before his battalion moved up to the Somme, Kettle wrote a letter to a friend saying that he had two chances of leaving – one on account of sickness and the other to take a staff appointment. 'I have chosen to stay with my comrades,' he wrote. 'The bombardment, destruction and bloodshed are beyond all imagination. Nor did I ever think that valour of simple men could be quite as beautiful as that of my Dublin Fusiliers.'[3] The extent of the bloodletting was brought home to Dalton in a chilling manner when he was walking along a trench. The ground seemed soft and soggy with what appeared to be stones here and there, and he kept slipping. He mentioned the stones underfoot to a sergeant who informed him that they were not stones – they were the remains of men killed in previous fighting.[4]

The Germans had a firm grip on Ginchy, and British commander Field Marshal Douglas Haig was determined that it would be captured. Previous attempts had been made to seize Ginchy by 7 Division, and they had come from the same direction, Delville Wood. The forces of 7 Division were withdrawn after suffering massive casualties. Now the British top brass decided to attack from another direction, from the south, throwing the 16th (Irish) Division into the fray. The Irish would attack from the newly-captured area around Guillemont. They would also mount an assault in greater strength than 7 Division. The weather was unfavourable – rain was falling. However, good fortune would favour the Irish, in that two new German divisions had been deployed in the sector and effective communications had not been established between them. As a result, the forces holding Ginchy lacked support.[5] This lack of coordination helped give the Irish the edge as they advanced, supported by artillery. Nevertheless, the attacking forces would suffer very heavy casualties.

Death of Tom Kettle

Dalton later recalled how he and Tom Kettle were both in the trenches at Trones Wood, opposite Guillemont, on the morning of 8 September 1916.[6] The mood was sombre. Their battalion had sustained heavy casualties from German shellfire the day before, losing about 200 men and seven officers. As they talked, an orderly arrived with a note for each officer: 'Be in readiness. Battalion will take up A and

B position in front of Guinchy [Ginchy] tonight at 12 midnight.' Kettle was in command of B Company while Dalton was second-in-command of A Company.

Dalton recalled in a letter: 'I was with Tom when he advanced to the position that night, and the stench of the dead that covered our road was so awful that we both used some foot-powder on our faces. When we reached our objective we dug ourselves in, and then, at five o'clock p.m. on the 9th, we attacked Guinchy' [sic]'.[7] It is unclear why the attack was timed for so late in the day. It may have been intended to deprive the enemy of sufficient daylight time to organize a counter-attack. It may also have been because the enemy expected a normal dawn offensive starting time.

The massed ranks of British artillery opened a rolling barrage as the Dubs left their trenches. Dalton recalled the moment that Kettle was hit.[8]

> I was just behind Tom when we went over the top. He was in a bent position, and a bullet got over a steel waistcoat that he wore and entered his heart. Well, he only lasted about one minute, and he had my crucifix in his hands. Then Boyd[9] took all the papers and things out of Tom's pockets in order to keep them for Mrs. Kettle, but poor Boyd was blown to atoms in a few minutes. The Welsh Guards buried Mr. Kettle's remains. Tom's death has been a big blow to the regiment, and I am afraid that I could not put in words my feelings on the subject.

In another letter Dalton wrote: 'Mr. Kettle died a grand and holy death — the death of a soldier and a true Christian.'[10] It is said that when Kettle's aged father Andrew heard the news that his son was missing in action, he responded: 'If Tom is dead, I don't want to live any longer.' True to his word, within two weeks he himself joined his son in death, passing away at eighty-three years of age.

Although there was no trace of the personal possessions that Tom Kettle had with him when killed, happily the poem that he wrote a few days before the battle survived. Perhaps fearing that the end was near, Kettle had written *To My Daughter Betty, The Gift of God* for his young daughter Elizabeth, born on 31 January 1913. The final, poignant lines are still regularly quoted:

> Know that we fools, now with the foolish dead,
> Died not for Flag, nor King, nor Emperor,
> But for a dream, born in a herdsman's shed,
> And for the Secret Scripture of the poor.

Dalton's daughter Audrey told the author that her father carried a copy of that poem in his wallet with him all his life, until the day he died.

The 8th and 9th battalions of the Dublin Fusiliers led the assault through Ginchy, their objective being the German support trench on the northern outskirts. The town, on a hill, had been well fortified by German engineers. It was defended by the 19th Bavarian Regiment, which had only recently arrived in the sector and was not fully familiar with the positions it was required to hold. About 200 of the German enemy surrendered, while others ran, pursued by the attackers. It was said that because of the loss of so many of their officers, the Irish soldiers, in hot pursuit of the enemy, carried on beyond the objective, and had to be brought back. Eventually the Irish consolidated their positions around the town.

Dalton's 9th Battalion suffered heavy losses in the attack on Ginchy. Many of the officers were killed or wounded, and Dalton, one of the most junior of the officers, had to take command of two companies – or what was left of the companies. He deployed these as best he could and sent a runner with a message back to command HQ that they were now in control of Ginchy. The order came back that they were to hold their position. The capture of Ginchy gave the 16th Division a prominent salient in the German lines, and it was only a matter of time before the Germans mounted a counter-attack. Bavarian infantry came in on the offensive at 18:20 and 21:00 and met stiff Irish resistance.

As Dalton and his men came under heavy fire, he deployed machine gun teams in key locations to discourage the enemy, even managing to take prisoners after he came face-to-face with enemy forces after dark. Dalton and his men held out until relieved after twenty-four hours by a battalion of the Welsh Guards. Dalton and another officer, 2nd Lieutenant Nicholas Hurst, a noted rugby player from a Church of Ireland family in Bantry, County Cork, were the only officers of the 9th Dublins to walk out of the battle relatively unscathed. The rest were killed, wounded or missing.[11] In the aftermath of the battle Dalton served as acting Captain.

For his actions on the day of Ginchy battle, Dalton was later awarded the Military Cross – his nickname afterwards would be 'Ginchy'. The full citation reads:

> At the capture of Guinchy [*sic*], on the 9th of September, 1916, he displayed great bravery and leadership in action. When, owing to the loss of officers, the men of two companies were left without leaders, he took command and led these companies to their final objective. After the withdrawal of another brigade and [while] the right flank of his battalion was in the rear, he carried out the protection of the flank, under intense fire, by the employment of machine-guns in selected commanding and successive positions. After dark, whilst going about supervising the consolidation of the position, he, with only one sergeant escorting, found himself confronted by a party of the enemy, consisting of one officer and twenty men. By his prompt determination the party were overawed and, after a few shots, threw up their arms and surrendered.

Many years later, Dalton would remember Ginchy as 'sad ... a glorious victory with terrific losses'.[12] The 16th Division suffered very heavy casualties in the period 3 September to 9 September – 224 officers and 4,090 men killed or wounded.[13]

Dalton was wounded in the fighting and was to spend time in hospital in France. While Dalton's father may have had misgivings about him joining the British Army in the first place, he seems to have had a considerable sense of pride about his son being injured heroically in the war against the Germans. A notice in the *Irish Independent* on 21 September 1916, that appeared to have been placed by the family, declared: 'Lieut. Emmet Dalton, Dublins, wounded, is a son of Mr J.F. Dalton J.P., 8 Upper St. Columba's road, and 2, Talbot St., Dublin.' The notice was accompanied by a photograph of a youthful Dalton in military uniform, sporting a military-style moustache.

Dalton received treatment for his wounds at The Liverpool Merchants Hospital at Étaples, France. It was one of a number of military hospitals situated in a sprawling base camp near the old town and port of Étaples, which lies at the mouth of the River Canche, in the Pas de Calais region of Picardy. He was one of the officers to receive a letter from a distraught Mrs Mary Kettle seeking details about her husband's death, and the possible location of his remains. On 14 October Dalton replied to Mrs Kettle, apologizing for the delay in answering the letter. 'I presume by now that you are utterly disgusted with me for failing to reply to your letter, but I assure you that if I had been in a fit condition I would have replied before now.' He described the last moments of Tom Kettle, clearly trying to be as sensitive and consoling as possible.

Although an articulate man, decades later, in his RTÉ interview with Cathal O'Shannon, Dalton would struggle to find the words to convey the horrors of the Battle of the Somme: 'It would be very hard to describe the Somme – I don't know if there has ever been a battle like it.' The butcher's bill for this long-running fight was enormous. It has been recorded that between 1 July and mid-November 1916, the British Army suffered a massive 432,000 casualties – an average of 3,600 for every day of the blood-soaked encounter.

Return to Dublin

Dalton, no doubt to the great relief of his family, was stationed in Dublin for a period following his treatment in hospital. His mother, in particular, fussed over him, sewing leather cuffs onto the sleeves of his uniform.[14] By early 1917, Dalton was attached to the 4th Battalion, RDF as an instructor in a musketry course. This was located at Bull Island, off the north Dublin suburbs of Clontarf and Dollymount, which was commandeered by the British Army in 1914 for a military training ground. A School of Musketry was established there complete with rifle ranges and facilities to teach trench warfare tactics. The clubhouse of the Royal Dublin Golf Club was taken over as quarters for officers. Dalton had probably established a reputation as a marksman to be selected as an instructor for this particular course.

In March, Dalton worked as an instructor on another course in his home city – an anti-gas attack course at the Irish Command School, Dublin. Both sides in the war mounted gas attacks, inflicting heavy casualties, and causing much fear and trepidation among troops targeted by chemical weapons.

Awarding of Military Medal by King George

A few weeks after giving the anti-gas course, Dalton travelled to London to collect his award for bravery from the British crown. On 2 May 1917, at Buckingham

Palace, King George V awarded a range of decorations to members of the British Army and Commonwealth forces, ranging from the Distinguished Service Cross to the Military Cross. Among the approximately seventy military personnel who received the Military Cross, there were just two from Irish regiments – Second Lieutenant Richard Marriott Watson, Royal Irish Rifles, and Second Lieutenant Emmet Dalton, of the Royal Dublin Fusiliers.[15] Dalton's luck held out and he would, of course, survive the war. Marriott-Watson, a poet and only son of the Australian-born writer, Henry Brereton Marriott-Watson, was killed the following March during the retreat from St. Quentin.

Decades later, Dalton reminisced to an American friend about the day he was presented with the Military Cross. Even though he had opposed the Easter Rising, it appears that nationalist sentiment engendered by the Rising had been having an effect on Dalton. The execution of the leaders, and their bravery in facing death, had stirred up public sympathy. He privately told journalist Howard Taubman about his feelings during the ceremony held in the presence of the King at Buckingham Palace. According to Taubman, the protocol was that when the riband with the Military Cross was hung around his neck, Dalton was to bow from the waist down in deference to the King. Thinking about the Easter Rebellion the previous year, he decided not to make the obeisance, and stayed standing ramrod straight in defiance of the court etiquette The moment the last presentation had been made, Dalton bolted from the room and left the palace.[16]

Dalton was promoted from 2nd Lieutenant to Lieutenant on 1 July 1917, and just over a week later was deployed abroad to Salonika, where allied forces were engaged in hostilities with the Bulgarians. He was now with the 6th Battalion, Leinster Regiment, having been transferred from the Royal Dublin Fusiliers. The Prince of Wales' Leinster Regiment had its home depot at Crinkill Barracks, Birr, in the Irish midlands, and drew its recruits largely from counties such as Longford, Westmeath, Offaly (King's County) and Laois (Queen's County). The regiment had been in the thick of the fighting at Gallipoli.

Bulgaria, which occupied a strategic position in the region, had entered the war on the side of the Central Powers, attacking Serbia in October 1915. The 10th (Irish) Division was among the Allied formations deployed to the region. The 6th and 1st Battalions of the Leinster Regiment were located in the Struma Valley. During his service in Salonika, Lieutenant Dalton, like many other Irish soldiers, contracted malaria. While in a rest camp he encountered a Scotsman who had been a professional golfer. The Scot instilled in Dalton an interest in golf that would develop into a life-long passion.[17] However, his first opportunity to test his skills on the green would come in an unlikely place, Egypt, a country not then noted for its golfing facilities.

War in the Middle East

In September 1917, the 10th (Irish) Division moved from Salonika to Egypt for service in the Middle East. The British top brass had decided that it was more urgent to confront the Turks in Palestine than the Bulgarians. It was on 14 September that men from the 6th Leinsters embarked on the steamer *Huntsgreen*. Five days later, after an uneventful voyage, they arrived at the ancient, bustling port of Alexandria. For Dalton and many of the Leinsters, this would be their first experience of the exotic world of Arabia. It would be an interesting period of service for Dalton, and he would learn about living under canvas in the desert and the rugged hills of the region, and the more mobile nature of the war in the Middle East.

On arrival at Alexandria, the 6th Leinsters boarded trains and travelled by way of Ismailia to Moascar where the battalion set up camp with other elements of the 10th Division. The battalion began a programme of desert route marches along with regular bathing in the salt water lakes of Ismailia which, it was hoped, would help cure the malaria that affected many of the men. Dalton would have first glimpsed the commander of the Egyptian Expeditionary Force (EEF), General Allenby, when the latter came to inspect the camp, with the men of the battalion lining up outside their tents. Then they marched along the Suez Canal, finally reaching Kantara on 2 October, where Dalton and his comrades put their surplus kit in storage. Allenby had been developing and upgrading railway facilities through the Sinai to facilitate the movement of troops to areas close to the front line. Dalton's battalion moved by train to Rafah, reaching it on 4 October. Training was carried out by the battalion. The water had to be piped from Kantara and was in short supply. Each man was limited strictly to three-quarters of a bottle a day 'for all purposes'.[18]

Allenby's forces moved into position and on 26 October the Third Battle of Gaza began, on the Gaza-Beersheba front. Dalton would not find himself in the front line at this stage – perhaps because of the malaria that infected many of the men, his battalion was assigned a logistics support role. The men of the 1st and 6th Leinsters were given an unglamorous but vital task – organizing camel convoys to carry water for the men and horses engaged in combat. Each camel carried two fifteen-gallon water tanks known as 'fanatis'. After the capture of Beersheba, the Leinsters moved up to the town itself. The historian of the Leinster Regiment has left a vivid account of horses almost mad with thirst at Beersheba, and being dragged away by exhausted men after they had the 'briefest drink' at the troughs.[19]

The 6th Leinsters was placed in reserve behind a small hill, as Allenby's forces continued the offensive on the Turkish positions. Some of the Leinsters had a bird's eye view of the fighting from observation positions on the hill. When the Turks were forced to retreat, the Leinsters moved up to occupy the Turkish trenches. On 5 November the two Leinster battalions joined the advance on Jerusalem, some forty miles northeast of Beersheba. It was a campaign of movement and manoeuvre, much different from the more static trench warfare that Dalton had experienced on the Western Front. They marched through hill country, bivouacking at night. Sometimes they came under sniper fire from the Turks, who were supported by German units. In one incident Dalton's superior, Lieutenant Colonel John Craske, commander of the 6th Leinsters, was wounded by a Turkish marksman.[20] The 29th Brigade with its two Leinster battalions was in support during some significant operations, including the capture of the Hareira Redoubt, a Turkish fortification, by 2nd Royal Irish Fusiliers of the 31st Brigade.

Turkish forces pulled out of the symbolically important city of Jerusalem, clearing the way for Allenby's forces to occupy the city. In a letter to a relative in the US, Dalton referred, with a note of pride, to the capture of Jerusalem on 9 December. He said that a couple of weeks ago they had taken Jerusalem and tomorrow 'we are going to do a big offensive, and I hope to come out of it alive'. He said he considered himself 'really lucky' to be alive after the amount of war he had seen.[21] The Ottoman Turks had captured Jerusalem in 1517. Now the city where Christ once walked was in the hands of the British – and an Irish division had played a role in its capture.

Bad weather delayed Allenby's next offensive to push the Ottoman Army further north. The 10th Division had to suffer through a bleak, rain-sodden Christmas in the district of Beit Sira, about twenty-five miles northwest of Jerusalem.[22] On St. Stephen's Day, the division attacked the Zeitun Ridge, a well-fortified Turkish position protected by numerous machine gun emplacements. Attacking troops had to negotiate steep ground and deep ravines or *wadis*. Dalton's battalion was fortunate. When they advanced to occupy a position at Shabuny, the 6th Leinsters found the Turks had fled, under enfilade fire from the 1st Leinsters and the 5th Connaught Rangers.

On 4 January 1918 the 6th Leinsters moved into an area around Suffa, northwest of Jerusalem, occupying part of the long line held by the Corps, and would stay there for some weeks, living among the stony, barren hills. Dalton was among those who lived in tents. With the occasional heavy rain it was not the ideal time to camp out. The work of the battalion included road making, disrupted by heavy falls of rain. Those not employed on road work were engaged in training.[23] One of the roles of the battalion was to repel any counter-attack by the Turks. Dalton, carried out extended reconnaissance patrols on horseback, shadowed by covering parties. Dalton gained considerable experience of negotiating his way on horseback through rough, rocky terrain and the local *wadis*.

Lieutenant Dalton's role was that of Assistant Adjutant, engaged in mainly administrative work, such as courts martial arrangements, and drawing maps of the positions held by the various units in the area. He was, apparently, an efficient typist, pounding away on a typewriter and producing circulars for the battalion.[24] From mid-January until the following April, Dalton kept a diary, written in small neat handwriting in a military notebook, using just one side of each page.[25] A picture emerges from his writings of a rather boyish figure, who regularly writes home to 'Mamma' and 'Pappa'. He was delighted to get letters from his parents, and also from his younger brothers Charlie and Brendan, and from friends. Like many a soldier at the front he read and re-read these precious letters. He was generous in sending a 'check' (he uses the American spelling) to his parents to buy presents 'for the boys'. Apart from writing to members of his family he also wrote to a young woman whom he calls 'Kittens' – possibly his childhood sweetheart Alice whom he would later marry. There were other female friends with whom he corresponded – Mai Broderick and May Doyle, as well as a person called Marnie.[26] From his diary and from other evidence,

Dalton emerges as a prolific letter writer, corresponding with relatives as far away as America.

For a young soldier in the desert hills, far away from home, letters assume enormous importance – the writing of them and the receiving of them. Dalton in his diary makes careful note of letters written and received. Some letters reached him literally months after being posted. He was often homesick, and felt particularly down or even irritable when the mail arrived and there was no letter for him. At one stage he remarked in his diary, 'I don't think I would feel so fed up as I do, if I could only see the dear folks at home occasionally...' However, he also reflects that 'there are fellows out here who have not been home for two years'.[27] Although Dalton was extremely busy at times, he also found spare time to write letters, read novels, or kick a football around. He tried to learn foreign languages but gave up Arabic and Russian as too difficult. To get photographs of loved ones or presents from home in the post was a great morale booster. He was delighted when plum pudding arrived and he shared it with his fellow officers. 'It was simply topping and everybody was pleased.' On another occasion he received the Christmas edition of *Our Boys*, the magazine produced by the Christian Brothers for their students – an event significant enough to be mentioned in his diary.

Dalton was diligent in fulfilling his religious duties, and attended 07:30 Mass every Sunday morning. He was still in his teenage years and his boyish exuberance emerges occasionally from entries in his diary – he notes that he cut the nose of the Padre, Father Burns, while they were playing a game of 'bombing each other'. There were times when he felt very down, and times also when he felt unwell or suffering from fever – possibly due to malaria.

To compensate for the homesickness, there were interesting sights to see. Jerusalem was not too far away, and was one of the places that soldiers stationed in the region liked to visit on leave. An entry in Dalton's diary indicates that he was particularly intrigued by the sights of the Holy City – he mentions doing a sketch of the Damascus Gate, which he sent to his father.[28] (In another entry he mentions sending drawings to his brother Charlie, probably the next best thing to sending photographs of local scenes. Another drawing, a self-portrait of himself in uniform and wearing a sun helmet, survives in his papers in the National Library.)

While Dalton's battalion was not engaged in combat at this period, there were regular reminders of the war. One day he saw an aerial fight between a German and a British aircraft – apparently the latter brought down the former without too much difficulty. In the latter part of January, Dalton received a grim reminder of the threat posed by German submarines to allied troopships, when 2nd Lieutenant O'Mahony joined the battalion – he was one of the survivors when the troopship *Aragon* was sunk by a German submarine outside the port of Alexandria on 30 December 1917, causing the deaths of more than 600. Dalton got a first-hand account of this horrific event from O'Mahony.[29]

There was a social side to a young officer's life in the hills. Visits were made to other battalions and regiments, and an officer going to Jerusalem or Cairo on leave would often bring back presents or souvenirs for his associates. Dalton notes that

Bill Cooke returned from Cairo 'with a good supply of cigarettes for me', and Major Graham returned from Jerusalem with souvenirs for his colleagues. 'Mullins got a lovely book of pressed flowers. Petrie got a lovely little box of polished olive wood.' Dalton himself received from Graham several postcards 'which I intend to send home today'. Lt. Colonel John Craske, the veteran battalion commander, seemed to take a paternal interest in the progress of his subordinate officers, and Dalton notes that Craske attended a dinner to celebrate the award to Captain Monaghan of the Military Cross.[30] There was one officer whom Dalton disliked, Major King, with whom he had arguments on those two ever-sensitive topics – politics and religion.

On 4 February Dalton undertook a long reconnaissance tour on horseback with Major King and Lieutenant Haile, and their first port of call was to 'Connaught Hill' – the headquarters of the 5th Battalion of the Connaught Rangers, which formed part of the 29th Brigade. Dalton and King paid a visit to Lt. Colonel Vincent M.B. Scully, commander of the battalion. Dalton formed the impression that Scully was rather 'fogged', that is uncertain, about his duties in the event of a Turkish counter-attack, a contingency which Dalton considered absurd as he believed the Turks did not have the courage to 'storm our present position'.[31] Dalton records how he and the other members of the party rode on, shadowed by a party providing protection, passing through Kurbetha Ibn Hareith and through the Wadi Eyub. This was an area of rocky hills, with stone walls, bridle paths and olive groves. They watered their horses at a well in a place described by Dalton as Job's Tomb. Because of a threatening storm they galloped towards home until the ground became very difficult, and he considered they were lucky to get back to base before the storm broke. On another reconnaissance tour, covering fifteen miles, Dalton rode the Adjutant's spirited horse, and observed that the animal 'had a mouth like iron and covered my hand with welts'.[32]

Exasperated by the intermittent heavy rain that sometimes penetrated his bivouac, Dalton remarks after once such occurrence that in the next war he will be a 'conscientious objector'. There seems to have been limited contact between the military and the Arab population. One day Dalton records that he accompanied the Medical Officer (MO) 'on his rounds of the natives'. On another occasion he encountered an Arab youth who had fled from the Turks, and for whom he felt sympathy. The youth, who spoke English, told how he was educated by the Christian Brothers – probably a reference to the De La Salle Brothers – in Jerusalem. The youth gave a graphic account of how the Turks 'robbed the people'. Dalton remarks that he felt for the youth because he was only sixteen years of age. He comments: 'I used think that Irish Catholics were the most oppressed but I have changed my opinion now.'[33]

After some weeks in Suffa, Dalton was made an Intelligence Officer (IO), in addition to his duties as Assistant Adjutant, but his work as IO seemed to consist largely of filing intelligence summaries from the division. Nevertheless, this experience would doubtless have given him insights into Allenby's strategy, and contributed to his military education, giving him a lasting appreciation of the value of intelligence in military operations. Some of the reports he received seem to have been of a very general nature, to do with matters like peace conferences and offensives on other fronts.[34]

Instructing at the Sniper School, El Arish

On 13 February Dalton records that he was informed by Captain Monaghan that Division had recommended him for good work in regard to Intelligence and that he would leave the Battalion on the 14th, the following day, to take up his next position as Instructor in sniping and intelligence duties at the Army Sniping School, El Arish, in the northern Sinai Desert in Egypt. Dalton had been in correspondence with one of the officers running the school, Captain Chalmers of the 3rd Dragoon Guards, apparently giving Chalmers the benefit of his experience as regards tactics. It also emerged that Dalton kept a notebook on scouting. Chalmers had written to Dalton in January thanking him for his information and asking for more, as he considered that the sniping school benefited from every little piece of information from those 'on the spot'.[35]

Dalton appears to have been popular with his fellow officers. On the night before his departure, there was a big attendance of officers from the battalion at a rousing send-off dinner in the mess. Dalton recorded that the main dish on the menu was 'kid' – a small goat that had been stolen from the 31st Field Ambulance 'whose mascot it was'. A plentiful supply of whiskey seems to have added further to the merriment. There was a sing-song and there were farewell speeches and toasts, and Dalton was given a rousing cheer.[36] Early next morning, Dalton set off on his long journey to El Arish. He was accompanied by two young fellow officers of the Leinsters, Lieutenants Cooke and Haile, who were being transferred from the infantry to the Royal Flying Corps (RFC) at Heliopolis, near Cairo. Dalton may also have been tempted to transfer – he would later reveal that he was of a mind to join the air force. For the first leg of the journey they travelled by road to Latrun, a distance of about twelve miles. A lorry later took them to Ramleigh (Ramallah) where they boarded the night train to Kantara.

After their journey through the Sinai, they arrived at Kantara, situated on the Suez Canal, early next morning. Kantara, formerly a small village with a few mud houses and a mosque on an ancient caravan route through the Sinai to Palestine, now accommodated a massive British military base camp and supply depot. Kantara had grown, due to the British war effort, into something resembling a modern metropolis, with miles of railway sidings, workshops, tarmac roads, electric light, cinemas, hospital facilities, churches and even a golf course. There were clubs, including a very efficient YMCA establishment, and Dalton records that he had a 'lovely breakfast' in the officers lounge there. Dalton was disappointed to find that most of his kit that had been put in storage at Kantara had disappeared, but he was issued with a tent and other items from the stores, including silk pyjamas. He was particularly pleased with the latter, describing the pyjamas, in the parlance of the day, as 'top hole'. After lunch in the mess, Dalton bade farewell to his travelling companions as they continued on their way 'in very good spirits' to Cairo.[37]

Dalton took a train to El Arish, with just one other officer in the carriage. Nurses got on at a stop en route and eventually Dalton tried to break the ice with the 'nicest looking' of them by offering her his 'British warm' – an officer's great coat – as it was cold. He was rebuffed, instantly regretting that he had spoken at all. However, another nurse asked him where he was going, leading to a general conversation that developed into a sing song which helped to pass the time.[38] It was late when Dalton arrived at El Arish. He began his duties at the school of instruction on 18 February, but found that his own services as a lecturer were not required until a new course started. He was told to assist Lieutenant Springay for the remaining week of the current course – Springay was giving a class on observation. Meanwhile, Dalton decided to take advantage of the golfing facilities at El Arish. On 23 February there is a simple entry in his diary, 'Played Golf'. This is the first record of Dalton playing the game that would take on a highly important role in his life. He played regularly during his stay in El Arish, and he would recall later that it was in Egypt that he played golf for the first time.

He had some leave and decided do some sightseeing. On 24 February he travelled to Cairo by train via Kantara, and checked into the luxurious Grand Continental Hotel on Opera Square. The Continental was then one of the great hotels in Cairo, renowned for its spacious and very elegant terrace area, where patrons could relax over drinks or a meal. The hotel was popular with members of the British armed forces – earlier in the war, as a young 2nd Lieutenant working in intelligence, T.E. Lawrence had resided there. Having spent a long period of storms and heavy rain living in a tent, Dalton must have revelled in the luxury of a comfortable bed in a good hotel. He records in his diary that he had breakfast in the hotel after a good night's sleep 'and a lovely hot bath'.[39] He went out to see the exotic sights of Cairo, and the following day continued with his sightseeing, visiting the other great hotel in Cairo, the historic Shepheard's Hotel, and also the fashionable café, Groppie's. Some of his fellow officers were also on leave, and he went about 'buying stuff' with 'Timmins and Billie Martin'. Some nurses from Alexandria, where important military hospital facilities were located, were also staying at the Continental, and Dalton had tea and dinner with them. He became particularly friendly with one of the nurses, Sister O'Brien, and he went for a [horse-drawn] garry drive with her, getting half-way to the pyramids. Dalton enjoyed the outing enormously, commenting in his diary that he had a 'top hole' time. He and his companion had coffee back at the hotel 'and went to our respective rooms'.[40] The next morning he took it easy in the hotel, playing a game of billiards. He met up with another officer from the 6th Leinsters who was also on leave, Captain Alan Brabazon (22) from a well-to-do Church of Ireland farming family in County Westmeath, and went to Groppie's for tea. (Brabazon was destined to die the following month from a sniper's bullet.) Dalton had lunch with another officer called Fry, and in the afternoon went to a social event organised by the wife of General Allenby.

Dalton records in his diary how he was introduced to Lady Allenby 'and had the pleasure of procuring a cup of tea for her'.[41] Probably impressed by Dalton's charm, she introduced him to Countess Hariaina Pacha, who was accompanied by her daughter. Dalton, who had an eye for attractive young women, was probably more interested in the daughter and he asked her to dance. As they took to the floor the young woman seemed to be mistaken about the identity of her dancing partner. She appeared to think Dalton was a French aristocrat, causing him some embarrassment by addressing him as 'Monsieur le Duc'. However, he admits that he did not really mind the fact that she was labouring under a slight delusion 'which my poor knowledge of French was unable to allay'.[42] (It is also possible that the young woman was having some fun at Dalton's expense.)

After his interesting break in Cairo, Dalton returned to El Arish. He resumed his instructor duties, and on 4 March, he mentioned in his diary his twentieth birthday. He felt 'lonely' but 'busy'. He would remain busy over the following weeks, although he still found time to play golf from time to time. As he concentrated on work, the entries in his diary became shorter and less detailed. The topics covered in the courses he gave included observation; scouting; intelligence summaries and aerial photographs. The latter topic indicated a particular interest on Dalton's part in air reconnaissance, and during the Irish Civil War he would show a particular interest in using aircraft to gain intelligence on opposing forces.

In an offensive in April, when the 6th Leinsters was tasked with taking a high peak area near the village of Kefr Ain, the battalion came under Turkish artillery and machine gun fire and suffered casualties. Among the injured were some of Dalton's officer colleagues, Lieutenant Hogan, 2nd Lieutenant McDonnell and Captain Powell. Dalton's sojourn at the school in El Arish meant that he missed out on these engagements with the enemy. While he probably would have wished to be where the action was, El Arish was a safer place in which to be located. Once again, from the point of view of survival, his luck had held out.

Dalton appears to have pleased his superiors in the way he performed as an instructor in the sniping school. A memorandum dated 22 May 1918 drawn up by Captain Percy H. Manbey on behalf of the Major commanding the El Arish School of Instruction, of which the sniping school was part, declared that Lieutenant Dalton has given 'entire satisfaction'.[43] The fourteen-week stint as a sniper instructor inspired Dalton to write a poem, *The Sniper*. He wrote it on 19 May, towards the end of the course during which he essentially taught men to stalk and kill the enemy. The poem is a grim reflection on the heavy responsibility on the shoulders of a marksman whose job it is to kill an enemy soldier. He knows that his shot will cause a woman's tears, and that a mother's heart will be torn apart. But he is also conscious that a comrade died at his side at dawn [at the hands of an enemy sniper], 'died with a gasp and nothing more...' He reflects that we are all marked with the hand of Cain. 'Thus shall it be, a life for a life...'[44] He closes with the Latin motto of the Royal Dublin Fusiliers, *Spectamur Agendo* – 'Let us be judged by our acts.'

Return to France

The British Army decided that it needed the 6th Leinsters on the Western Front. On 23 May Dalton and his battalion boarded the vessel *Ormonde* at Port Said and sailed for France, arriving in Marseilles on 1 June. The battalion travelled by train to

Aire in northern France, near the border with Belgium, and set up camp. The usual training and fatigue work was carried out, and anti-malaria quinine treatment was administered.[45] One of the great advantages of the transfer of the 6th Leinsters to northern France was that all ranks became eligible for leave – some had been serving continuously abroad for three years.[46] Dalton was promoted to Captain on 3 July, and was also given the opportunity to visit Ireland on leave.

In the meantime Dalton's skills as an instructor were called on once again – in July he gave a Lewis gun course to newly-arrived American troops at the Samer Training Area near Boulogne.[47] They were part of the rapidly expanding American Expeditionary Force preparing to fight on the Western Front. It was decided that those American units deployed on the British front would use certain British weapons, such as the Vickers and Lewis machine guns, as opposed to their own American-supplied weapons. As a result, American officers and non-commissioned officers needed instruction in the British weapons so that they could, in turn, instruct their own men. Captain Dalton, ever conscious of his American birth, was clearly very pleased to meet the American military men he instructed. To ease them into combat conditions, American units were sent for further training with British forces in front line positions, and there is an indication that Dalton was in action with American troops around this period. In a letter to his American cousin, Frances O'Brien he said that he had the opportunity of fighting alongside United States troops, and in a tribute to their bravery said it was 'glorious' to see how the American soldiers fought.[48] On 29 June 1918, the Commandant of the VII Corps Lewis Gun School recommended Dalton as 'a good instructor'.[49]

In his 4 August letter to his cousin, Dalton wrote that he had received two weeks leave to go home to Ireland, and that he was about to transfer to the Royal Air Force (RAF), as he believed nothing could equal the difficulties and dreadfulness of an infantry soldier's life. As indicated above, while stationed in Palestine, two of his fellow officers had transferred to the air force, and he may have considered following in their footsteps. Flying also probably appealed to his spirit of adventure. It is unclear if Dalton pressed ahead with an attempt to transfer to the RAF – certainly, he remained in the infantry until demobilized, but in his later army service in Ireland, he would show a keen interest in military aviation and have an appreciation of the value of air support in military operations.

On 10 August, word came through that the 6th Leinsters battalion was to be disbanded. Later in the year, officers and men would go to other regiments such as the Connaught Rangers, while others, including Captain Dalton, transferred to the 2nd Battalion of the Leinsters. Meanwhile, in the latter part of August, Dalton went home to Ireland for a badly-needed two-week break. On 1 October, Dalton officially joined[50] the 2nd Leinsters who were in Belgium at this period, taking part in combat operations as the war ground to a close. Once again, Dalton was deployed with a fighting unit. Lieutenant Francis C. Hitchcock of the 2nd Leinsters recorded in his diary for 4 October that heavy rain fell all day and a new draft of officers arrived.'[51] It is likely that Dalton was part of this draft. (Hitchcock would later turn his diary into a book, *Stand To: A Diary of the Trenches, 1915–1918*.[52]

It remains one of the best memoirs to emerge from the Great War, written with humour and empathy, and giving a most vivid day-to-day account of life as a junior officer in a time of war.)

The battalion moved to Ypres on 5 October. The British II Corps, in alliance with French and Belgian forces, was preparing a major assault on the German lines. The 2nd Leinsters were now part of the 88th Brigade of the 29th Division of II Corps. Hitchcock noted in his diary for 5 October: 'At 5 p.m. the battalion paraded and moved off for Ypres for another offensive. It was raining heavily when they paraded and marched off.'[53] On 13 October the battalion moved into position in trenches for the attack the following day. There was a heavy fog as the attack went in. Dalton's battalion, 2nd Leinsters, was deployed among the advance troops of the 88th Brigade, fighting in the Ledeghem sector near Courtrai. Details are unavailable of Dalton's role in the attack. During the fighting on 14 October, two members of the battalion carried out actions that would later win them the Victoria Cross, the highest British award for valour. They were men who Dalton would get to know quite well: Scots-born Sergeant John O'Neill, from Airdrie, Lanarkshire, and Private Martin Moffat, from Sligo. The liberation of the village of Ledeghem by the 2nd Leinsters and other elements of the 29th Division was still being commemorated annually in recent years by local dignitaries and members of the Leinster Regiment Association.

Deployment to Germany

Dalton went on sick leave for the first three weeks of November 1918.[54] Meanwhile, after four long years the war was finally drawing to a close. Lieutenant Hitchcock recorded in his diary for 10 November that he and men of the 2nd Leinsters were marching to a rendezvous at the village of Arc-Anière when the Brigadier came galloping up to call out: 'The War is over! The Kaiser has abdicated.'[55] On the following day, 11 November, the Armistice came into force. As the war ended, all over Europe and further afield, one can imagine how parents and loved ones of combatants experienced an enormous sense of relief. Among many there was probably also a sense of anti-climax, as they wondered what had been achieved by such carnage. From later in November, until the following January, Captain Dalton was stationed in northern France. He was with the 'L' Infantry Base Depot (IBD), Calais.[56] Hitchcock also spent some time at an IBD in Calais, in August 1918. In his memoir, he described the depot as being located 'on the high ground overlooking the old historical town of Calais'. Accommodation was in tents, around which deep trenches ran at intervals in case of an air raid. The camp had suffered some direct hits 'and numerous casualties'. There was an officers' club where meals were provided.[57]

As Captain Dalton found, there was a social side to life in the depot. Among Dalton's papers at the National Library in Dublin is a programme for a dinner dance at the 'L' IBD, Calais on 3 January 1919. Listed on the programme for the evening are some of the popular dances of the day – including the Waltz, One Step, Veleta and Lancers. On the back of the programme, a number of officers signed their names, with regiments also given – they include Irish regiments, the Royal Dublin Fusiliers and the Leinsters, and English regiments such as the Essex and the Suffolk.[58] No doubt, the end of the war added to the festive atmosphere. A few days later, on 6 January, Dalton entered Germany to serve with the 2nd Leinsters, as part of the Allies' Army of Occupation of the Rhineland.[59] (The occupation was mandated by the Armistice, and was carried out by French, Belgian, American and British troops.) In early 1919, Dalton was with a unit of the 2nd Leinsters stationed in a quiet rural village called Dhunn, about eighteen miles northeast of Cologne. This was in the outpost area occupied by the 88th Brigade. Lieutenant Hitchcock, who had been stationed here for a period and departed before Dalton arrived, found the area depressing. Platoons were billeted in 'very dirty isolated farms'. It was also 'bitterly cold and rained continually'.

Lieutenant Hitchcock was delighted to get orders to leave this bleak area peopled by hard-working farmers. He noted that, before departure, they received official news in December of the award of two Victoria Crosses to the battalion.[60] The following month, January, somebody had the idea of gathering together, for a photograph, members of 'D' Company of the battalion who had been awarded decorations for bravery. The picture was taken outdoors, in a field or garden with a row of tall trees in the background. It is a most remarkable photograph and still survives as a treasured memento in the possession of Emmet Dalton's daughter Audrey. It shows Dalton and Captain John Moran, both recipients of the Military Cross, with the two winners of the Victoria Cross, Sergeant O'Neill and Private Moffat.

While Dalton was stationed at Dhunn with 'D' Company, 2nd Leinsters, he spent time in training and exercises, which no doubt helped to further develop his military expertise. On 14 February 1919, Dalton drew up Operation Orders for the company as part of a battalion exercise involving an advance on the ancient town of Radevormwald.[61] (Although Dalton had been promoted to Captain or acting Captain, he describes himself as 'Lieut. J.E. Dalton' on the handwritten document, and commanding officer of the company.) 'D' Company was to form the advance guard of the battalion advance, and he deployed elements of the company in various roles, in accordance with British military doctrine, outlining the relevant map references. Second Lieutenant Dorgan, with numbers 1 and 2 Sections and a Lewis Gun, was to be in the lead, acting in a 'Point' role. Flankers would be provided by no. 3 Section, while Lieutenant Johnson and no. 14 Platoon would form the Vanguard. The Main Guard would consist of two Platoons under the O.C. and his second in command. There would also be Connecting Files, provided by a Section, while two runners, Private Hart and Private Martin Moffat VC, would report to the Battalion HQ and act as Liaison. Experience in such exercises involving the deployment of infantry forces during military manoeuvres would, no doubt, come in useful when Dalton went on to become a senior officer in the National Army during the Irish Civil War. The experience would have been especially relevant as Dalton deployed his forces for the advance on Cork following seaborne landings in August 1922.

While stationed in the Cologne region, Emmet Dalton had a poignant task to fulfil. He went in search of a grave – the last resting place of a close friend, a fellow

Irish officer who had been wounded, captured by the Germans and then died as a prisoner of war in October 1918, just before the Armistice. John Kemmy Boyle was, like Dalton, a northside Dubliner, and a fellow student at O'Connell School. The two men had both joined the Royal Dublin Fusiliers in 1916.

Already highly decorated, on 24 March 1918 Boyle was wounded and taken prisoner by the Germans while serving with 2nd Royal Irish Rifles (RIR). He died in a German Prisoner of War camp of pneumonia just three weeks before the Armistice. He was twenty-one years old. His remains lie in a war cemetery in Germany – Cologne Southern Cemetery. Dalton must, by now, have become used to comrades being killed in the war, but Boyle's death appears to have affected him deeply. He was so moved that he wrote a very emotional seven-verse poem in memory of his dead friend – the handwritten text, in capital letters, on a single sheet of paper, is still preserved within the pages of his diary, among his papers at the National Library in Dublin.[62] The poem is titled 'Lieut. John K. Boyle M.C., My Dearest & Best Friend R.I.P.', and it is signed at the bottom, 'J. Emmet Dalton'. The poem is undated, but the opening lines indicate that Dalton was inspired to write the verses after he found Boyle's grave in Germany. 'At last I have found your lowly place of rest...' In the poem, Dalton reflects on his friend living in the 'Hunnish Gaol' for months and then dying with no mother or sweetheart or friend by his side. The tough-minded soldier-poet shows a compassionate, sensitive side in these lines in memory of his friend.

As Dalton was being demobilized, he received the usual letter from the British War Office to say that he was released from military duty. In his case, the release was from 4 April 1919. The letter stated that he would be permitted to wear uniform for one month only after date of release, to enable him to obtain plain clothes, but this would not entitle him to a concession voucher while travelling.[63] The War Office sent the letter to Dalton at his father's business address, 15 Wicklow Street, Dublin, where Dalton senior operated an importing concern. (The office would later move to 12 Wicklow Street.) The authorities had been informed that after leaving the army, Emmet would be working for his father on a 'profit sharing' basis.

Dalton's service as an officer in the British Army, while often difficult and sometimes dangerous, had broadened his horizons. He had learned the art of soldiering, the finer points of tactics, strategy and leadership, and had developed abilities as a military instructor. He had quickly matured and acquired new skills – including horse riding. He had been to interesting places, including the Middle East. He had encountered people from outside his Irish Catholic middle-class environment. Among them were men from the 'other' community in Ireland, the Protestants, including members of the landed gentry, the middle class and the farming community. It had been a very interesting and challenging time in his life, interspersed with moments of great tragedy and trauma. Twenty-one year-old Emmet Dalton was now returning to a country in turmoil – the Great War had ended but his war-fighting days were far from over.

CHAPTER THREE

IRA Activities

A fter his service in the Great War, Emmet Dalton returned home to a very different Ireland. The movement for Irish independence was gaining momentum. Following the suppression of the Easter Rising, the Volunteers had been re-formed and Dalton's younger brother Charlie had joined in December 1917. He became a member of F Company, 2nd Battalion in Dublin, at only fourteen years of age. He would later, with boyish pride, come to possess his own personal weapon – a German-made Mauser pistol which Emmet had brought home as a souvenir.[1] Charlie grew more deeply involved in the movement as part of the IRA's intelligence operations overseen by Michael Collins. Emmet would also be drawn into republican activities.

It was a time of political turmoil. The separatist Sinn Féin movement rejected the Westminster parliament and instead set up an independent Irish legislative assembly. The party had won a strong majority in the December 1918 general election, and on 21 January 1919 the Sinn Féin elected representatives (Teachtaí Dála – TDs) met in Dublin as the first Dáil Éireann. Later in the year, the British would seek to suppress the assembly. On the very day that the first Dáil met, what are generally seen as the first shots of the War of Independence were fired in Soloheadbeg, County Tipperary. A group of IRA men led by Dan Breen and Sean Treacy shot dead two members of the Royal Irish Constabulary (RIC) during an operation to seize gelignite being escorted by the armed policemen. It was claimed that the constables had resisted. In a statement to the BMH, Breen said: 'Treacy had stated to me that the only way to start a war was to kill someone, and we wanted to start a war, so we intended to kill some of the police whom we looked upon as the foremost and most important branch of the enemy forces which were holding the country in subjection.'[2]

On his return to Dublin, Emmet had resumed his studies. With the aid of a military education grant he studied engineering for about a year at the Royal

College of Science. He also worked for a period as a temporary clerk with the Office of Public Works.[3] Return from the war also gave him the opportunity to pursue his sports interests. He joined Bohemians soccer club, located in Phibsboro not far from his Dublin home, and played with the club for a season.

In early 1920 Charlie Dalton was asked to join the IRA's GHQ Intelligence Unit, reporting to Liam Tobin, Deputy Director of Intelligence, at an office in Crow Street, Dublin. It was to be the beginning of a notable association with Tobin over the following years. His duties were outlined to him by the Assistant Director of Intelligence, Tom Cullen, who was in daily touch with the Director, Michael Collins.[4] Dalton's role included tracing the activities of enemy agents and spies, establishing contacts among individuals in government service, keeping files on intelligence targets and participating in active service operations arising out of intelligence gathering. One of the central aims of the Intelligence Department was to intercept government and crown forces' communications.

In October 1920 Charlie Dalton and another Volunteer opened fire on British soldiers who were deployed at Binn's Bridge in his home area of Drumcondra as part of a cordon. Dalton wanted to disrupt the cordon to allow Volunteers returning from an operation in the city centre to get through. Two soldiers were killed, while he and his colleague escaped along a railway embankment and emerged from it close to his home at Upper St. Columba's Road. Later that evening Charlie was on his way home when he spotted a passing touring car with a number of men in plain clothes. He was astonished to see the car pull up in front of his house. When they could not find Charlie they arrested Emmet instead, although it appears his detention was only temporary. No doubt his discharge papers showing he had been a British officer in the Great War proved useful. Charlie believed a neighbour saw him coming down from the railway and tipped off the authorities.[5] Because of the raid, Charlie thought it advisable to stay away from home. The attack resulted in the Dalton family, including Emmet, coming to the attention of the authorities.

Bloody Sunday

As a member of Michael Collins's intelligence staff, Charlie Dalton was one of the Volunteers closely involved in gathering information on British intelligence officers living at boarding houses, flats and hotels around Dublin. It was a period when Collins was becoming increasingly concerned about what he saw as a major threat from the British secret service. It was decided to launch a pre-emptive strike against members of a group known as the 'Cairo Gang'. Collins chose 9 am on 21 November 1920 as the moment to strike, targeting addresses across the city, in a day that would go down in history as Bloody Sunday. Members of Collins's special unit, the Squad, were deployed with Volunteers from the Dublin Brigade. Charlie Dalton was only seventeen years old at the time, an impressionable youth, and he would later recall his great anxiety in advance of the operation. The night before the raids, Charlie shared a hideout with a number of other Volunteers, including future Taoiseach Sean Lemass. Lemass, who participated in the Bloody Sunday shootings, believed that these activities affected Charlie's nerves.

Charlie was not one of the men who would actually pull the trigger on the day – he was sent to gather up any documents relating to intelligence. He accompanied the gunmen to a house at 28 Upper Pembroke Street where men were to be shot. Charlie had played a particular role in gathering advance information to help target the doomed officers by befriending a young woman who worked as a servant in the house. Two officers were shot dead and four wounded, one of whom died the following December. The memory of the shootings would remain with Charlie. Altogether fourteen members of British intelligence, or suspected members, were shot dead in Dublin that morning. It would later emerge that not all were intelligence officers. Some were shot in their pyjamas or in the presence of their wives. On the afternoon of the Bloody Sunday killings, in revenge for the massacre, the Auxiliaries fired on the crowd at a match in Croke Park, killing ten and injuring about sixty, four of whom later died. In Dublin Castle, two IRA prisoners, Dick McKee and Peadar Clancy, as well as a young man Conor Clune, who was not involved in the IRA, were killed. The classic excuse was given, that they were 'shot while trying to escape'. In nationalist Ireland, nobody believed it.

After the assassination of the British officers, Charlie Dalton was in a state of great nervous agitation. One of his colleagues Matty McDonald said Charlie could not sleep on the night of Bloody Sunday: 'He thought he could hear the gurgling of the officers' blood and he kept awake all night until we told him a tap was running somewhere.'[6] Sean Lemass was present and was also concerned about Charlie's state. In later life Charlie Dalton was a very troubled man, and experienced persistent mental health problems that required spells in hospital under psychiatric care. Emmet attributed Charlie's troubles to his youthful involvement with the Squad.

Raid on the Dalton Home

In early December, in the wake of the Bloody Sunday killings, there was another raid on the Dalton home. In his memoir, Charlie gave an account of the raid as told to him by his mother.[7] It was after midnight, and everyone in the household had gone to bed. Lorries could be heard coming up the road and then a loud knocking on the door. Emmet went down to answer the door. There was a sound of men charging up the stairs. The door to the bedroom of Mr and Mrs Dalton burst open and about a dozen men entered the room. They began searching the room and throwing questions at the couple. They were looking for Charlie. Mr Dalton said, 'Do you know who I am?' He informed the raiding party, a mixture of Auxiliaries and military officers, that he was a Justice of the Peace. They did not seem impressed. They took away James F. Dalton and Emmet. Mrs Dalton spent the next couple of days trying to establish the whereabouts of her husband and son. Eventually she found they had been taken to Collinstown Aerodrome north of Dublin for questioning. Emmet later recalled that as he and his father were being taken away, the Auxiliaries fired a couple of shots in the air. His father had a habit of blowing his nose loudly and now proceeded to do so – apparently as a signal to his wife that he was alright, that he had not been shot.[8]

Prisoners arrested after raids or by military night patrols were often processed at a detention centre at Collinstown. An IRA man who was being held there, Joseph Lawless, who would later serve as an officer in the National Army during the Civil War, recalled two of the prisoners to whom they were introduced in this way – one was Emmet Dalton, and the other Peadar Kearney, who wrote the lyrics for *The Soldier's Song* (*Amhrán na bhFiann*) which became Ireland's National Anthem. Dalton apparently secured his release by a plea of mistaken identity and a display of his British Army discharge papers.[9]

The British intelligence officers in Dublin Castle began compiling a file on Emmet. According to this file, Emmet and his father were arrested on 9 December and released on 18 December. 'Dagger, bayonet, helmet and seditious documents were found in the house when they were arrested,' the file stated.[10] However, no charges were brought against the two. Apart from the documents, the items listed may well have been war souvenirs brought back to Ireland by Emmet. The elder Dalton's status as a Justice of the Peace and Emmet's service to the British empire in the Great War may have helped to secure their release. It appears from the intelligence file that while the British were aware of Charlie's intelligence activities their information was limited. The file noted: 'Either this man [Emmet] or his brother Charles, who is believed to be an IRA Secret Service man, was with a Flying Column.' The file added: 'Sister a courier.' This may be a reference to Nuala who was aged only seven at the time.

While in detention, James F. Dalton acted as 'Chaplain' to the other prisoners by leading the Rosary. Emmet made use of his military training to drill his fellow-prisoners. They were both incensed over being detained. Emmet would later tell, with some amusement, how his father's role as 'Chaplain' was short-lived. They were placed in a hut with up to eighteen other men, and on the first night the Volunteer in charge called for night prayers and everyone knelt down and said their prayers before going to bed. The next day Dalton senior asked if he, as the older man, could give out the prayers and this was agreed. That night he proceeded to give out the rosary, with a homily on each mystery. This was clearly too much for detainees who were delayed in going to bed – they just wanted to get to sleep. The next day some of the hut inmates got together and it was decided that in future the prayers would be given out in Irish. As James F. Dalton did not have the language, he was excluded from leading the prayers, much to the relief of inmates. It was a diplomatic way of dealing with the problem.[11]

It was unusual for a duo with such a respectable background, a JP and his war hero son who had served as a British Army officer, to be pulled in for questioning. The *Irish Independent* reported the arrests with the headline 'Ex-Army Captain and J.P. Arrested'.[12] When Charlie Dalton reported on the raid on his family home to Liam Tobin, the Deputy Director of Intelligence, Tobin told him he already knew all about it. Tobin and Michael Collins and one or two staff officers happened to be spending the night in a house overlooking the Dalton residence, and observed the raid and all the commotion. As a result they had a rather sleepless night, with the enemy so close at hand.[13]

Training the IRA

In late 1920 Emmet Dalton became involved in training the IRA. Oscar Traynor, Commander of the Dublin Brigade, was seeking to improve the level of training in the Volunteers. J.J. 'Ginger' O'Connell was Director of Training but he had also been appointed Assistant Chief of Staff, and found it difficult to give enough time to the training role. O'Connell, who had served in the US armed forces, asked Traynor to keep an eye out for somebody who could replace him as Director of Training. Charlie Dalton had been telling Traynor of the outstanding abilities of his brother Emmet who had fought in the British Army all through the Great War and who was sympathetic to the Volunteers. A newspaper profile written in the summer of 1922 suggested that Dalton had to 'fight his way' into the movement, owing to the reluctance of senior leaders to accept a former officer in the British Army, though they quickly recognized his resourcefulness.[14] The fact that Emmet already had a brother active in the Volunteers may have helped dispel any lingering doubts about his bona fides.

Traynor asked Charlie to bring in Emmet for an interview. It was not unknown for Irishmen who had fought for the British in the Great War to throw in their lot with the Volunteers, the West Cork guerrilla leader Tom Barry being a notable example. When Emmet Dalton came in for interview, Traynor asked him if he would be prepared to give a series of lectures to members of the Dublin Brigade. He replied he would be willing to do so.

He began lecturing members of different battalions, with map-reading one of the areas covered. One of those he encountered during this work was his former school friend, Sean Lemass. O'Connell attended some of the lectures and reported back that he was impressed by Dalton's abilities.[15] Dalton became Assistant Director of Training in the IRA General Headquarters staff, and later assumed the role of Director of Training, around June 1921. Meanwhile, he dropped out of his engineering course, and also left his temporary job in the Office of Public Works. Dalton's previous military experience had included roles as an instructor, which made him a valuable addition to the GHQ staff. O'Connell introduced him to various senior figures in the Volunteers, including the Chief of Staff, Richard Mulcahy. He got to know Piaras Béaslaí, the editor of the Volunteers' journal, *An t-Óglach*, and in February 1921 helped him secure an office on North Great George's Street. A disadvantage was that the room could only be used during the day – by night it was used for dancing classes.[16]

A young Volunteer, Gerald Davis, attended lectures by Dalton. In early 1921 IRA Headquarters asked for volunteers to go down the country as organizers. The Headquarters staff particularly desired to use students for this work. Davis was at the National University in Dublin and he and other students in the movement offered their services. They were interviewed by senior IRA figures Dick Mulcahy and Oscar Traynor and instructed to attend a series of lectures in a building somewhere near Amiens Street. Among those who lectured them were Emmet Dalton and his brother Charlie, Ernie O'Malley, 'Ginger' O'Connell and Rory O'Connor. The lectures covered 'guerilla warfare, engineering, the construction of land mines and the use of arms and so forth'. The course involved about a week of lectures.[17]

Apart from his expertise in giving lectures to Dublin Brigade personnel, Emmet Dalton assumed another useful role as impersonator of a British Army officer. Shortly after taking up his lecturing duties, there was a raid on the brigade headquarters. The building, sometimes known as the Plaza Hotel, was located at 6 Gardiner's Row (now known as Gardiner Row), which also housed the offices of the Irish Engineering, Electrical, Shipbuilding and Foundry Trade Union. Oscar Traynor, Christopher 'Kit' O'Malley, Adjutant, and Dalton were all present in the HQ office. It was located in an area of the building which, they hoped, would not be found by the troops, but they had no guarantee that their hideaway would remain undetected. They had hidden away their papers and were waiting for the troops to burst in, when Dalton suggested that the best thing to do was to go down and 'brazen it out'. With Dalton leading the way, they went down to the hallway where Dalton talked first to a soldier, and then to an officer, and the two got to the stage of laughing.[18] Eventually Dalton said to his companions, 'Come along, men' and they left the building and proceeded on their way, only to be held up by soldiers at the corner of nearby Findlater's Church. Again, Dalton talked to a British officer and they were passed safely through the cordon. Traynor later described how Dalton, because of his general appearance, deceived the British officers into believing that he also was a British officer, engaged on work about which the least said the better. Traynor commented: 'There can be little doubt that, due to Dalton's presence, we managed to evade arrest on that occasion.'[19]

As he became more involved with the IRA, Dalton was living away from home, effectively on the run. For a period he lay low in the secluded, scenic environs of Howth, County Dublin, beside the sea, with other IRA members such as Tom Flood and Christopher O'Malley. At some stage in 1921, while the War of Independence was still in progress, Dalton made a return journey to O'Connell School where he met Brother Allen. According to a story told by Brother Allen in later life, Dalton said he had a particular favour to ask of the Brother – he wanted a place to store a ton of coal.[20] He said his father and mother, unknown to each other, had each ordered a ton of coal and they had no space to store the extra fuel. Brother Allen agreed to help. Dalton duly delivered the ton of coal, in sacks, and it was stored in the basement furnace area of the school, separate from the Brothers' coal. Subsequently, Dalton returned to take away the coal. Then an extraordinary thing happened – there was a raid by the British on O'Connell's, and members of the raiding party went straight to the furnace area to search it. Brother Allen later learned that the sacks contained not just coal, but sticks of gelignite, which Dalton was hiding away for the IRA. Apparently, Brother Allen had a theory that the coal was removed after Dalton got a tip about the upcoming raid from one of Michael Collins's informants in Dublin Castle.

Dalton Escorts Unionist Leader James Craig to See De Valera

It was a period when Emmet Dalton was called on to carry out special tasks for the movement. In early May 1921 he was deployed for a particularly sensitive operation to escort Unionist leader, Sir James Craig, on a secret visit to see Dáil President Éamon de Valera at a private house in a north Dublin suburb. This was several weeks before the Truce that would bring a formal end to hostilities in the War of Independence. Craig showed particular courage in undertaking the visit. In coming to Dublin he was entering what some Unionists would have seen as the lion's den. The meeting between the two men was arranged by a senior British official in Dublin Castle, Alfred 'Andy' Cope, acting with the blessing of British Prime Minister Lloyd George. He was opening lines of communication with senior Irish republicans to find an end to the conflict. Cope secured a guarantee from Sinn Féin of a 'safe conduct' for Craig as he went to see de Valera.

Craig and his wife came to Dublin without any escort and stayed at the Private Secretary's Lodge in the Phoenix Park. On the morning of 6 May, Cope drove Craig to the home of a leading judge, Sir James O'Connor, on Northumberland Road. Here he was met by the prominent Sinn Féin priest, Father Michael O'Flanagan. According to Craig's later account, two Sinn Féiners, 'armed to the teeth', suggested he accompany them to an unnamed location where de Valera was waiting to see him. Craig set off in a car with the two men and a driver, and he would later describe them as 'three of the worst looking toughs I have ever seen'.[21]

Emmet Dalton would later confirm that he himself was one of the men who escorted Craig on this secret trip to see Dev. However, Dalton's military style moustache and officer-style bearing hardly qualified him as a villainous 'tough'. In an account given to historian Calton Younger, Dalton said he sat in the car beside Craig and advised him to pass himself off as his secretary if they were stopped by Crown forces. In the event of trouble, Craig would be 'first to go'. Many years later, Dalton expressed admiration for Craig's courage.[22]

Another member of the escort was a young republican, Sean Harling, who worked for Dáil Éireann. He usually helped organize the logistics and security arrangements when President Éamon de Valera received VIP visitors or journalists from abroad. In testimony to the Bureau of Military History, Harling does not mention Dalton in connection with the Craig trip, but identified Joe Hyland as the driver of the car.[23] A taxi-driver, Hyland was Michael Collins's 'wheelman', and well-used to clandestine operations.

According to the account given by Craig's biographer, St. John Ervine, the car carrying the Unionist leader stopped en route at a canal bridge, and Craig was asked to alight. A barge was passing under the bridge, and Craig inquired, no doubt facetiously, if the journey was to continue by water. In fact they were changing to another car on the other side of the bridge – probably as a security precaution. St. John Ervine states that Craig thought he was being driven to County Wicklow, and suggests he was taken by a roundabout route so that he would not know his actual location. However, Harling in his Witness Statement, states that Craig asked him, while they were passing through the north Dublin suburb of Clontarf, would it be indiscreet of him to inquire where he was now. 'So I said, "No Sir, you are in Clontarf." He said, "Oh, this is where King Brian [Boru] fought the Danes."'

Craig was brought to a house called Belvidere, on the Howth Road, Clontarf, occupied by a solicitor, Tom Green. This was the 'safe house' where de Valera was waiting to receive his visitor. It was a large, luxurious, detached residence set in spacious gardens. Craig's biographer says the Unionist leader saw a number of men with picks and shovels 'pretending' to repair the road outside the house, but who were clearly 'guarding' de Valera. St. John Ervine describes how the 'three toughs', followed by Craig, entered the house and met de Valera standing on the threshold of the sitting room. This may have been Dalton's first meeting with Dev, whom Dalton would later come to despise, considering him the prime cause of Ireland's Civil War.

While a meeting between the leaders of two opposing traditions on the island of Ireland was in itself a positive development, there was little immediate result from the encounter between Craig and de Valera. According to Craig's later account to his wife, de Valera began to talk, reaching the eleventh-century era of Brian Boru after 'a half hour', and after another half hour, the era of 'some king a century or two later'. 'By this time I was getting tired, for de Valera hadn't begun to reach the point at issue. Fortunately, a fine Kerry Blue entered the room and enabled me to change the conversation…'[24] M.J. MacManus, who wrote a sympathetic biography of de Valera, had a different version of events, saying that de Valera had to do almost all the talking because Craig said so little: 'De Valera welcomed the opportunity for an exchange of views, but found that he had to do most of the talking. The dour Northerner was a man of few words. He lit his pipe and smoked and listened. De Valera gave him some geography, a certain amount of economics, and quite a lot of history. Sir James smoked and smoked, a perfect picture of the strong, silent man…'[25]

The two men agreed on a brief statement to the press to record the fact that they had met. Craig wrote the statement on a piece of paper torn from a copy of the *Freeman's Journal* newspaper and de Valera wrote the agreed text on another piece of paper. Emmet Dalton would describe later how Craig, after the meeting, told him that he found de Valera 'impossible'.[26] Craig was driven back to the home of Sir James O'Connor, where O'Connor and Cope were waiting anxiously for his return. Craig and Cope travelled on to the Secretary's Lodge in the Phoenix Park, where Lady Craigavon was waiting even more anxiously for her husband to come back. Years later, after her husband's death, she still retained the scrap of paper from the *Freeman's Journal* on which Craig had written the statement.

Dalton's companion on this occasion, Sean Harling, went on to win his own place in the history of Irish intrigue. Harling, who was interned during the Civil War, apparently went on to work as an undercover intelligence agent for the Free State police force, the Garda Síochána. He claimed that on returning to his Dublin home at Dartry Road one evening in January 1928, he was fired on by two men, and that he returned fire, mortally wounding one of his assailants. The dead man was Timothy Coughlan, an IRA man believed to have been part of the three-man gang who had assassinated Government Minister Kevin O'Higgins the previous year. It was found that Coughlan had been shot in the back of the head and still had a cigarette in his mouth. A tribunal of inquiry found that Harling had acted in self-defence.

Meeting Michael Collins, and Attempted Rescue of Sean MacEoin

Some time after he had joined the IRA Emmet Dalton met the man who was to have a profound effect on his life – Michael Collins. Dalton was introduced to Collins at Devlin's public house, one of Collins's regular haunts. Dalton was very impressed by the man known affectionately as the 'Big Fellow'. Apparently Collins was introduced to Dalton only by his nickname – the name 'Michael Collins' was not used at all during this first encounter. There were also code names for the various hostelries that Collins frequented. So far as Dalton could recall, Vaughan's Hotel was 'joint number one', Devlin's was 'joint number two' and nearby Kirwan's pub was 'joint number three'. It appears that the two men did not have much to talk about during that first meeting but Collins said they would meet again.[27]

The next meeting with Collins resulted in Dalton taking a lead role in one of the most hazardous episodes of his career – the attempt to rescue senior IRA commander Sean MacEoin from Mountjoy Prison. It was an operation that also involved Emmet's brother Charlie. Even though Charlie was a member of Collins's intelligence apparatus, and had taken part in the Bloody Sunday operation, he only knew Collins to see. His first face-to-face meeting with Collins did not happen until April 1921, when the operation to 'spring' MacEoin from prison was being organized.

Collins was particularly anxious to rescue MacEoin. Known as 'The Blacksmith of Ballinalee', MacEoin was one of the more notable guerrilla fighters during the War of Independence. He operated in County Longford and was facing trial by military court and an almost certain death sentence. Ironically, he was an IRA leader who acted with particular chivalry towards enemy prisoners. Emmet Dalton described MacEoin as having 'brought a glimmer of decency into a dark and sordid era'.[28]

To 'spring' MacEoin from Mountjoy Prison, Collins came up with the idea of hi-jacking a British Army armoured car and have one of their people impersonate a British officer in the prison. MacEoin would then be taken away to safety. Collins devised the plan after being told that the crew of an armoured car regularly breached security regulations by emerging from the vehicle at a particular location and leaving the door open. This made the car's seizure a real possibility. But who could impersonate a British officer?

Traynor suggested Emmet Dalton to Collins, who asked to meet him. As mentioned, the two had previously been introduced at Devlin's pub. When the war hero met the Big Fellow once again, Collins was immediately struck by the fact that Dalton was 'made for the job'.[29] According to Traynor, Dalton spoke with the required 'affected accent' of the British officer, was very neat and debonair and wore a small, fair moustache, of the type favoured by the officer class. Collins explained that Dalton would dress up as a British officer and bluff his way into Mountjoy in a hi-jacked armoured car to rescue MacEoin. Privately, Dalton thought the plan was 'insane', according to his later account, but such was Collins's enthusiasm that he decided to go along with the proposal.[30] When Dalton agreed to take part, Collins shook his hand warmly, and assured him he would have the backing of the entire Volunteer organization. Collins went on to have regular meetings with Dalton as part of the planning process for the rescue.

A bond developed between the two men. Clearly, Collins saw in Emmet Dalton a brave, dynamic young man who could handle major tasks. He obviously respected Dalton's military experience, his coolness and his 'can-do' attitude, and would entrust Dalton with a range of crucial tasks over the following year. Dalton, for his part, looked up to Collins. Dalton would write later of Collins that he never knew a man to possess such an amazing personality – he described Collins as a severe taskmaster but with his mesmeric personality the Big Fellow 'could make the weakest of us feel strong with the overflow of his courage'.[31]

In late April 1921 Charlie Dalton was called in by the Assistant Director of Intelligence, Tom Cullen, to discuss with Collins his part in the upcoming rescue. Charlie recalled later that he was 'overawed' to be in the presence of Collins, and felt annoyed with himself that he was not at ease as he wanted to make a 'good impression'.[32]

Collins had received information from Michael Lynch, the Superintendent of the Dublin Corporation abattoir, who was also an on-the-run Volunteer officer. British soldiers in lorries, escorted by an armoured car, called to the slaughter house on Aughrim Street, off the North Circular Road, early every morning to collect meat.[33] The military killed their own cattle at the abattoir, prepared the meat there, which was then taken back in lorries to military base facilities to feed the soldiers. The fact that the crew had a habit of leaving the armoured car while soldiers were dressing the meat or having breakfast meant that the vehicle was vulnerable to seizure. Charlie Dalton's role was to keep surveillance on the soldiers at the abattoir, and to assess the feasibility of the car's seizure. He reported back to Collins that he believed the operation could be successful.

A rescue plan was drawn up. Dressed as British officers, Emmet Dalton and Joe Leonard would enter Mountjoy in the hi-jacked armoured car and convince the prison authorities that they were transferring MacEoin. The two rescuers would wear uniforms that Dalton retained from his service as an officer in the British Army. Emmet Dalton would lead this part of the operation. As part of the preparation, Collins held a meeting at Jim Kirwan's public house. Dalton and Leonard attended, and met a sympathetic Mountjoy Prison warder – probably Peadar Breslin. The warder gave them full information about the position of military guards, meal times and relief times for police and Auxiliaries.[34]

When Dalton found that the armoured car to be hi-jacked was a Peerless model, equipped with two Hotchkiss machine guns, he set about trying to locate two Volunteers who would be capable of using the Hotchkiss.[35] This was a weapon which, he knew from experience, was mainly used by the British Cavalry in the Great War. He had no personal experience of using the weapon himself. He knew a man called Jack McSweeney who had been a pilot in the British air force and found that McSweeney had a working knowledge of the Hotchkiss and, more importantly, was 'sound' as regards his national outlook. McSweeney went along with Dalton to a meeting with the two Volunteers who were to act as gunners in the armoured car, and with the aid of blackboard diagrams, instructed them in the operation of the gun. Dalton admitted it was the best that could be done in the absence of an actual Hotchkiss machine gun. (McSweeney later helped Dalton procure an aircraft during the Anglo-Irish Treaty talks held in London during late 1921, which would fly Collins back to Ireland in the event of an emergency.)

The rescue attempt was a high-risk operation. Mountjoy Prison was a heavily-guarded, high-security facility. While outwardly calm, Emmet Dalton feared he might not come out alive. Being a devout Catholic, he took the precaution of going to Confession.[36] Dalton later recalled Collins' briefing on the rescue plans to participants. When Collins detailed the arrangements 'he seemed to have made molehills of mountainous difficulties'. Dalton went on: 'His "God Speed" when our little party set out was in itself a tonic to cheer us.'[37]

Members of Michael Collins's Squad, the Active Service Unit and of the intelligence staff were mobilized for the rescue. Charlie Dalton was stationed in the home of the abattoir superintendent. For three days he kept vigil on the slaughterhouse while the others lay in wait. On the morning of 12 May 1921, he saw the armoured car crew step out of the vehicle. Recognizing the time had come to strike, he signalled the others by raising a window blind. Paddy O'Daly led an IRA party into the abattoir, where they shouted 'hands up'. One soldier was fired on when, apparently, he failed to comply immediately with instructions – he may have showed resistance or may simply have hesitated. He was seriously wounded and died later of his injuries.[38] Meanwhile, Charlie Dalton ran to a nearby house to breathlessly tell his brother and Joe Leonard that the operation had been launched. The two men already wore their British Army uniforms. The house, An Grianán, on the corner of Ellesmere Avenue and North Circular Road, was occupied by two elderly ladies. Probably fearing the worst, the women knelt in anxious prayer as Dalton and Leonard left the house. The Peerless armoured car, equipped with two machine guns, was commandeered, with Pat McCrea, the Squad's premier 'wheelman' driving, and Bill Stapleton as his assistant. McCrea had never driven a vehicle like this. Also in the IRA group were Sean Caffrey; machine gunner Peter Gough, who had served in a machine gun unit in the British Army during the Great War, and Tom Keogh whose coolness was regarded as an important asset. They wore British Army caps and dungarees. Meanwhile at the abattoir, soldiers and staff were held at gunpoint by members of the IRA group until the armoured car was well on its way – then they themselves withdrew.

McCrea drove the car along the North Circular Road to Hanlon's Corner where Emmet Dalton and Joe Leonard were waiting. McCrea's co-driver Bill Stapleton gave the pre-arranged signal – a white handkerchief waved out the window of the car – and the two 'officers' were quickly on board. With seven now in the vehicle, it was a tight squeeze. When the armoured car drove up to the prison, the car horn was sounded and a warder looked out through the grille and then emerged from the wicket gate. With an air of authority, Dalton waved an official-looking document, and demanded immediate access to the prison. The main gates were opened and the armoured car drove through. The gates closed behind them but McCrea managed to reverse and to park the vehicle in such a way that the two inner gates of the jail could not be closed. Meanwhile, a separate group of Volunteers hung about outside the prison to open the front gates when the time came for the car to escape.[39]

Leonard had been a prisoner in Mountjoy. A warder was clearly startled when he recognized Leonard in his British Army uniform but does not appear to have raised the alarm. Dalton was approached by the Chief Warder who asked him why he was there, and Dalton replied that he had come to see the prisoner 'McKeon' (MacEoin). Dalton and Leonard made their way into the prison with the help of their inside man, warder Peadar Breslin. MacEoin had already been tipped off by Breslin to expect a rescue attempt. The original plan was that MacEoin would contrive to get himself in the Governor's office at the time the rescuers came in. They would then leave together. Unfortunately, police in the prison introduced an additional security check on the prisoners which prevented MacEoin getting to the Governor's office in time.[40] Dalton carried with him duplicate keys to the doors of the wing and the cell where MacEoin was being held. The keys had been made for Michael Collins from impressions supplied to him by a sympathetic warder, possibly Breslin.[41]

Dalton and Leonard passed into the central section, or 'diamond' where blocks converged. They were on their way to MacEoin's cell in C (I) Wing when the Chief Warder again approached Dalton and stopped him, asking him again what his mission was. Dalton told him he needed to see MacEoin to read to him a statement of evidence. The warder said he could not interview the prisoner – he had first to go and see the Governor and get permission. Governor Charles Munro, brother of Hector Munro, the short story writer with the pen name Saki, was an essentially humane man. He had brought in a rule that military officers had to check with him first before seeing a prisoner. The rule had been introduced after prisoners had complained of being abused by visiting army officers.

Dalton and Leonard were shown by the Chief Warder into the Governor's office. He introduced the visitors and then departed. Now the two 'officers' met with another setback – the Governor was not alone. The Deputy Governor and the prison medical officer, Dr. Hackett, were also there. Dalton saluted the Governor, who greeted the visitors pleasantly. Emulating the clipped tones of a British officer, Dalton explained his mission, requesting that he should be allowed to go and see MacEoin, or that MacEoin should be brought to the office. He handed over a forged 'prisoner transfer' document ordering MacEoin to be taken from Mountjoy to Dublin Castle. The Governor read the document and went to pick up the telephone to phone Dublin Castle to confirm the order. Leonard immediately sprang forward and knocked the telephone out of his hand while Dalton produced his revolver, saying 'Hands up, gentlemen please.' The governor and his colleagues were so shocked they did not immediately comply. Leonard addressed them more forcefully. 'Put up your f…ing hands.' The three raised their hands and the Governor was so astonished at this turn of events that his monocle fell from his eye, and broke on his desk. It was one of those details that stayed engraved in Dalton's memory.

Dalton told Leonard to tie up the three men. Leonard asked with what should he tie them up. Dalton said to take their handkerchiefs and tie their hands behind their back. Leonard proceeded to do so. Dalton's idea was that he would put his head out the door and ask for MacEoin to be sent to the Governor's office immediately. Just then, they were startled to hear the sound of gunfire.

Mingling with a large crowd of people waiting outside the prison to visit relatives were members of a second section of the rescue group – Frank Bolster, Tom Walsh, and Cumann na mBan member Áine Malone, who carried a prisoner's parcel.[42] When the wicket gate was opened to allow the parcel to pass through, Bolster and Walsh drew revolvers and grabbed the gate-keeper's keys. They then opened the main gate, to facilitate the escape of the party inside the jail. A sentry on the roof saw the commotion and fired a shot that wounded Walsh in the hand, thus raising the alarm. Before the sentry could fire again, Tom Keogh shot him dead from inside the courtyard with a Mauser C96 'Peter the Painter' pistol. The soldier's rifle fell to the ground and was picked up by Bill Stapleton.

Dalton and Leonard heard the gunfire in the Governor's office. They knew now that they had to abandon the rescue operation. In his RTÉ interview with Pádraigh Ó Raghallaigh, Dalton recalled turning to Leonard and saying, 'Let's get out of here.' They managed to lock their captives into the office as they emerged into a corridor full of Auxiliaries and warders milling around, clearly on full alert due to the gunfire. Dalton murmured to Leonard, 'For God's sake, don't run.' They walked out into the yard where Pat McCrea was ready to drive off. McCrea was relieved to see them but disappointed that MacEoin was not with them. McCrea recalled that they asked, 'Who the hell started shooting?', and said it had spoiled the job.[43] Dalton ensured that everyone was on board. Then Dalton realized there was little room for himself inside the vehicle. He and Frank Bolster sat on the outside, at the back. Dalton remained calm and said to McCrea, 'Pat, home please' or words to that effect – like a gentleman addressing his chauffeur. With little time to spare McCrea drove out through the front gate and down the avenue to the North Circular Road. A troop of British soldiers ran out after the vehicle but did not open fire – apparently they thought the occupants of the car were British Army personnel. The British later reported that the car, with its occupants, 'still unrecognized as hostile, was permitted to depart'.[44]

The armoured car moved south down the North Circular Road. As he sat outside at the back of the vehicle, Dalton lit a cigarette. Meanwhile, the Governor, locked in his office, managed to break a window to raise the alarm, and also phoned military headquarters. Soon troops in lorries were out on the streets looking for the armoured car.[45] McCrea, still at the wheel of the vehicle, drove to a rendezvous in the area of North Richmond Street, off the North Circular Road, where O'Connell School was located. Michael Lynch, the abattoir superintendent who had supplied vital intelligence for the rescue operation, was there when the armoured car arrived. He later recalled Emmet Dalton sitting on the platform at the back of the car, 'lying back as an immaculate British officer, with his knees crossed and smoking a cigarette'.[46] 'I can never forget that moment,' Lynch said of Dalton's cool attitude.

'He was completely unperturbed even though only a few moments before he had undergone an experience that would have driven most men crazy. Let me say at once that this was no pose, no bravado, but sheer unadulterated nerve.'[47]

Meanwhile, Paddy O'Daly arrived on a push bike with the wounded Walsh, blood streaming from his hand, hanging on the back of the bicycle. Lynch provided some emergency first aid, bandaging Walsh's wound. As often happens in Dublin when an unusual event occurs, a crowd of children gathered. One urchin said to Lynch, 'Hey, Sir. Give me the wounded man. I live around here and we'll look after him.' Lynch thought it was time that Dalton should get away from the area as quickly as possible. He asked Dalton if he was going to stay there all day. 'No,' Dalton replied, 'I might as well get off and get out of these duds.'[48]

Standing by at the rendezvous, in his taxi, was Joe Hyland, Michael Collins's faithful driver. The original plan was that he would drive Sean MacEoin to a secure hiding place. Now his job was to take Dalton, Leonard and Walsh away to safety. He drove the three men to the pleasant seaside area of Howth, a safe distance away from the excitement. As previously mentioned, Dalton had been staying at a house in Howth with other Volunteers. Hyland dropped off his three passengers at a secluded convent, Stella Maris, on Howth peninsula, run by the Sisters of Charity. Leonard's sister had friends at the convent, set in spacious grounds with woodland paths and a panoramic view of the sea.

A nun was initially startled to open the door and find two men in British Army uniform on the doorstep. All was explained and the callers were welcomed into the convent. Walsh received further treatment for his wound, and the visitors were given tea, served in the convent's best china. Dalton and Leonard needed to change from their British Army uniforms into civilian clothes. A messenger was sent to Cassidy's public house on Howth Summit and returned with two suits. Now in civilian clothes, Dalton and Leonard returned to Dublin city centre by tram.

Pat McCrea ran into problems with the armoured car after dropping off three of his passengers at North Richmond Street. His experience was mainly with Ford cars, and he did not realize that the armour plates covering the radiator should have been opened while the car was moving. As a result, the engine badly overheated and the vehicle ground to a halt in the seaside suburb of Clontarf. The original plan had been to drive the armoured car to a farm between Swords and Malahide, in the Fingal Brigade area, where it would be hidden in a barn but now the vehicle had to be abandoned.[49] The crew stripped the vehicle of its two Hotchkiss machine guns and ammunition belts, set fire to the engine, and made their getaway with the machine guns and the rifle dropped by the shot sentry. The British were so concerned about the loss of the armoured car that they deployed a low-flying aircraft to search for it. The vehicle was eventually located on a secluded road near Clontarf railway station, and towed back to town. Meanwhile, the placid and iron-nerved McCrea returned to his day job delivering groceries on behalf of his brother (a merchant on South Great George's Street) to the Auxiliaries in Portobello Barracks. He is said to have been 'quietly amused' by the furore caused there by his activities earlier that day.[50] The following day, Sunday, Charlie Dalton went to see Pat McCrea to find out what went wrong with the operation, and was pleased to find Emmet with him. Emmet told him it was 'hopeless' from the moment the firing started – if that had been delayed for a couple of minutes they might have got MacEoin out.[51]

Members of the IRA group were extremely lucky to escape, but they were devastated at the failure to rescue MacEoin. On the evening of the rescue attempt Dalton met Collins who was also deeply disappointed, but even then Dalton found the Big Fellow 'was generous in his thanks for the effort that had been made'.[52] He told Dalton that he would always consider it 'a successful failure'. Collins was clearly impressed by Dalton's performance – all that could have been done, had been done. For his part, Dalton felt that Collins had come to trust him and thereafter Dalton had 'infinite faith' in Collins.[53] It was the beginning of a close, working relationship between the two men. The operation had enhanced Dalton's reputation for courage and coolness under pressure. He himself insisted that it was Collins's leadership qualities that encouraged people like himself to undertake major operations that they would otherwise have had their doubts about.

As it turned out, the IRA gained considerable publicity and prestige from the daring rescue attempt. *The Times* described the rescue operation as 'the most daring coup yet effected by Republicans in Dublin'.[54] Details of the identity of the soldiers who were killed during the rescue attempt did not immediately enter the public domain. The soldier fatally wounded in the abattoir was identified in recent years as Private Albert George Saggers (20), of the Royal Army Service Corps, of Stanstead, England.[55]

Had Dalton and Leonard been captured they could have faced a draconian sentence in a military court. The hi-jacking of the armoured car was a matter of great concern to the British military commander in Ireland, General Macready. He reported on the incident in one of his regular weekly reports to the War Office and the Cabinet. Macready said that a court of enquiry was being held. The whole incident had caused him to consider seriously 'the adequacy of the personnel at present available for manning the armoured cars...'[56] Meanwhile, security arrangements were tightened, with instructions issued to the British military that armed men or armoured cars were not to be allowed to enter any barracks or quarters until their identity had been thoroughly established.[57]

MacEoin went on trial in a military court on 14 June and, as expected, was sentenced to death. Michael Collins insisted on MacEoin being released when arrangements for truce negotiations with the British were being put in place later in 1921. In later years, Emmet Dalton commented on the rescue attempt: 'It was, I suppose, suicidal but it nearly came off, probably because it was so outrageously silly.'[58] Dalton and other members of the IRA rescue group remained loyal to Collins and some, like Dalton himself and Paddy O'Daly, would play significant roles on the Free State side in the ensuing Civil War. The sole woman participant in the rescue attempt, Áine Malone, a glamorous young Dubliner who had been shot in the hip while carrying dispatches during the 1916 Rising, took the republican side in the Civil War.[59]

Eventually, the British identified Emmet Dalton as one of the bogus British officers who had entered Mountjoy in the attempt to 'spring' MacEoin. In the months following the Truce, Dalton's name entered the public domain in connection with the operation. If the British did not know already, they knew it now. The Dublin Castle file on Dalton includes two press clippings from 1922 that refer to Dalton's role in the affair. The British also suspected Dalton's involvement in organizing the February 1921 escape of three republican prisoners from Kilmainham Jail, Frank Teeling, Simon Donnelly, and Ernie O'Malley. The Dublin Castle file details a conversation between a British officer and 'a captain of the republicans' in which the latter claims that Dalton was responsible for the escape.

According to the report, the whole Kilmainham escape 'was arranged by Major General Dalton' (his Civil War rank). The republican referred to Dalton as an ex-British officer, and said Dalton drove up to Kilmainham Jail in a lorry about an hour before the escape, dressed as a British officer, and entered the jail. He also said that Dalton had entered Kilmainham Jail 'several times', dressed as a 'British officer'.[60] The British Administration appeared to give credence to this account, and included the remark in Dalton's file. In the file there is a summary of Dalton's career which includes the remark: 'Organized the escape from Kilmainham Prison of one TEELING a prisoner convicted of murder and awaiting execution... Said to have been responsible for many of the escapes from prisons and is regarded as an expert at such work.' However, Ernie O'Malley's first-hand account of the escape from Kilmainham in his book *On Another Man's Wound*, makes no reference to any role by Dalton in the escape, nor to anyone entering the prison posing as a British officer. Other IRA documentation does not mention Dalton in this regard either.

Attack on the Custom House

In the earlier part of 1921, members of the Dáil Cabinet decided to strike a major blow at British administration in Ireland by destroying the Custom House by the banks of the Liffey in Dublin. The period building housed important government files and a number of Departments, including Inland Revenue, Local Government, and the Stamp Office. It was one of the biggest operations mounted by the IRA during the War of Independence. The attack was launched on 25 May 1921 by a force of about 120 Volunteers under Commandant Tom Ennis, commander of the 2nd Battalion of the Dublin Brigade. After the raiders struck, there were delays in getting the staff to leave the building. As a result the Volunteers were still on the scene when Crown forces arrived – a unit of Black and Tans backed up by military and armoured cars. While the IRA succeeded in its objective of burning the Custom House, it was a disaster for the organization. Most of the Volunteers who took part were captured and five were killed in the fighting, including two brothers, Paddy and Stephen O'Reilly. Ennis was shot in the leg and the hip and was lucky to get away. Jim Slattery, one of the members of Michael Collins's Squad who took part in the operation, also got away but lost a hand as a result of injuries. Among the civilian casualties was the caretaker, Mr. F.M. Davis who was fatally wounded after he apparently tried to raise the alarm – he was due to retire the following August. A colleague heard the dying family man say: 'Who will look after my boys?'[61]

Dalton was not involved in the Custom House operation or in the planning of it but he monitored developments from the headquarters of the Dublin Brigade, with the brigade adjutant Christy O'Malley. Word came through that the operation had gone awry and that many of the Volunteers had been captured. Dalton and his colleagues tried to organize a force to mount a diversion that would enable the escape of Volunteers who had been lined up by the British but at short notice they could not find anyone available.[62]

Shortly after the Custom House operation, Dalton called to the Gresham Hotel to see a visitor from America, James Brendan Connolly, who was Commissioner for the American Committee for the Relief in Ireland. Connolly, son of an Irish-speaking immigrant from the Aran Islands, came from Dalton's home state of Massachusetts and this probably made Dalton all the more eager to meet him. They discussed how Connolly could help in publicizing the IRA's achievements – Dalton told him to contact republican publicist Erskine Childers who had the records of the IRA 'in the field'. They also discussed the serious wounds suffered by the Commandant of the Dublin Brigade, Tom Ennis, in the attack on the Custom House. Clearly, Dalton feared the worst and remarked, 'He can't live'.[63] In fact Ennis would survive to fight alongside Dalton in the Civil War.

Dalton wrote a detailed report on the Custom House operation which included an analysis of what went wrong from a military point of view. He concluded that the main force had inadequate protection: 'A force can be regarded as secure from surprise only when protection is furnished in every direction from which attack is possible.' He commented that ambush parties should have been posted at all likely routes for the purpose of holding up the enemy advance and thus gaining time. However, he did praise Commandant Tom Ennis for the initiative he showed in turning 'what might have been a failure into success'.[64] Looking back on the operation in later years Dalton saw the capture of so many Volunteers and the deaths of others as a very grave blow to the Dublin Brigade. In his view, the Volunteers in Dublin were in a hopeless position, there was no fighting force left and there was a lack of arms.[65] For this reason he would welcome the Truce between the British and the IRA that was now not far off – it would be concluded just a few weeks later.

The Arrival of the Thompson Guns

There was considerable excitement in the upper ranks of the IRA when the first Thompson sub-machine guns were smuggled in from the United States. Harry Boland, the Irish representative in the US, was involved in procuring the weapons. Just a few guns were brought in after a major consignment was seized in America.[66] The Thompson guns that made their way to Ireland, while of great interest to the movement, would not have been sufficient to solve the arms shortage which in Dalton's view had greatly impaired the capabilities of the Volunteers.

Dalton was one of the IRA GHQ members to examine the rapid-fire sub-machine guns that were imported from the US. In Dublin, he liaised with two Irish-

American former officers of the US armed forces, Major James Dineen and Captain Patrick Cronin. They had arrived from Chicago to give classes in the maintenance, dismantling and firing of the weapon. Both men would later become officers in the Free State Army. P.J. Paul[67] recalled being brought to a room in University College Dublin, probably some time in May 1921, and there meeting Emmet Dalton, as well as two American instructors, and shown a Thompson. According to Paul, the name on the door where the meeting took place was 'Owen MacNeill' – probably a reference to Professor Eoin MacNeill, the noted academic, Gaelic League founder, and later government minister.

Dalton was also present when Michael Collins and a prominent figure in Collins' Squad were shown a Thompson. The weapon had been brought to the Dublin home of a republican family, and examined and assembled. According to Catherine Rooney[68] those present were Collins, Dalton and Paddy Daly. She recalled that after some time the men left and went to Marino where they tried out the gun. Emmet Dalton's brother Charlie was equipped with a Thompson when he took part in an ambush of British troops travelling by train through his home area of Drumcondra on 16 June 1921. It was part of an attempt to carry out a number of attacks so that the British would not know how the ranks of the Volunteers had been depleted by the arrests made during the Custom House operation.[69] Charlie Dalton believed it was the first time that the two new Thompson guns that had been smuggled into Ireland were brought into action, although he did not manage to fire his own weapon as the target only presented itself briefly.

Emmet Dalton came to know the boisterous, playful side of Michael Collins. In later years he recalled how, 'at the very height of the struggle and curfew', he himself, Collins and Gearóid O'Sullivan were staying the night at the small, private Munster Hotel, run by Miss McCarthy. (The hotel at 44 Mountjoy Street in Dublin's north inner city, was a favourite Collins 'safe house'.) Collins sabotaged the bed that O'Sullivan was to occupy, so that it collapsed under his weight, causing the Big Fellow to laugh uproariously. In case Dalton felt left out of the merriment, Collins threw Dalton's shoes through the open window and into the street.[70] Crown forces were patrolling the neighbourhood and Dalton may have had some reservations about the Big Fellow's prank as he ventured out to recover his footwear.

Truce in the War of Independence

Emmet Dalton would recall in later life that he was surprised when he heard, in the summer of 1921, that there might be a Truce in the War of Independence. Following talks between the leaders on both sides, a Truce was agreed, and it came into operation on 11 July 1921. According to Dalton, he and other members of the IRA general staff were pleased at the decision to call a Truce. He considered that their fighting force in Dublin had been severely reduced as a result of so many of their men being captured in the Custom House operation. He estimated that 60 per cent of the fighting force had been taken prisoner at the Custom House. It was a severe setback.[71]

As part of the Truce a liaison system was set up between the IRA and the British civil and military authorities in Ireland to monitor the observation of the Truce.

Dalton apparently became Assistant Chief Liaison Officer and Dublin Brigade Liaison Officer.[72] He would later assume the very powerful position of Chief Liaison Officer. Dalton continued with his role as Director of Training in IRA GHQ. The IRA began to train openly rather than covertly as was the case previously. Dalton organized 'a complete training programme for the whole country', according to J.J. 'Ginger' O'Connell.[73] One of Dalton's roles was to organize training camps and appoint instructors. For this task Dalton sought Irish Volunteers with British military experience. In his memoir, *Dublin Made Me*, Todd Andrews recalled going along to meet Dalton in a 'miserable gloomy' room in the building known as the Plaza Hotel. He had heard about Dalton but was surprised at how youthful the Director of Training looked. Nevertheless, there was no mistaking the 'air of authority he exuded', despite his quiet and pleasant manner.[74] Dalton told him to take charge of a training camp for senior officers of the Donegal Brigade, at Dungloe. He was assisted by a former British Army sergeant. Details of the course were set out in the official curriculum. Andrews had his doubts about the sergeant who seemed to have more interest in drink than in republican politics, and the instructor was ultimately sent back to Dublin as 'unsuitable'.

One of those impressed by Dalton's performance as Director of Training was Seamus Finn from County Meath, who was Vice O/C and Director of Training of the 1st Eastern Division of the IRA. In his statement to the BMH, Finn said: 'I believe I have never met anyone so efficient in my life. He was a pale faced, slightly-built man, but gave one the impression of being made of whalebone. I was very impressed by him and I was not alone in that.' Finn told how, following the Truce, a divisional or central camp was established at Ballymacoll outside Dunboyne, and Dalton sent down two training officers. 'This camp was kept going right through the Truce period, and was not closed until the British withdrew their troops from the country altogether, and our men took over and occupied the barracks which they vacated.'[75] Dalton approached a former schoolmate at O'Connell's, John Harrington, who had been active in the IRA, to run a training camp at Sligo. Harrington declined the offer, considering that he would be of greater value in an intelligence role in Dublin if hostilities were resumed.[76]

William Corri, from an Irish-Italian family in Ringsend, Dublin, was one of the men with previous military experience who was recruited by Dalton to give instruction to the Volunteers. Corri, who stood out among the Volunteers because of his Latin looks, came from a most artistic family – his forebears included opera singers, composers and a prominent landscape painter. He had served in the British Army in the Great War in Salonika, Belgium and France. After returning to Dublin he joined the Volunteers, becoming a member of E Company, I Battalion, having previously been rejected by the commander of another unit because of his service in the British Army. He took part in raids and ambushes in Dublin, and was chosen by Dalton for a reformed Active Service Unit (ASU) after the original force's decimation in the Custom House operation. After the Truce he became a member of GHQ training staff, and instructed officers at training camps in north Roscommon and County Mayo; at Dunboyne, County Meath and at Mulhuddart and Loughlinstown in County Dublin.[77] Corri would take the Free State side in the Civil War, and served as governor of the Gormanstown prison camp and of Kilmainham Prison. In later years he continued his contact with Dalton through the Association of the Old Dublin Brigade.

During the summer of 1921 Dalton spent several weeks running an IRA training camp in the Dublin Mountains. Groups of Volunteers would arrive for a ten-day course, centred on a very remote hunting lodge, Glenasmole Lodge, in the scenic, wooded valley of Glenasmole. For many trainees, such training courses, apart from providing military instruction, would have been a welcome break from normal routine, providing a change of scene, a sense of camaraderie, and a stay in a stunning location. Located on the very edge of mountain moorland and heather, the lodge was well chosen for a military training camp. Dalton was pleased with the courses.[78]

Glenasmole Lodge was the hillside retreat of a prominent Anglo-Irish businessman, Charles Wisdom Hely who had been a Justice of the Peace and whose main residence was at Rathgar, Dublin. It is unclear under what conditions the IRA used his hillside retreat – Hely later re-assumed the use of the lodge. (Wisdom Hely and his printing and stationary business on Dame Street are mentioned in James Joyce's novel *Ulysses*. The character Leopold Bloom used to work at Hely's but was sacked because he kept making suggestions to Wisdom Hely as to how to improve the business.) During 1921 another IRA officer Paddy O'Brien worked as an assistant to Dalton in running courses at the Glenasmole camp and he and Dalton got to know each other well. The two men would take opposite sides in the Civil War. Among the instructors at the Glenasmole camp were the two Americans who had initiated the Volunteers into the use of the Thompson sub-machine gun, Major James Dineen and Captain Patrick Cronin. At Glenasmole, they specialised in instruction in the Thompson gun, and one can imagine how the hillside echoed to the staccato sound of the weapon as it was fired during training. Both men were useful additions to the IRA training staff. Dineen was born in Limerick and had served seventeen years in the US armed forces. He took part in operations against the Mexican revolutionary Pancho Villa and in the Great War in France he had been wounded.

During the period of the Truce, the IRA continued to maintain its organization in case hostilities resumed, and plans were formulated for a uniformed army. Ernie O'Malley recalled how, in the period following the Truce, he was called to Dublin for a meeting of senior IRA officers, in August 1921. Among those present were Michael Collins, Director of Intelligence; Richard Mulcahy, Chief of Staff; Eoin O'Duffy, Deputy Chief of Staff, and Emmet Dalton, Director of Training. Officers from the provinces gave a report on developments in their areas. The question of wearing uniforms was discussed – most were in favour.[79] Elements of the IRA were about to move from a guerrilla force to a conventional army.

Getting to Know Senior Figures in the Republican Movement

After joining the General Headquarters staff of the IRA, Dalton came to know some of the leading figures in the independence movement. He became friends with Harry Boland, who had been imprisoned after the 1916 Rising, later becoming Sinn Féin party secretary, and TD for South Roscommon in the First Dáil. Boland also served for a period as President of the Supreme Council of the secretive Irish Republican Brotherhood and was to be a republican envoy to the United States from May 1919 to December 1921. Dalton witnessed the competition for the affections of Kitty Kiernan between Boland and the latter's good friend Michael Collins, a contest that the Big Fellow would ultimately win. After Boland returned from the United States in August 1921, Dalton tagged along when Boland, Collins and Sean MacEoin showed up in Granard, County Longford where Kitty lived. Boland's biographer comments that Dalton was a 'congenial novelty in the inner circle'.[80]

Dalton was also a guest at the wedding of Tom Barry and Leslie Price in Dublin on 22 August 1921. The guest list reads like a 'Who's Who' of the Irish republican movement at the time, and included Michael Collins, Éamon de Valera, Harry Boland, Eoin O'Duffy, Countess Markievicz and Mary McSwiney. The best man was Liam Deasy. The wedding reception was held at Vaughan's Hotel, Parnell Square, a favourite haunt of Michael Collins. Some of those at the happy event would later take leading roles on opposite sides in the Civil War. Ironically, on the first anniversary of the wedding, Michael Collins would die at Bealnablath, County Cork, in an ambush organized with the approval of the groom's best man Liam Deasy.

During the Truce period, in his capacity as Training Officer, Dalton came to know Tom Barry well – he visited the West Cork area and was shown around by Barry. He would later recall that he had a 'good acquaintance with West Cork'.[81] This knowledge would come in useful during the Civil War, when the region formed part of the battleground between Dalton's troops and republican fighters, who included leaders such as Barry. With his personal charm, Dalton made an impression on Kitty Kiernan and her sister Maud, and became friendly with them. Maud seemed to take an interest in Dalton's love life. By late 1921 Emmet was clearly deeply committed to his sweetheart Alice whom he would marry the following year. But there may have been other romances in the meantime. Maud, in a letter to Harry Boland in December 1921, said she believed Emmet has fallen in love again. 'I hope this will be the final one.'[82] In October 1922 Maud herself would marry Gearóid O'Sullivan, who was friendly with Emmet and very close to Michael Collins. O'Sullivan would serve as Adjutant General of the National Army during the Civil War and in later life became a successful barrister and member of the Dáil.

Dalton attended the wedding of Kitty Kiernan's glamorous sister Helen when she married County Fermanagh solicitor Paul McGovern. Collins had originally been attracted to Helen but transferred his affections to Kitty when Helen chose McGovern instead. While in London with the Treaty delegation in October 1921, Dalton took time to write to Harry Boland that the wedding was a 'huge success', and commented on how well Kitty looked.[83] The McGovern marriage broke up in 1925, and Helen ran a successful fish restaurant on Duke Street, Dublin, known as 'The Dive'. One of her grandsons is the actor Barry McGovern,[84] who happened to play the role of the Big Fellow's great opponent, Éamon de Valera, in the 1991 RTÉ-BBC historical film, *The Treaty*.

Playing Soccer and Golf

Emmet Dalton loved football and he played with Bohemians after returning to Dublin from the Great War. He is said to have joined the club in 1919 and played for a season. According to author Ulick O'Connor, Dalton frequently played matches against British regiments behind the barbed wire that had been erected 'to keep men of his kind from entering for purposes other than sport'.[85] Said Ulick: 'He told me they [the British] would not know you in your togs.' He added that Dalton was a 'great soccer player'. Ulick got to know Dalton well in the 1950s while interviewing him in connection with research for his biography of the poet, writer and surgeon Oliver St. John Gogarty.[86] They would meet in the Shelbourne Hotel when Dalton made trips to Dublin from his home in London. Dalton and Gogarty had been good friends. Ulick said that during the War of Independence, Dalton played a part in bringing wounded IRA men to Gogarty's house in Ely Place in Dublin for medical assistance.[87] 'Gogarty used to do operations on IRA men in trouble,' said Ulick, adding that if Gogarty had been caught by the authorities he would have been in serious trouble.

Dalton was also to indulge his passion for golf. Having played the game in El Arish in the Sinai desert, he was eager to develop his skills in the greener pastures of Ireland after being demobilized. It is unclear when exactly he joined the Hermitage club in the Lucan area of County Dublin, which had been founded in 1905. Hermitage enjoys a magnificent location, an oasis of greenery and woodlands just a few miles from the city. The lands slope down to the River Liffey and there are panoramic views across the green river valley. Over the years the game of golf in general, and his membership of Hermitage in particular, would play a very important role in Dalton's life. Dalton quickly achieved scratch status, and a golfing journalist who interviewed him in later years attributed his golfing skills partly to his ability as a marksman while in the military. The journalist wrote that 'great accuracy with a rifle stood to him in his golf as it is his wonderful accurate "shooting" as the Yankees have it, that has brought him to scratch.'[88] Dalton's avid interest in sport probably provided him with a welcome outlet as he faced into a challenging period, during which he would work more closely with a demanding taskmaster, Michael Collins.

CHAPTER FOUR

Treaty Talks

Emmet Dalton's revolutionary star was clearly in the ascendant. At one stage in 1921 there was some indication from republican leader Harry Boland that Dalton might be sent to America as a special emissary. Visiting Boston, Massachusetts in November that year, Boland described Dalton as, 'one of the big men in the fight for Irish freedom', who had proven his worth both on the field of battle and in assisting in the planning of the Anglo-Irish peace treaty.[1]

Michael Collins thought highly enough of Emmet Dalton's abilities to entrust him with sensitive missions. Perhaps none was more important than the Anglo-Irish Treaty negotiations, held between representatives of Dáil Éireann and British government cabinet ministers. The Irish delegation was faced with the unenviable task of trying to secure Irish independence, as well as preventing partition of the island. Michael Collins was tasked as a representative, while serving as Minister of Finance in the Dáil government and IRA Director of Intelligence. He would join his fellow delegates Arthur Griffith, Eamonn Duggan, George Gavan Duffy and Robert Barton.

Later in life, Dalton said he never liked the idea of Collins travelling to London for the Treaty negotiations. The crown forces dearly wanted to get their hands on Collins during the Anglo-Irish War. Now the Big Fellow was emerging out of the shadows and into danger. Even within the IRA, many members did not know what he looked like. There was also the possibility that comrades of British personnel who had been killed on Collins's orders might be tempted to take revenge – memories of Bloody Sunday were still raw. Dalton said fellow members of the GHQ staff were 'gravely concerned' over the safety of Michael Collins in England.[2]

Collins did not consider himself the right person to go to London as Dalton emphasized in later years. Dalton was present at a meeting of the General Headquarters Staff when Collins revealed that he had been selected. Collins was adamant that it was not his job or his place to go – he felt it would be more appropriate for Dáil President Éamon de Valera to go, and leave Collins to carry on the work he knew best.[3] De Valera considered it more appropriate that he himself stay at home. Despite his misgivings, Collins ultimately agreed to go.

Dalton had his doubts as to whether there would be a successful outcome to the talks. There were also fears that should the Treaty negotiations break down while Collins was in London, 'the entire Irish Army position would be jeopardised'. According to Dalton, he and Collins decided to place an aircraft in readiness should the talks break down and it proved necessary to fly Collins back to Ireland. Dalton set about formulating a plan.[4]

He contacted Waterford-born Jack McSweeney, who had been a pilot with 50 Squadron of the Royal Flying Corps (RFC) during the Great War. As previously mentioned, Dalton had met McSweeeney while researching the Hotchkiss machine gun in the prelude to the Sean MacEoin rescue operation. Dalton also put out feelers through the Dublin Brigade. Fourth Battalion Commandant Sean Dowling recommended another former RFC pilot, Charles Russell. The Dublin native enjoyed a remarkable flying career, and became a pioneer of Irish aviation. Russell had served with 65 Squadron of the RFC in France during the Great War and was later an instructor in aerobatics. He had flown extensively in the United States and in Canada, where he carried out an aerial survey between Toronto and Niagara for the Canadian Electric Power Commission.[5] Dalton had a long talk with McSweeney and Russell and, after being satisfied of their loyalty to the republican cause, he sent them to England to buy a suitable aircraft. Russell's time as an aviator in Canada gave him a 'cover' story – he would purport to be procuring an aircraft for a Canadian forestry department.

The aircraft had to be suitable for carrying passengers and freight, and with an eye to future use by Irish armed forces, it also had to be suitable for military purposes, including bombing missions. The two young men spoke to representatives of a number of aircraft manufacturers, Avro & Co., Martinsyde & Co., Short Bros., Vickers Ltd., and De Havilland & Co.[6]

The type of aircraft they ultimately purchased was a Martinsyde Type A, Mark 2, four-seater bi-plane. This aircraft was powered by a Rolls Royce engine, had a range of 550 miles, a cruising speed of 100 miles per hour, and cost £2,600.[7] The transaction occurred during the Treaty negotiations, and it was held on stand-by at Croydon Aerodrome, the gateway for international flights to and from London. Russell and McSweeney took several practice flights to familiarize themselves with the machine. When the aerodrome people became impatient at the delay in removing the aircraft from their facilities, Russell, after each practice flight, kept complaining of 'right wing low' or 'left wing low' or 'unsatisfactory rudder' by way of explaining the delay.[8]

Dalton showed his usual meticulous attention to detail in planning how the aircraft could land safely in the greater Dublin area if Collins had to make a quick getaway. It was proposed that Russell would be the pilot for the flight to Ireland, while McSweeney would be deployed at the landing ground to prepare the runway and arrange re-fuelling. The plane would fly from London, across the Irish Sea, and ultimately land at Leopardstown racecourse.[9]

Collins, of course, did not have to make an emergency getaway from London, but the aircraft did serve a useful purpose. It was taken to Baldonnel, near Dublin, the airfield chosen to be the base of the air division of the new National Army, and was the first military aircraft acquired by new Irish state. Its purchase can be seen as the birth of the Irish Air Corps. Dalton later stated with pride, 'From this beginning grew what is now known as the Irish Air Force.'[10]

Dalton Joins the IRB and Goes to London with Collins

Before Emmet Dalton departed for London with Michael Collins for the Treaty negotiations, he went through an important procedure. He was sworn into the secret, oath-bound organization, the Irish Republican Brotherhood (IRB). It was decided at a meeting of the Dublin County Board of the IRB on 6 October that Dalton should be accepted as a member.[11] Founded in the nineteenth century, the IRB was dedicated to the establishment of an Irish republic by any means necessary. Collins had become President of the Supreme Council of the IRB in the summer of 1920, and perhaps he wanted Dalton to join the organization before assisting with the sensitive Treaty talks. The Catholic Church did not approve of secret, oath-bound societies such as the IRB. Dalton later told of being refused Confession by a priest on the basis of his IRB membership. However, during the revolutionary period a man refused the Sacraments by one priest could often find another willing to turn a blind eye. In Dalton's case the obliging cleric who heard his Confession and gave absolution happened to be a Jesuit.[12]

Most of the Irish delegation, of which Arthur Griffith was chairman, arrived in London on 8 October for the Treaty talks that would decide the future relationship between Ireland and Britain. Collins, accompanied by Dalton and a small entourage, travelled on the mail boat from Dun Laoghaire the following evening. Collins had brought some of his most trusted intelligence operatives and members of the Squad. They would act as bodyguards and couriers. Collins, full of nervous energy, found it difficult to sit still on the voyage. Dalton remembered him pacing the ship deck, full of his own thoughts, and looking gloomy. Dalton spent time with him on deck, and one of Collins's remarks stuck in Dalton's memory: 'How am I expected to get people out of the strait-jackets they have themselves secured?'[13] No doubt Collins recognized that he would disappoint uncompromising republicans back home.

Two senior officials from Dublin Castle, Under-Secretaries Sir John Anderson and Alfred Cope, crossed on the same mail boat. When Cope found Collins could not get a sleeping compartment on the train from Holyhead to London (the party did not book in advance), he insisted Collins take his. Dalton and Cope spent the night in the reserved compartment of a first-class carriage. Dalton said he often wondered who had learned most from the other during the long journey to London.[14] Cope probably knew already about Dalton's background as a British Army officer and holder of the Military Cross – perhaps during the night he found out more about the motivation of a young man who had fought for the British and then changed sides. They arrived in Euston, London about five o'clock on the morning of 10 October, the day before Collins was to meet British Prime Minister David Lloyd George at his residence, 10 Downing Street.

The Irish had rented two houses for the Treaty talks. Most of the delegation and the staff were based at 22 Hans Place, near the renowned Harrods department store. Collins and key members of his own circle, including Dalton, were based at Grosvenor House, 15 Cadogan Gardens, Kensington, a short walk away from Hans Place. Though he had been reluctant to attend the London talks, Collins appeared pleased to be surrounded by men who were part of his close circle. A member of the Irish delegation, Robert Barton, said that meetings of the delegation were held in Hans Place but Collins carried out his functions as Director of Intelligence in Grosvenor House. He recalled that those based with Collins at this location were Emmet Dalton, Diarmuid O'Hegarty, Tom Cullen, Ned Broy 'and a number of others'. In his statement to the BMH, Barton said: 'Collins took all these over himself, partly by way of protection and partly by way of keeping in touch with things at home. They were passing backwards and forwards with information all the time. Remember, you could not trust even the postman, the King's messenger.'[15]

Collins availed of Dalton's military expertise in side-talks with the British on defence matters. Dalton also acted as adviser on IRA and British compliance with the Truce, which was still in place. On the opening day of the Treaty negotiations, the Irish delegation, with their staff members, set off for 10 Downing Street, in a fleet of Rolls Royce cars. Most of the delegates were in the first car. Collins travelled in the second car with Dalton and key members of the intelligence staff – Liam Tobin, Tom Cullen, Joe Dolan and Joe Guilfoyle. When Collins and the other delegates arrived at the barricaded entrance to 10 Downing Street, they found a big crowd of Irish exiles assembled, many of them on their knees praying. Dalton received special attention from some of the press cameramen. He did not realize that they had noticed the butt of his revolver protruding from his hip pocket.[16] Observing the arrival of Collins and his men was one of the Irish delegation secretaries, Kathleen Napoli McKenna, who remembered seeing 'Emmet Dalton, handsome as a Wild West cinema star, the butt of a service rifle [sic] peeping from his hip pocket, all alert.'[17]

It might have been assumed that Dalton, in addition to his advisory duties, was acting as a bodyguard for Collins, in light of the fact that he was armed with a .45 service revolver. However, according to Dalton's daughter Audrey, Dalton always insisted that he was not there as a bodyguard, but as a member of the defence committee. Nevertheless, Dalton was concerned about Collins's security while in London, as evidenced by his role in the air escape plan. Even as an adviser, Dalton would have been useful to have around in the event of a threat to Collins. Dalton was frequently at Collins's side. One of the photographs from the period shows Dalton and Collins, smiling shyly for the camera, sitting in the open-topped back of a motor car, looking like dashing, well-dressed young men about town.

Talks with the British

As they negotiated on the future of Ireland, the Irish delegates were up against a British side headed by Prime Minister David Lloyd George, genial, charming but ruthless. Collins had side meetings with the British on finance, defence and observance of the truce. For the defence talks, apart from Dalton, Collins's team included other senior military men, Eoin O'Duffy and J.J. 'Ginger' O'Connell, and the Irish delegation secretary, Erskine Childers. The latter wrote the best-selling thriller *Riddle of the Sands*, had delivered the Volunteer rifles to Howth in 1914 and also had considerable expertise from his service as a Royal Navy officer. Dalton and Collins came to distrust Childers, who later took an anti-Treaty stance.

On the issue of defence, Collins spent much time arguing with Air Marshal Hugh Trenchard, head of the Royal Air Force, and Admiral David Beatty, head of the Royal Navy. He tried to convince them that controlling Ireland in a naval war was not very important. Security cooperation with Ireland, he argued, would be best achieved on the basis of Irish neutrality, rather than as a subordinate country within the British empire.[18] Dalton attended his first meeting on defence on 13 October. He accompanied Collins to a meeting at the Colonial Office with the formidable and very abrasive Colonial Secretary, Winston Churchill. Erskine Childers also attended this informal meeting of the Air and Naval Defence Committee. Churchill was accompanied by the Royal Navy's Admiral Beatty and Captain B.E. Domville.[19] Dalton took advantage of the opportunity to break the ice with Churchill and to make a personal assessment of the man.

A further meeting of the committee was held on 17 October at the Offices of the Cabinet, 2 Whitehall Gardens. On this occasion Collins brought his full defence team – Dalton, O'Connell, O'Duffy and Childers, with Diarmuid O'Hegarty as secretary. Churchill was accompanied by Sir Laming Worthington Evans, Secretary of State for War. The two had a formidable array of advisers – Sir Hugh Trenchard, Vice-Admiral Sir Osmond de Beauvoir Brock, Captain F. E. Grant and Captain Domville, with Tom Jones and Lionel Curtis acting as secretaries. The two sides met again the following morning at the Colonial Office.[20] In later years Dalton reflected that on facing Churchill's team across the conference table, he reckoned his own side could have done with some reserves. Nevertheless he believed that what they lacked in numbers they made up with Collins's 'dominant courage and determination'.[21] Dalton indicated in a letter how busy he had been in recent days, 'looking after Mick', and arguing with Winston Churchill and Admiral Beatty.[22]

In pursuing talks with the British on defence, Collins decided that he needed support from the West Cork guerrilla leader Tom Barry. Dalton recalled how one night, on the way home from a fiery encounter with the British delegation, Collins told him, 'I wish I had Tom Barry over here.' Dalton told the writer Meda Ryan that on his next visit to Dublin, Collins sent word to Barry to go to London, which he did. In the evenings, at Hans Place, Collins and the negotiators listened to Barry's opinion on military aspects of the negotiations.[23] Despite Collins's reluctance to go to London for the negotiations, Dalton gained the impression that the British were more than happy to have him there, because they saw him as the militant force controlling what happened in Ireland.[24] It made sense for the British to try to do a deal with the senior figure perceived to be the hardliner who wielded the real power back home.

Dalton was present when Collins had a confrontation with Churchill, who had challenged the Irish side over what he described as breaches of the Truce. Collins became increasingly irritated as Churchill outlined a seemingly endless list of incidents in which, he said, the Truce had been broken. Collins scribbled a note to Dalton, asking if they had 'any answer' to Churchill's points. Dalton, never one for subterfuge or evasion, scribbled, 'No answer'. Collins remained quiet for a while as Churchill pressed on with his tirade. Suddenly Collins thumped the table, surprising all present, including Churchill, who was stunned into silence. Collins had the ability to take the sting out of a remark or gesture by a mischievous grin and he used the technique on this occasion. Churchill looked at Collins, saw the Big Fellow grinning, and began to grin as well.[25] The tension had been defused. Churchill had been tricked into ceasing his verbal tirade, even though it was clear that Collins had no answer to the accusations being made.

Collins took time off from pressing duties to write letters to his sweetheart, Kitty Kiernan back in Ireland. She seemed to like Dalton, and in one of her letters to Collins in London, dated 17 October, she inquired after Emmet and the others in Collins's entourage.[26] Even though Collins worked extremely hard, once he was ensconced with his friends at Grosvenor House there was bound to be horseplay and practical jokes, as Dalton himself would discover. Some of the beds in the house had legs that were hinged, and Collins liked to bend them back during the night so that the occupants would find themselves sleeping at an angle to the floor. In his practical way, Dalton decided on a way of dealing with the situation. Ned Broy looked into Dalton's room one night and saw him sleeping at an angle to the floor. Dalton explained that Collins would come in and bend the legs later, so he decided to bend them himself.[27]

Through Collins, Dalton became friendly with Lady Lavery, the glamorous American-born high society hostess and wife of the prestigious painter Sir John Lavery. She became a great admirer of the Big Fellow, and introduced him to some members of her influential social circle. Hazel Lavery also liked to entertain Cabinet ministers such as Winston Churchill and Prime Minister Lloyd George, and other important figures at her palatial Kensington home, 5 Cromwell Place. In Dalton's view, she was a very useful contact for Collins in his role as Director of Intelligence. Through her, he was able to get useful inside information, and also feed her items to ensure they got back to the right people.[28] There has been much speculation as to whether Collins and Lady Lavery had an affair. In an interview in 1974 with the writer Meda Ryan, Dalton said that Collins 'liked Hazel, everybody did', but that was all there was to it. Dalton claimed Collins would never put himself in the position where he could be blackmailed, either by people from his own side or by the British.[29] However, as will be explained, the actual situation may have been much more complicated.

In a draft article written in 1946 for the twenty-fifth anniversary of the signing of the Treaty, and apparently unpublished, Dalton said that he had listened over the years to 'scurrilous and malign statements' concerning the private lives of the delegates in London during the negotiations.[30] He may have been referring to rumours about the Collins/Lady Lavery relationship. He said he always felt that such absurd remarks were unworthy of rebuttal. He went on to present a picture of Collins that contradicted any 'scurrilous' statements that might have been made. He referred to a particular aspect of the Big Fellow's routine in London – the 'daily visits by Michael Collins to a place of worship where he humbly prayed for guidance and divine inspiration…' During the Treaty talks, Collins would often attend early morning Mass at the Church of St. Mary, Cadogan Place, or Brompton Oratory. Dalton, a religious man himself, was clearly impressed by Collins's piety while immersed in talks on the future of Ireland.

As the negotiations dragged on, Dalton observed how the stress took its toll on Collins. He recalled that one morning Collins was in an 'impossible' mood and had snapped at the ever-faithful Diarmuid O'Hegarty. Dalton described O'Hegarty as a brilliant and indefatigable worker, like Collins himself, and believed there was none closer to Collins.[31] The fact that Collins could turn on his friend in a moment of exasperation was an indication of the strain under which he was operating.

Sometimes the stress was relieved by horseplay. Kathleen Napoli McKenna has described how, during a banquet at Hans Place, Collins arrived with his entourage, including Dalton, Tobin, Cullen, Guilfoyle and Dolan. She recalled that they were a 'happy, boisterous crowd', and that they began throwing cushions at each other, then oranges, apples and nuts from the table. As a former British Army officer with a belief in military discipline, Dalton's enthusiasm for such activities was perhaps more restrained. On another night, Collins was involved in horseplay on the top floor at the house on Cadogan Gardens in which some furniture was broken. Joe McGrath, accountant to the delegation, was not amused when he came from Hans Place to inspect the damage. [32]

Part of Dalton's role as IRA Director of Training was to contribute training material to the Volunteer publication, *An t-Óglach*, edited by Piaras Béaslaí. At one stage, Béaslaí was unhappy with the level of cooperation he was getting from Dalton, and in his forthright way made his displeasure known. Dalton, as a member of Collins's entourage in London, obviously had more pressing concerns at the time. In November 1921 Béaslaí wrote to Dalton complaining he was getting 'no help' from the Training Department with regard to training matter for *An t-Óglach*. Béaslaí said he had to publish material on his own responsibility 'with the danger of publishing unsuitable matter'. He suggested that Dalton send him some books with relevant material marked that he could use for producing training material for the newspaper. It appears that to mollify the prickly editor, Dalton immediately arranged for an article to be sent to him but this only served to further agitate Béaslaí. Dalton was normally highly efficient, but it emerged that the article he had submitted had been published a few weeks previously. Béaslaí returned the article to Dalton pointing out icily that it had already appeared in the 21 October issue.[33] (The two training articles that appeared in this issue concerned the use of cover by troops advancing to the attack, and the care and use of the revolver.)

While Dalton seemed to remain in awe of Michael Collins, he could be very outspoken in voicing criticisms of shortcomings that he encountered. The historian

Charles Townshend suggests that Dalton may have authored a paper written in late November 1921 that argued, in the event of the war being renewed, there should be more concerted action against the enemy civil administration. The paper was also notable for the stringent criticism it contained of the republican civil administration, claiming that no single Government Department had been of the slightest assistance to the Army and some had been a 'serious drag'. The Publicity Department was the only one 'pulling its weight'. The writer argued that in future ineffective officials must be sacked – after all, inadequate army officers were 'dismissed every week'.[34]

Meanwhile, the Treaty negotiations were dragging on. The talks ultimately took nearly two months to conclude. Dalton travelled back and forth between London and Dublin during this period. On 20 November there was a big procession from Dublin city centre to Glasnevin Cemetery to commemorate the first anniversary of the deaths in Dublin Castle of the two IRA men, Richard McKee and Peadar Clancy. The Dublin Castle file on Dalton recorded that he, along with Richard Mulcahy and other officers of the IRA, placed wreathes on the graves of the two men.[35] Towards the end of the Treaty talks, on 26 November, the Publicity Department of Dáil Éireann announced that the Acting Chief Liaison Officer will be Commandant J.E. Dalton 'to whom all communications should be addressed at the Gresham Hotel, Dublin'.

Finally, the Treaty was signed in the early hours of the morning on 6 December 1921. It provided for the establishment, within a year, of an Irish Free State as a self-governing dominion within the British Commonwealth, a decision that would spark turmoil in Ireland as it fell short of the independent republic for which the IRA had fought. Collins and his pro-Treaty supporters saw the Treaty as a stepping stone to the republic.

The question arises as to Dalton's location on the night the Treaty was signed. In old age, he said in an interview he was in Dublin as he had been appointed Chief Liaison Officer.[36] There is another unconfirmed account of him being among those with Griffith at Hans Place on the night of the signing. According to this account, Griffith wrote a brief press statement about the momentous event that had occurred and gave the handwritten note to Dalton so he could pass on the details to the press.[37] Griffith's statement read: 'I have signed a Treaty of Peace between Ireland and Great Britain. I believe that Treaty will lay the foundations of peace and friendship between the two nations. What I have signed I shall stand by in the belief that the end of the conflict of centuries is at hand.' Griffith's handwritten note survived in the possession of the Dalton family, and was deposited by Emmet's brother Charlie with the National Museum in December 1949.[38] Griffith's statement was carried in full in the *Irish Independent*, as part of the newspaper's extensive coverage of the signing of the Treaty.[39] The newspaper also noted that it was stated that Mr Michael Collins is 'in absolute agreement with Mr Griffith's statement'.

Following the signing of the Treaty, there appears, from Dalton's later account, to have been a sense of relief, even of euphoria, among members of the Irish delegation when they returned to Ireland. However, difficulties soon surfaced, with de Valera and two ministers, Cathal Brugha and Austin Stack, opposing the settlement terms. Dalton later wrote that when the delegates returned to Dublin in triumph, 'their ardour was soon dampened by the unpredictable attitude adopted by Mr de Valera – he seemed to change from day to day'. Dalton described his sympathy for Collins, faced with this situation, and then having to endure the Dáil debates on the Treaty. 'Poor Collins! How he must have suffered during the Treaty debates in University College.'[40]

In old age, Dalton rejected various arguments that were advanced against the Treaty, which involved an oath of faithfulness to the King. One of the arguments against the Treaty was that it had been concluded under duress, following a threat by Lloyd George to renew the war if it was not signed. In an obvious reference to this argument, Dalton said in an RTÉ interview with Pádraigh Ó Raghallaigh that he did not accept Collins had signed the Treaty under duress. He said that nothing that Collins ever did would indicate that he signed 'for expediency or under duress or under a threat'. 'He signed because it was the right thing to do.' While the Treaty arrangements fell short of the Republic, he knew that Collins himself felt they had gained a great deal more than they had a right to expect. He sincerely believed the Treaty was the 'breaking of the ice' that could lead to complete and absolute freedom.[41] After returning to Dublin, Collins was facing into a maelstrom, with elements of the republican movement mounting vehement opposition to the Treaty – these differences would ultimately explode into Civil War. Dalton, for his part, was also facing an enormous challenge as he pressed ahead with his work as the IRA's Chief Liaison Officer with the British.

CHAPTER FIVE

Liaising with the British

General Sir Nevil Macready, commander of the British forces in Ireland, was clearly intrigued by the IRA's Chief Liaison Officer who was tasked with resolving the myriad complex issues arising from the Truce. No doubt it came as a surprise to Macready that the despised 'Shinners' would appoint an officer with a distinguished record in the British Army in the Great War, and a recipient of the Military Cross. Macready became aware that his own forces had arrested Dalton and his father back in December 1920, following the assassination of British officers on Bloody Sunday. The details were in the intelligence file on Dalton kept by the secret service people at Dublin Castle. It is unclear if Macready was aware at this stage that Dalton was also one of the imposters who bluffed their way into Mountjoy Prison a few months previously in a hi-jacked armoured car in an attempt to 'spring' Sean MacEoin – an operation that had caused much aggravation for the British commander. Information about Dalton's role in this affair would emerge into the public domain later in the year.

Macready seems to have accepted the self-confident, personable, courteous young man as someone he could do business with. Macready, son of the noted actor William Charles Macready, had himself served in the Great War in France so at least he had something in common with Dalton. Macready considered Dalton's appointment to be of such interest that he provided details of the new Liaison Officer in one of his weekly dispatches to the War Office, which were routinely circulated to Lloyd George's Cabinet.[1] It would appear that word of Dalton's background as a Ginchy war hero spread quickly among senior officials in the close-knit British establishment in Dublin. No doubt a certain respect was accorded to Dalton as a result – but mutual reserve and wariness also persisted.

One of the first issues that Macready's people raised with Dalton was a rather minor one, but Macready was clearly impressed by the way that Dalton dealt with it. Two officers' chargers and two draught horses of the Sherwood Foresters had been seized by 'armed civilians' at Clonakilty, County Cork. The four horses were returned after the matter was referred to the Chief Liaison Officer. Macready observed approvingly that the new liaison representative 'is making greater efforts to insist on the observation of the terms of the truce than his predecessor'.[2] Macready also recorded that Dalton had promised to make inquiries into the case of a Private Coe of the Essex Regiment who had been held captive for eight days after being kidnapped in Cork. The IRA liaison office in the Gresham also, around this period, showed that it was prepared to cooperate fully in matters of prisoner parole. The Publicity Department of the Dáil announced that Volunteer Michael McElligot had given himself up to the Governor of Mountjoy Prison on the order of the Chief Liaison Officer, in order to avoid any misunderstanding after the British alleged he had escaped from jail by breaking parole.[3] McElligot returned to jail on 1 December, the day that Dalton formally assumed the post of Chief Liaison Officer.

Dalton had assumed an onerous position. The job required a great variety of skills, including those more often associated with the diplomat, the senior civil servant, the lawyer, the politician and the policeman. It required an ability to see 'the big picture', while still being able to focus on the most minute detail. It meant dealing on sensitive matters to do with the Truce with senior officials in Dublin Castle and the British military command in Ireland, as well as senior figures in the Dáil and the IRA, and of course with the National Army as the pro-Treaty element of the IRA was soon to become. Dalton was still a very young man but he showed considerable maturity and tact in carrying out the functions of a demanding and highly challenging job.

Issues to be dealt with in Dalton's office could range from the mundane – the expenses claimed by local liaison officers, for instance, or requests for headed notepaper – to matters of great national significance that could seriously threaten the Truce, such as the abduction and execution by republican forces in County Cork of three British Army officers in April. He also had to deal with the treatment of Irish prisoners still in British custody. He raised issues to do with prisoners still detained who, he insisted, should have been released. With his background as a member of the General Headquarters staff of the IRA, he was also conscious of various prisoners held by the British who, he feared, were in particular danger. Among the Volunteers captured at the burning of the Custom House were men involved in the Bloody Sunday assassinations. He later told how, after taking up the post, he made it a priority to get these men out on parole as fast as possible in case there was a breakdown in the Truce. He succeeded in doing so, and considered it one of his real achievements in the new job.[4] Dealing with law enforcement issues on a day-to-day basis, among the bodies Dalton liaised with were the IRA's policing element, the Irish Republican Police (IRP); the Dublin Metropolitan Police (DMP) a mainly unarmed force that had survived from the British era, and the newly-established Criminal Investigation Department (CID) at Oriel House in Dublin, which investigated 'ordinary' crime as well as 'political' crime or subversion, and had an intelligence role, with links to Military Intelligence. He also had to deal with the Royal Irish Constabulary (RIC) while that body was still in existence. (It was fully disbanded by April 1922.) Members of the public regularly contacted the Liaison authorities in connection with their own problems, grievances or anxieties. Among the issues raised were queries by relatives about the fate of loved ones who had been 'disappeared' during the Troubles. It would appear that Dalton was able to secure the release of at least two Crown officials abducted by armed men during the Truce.

Dalton mainly liaised with the Under Secretary for Ireland, Sir John Anderson and Joint Assistant Under Secretary, Alfred 'Andy' Cope – more often the latter, as Cope had a particular role in liaison work. Dalton also had dealings with other castle officials such as Walter Doolin and the urbane Mark Sturgis. Another official with whom Dalton became familiar was Norman Loughnane, born in England but with Irish Catholic family connections in counties Tipperary and Galway. Loughnane would have had a personal understanding of the atrocities committed by the crown forces during the Anglo-Irish War. He was related to two brothers, Patrick and Henry Loughnane, who were tortured and murdered after being arrested by crown forces near Gort, County Galway in November 1920. Both were members of the IRA.

On the military side Dalton liaised with General Macready, mostly through his main staff officer, Colonel J.E. Brind. Brind had served in the Boer War and the Great War and was the son of a Connaught Rangers officer. (Brind was described as having 'a face as red and as round as a well-shaped tomato' by Patrick Moylett, to whom a teenage Dalton had delivered rifles in 1914.)[5] Dalton also dealt with IRA liaison officers appointed at local levels around the country. He maintained close contact with Michael Collins. When Collins wanted to confer with a senior British official such as Alfred Cope, it was often Dalton who set up the meeting.[6]

Dalton used psychological tactics to boost the power, influence and prestige of his office vis-à-vis the British. According to his later account, his predecessors in the role of Chief Liaison Officer attended meetings with the British on British 'home territory', at Dublin Castle or at British military headquarters. Dalton insisted that the British return visits to him at his office in the Gresham Hotel. In the case of Macready, it meant that the general would have to travel to the hotel in central Dublin to confer with Dalton. He would be conspicuous in his military uniform and there would be security issues involved. Dalton knew that the general was being put under duress and that it would be to his own advantage to say to Macready after he had come to the Gresham that he (Dalton) would in future go and see the commander for meetings, to save him the trouble of coming into town. Dalton reckoned that by doing Macready a favour in this way, he might get concessions in turn from the general – he believed the tactic ultimately paid off.[7]

Members of the Liaison Staff occupied a two-room suite, Room 56, on the first floor of the Gresham, one of Dublin's best hotels, located on Sackville Street (now O'Connell Street). The office later moved to Government Buildings. Dalton's main assistant was a young IRA officer from the north of Ireland, Captain Charles McAllister, who acted as Assistant Liaison Officer. Dalton received a steady stream of callers at the office. One of the visitors was Alfred Cope, often seen as

Prime Minister Lloyd George's personal representative in Dublin Castle – Cope had already been dealing regularly with Dalton's predecessor, Eamon Duggan. As mentioned earlier, Dalton had met Cope on the way to London with Michael Collins for the Treaty talks the previous October. Collins also visited Dalton at the Gresham. In addition, there was a stream of individuals seeking job opportunities in the new state. The young Dublin IRA officer Todd Andrews worked under Dalton. He later recalled that even though he had been born close to the Gresham, it had never occurred to him that he would ever enter the hotel. So far as he was concerned, only 'wealthy people from the country or abroad' frequented such an establishment. When he reported to Dalton at the Gresham he noted 'rich drapes, sumptuous armchairs, deep carpets' that were on a scale outside his experience. He thought it was a 'highly improbable ambiance' for an IRA headquarters staff.[8]

In an undated memo preserved in the Military Archives, Dalton said that the liaison work entailed 'constant touch with the British authorities, and as such, demanded the most careful handling'. He recalled that many of the incidents dealt with were of particular importance, as for example, 'the burning of Rathkeale Workhouse, the Tipperary and Kesh arms seizures', and the 'period of the paroles and releases of our prisoners in British custody'. Apart from this, less serious incidents 'were cropping up every day, and at times almost every hour of the day'.[9] (The Rathkeale Workhouse incident is referred to below. The 'Tipperary arms seizure' refers to the theft of more than thirty rifles and other materiel from British army hutments near the military barracks in Tipperary town in November 1921. The Kesh arms seizure refers to a raid on Kesh police barracks, County Fermanagh on 15 November.)

Dalton described the demanding nature of the work: 'Following the signing of the Treaty in England, a most unprecedented outburst of brigandism swept the whole country.' Armed hold-ups and motor thefts happened daily. One day, his office had six reports of motor car thefts. Because the Criminal Investigation Department (CID) was not yet functioning, police work was directed from his headquarters. Many of the missing cars were recovered, and convictions obtained. Despite the Truce, 'attacks upon British forces were of such frequent occurrence as to render Liaison work almost impossible'. Dalton praised the local Liaison Officers working around the country, and for the way they showed wisdom and courage in carrying out tasks of an extremely delicate nature. Dalton said he regretted to say that many of them were looked on as traitors 'by our own side' on account of their association with 'the then British enemy'. Dalton appointed a few of the IRA liaison officers who worked at local level around the country, selecting bright, young, and educated men whom he knew he could trust. As IRA Director of Training he had given military instruction classes to Volunteers who were students at St. Patrick's College, Drumcondra, where they were preparing for a career in teaching. These men had returned to their respective home areas, giving Dalton a readymade network of capable contacts who could be used for liaison work.[10]

General Macready did not share Dalton's high opinion of the Liaison Officers at the local level. He later commented in his memoirs:

I had hoped that the persons nominated to act in liaison with the General Officers throughout the country would have helped smooth over the difficulties that arose almost daily, but unfortunately the men chosen by Sinn Féin for this work were persons who appeared determined to do everything to irritate and annoy the officers with whom they were in touch, losing no opportunity of posing to the public as the ruling power in the country.[11]

Another difficulty that troubled Macready was that the IRA liaison officials used notepaper headed 'Irish Republican Army' and 'after their signatures added an Army rank, generally that of General'. (In fact it was the Irish language version of IRA, 'Óglaigh na hÉireann' that appeared on the notepaper – a gesture that was even less likely to find favour with the British commander.) Macready recalled in his memoirs that he passed word to his Divisional Generals that 'neither the IRA nor any military rank could be recognized by us, because if the peace negotiations broke down, the Irish would at once argue that we had recognized their Army status and claim to be treated as belligerents'. He remarked that so difficult did the liaison business become that it soon broke down so far as the Army was concerned, and communications were carried on 'through the civil authorities at the Castle [Dublin Castle]'. The disruption of communications at local level placed an even greater burden on the Liaison office in Dublin. (This reluctance by Macready to recognize military ranks appeared to apply subsequently not only to the anti-Treaty IRA but to the forces of the new Provisional Government. In Macready's communications to the War Office the military ranks of the new Free State officers were frequently put in inverted commas.)

Mark Sturgis, Joint Assistant Under Secretary with the British Administration in Dublin Castle, detailed his first encounter with Emmet Dalton on 24 November 1921. Sturgis was clearly not particularly pleased at having to start all over again with another emissary, and commented that he never heard of this man Dalton before, that he looked very young. With his English upper-class consciousness, Sturgis also noted that Dalton did not talk like a 'countryman'. He came across to Sturgis as a 'forceful' young man, and educated.[12] On 1 December Sturgis recorded with obvious surprise that he had been told by Macready that Dalton had been an officer in 'the Munsters' [sic] and had got the Military Cross in the war. Sturgis reckoned that Dalton must have had a pretty strong conviction to join the IRA, and thought it a pity that he had got mixed up with 'such a crowd'.

Early on in his role as Chief Liaison Officer, Dalton was faced with a serious incident, the aftermath of the burning of Rathkeale Workhouse in County Limerick in late November 1921. The building had been occupied by the IRA, and the British military authorities in Limerick indicated that they wanted to occupy the building with their own forces. Rather than let the British take over the workhouse, the IRA burned it, which was referred to as a 'breach of the truce' in some newspaper reporting. After the burning, the British military informed Dalton that London had instructed the army to postpone any attempt to occupy the building. In a memo in the Military Archives obviously written by Dalton, he remarked that the incident of the 'wire arriving late' appeared to be a game 'to place us in the wrong and to give them every advantage regarding publicity'.[13] The incident occurred at a particularly sensitive time, in the final stages of the Treaty talks in London but there was no disruption of the negotiations.

There were internal differences and tensions among some of the British with whom Dalton was dealing. Alfred Cope came from a modest background and was a former detective with the British customs service. With the covert encouragement of Prime Minister Lloyd George, he had opened up a 'back channel' with the Irish leaders and played an important role in bringing about a Truce. He established a rapport with Michael Collins and Arthur Griffith and helped to persuade the plenipotentiaries to accept the Anglo-Irish Treaty. He was distrusted by some in the British military and police who regarded him as a 'Shinn' (Sinn Féin supporter or sympathizer). Cope's colleague in Dublin Castle, Mark Sturgis, was one of those who thought that Cope was mixing too easily with the Sinn Féiners. Sturgis loved to move in high social circles, and his connections were in stark contrast to Cope's more proletarian origins. Educated at Eton and Oxford, and married to Lady Rachel (the daughter of Lord Wharncliffe), Sturgis kept a detailed and sometimes indiscreet diary about the final period of the British administration. In the diary we get a glimpse of the social life he enjoyed – outings to the racecourses; horse riding in the Phoenix Park; dining in the Vice-Regal lodge, official residence of the Lord Lieutenant; or visiting landed gentry friends in the magnificent mansion at Powerscourt demesne. There was official correspondence between Sturgis and Dalton, some of which survives.

Dalton's Work Load as Chief Liaison Officer

Dalton's office dealt with a considerable volume of correspondence. With limited staff, it was not always easy to keep track of all documentation. At one stage Dalton sent a handwritten note to the Adjutant General of the National Army apologizing for a wire being apparently mislaid. A very wide variety of tasks and queries landed on Dalton's desk, not all involving great matters of state.

The following are some random examples of the types of cases he handled. Dalton asked for the return of bicycles that had been seized when 15 IRA Volunteers were arrested on the South Circular Road, Dublin on 15 September 1920. He received a reply from a Dublin Castle official that the British military would return the bicycles. He was less successful in another request made on behalf of the Superintendent of the Grangegorman Mental Hospital in north Dublin. Dalton asked the British military authorities to return hospital recreational grounds that had been commandeered for soldiers to play games. The military were reluctant to comply with the request immediately, as withdrawal from various bases meant that such recreational facilities were in short supply. Ultimately, Dalton reassured the hospital authorities that they would get the grounds back shortly, as the British were evacuating Ireland anyway.

On another occasion the British sought the return of a Private Ingram of the 13th Hussars who had deserted from his unit at the Curragh. They believed he had joined the IRA (i.e. the National Army) at Longford. Dalton wrote to General Sean MacEoin to check if Ingram was serving under his command. The British asked Dalton for help in tracing a certain witness, Garrett Russell of Ennistymon, County Clare, who was to give evidence against an RIC constable in a British court martial. The constable was accused of throwing a bomb in the street that injured children. Dalton made inquiries but could not locate the witness.[14]

Dalton received complaints from the British military about their vehicles being hi-jacked or stolen by the IRA. Dalton's attitude was that if any vehicles were seized it was a breach of the Truce, and had to be given back. In a letter to the O.C. Dublin Brigade in December 1921, Dalton referred to a Ford car, property of 'the enemy' that had been taken in Talbot Street 'presumably by our forces'. He stated that if the vehicle 'is in our hands at the moment, it must be returned'.[15] The Brigade Adjutant assured Dalton that he had made extensive inquiries and found that the car had not been taken by any member of the Brigade.

In one particular case a Crossley tender was hi-jacked at Crumlin, Dublin in December 1921, and Dalton checked as usual with the IRA. He was assured by the O.C. Dublin Brigade that none of his men was responsible. On this basis, Dalton assured the British that the IRA was not involved and the British took him at his word. However, there was a further development in the saga when the Crossley tender driver insisted that the man who took his vehicle was one and the same as the IRA officer who seized three tenders from him in the same area of Crumlin on 25 April 1921 in the period before the Truce. The driver's commanding officer came to see Dalton and suggested that the driver and the IRA officer be brought face to face to clarify the situation. Dalton wrote to the O.C. Dublin Brigade passing on the British officer's request, concluding: 'I do not know if you will agree with this or not, and I would be glad to hear what you have to say about it.'[16] There is no indication in the correspondence as to how the issue was resolved. On another occasion, in a letter to Captain Lashmer Whistler, a member of Dalton's Liaison Office (possibly Captain McAllister) said he had decided to conduct investigations personally into the theft of vehicles and asked the British if he could 'cross-examine' the drivers of lorries and cars at the time of capture – possibly an indication that the Liaison office personnel were sceptical as to some aspects of complaints about vehicles being taken by armed men.[17] The response is unavailable from the remarkable 'Bolo' Whistler, who was one of the military men sent to Ireland to replace the officers who had been assassinated on Bloody Sunday in November 1920. He would go on to have a distinguished military career, serving in Egypt and Libya during the Second World War, and rising to the post of General Officer Commanding, 3rd Infantry Division (Northwestern Europe) in 1944.

Dalton received details of complaints from individual citizens who, from the details supplied, were clearly of Anglo-Irish background or had served as British Army officers. Some, with traditional loyalties to Britain, were faced with the withdrawal of the traditional law and order measures enforced by the RIC and were feeling vulnerable. Officials in Dublin Castle clearly felt a sense of obligation towards them. On 27 January, Dublin Castle official Walter Doolin reported an incident in which a number of armed men called to the home of General Holmes, near Nenagh, County Tipperary, seized his car and drove it away. Brigadier General H.C. Holmes, aged 60 at the time of the incident, had done the empire some service – he had served in the British Army in the turbulent Northwest Frontier region of India in the late 1890s, then in the Boer War and the Great War. The men told Holmes they were from the IRA and Doolin clearly believed this was the case – he also seemed to believe that Dalton had the necessary local contacts with the IRA, and the necessary influence, to get the car back. Doolin added in a handwritten note: 'Doubtless you will arrange for its return?' In a similar note on the same date, Doolin also asked for assistance in retrieving a motor car seized by armed men from Captain W.R. Roe in the Roscrea area of County Tipperary.[18]

For Dalton, getting in touch with IRA commanders in more remote areas could pose challenges, in light of the fact that few people had telephones. A noted republican activist in Mallow, County Cork, Siobhan Lankford, who would take the anti-Treaty side in the Civil War, described Dalton's system of communicating with the IRA in her region. A woman in Mallow, Mrs Mortell, had a telephone, and on getting a telephone message from Dalton, she would send her son Denis to bring Ms Lankford to the phone so that she could talk to Dalton when he rang again.[19] Ms Lankford would then arrange for the message from Dalton to be relayed by courier to the officer for whom it was destined, in any part of the county. The courier might travel on bicycle, motor bike or possibly even on horseback.

David Neligan and the Coded Letter

After Dalton moved into his office at the Gresham he was asked to assist in at least one covert operation by David Neligan, who was one of Michael Collins's spies in Dublin Castle. Neligan had passed information to Collins while serving as a detective with the G2 intelligence unit of the Dublin Metropolitan Police and later while serving with the British secret service in Dublin Castle. Even in the wake of the Truce, Alfred Cope and other senior officials in Dublin Castle were unaware that Neligan was one of Collins's key informants. Neligan collected his British secret service pension up to his death in 1983. In later life Neligan recalled visiting the Gresham Hotel to seek Dalton's assistance on a particularly sensitive matter. As he approached Dalton's office in the Gresham, Neligan was startled by the voice of Alfred Cope whom he knew well. He spotted Cope leaving Dalton's room, saying 'Goodbye, Captain'. Neligan ducked into a bedroom until the coast was clear. Dalton asked him: 'Where did you come out of? Did you see Cope?' Neligan had been given an important letter by a secret service chief in Dublin Castle, Count Sévigné – believed to be a pseudonym – to deliver to England. In true 'cloak and dagger' style, he was told a woman would meet him off the boat at Holyhead and give him details as to the rendezvous with a man in London, to whom he was to hand the letter.[20]

Neligan wanted Dalton's help in arranging for the envelope to be opened so that the letter could be examined for intelligence purposes. It would then be re-sealed so that nobody would know the letter had been tampered with. Dalton knew the man who could assist. The letter was sent to Pat Moynihan, a post office investigator who had also been part of Collins's secret intelligence network and who later became a director of the Criminal Investigation Department at Oriel House. Moynihan was an expert in such matters and he succeeded in opening the envelope. He found the letter was in a code which he was unable to break in the time available. The letter was re-sealed, giving no sign it had been opened. Neligan sailed across to Holyhead, with two men from Michael Collins's Squad assigned to shadow him. At Holyhead a woman with hennaed hair met him and gave him a letter which directed him to a London hotel.

Neligan duly delivered Count Sévigné's letter to 'a fine old fellow', who answered to the name of Wooley. Wooley pointed out two good-looking young women in the hotel, who he referred to as 'the two birds'. Wooley said he was going to have one of them for the weekend and the other one was Neligan's. Was it a trap or a test? Whatever the motivation behind the offer, Neligan declined, making up a story that there was another woman, who was very jealous, waiting for him back at his own hotel. To use a popular phrase, he made his excuses and left. It appears that the mystery surrounding the contents of the coded letter was never solved.

Dalton's assistant, Captain McAllister, was apparently travelling with Alfred Cope in his car one day when they were confronted by anti-Treaty republicans who commandeered the vehicle. According to General Macready in his memoirs, Cope pursued the thieves in another car and put a bullet through the chest of the man driving his own car and recovered it.[21] According to David Neligan, who had by now become a senior figure in the Free State 'special branch', it was a squad from Oriel House that shot the car thief. The man was wounded in the shoulder and taken to hospital, and the car was recovered. The squad was deployed after Cope came to Oriel House to complain that his car had been seized by armed men while travelling with Captain McAllister.[22] It appears that the presence of Dalton's colleague gave no immunity to Cope in the eyes of the republicans – another indication of rising tension in the wake of the Treaty.

The Missing

The Liaison authorities received requests for assistance in clarifying the fate of some of those who were taken away by armed men during the Anglo-Irish War and never seen again. On 28 November 1921 a firm of solicitors with offices in Cork city and Skibbereen, Travers Wolfe, raised the issue of Mrs Bridget Noble, from Ardgroom, County Cork. The letter to Captain Thomas Healy, the Liaison Officer in Bandon, which was forwarded to the office in Dublin, stated that Mrs Noble had been taken from her home by the IRA the previous February, 'and since then, she has not been heard of'. The letter went on: 'Her husband is most anxious to know whether she is alive or not. He wrote your predecessor but had no reply.'[23]

Apparently, Mrs Noble was a Catholic married to a Scotsman, a cooper by trade, Alexander Noble. It is presumed that she was accused of being an informer, executed, and her body disposed of in a secret location. In some such cases bodies were later recovered, in other cases they were never found, imposing additional agony on grieving relatives. There is no indication that Mrs Noble's remains were ever located.

Unfortunately for the relatives of persons like Mrs Noble who were 'disappeared' before the Truce, these cases were outside the remit of the Liaison staff. They were only authorized to deal with incidents that occurred after the Truce. There was no provision for intervention in pre-Truce cases in the liaison system that Dalton inherited. Dalton was not an inhumane man, but perhaps there was a limit to what he could accomplish. (In his later role as a commander in Cork during the Civil War in September 1922, Dalton arranged for his Intelligence Officer to clarify the fate of George Horgan who had been abducted from his Cork home in December 1920. It was established that he had been shot as a spy by the IRA and buried in a wooded area. The information was conveyed to Defence Minister, General Mulcahy.[24])

In another case of a 'disappeared' person, John Daly, Enfield, County Meath wrote to the IRA Liaison Officer at Nenagh, County Tipperary asking for any information that could be provided about his son, Joseph Daly, RIC, who was stationed at Silvermines, County Tipperary and who was missing since 14 May 1921. The Liaison Officer, Commandant E. Quinlan, who covered Tipperary North Riding, noted in a report to the Liaison office in Dublin that he replied stating that this matter 'did not come within the scope of my duties as I was only appointed to deal with breaches of the Truce'.[25] Constable Daly and another policeman, Constable Thomas Gallivan, both aged 20, were reported missing around the same time and were presumed to have been killed, and their bodies secretly buried.[26]

Dalton was apparently able to follow up another case raised by Travers Wolfe with Captain Healy, as the incident happened after the Truce. An elderly Church of Ireland widow, Mrs Sweetnam, from Lissanoohig, Skibbereen had received a letter purporting to come from the IRA with an apparent eviction threat.[27] In February 1921 her husband Mathew had been shot dead in front of her by the IRA. A Church of Ireland neighbour, William Connell, was shot dead the same night. It was reported that the two farmers had given evidence in court against IRA arms fund collectors.[28] A local IRA officer later told the BMH that an order was received that the two men be executed 'and their lands forfeited'.[29] Dalton's office informed Captain Healy that the matter was 'receiving attention'.[30]

In the transition from the jurisdiction of the crown forces to the jurisdiction of the forces of the Irish Provisional Government, there was sometimes confusion over how a particular crime or alleged crime should be investigated or brought to trial. One incident dealt with by Dalton illustrates the kind of problem that could arise. In January 1922, he was informed of an alleged indecent assault of a 21-year-old woman by two British soldiers from a cavalry unit at the Curragh. The woman told of encountering the two privates on horseback near Clane, County Kildare in December 1921. She said that one soldier dismounted, knocked her down and indecently assaulted her, and when she tried to resist, he beat her, injuring her eye. The other soldier failed to intervene, and warned his colleague that a car was approaching. The two soldiers from 3 Cavalry Brigade were arrested by the Irish Republican Police and then handed over to the British military authorities. The military set up a tribunal to try the case and in January the Liaison Officer in Naas, Captain Liam Murphy consulted with Dalton as to whether the IRA police should give evidence in the British military court. Dalton pragmatically suggested that a summary of the evidence could be given to the British and this, with identification of the culprits by the young woman, should result in a conviction. Ultimately it appears that neither the woman nor the Irish Republican Police attended the tribunal. Alfred Cope wrote to Dalton asking him to request his local representative to induce the witnesses, 'especially the girl', to attend. Dalton checked with his own Minister for Home Affairs, Eamon Duggan, and was informed that the 'enemy soldiery' should not have been handed over to the Military Authorities as the latter had no power to deal with 'ordinary criminal offences'. The letter from the Minister's office added: 'If the girl refuses to give evidence – that ends the matter.'[31] It appears that the British military authorities, for lack of witnesses to testify, withdrew the charges against the two soldiers.

IRA Prisoners, and Treaty Tensions

One of Emmet Dalton's duties as Chief Liaison Officer was to deal with the grievances of republican prisoners still being held by the British, some of whom would not be released until the Treaty had been ratified. One such prisoner was John Donnelly, from Holles Street, Dublin, who had been sentenced to death at a court martial for killing two members of the crown forces during an ambush at Brunswick Street. Parcels were stopped by the prison authorities and he and other prisoners went on hunger strike. During the strike, Dalton entered the prison as Chief Liaison Officer to see what had caused the problem. He interceded with the authorities and the men got their parcels back, and the freedom of the prison, on the understanding that they would not try to escape.[32] Much had changed since Dalton's previous visit to Mountjoy when he had tried to 'spring' Sean MacEoin. Donnelly had been in prison with MacEoin during the rescue attempt and heard the gunfire that day. He was ultimately freed after the Treaty had been ratified.

On 8 December Sturgis recorded in his diary that he had an interesting talk with Dalton the night before. Dalton was of the view that there would be decided opposition in the Dáil to the ratification of the Treaty, but that this diehard minority would be snowed under, that there would be no armed revolt. Subsequent events showed that this was over-optimistic. As regards anti-Treaty activity in Cork, Sturgis quoted Dalton as saying that Cork never forgave itself for failing to move in 1916, and had been 'getting even with Dublin ever since...'[33] The debates would begin on 14 December, and run until 7 January 1922.

Meanwhile, as the situation deteriorated, Sturgis wrote on 10 December that Dalton was 'badly rattled', apparently by trouble in Thurles the evening before, when a bomb was thrown at a train carrying released republican prisoners from Ballykinlar Camp. One of the injured ex-prisoners, Declan Horton, later died.[34] A local IRA intelligence officer believed an RIC sergeant, Thomas Enright, carried out the attack.[35] Commandant Dalton issued a statement through the Publicity Department of Dáil Éireann stating that he had received an assurance of regret and also an intimation from the British authorities 'that they intend to take immediate disciplinary action with the perpetrators of the bombing outrage at Thurles'. He added: 'I believe that this sincere effort to maintain the truce will have good results.' The Associated Press news agency quoted him as saying: 'Provocation of this nature should at no time be regarded as justification of action by our people which would constitute a breach of the truce.'[36]

Attacks on the RIC

Despite the Truce, gunmen continued to target members and former members of the Crown forces, and there was a series of murders. In some cases the attacks may have been motivated by revenge. On 12 December two RIC men were attacked in Ballybunion, County Kerry, resulting in the death of Sergeant John Maher and the serious wounding of Constable Gallagher. On 14 December Sergeant Thomas Enright was shot dead in Kilmallock, County Limerick where he had been attending a coursing meeting in plain clothes; a constable called Timoney was injured. County Kerry-born Enright had fought in the First World War as a member of the Canadian forces. Sturgis wrote to Dalton on 16 December urging Sinn Féin to repudiate the attacks. Sturgis referred to the frame of mind of police 'who see men with whom they were "at war" a few month ago walking around openly, protected by the Truce, while they themselves feel they are not immune from attack and assassination...'[37]

Dalton issued a statement expressing dismay and regret over the shootings, and saying he had confidence that such deeds 'are not the acts of members of the IRA' but are the acts of 'cowardly individuals' who sought to give the impression that their misdeeds were the actions of IRA soldiers. Should the actions be proven to be the work of IRA members, the General Staff had decided 'to take the most drastic action against the perpetrators'.[38] In fact Martin Meade, a member of the East Limerick Brigade of the IRA later admitted in a statement to the BMH that he was involved in shooting Sergeant Enright because 'he was particularly active and bitter against our men, on one occasion bombing some of our captured men'. The latter comment seems to be a reference to the bombing of the train at Thurles, although it is unclear what evidence existed that Enright was involved. It might have been tempting to assume that the murder of RIC men during the Truce was the work of anti-Treaty republicans – in this case at least, the perpetrator would go on to take the Free State side in the Civil War.

Tensions at the Squad Dance

There was a social side to being associated with Michael Collins, and in December 1921 there was a 'Squad' dance held at the Summit Inn on top of Howth Hill. It was an evening when some of Collins's most formidable gunmen were engaged in the gentle arts of the ballroom, practising nothing more lethal than the Waltz or the One Step. Dalton, who liked to socialize, drove out to the event in his motor car, giving a lift to two other IRA members, Sean Dowling and Andy Cooney. Dalton was particularly friendly with Dowling, who was one of the intellectuals in the republican movement, and would later qualify as a dentist. He had attended St. Enda's, the school founded by Pádraig Pearse and had studied English literature at University College Dublin under Thomas MacDonagh. The Howth dance was held after the Treaty had been signed, and Andy Cooney was emerging as anti-Treaty. Cooney later described the social event as 'a strangely awkward dance' – it was evident that his views on the Treaty were becoming known.[39]

Political differences were becoming noticeable, even at social events, and there was a slight element of tension in the air. An attractive young woman from County Kerry, Madge Clifford was at the dance. She would take the republican side in the Civil War, and was destined to have a rather tense encounter with Dalton after he captured the County Wicklow town of Baltinglass. Also present was Frank Thornton, an important member of Collins's intelligence staff who would serve as an officer in the Free State Army in the Civil War. As for Dalton's two travelling companions, Dowling and Cooney, they would both take the anti-Treaty side.

Dalton, in his capacity as Chief Liaison Officer, was among those present in the Mansion House, Dublin when leading politicians, including Ministers and TDs and other figures gathered on Tuesday, 13 December, prior to the opening of the Treaty debate at University College the following day. Among the gathering were figures from both sides of the Treaty debate. Arthur Griffith, Michael Collins and W.T. Cosgrave were among those supporting the Treaty, while the opponents of the measure included Éamon de Valera and Liam Mellows. A crowd gathered outside the Mansion House, and there was a general air of expectancy. There was a large contingent of journalists in town, including reporters from England, the Continent and as far away as the United States. The final vote on the Treaty, on which so much depended and which would shape the Ireland of the future, would not come until almost four weeks later.

Case of Kidnapped Journalist

One of the journalists who came to Ireland to cover the Treaty debate was an English pressman, A.B. Kay, special correspondent for *The Times* of London. He fell foul of senior republicans in Cork over an article he wrote, and was abducted in Dublin. Dalton was landed with the task of securing Kay's release. Arthur Brown Kay, a 38-year-old married man and a native of Skipton, Yorkshire, was a highly experienced journalist who had been Editor of the Bradford *Daily Telegraph* before joining the Manchester staff of *The Times* in 1920. In a dispatch to his newspaper in late December 1921, he had described his impression, from visiting the Cork region, that most people favoured the Treaty settlement. He quoted an unnamed officer in the Irish Army [IRA] as saying: 'If we had to go to war again, what better terms should we win?'[40] In what would emerge as an over-optimistic assessment, Kay believed that IRA members in Cork, while critical of plenipotentiaries, would honour the Treaty. Unfortunately for Kay, his comments had been picked up by an Irish newspaper and he discovered that some senior republicans in the Cork area had taken serious issue with his article. Kay received a warning that they were after him and he hurriedly left Cork, coming straight to Dublin, where he apparently got in touch with Emmet Dalton. It appears that Dalton contacted sources in Cork and informed Kay that it would not be safe for him to return there, but he would be secure in Dublin.

Dalton's assessment that Kay would be safe in Dublin proved over-optimistic. Some time after their conversation, on 4 January, Kay was abducted by armed men from a dining room at a shop on Leeson Street in south Dublin city where he was lunching with other British correspondents. The journalists were on a break while covering the Treaty debates in the Dáil, which was meeting in University College on nearby Earlsfort Terrace. Cork City IRA commanders Dan 'Sandow' O'Donovan (nicknamed after the famous German bodybuilder) and Mick Murphy, both prominent GAA players, bundled Kay into a Rolls Royce sedan driven by Jim Gray, and sped off.[41]

Members of the world's press assigned to Dublin for the Treaty debates were outraged by the kidnapping. They held an emergency meeting and issued a statement protesting 'in the most emphatic manner against the outrage perpetrated on one of our colleagues'. The Dáil Government began moves to secure the release of the journalist and *The Times* reported that Michael Collins 'was up most of the night' trying to resolve the issue. The matter was referred to in the Dáil by Desmond FitzGerald, Minister for Publicity, who condemned the kidnappers as 'criminals'.

Kay was taken by car to County Cork and brought to a remote farmhouse where he was interrogated by a military court of inquiry. The court had been convened by Sean O'Hegarty, Commander of the IRA's Cork No 1 Brigade who was apparently anti-Treaty but who would, in fact, take a neutral stance in the ensuing Civil War. According to Kay, he was accused of publishing news concerning the IRA in Cork that had not been authorized. He was also accused of setting forth views that did not represent the views of the Army in Cork. He was, apparently, not under threat of being executed but was faced with 'deportation' from Ireland. With, perhaps, a little hair-splitting involved, Kay signed a statement that satisfied his captors and he was free to go. Meanwhile, Collins sent trusted members of the Squad to Mallow with an order for Kay's release and to ensure he was brought back safely to Dublin.[42] Dalton got word that Kay was released and was being brought back to Dublin by car. In a follow-up article for *The Times*, Kay paid tribute to the 'courtesy' shown by his captors and by those who escorted him back to the capital, and said that on arriving in Dublin he learned that liaison officer Emmet Dalton had proposed to offer himself as a hostage to the British for his safe return, 'for which I thank him'.[43] It is unclear what Dalton hoped to achieve by offering himself as a hostage – the gesture may have had more symbolic than practical significance.

On the issue of freedom of expression, Dalton would also receive complaints, from a professor at University College Cork (UCC), Alfred O'Rahilly, that a pamphlet he had written in support of the Treaty had been suppressed by the IRA in Cork. O'Rahilly, never a man to mince his words, had made a charge of 'linguistic pedantry' against those had made the term 'republic' all-important. IRA men had gone to the printers, seized the pamphlets and dismantled the type. O'Rahilly, who had studied for the priesthood in the Jesuits, was an outspoken character who would not accept being silenced. As in the case of the action taken against Mr Kay, it emerged that the IRA officer responsible for the suppression of O'Rahilly's pamphlet was Sean O'Hegarty. Liam Lynch, then O.C. 1st Southern Division of the IRA, wrote to General Mulcahy on 4 January stating that he agreed with the seizure of the pamphlet.[44]

As for Arthur Kay, he was released just in time to be available to cover, the following day, one of the defining events in modern Irish history, an event that would impact on the lives of so many of those who were part of the IRA and on the lives of many ordinary Irish people. It was to unleash a bitter, fratricidal conflict that afflicted Irish politics for generations. That event was the vote in the Dáil on the Anglo-Irish Treaty, which took place on 7 January 1922, and which sundered Irish Republicanism, culminating six months later in civil war.

Anglo-Irish Treaty Approved By Narrow Dáil Majority

The Anglo-Irish Treaty was ratified by the Dáil by a narrow majority – 64 in favour, 57 against. Under the Treaty, Ireland would become a self-governing dominion within the British Empire, and British forces would withdraw. The six-county state of Northern Ireland, which had been set up by Westminster's Government of Ireland Act, 1920, could opt to join up with the South. If not, the boundaries of Northern Ireland would be decided by a Boundary Commission. The northern state, which had a Protestant, Unionist majority, was destined to remain part of the United Kingdom.

A major focus of the Treaty debates had been on the question of the oath of allegiance, which members of the Dáil and Senate were required to take. The first part of the oath declared allegiance to the Irish Free State. The secondary part of the oath declared faithfulness to the King and his heirs. The King remained as head of state, and this was anathema to republicans. The establishment of a state within the British Empire was considered by anti-Treatyites a betrayal of the Irish Republic declared in 1916. Michael Collins insisted it was the best deal that could be achieved and that it was a 'stepping stone' to the republic. Éamon de Valera, who rejected the Treaty, resigned as President of the Dáil and was replaced by Arthur Griffith.

Most members of the IRA's General Headquarters staff, including Dalton, accepted the Treaty. Rory O'Connor, Director of Engineering and Liam Mellows, Director of Purchases, were against it. A majority of rank-and-file members of the IRA rejected the Treaty but a general election in June 1922 would indicate only minority support for the anti-Treaty position. Clearly many Irish people, whatever their views on the oath, were tired of war and conflict and craved stability and an end to violence. Some took the pragmatic view that what was often described as the 'oath of allegiance to the king' was simply a verbal formula. Dalton himself never showed any equivocation or hesitation about taking the pro-Treaty side. He was more than happy to follow the lead of the man he hero-worshipped, Michael Collins. Dalton took the simple view that the Treaty had been ratified by the Dáil, and that this gave the Treaty legitimacy. He believed that a decision made by a majority of the people's elected representatives had to be respected – that was the way that parliaments worked; parliamentary democracy did not allow for a minority to hold sway over the majority. He came to consider those who took up arms against the majority decision of the Dáil to be engaged in treachery, and referred to them as 'Mutineers'.

Following the ratification of the Treaty, there was more work in store for Dalton. British forces were set to pull out of their bases and posts in Ireland (with the exception of the six northeastern counties which retained the connection with Britain). Dalton's Liaison office became the Evacuation office, although he continued with his Liaison work. Supervising the British withdrawal would present another new challenge for Dalton.

CHAPTER SIX

Evacuation of Crown Forces

Emmet Dalton deployed members of the new National Army for the major logistical task of taking over facilities from the British forces who were withdrawing from Ireland. There was much detailed work involved. Dalton had to oversee, for instance, the checking of inventories of items to be left behind in military installations as the British pulled out. The evacuation of Royal Irish Constabulary barracks also came within his remit. As divisions developed between the pro- and anti-Treaty forces, concerns developed over which side occupied a particular facility after takeover from the crown forces.

The police and military equipment left behind was taken over by Dalton or his representatives, and helped to equip the nascent forces of the new state. On 9 February the Secretary of State for the Colonies, Winston Churchill, told the House of Commons that no munitions or stores of any kind have been given or sold to the Irish Republican Army, 'but a quantity of police arms and ammunition and motor transport, and of military and police stores have been taken over by the Provisional Government of the Irish Free State subject to a valuation'.[1]

Public ceremonies marked the takeover of major facilities in Dublin, involving Dalton and other senior figures from the pro-Treaty side. They were clearly proud of being present and of the evacuation that had been achieved. Newspaper and newsreel personnel were facilitated to cover these events as senior pro-Treaty figures were clearly conscious of the political, 'public relations' and propaganda value of these ceremonies and seemed eager to proclaim the message – we are getting results on foot of the Treaty, the British are moving out and 'our lads' are moving in.

Dalton had the privilege of participating in major historical events, such as the takeover of Dublin Castle on 15 January 1922. Dublin Castle had for centuries been the nerve centre of British rule in Ireland and now it was being taken over by members of a native Irish government, albeit one that was still within the Commonwealth. (In fact British officials and crown forces did not complete their withdrawal from the castle until the following August.) Collins effectively played down the fact that legally he was being installed in office as head of the new Provisional Government by the Lord Lieutenant, Viscount FitzAlan. Collins preferred to see the occasion as the handover of the seat of power to a native Irish government.

On a cold, winter's day, large crowds gathered to see the dignitaries arrive for the handover. In the Lower Castle Yard groups of soldiers, military police and Auxiliary police also watched. The Dublin Metropolitan Police kept the crowds back on Dame Street. Then a burst of cheering heralded the arrival of three taxis carrying Collins and his government colleagues. The cars swept through the eastern archway and around to the entrance to the Chief Secretary's office. The *Irish Times* observed that shortly after Collins arrived there came a number of senior officials of most of the government departments, as well as Emmet Dalton, 'Chief Liaison Officer of the Irish Republican Army'. These men entered the castle 'almost unobserved'.[2] Newsreel footage indicates that Dalton seems to have been the only one on the Irish side to have worn a rather proletarian cap – the others wore hats. In the Council Chamber, the Lord Lieutenant, Lord FitzAlan met with Collins and the other Irish Ministers. After about a half hour, the officials left quietly, followed by Collins and his government colleagues. It was reported that Collins looked pleased and, as usual, was first into the taxi. Dalton also looked pleased – newsreel footage shows him smiling and turning around to chat to another member of the Irish group as they emerged in the courtyard. That night a proclamation was issued formally establishing the Irish Provisional Government. The members of the new government were Michael Collins (Chairman and Minister for Finance), William T. Cosgrave, Eamon Duggan, Patrick Hogan, Fionan Lynch, Joseph McGrath, Eoin MacNeill and Kevin O'Higgins.

In 1919 Michael Collins had helped raise a National Loan to finance the work of the new government. The British had tried to suppress the loan and had seized lists of subscribers. As he set about his work as Minister of Finance in the new Provisional Government, Collins was anxious to retrieve the lists. He sent a note to Dalton instructing him, as Chief Liaison Officer, to urgently raise the matter with Dublin Castle official Alfred Cope: 'Will you get on to Cope at once please and ask him what he has done with my Loan lists. I have not heard of them for some time and I want them badly and urgently.'[3]

Probably also at the behest of Collins, Dalton apparently conveyed concerns to Cope about the British removal of Dublin Castle files to England as they prepared to pull out of Ireland. In a letter to Dalton, Cope gave an assurance that the only papers being removed from the Castle to London were 'confidential papers relating to the political movement in this country'. He insisted that the removal of such papers 'will not hamper the future administration'. He said that if any person applied for the return of papers seized in police raids during the conflict, their requests would be considered.[4] Before the British withdrawal later in 1922, there were reports of files being burned at Dublin Castle – the speculation was that these were sensitive intelligence files with details of informants and similar secret information.[5] Large quantities of other files relating to the RIC and security matters were taken to London. It would later emerge, among these items were intelligence files on prominent individuals, including the Dublin Castle file on Dalton himself.

According to David Neligan, one of Michael Collins's key informants in Dublin Castle, when the British were about to leave the castle, Collins wanted them to leave their secret contemporary records behind, but they refused: 'They burned many of them in the Castle. The residue they packed securely for transfer.' Neligan claimed Collins planned to seize these files, but found them too well-protected to make a move.[6]

A few days after the formation of the Provisional Government, Dalton helped end a brief hunger strike by twenty-nine republican prisoners in Derry Prison, across the new border in Northern Ireland. It was reported that Dalton, as Chief Liaison Officer, told Commandant Shields, the local Liaison Officer for Derry, to instruct the men to end the strike. Shields went to the prison, met the Governor and then interviewed the leader of the hunger strikers.[7] As a result of the instructions that were conveyed, the men agreed to resume taking food after a twenty-four-hour fast. It was reported that the 'early release' of the men was expected. Dalton was portrayed in news reports as a man of considerable authority who could bring an end to a hunger strike – presumably on the basis of guarantees given in regard to early release. However, Dalton in his letter to Shields made it clear that the decision to end the hunger strike came from the Chief of Staff.[8]

As Dalton continued with his work as Chief Liaison Officer, the British had reason to appreciate his troubleshooting skills, especially in regard to gaining the release of crown officials who had been abducted despite the Truce. On 22 January, Lewis J. Watters, Crown Solicitor for Kilkenny, was abducted from his home by armed men and taken away to an unknown destination. The following day, Anthony Carroll, Crown Solicitor in County Cork, was kidnapped while on his way to attend Fermoy Petty Sessions. The Chief Secretary, Sir Hamar Greenwood informed the Cabinet in London on 2 February, that 'both these gentlemen have since been released as a result of representations made to the Chief Sinn Fein Liaison Officer, who has given an assurance that the offenders have been punished.'[9] The following day a note of approval was added to the intelligence file on Dalton at Dublin Castle. 'Since the signing of the [Treaty] agreement, [Dalton] has shown himself on the side of Law and Order and desirous of co-operating with us for this end.'[10]

An issue arose in early 1922 in regard to the remains of men executed by the British during the War of Independence. Dalton received a letter from a Mrs Quinlan, mother of Patrick Maher, who was hanged at Mountjoy Prison, and buried in the prison grounds, in accordance with the Capital Punishment Act. Mrs Quinlan wanted the remains of her son exhumed and removed from the prison for re-burial. In a letter dated 27 January 1922, Dalton wrote to Michael Collins about the matter. He explained the wishes of Mrs Quinlan, and pointed out that in all probability he may expect other similar requests. Collins was sympathetic to the idea of the men's remains being returned to relatives for re-burial. Dalton, in a handwritten note, recorded that he received a telephone call (presumably from Collins) stating that the whole matter of the remains of the executed men will be taken up at the same time. 'Of course it will be a very big task.'[11] However, the issue was deferred with the outbreak of the Civil War. Ultimately, it would not be until 2001 that the remains of ten men hanged at Mountjoy Prison in the period October 1920 to June 1921 would be exhumed for re-burial.

Takeover of Beggar's Bush

There was a significant development when the feared British paramilitary police, the Auxiliaries, a force of ex-officers who had been sent to Ireland to support the RIC departed from Beggar's Bush barracks on Haddington Road, Dublin. The way was now open for Irish forces to occupy Beggar's Bush, a walled, stone-built fortress dating from 1827. Dalton was present with other officers when an IRA column, in new green uniforms, marched into the base on 1 February. This was to be the nucleus of the new National Army, and for a period Beggar's Bush (often referred to as 'The Bush') would be the location of army headquarters. The IRA contingent, composed of about 45 Active Service Unit members of the Dublin Brigade of the IRA had assembled at the Phoenix Park and formed up with fixed bayonets. Headed by Paddy O'Daly and led by a band of kilted pipers, the contingent, known as the Dublin Guard, marched into central Dublin. There was much excitement among the public at the appearance of the first unit of the new regular army, and much cheering. Michael Collins and other figures from the Provisional Government came out to the steps of City Hall, and Collins took the salute as the troops marched past. It was an emotional moment.

At Beggar's Bush, the troops paraded on the square in the presence of Richard Mulcahy, Minister for Defence; General Eoin O'Duffy, Chief of Staff, and a number of other officers, including Commandant Dalton. It was a proud moment for Dalton. He knew some of the men who had marched in, including Joe Leonard, who had entered Mountjoy with him in the attempt to 'spring' Sean MacEoin, and Vinny Byrne, one of Michael Collins's most faithful disciples. In the background, looking on, was the senior British official Alfred Cope, as well as some British officers in plain clothes and members of the RIC.[12] By the following May the contingent in Beggar's Bush had expanded into a brigade.

On 2 February Dalton had another encounter with Sir James Craig, Northern Ireland's first Premier, whom Dalton had accompanied on his secret visit to de Valera in Dublin prior to the Truce. Now as Chief Liaison Officer, Dalton openly escorted the Ulster Premier and his entourage into City Hall in Dublin to meet Michael Collins, as Chairman of the Provisional Government. A crowd had assembled to see the dignitaries arrive by motor car, and Craig made a valiant effort to smile pleasantly as he posed for photographers and newsreel cameras. Newsreel footage shows Craig and his colleagues dressed formally in overcoats and hats, while Dalton is attired more informally in trench coat and cap as he shows them up the steps to City Hall. (Craig was accompanied by Captain Herbert Dixon MP and Colonel Spender, Secretary to the Northern Cabinet.) The purpose of the meeting was to discuss the role of the Boundary Commission, which formed part of the Anglo-Irish Treaty. After more than three hours of talks there seemed to be little agreement between the two sides. It is unclear if Craig recognized Dalton from their previous encounter.

Dalton was, by background and instinct, a supporter of law and order, especially now that the Truce was in force, and the Provisional Government had been formed following Dáil approval of the Anglo-Irish Treaty. In early 1922 he became particularly irked by the level of lawlessness in counties Mayo and Sligo. He vented his annoyance in a letter dated 10 February to 'M.D' probably the Minister for Defence, General Mulcahy. Dalton pointed out that he had previously complained about the 'daily increasing wave of crime and outrage in the counties of Mayo and Sligo'. He went on:

> Since that date there has been no abatement, and robbery, lawlessness, and indiscipline is rampant. Since that date some half a dozen motor cars have been stolen. A Crossley Tender of police, who were being demobilized was ambushed, and now I hear of the capture and detention of a District Inspector. I have given the A.G. [Adjutant General] particulars of these incidents, but I feel it my duty to inform you of the present state of affairs in the West.[13]

Dalton appears to have had a role in arranging armed escorts for cash deliveries in Dublin. At a meeting in February 1922, Dublin County Council was told that following a robbery of £410 from one of its pay clerks, armed escorts had been provided, and the Chief Liaison Officer indicated that any contribution the Council considered reasonable to the Criminal Investigation Fund would be accepted.[14] (This would suggest that the escorts came from the Criminal Investigation Department at Oriel House.)

Dalton did not suffer fools gladly. While generally polite and courteous, he could be very outspoken in his views even with persons of considerable rank, if he considered they were being foolish, misguided or obtuse. An example of Dalton's impatience can be found in a letter he wrote to the then Minister for External Affairs, George Gavan Duffy in February 1922.[15] Apparently Dalton had received a request for assistance in regard to a man called Kraatz, and he did not consider this was an appropriate matter for him to deal with. In his letter to the Minister he said he thinks 'it would be more business-like if you took up the matter direct with Dublin Castle'. He went on:

> You will understand that I am not in a position to know, or find out, if Kraatz is a desirable person and if he should be allowed to return at all. Provided you can satisfy yourself that he is, it would be an easy

matter for you to take up with the Castle authorities, with a view to securing the necessary passports.

In addition to his liaison and evacuation work, Dalton retained his position as Director of Training in the National Army. In the latter capacity he attended meetings of the GHQ although, because of pressure of work, for a period he had to delegate training duties to another officer.[16] Nevertheless, he played an important role developing and training the new military force of the Provisional Government. An Aviation Department was established as a subsidiary department to Dalton's Training Branch at Beggar's Bush – he had, after all, been instrumental in procuring the first aircraft to be deployed by the Irish armed forces. He recalled later that Charles Russell and Jack McSweeney, who also played a key role in the acquisition, helped draw up 'plans and suggestions' for the airplane in the Aviation Department.[17]

General Macready reported to the War Office that as far as could be ascertained, the intention of the Provisional Government was to build up an army of about 25,000 from units of the IRA that could be relied on. 'In order to carry out this plan, parties of about 100 men from selected IRA Units are now being sent to Beggar's Bush, Dublin for training. The period of training is about one month, at the expiration of which the men are supplied with uniform and equipment and are sent back to their areas to take over local barracks and thus form the nucleus of the new military forces.' Macready added that the system of training was based on that 'set forth in our War Office manuals'.[18]

Men who had been Volunteers in the pre-Truce IRA could apply to join the army and some who had been active in Britain in the republican movement came to Dublin to enlist. They included men who had at various times served prison sentences in Britain for republican activity. One was John McPeak, from an Irish-Scots background, who later served with Dalton at Bealnablath. Another was John Pinkman who would go on to write a valuable memoir of his experiences in the Civil War. A third man was Pinkman's friend, Paddy Lowe, who was shot dead in Capel Street during the siege of the Four Courts at the start of the Civil War.

The Provisional Government faced a challenge in building the new army. In the pro-Treaty General Headquarters of the IRA which formed the leadership of the new military force, there were some highly competent officers but only two with previous conventional military experience – Emmet Dalton and J.J. 'Ginger' O'Connell. Of the two, Dalton, with his combat roles in the Great War, was the more experienced. O'Connell had served for two years (1912–4) as a member of the renowned, largely Irish, 'Fighting 69th' Regiment of the part-time New York National Guard.

Other men with previous military experience gained senior positions in the new National Army. One was John T. Prout, a native of Dundrum, County Tipperary who, after emigrating to America served as an officer with the Fighting 69th Regiment on the Mexican border in the campaign against Pancho Villa. He was later decorated by the US and French governments for valour in the Great War, at the end of which he commanded an all-black unit, the 370th Regiment. On his return to Tipperary he acted as an IRA instructor before joining the National Army. Another officer was William R.E. Murphy from County Wexford who attained the rank of Lieutenant Colonel while commanding a British battalion in the Great War. He was awarded the Military Cross and was later recruited by Michael Collins to serve as a senior officer in the new National Army.

During this period the Provisional Government forces moved from the easy informality of the pre-Truce Volunteer guerrilla forces to the more hierarchical structure of a conventional army, composed of officers and 'other ranks', with soldiers being required to address an officer as 'Sir', as in the British Army. Officers would be appointed, rather than elected by the Volunteers as often happened in the pre-Truce IRA. Dalton helped design the uniform of the new force. He told Cathal O'Shannon that he devised the idea of the high collar, after the style of the French and the Americans. Pragmatically, he hoped to avoid difficulties surrounding the use of collars and ties.[19]

Dalton underwent swift promotion – no doubt largely because of his previous military experience. In February 1922, in one of his weekly reports to the War Office that was circulated to the Cabinet, General Macready remarked on the senior military titles being given to young men in the new 'Irish Military organization'. Macready wrote:

> Rapid promotion and multiplicity of titles appear to be the order of the day in the new Irish Military organisation. Commandants General who were never heard of until after the 'Truce' on the 11th July [1921], are now frequently met with, and Colonels, Commandants and even Major Generals are now beginning to appear. One J.E. Dalton, a young man of apparently some 25 years, who took Mr. Duggan's place as Chief Liaison Officer, has now blossomed into a Major General...[20]

Dalton was one of those who met Joe McGarrity, a key figure in the Irish revolutionary movement in America, who came to Ireland in early 1922 to see if there was a way of resolving the differences between those on opposing sides in the Treaty divide. McGarrity, who took an anti-Treaty stance himself, had meetings in Dublin with members of the Supreme Council of the Irish Republican Brotherhood (IRB). He liaised closely with Harry Boland, one of a minority of IRB Supreme Council members to oppose the Treaty. On 22 February there was a farewell IRB dinner for McGarrity at the Dolphin Hotel and Restaurant in East Essex Street, attended by Boland and other guests, including another Supreme Council member Sean Ó Murthuile. Also present was Emmet Dalton – probably in his capacity as an IRB member.[21] Another guest was the former American army officer and Thompson gunrunner, James Dineen, who had served on Dalton's IRA training staff. McGarrity had been involved in the procurement of the Thompson guns in the United States. Dineen now held the rank of Lieutenant Commandant in the National Army headquarters. McGarrity returned to America with no resolution to the Treaty differences in sight. Just a few months later Dalton returned to the Dolphin, located just off the Liffey quays, when the hotel became his forward command headquarters for the artillery attack on the Four Courts garrison of the anti-Treaty forces.

Dalton had an extremely heavy work-load in this period, immersed as he was in the liaison and evacuation work, while retaining overall responsibility for training. In addition, with his social skills, he was called on by Michael Collins to represent him on at least one public occasion. The Dublin Port and Docks Board held a lunch in March to mark a move to build a new wharf at Alexandra Basin. Among the guests were Dalton, representing Collins; Ernest Blythe, Minister for Trade; Alderman Cosgrave, Minister for Local Government, and Joe McGrath, Minister for Labour.[22] Dalton and McGrath would become very close friends sharing an interest in common – a passion for horse racing.

Treaty Tension Mounts

As Dalton supervised the takeover of military and police facilities around the country, it became increasingly difficult to ensure that it was only pro-Treaty elements of the IRA, as opposed to anti-Treaty, who occupied the facilities. It was also unclear whether individual members of the IRA intended to support the Treaty. One of Dalton's emissaries in organizing the logistical arrangements for the takeover of facilities from the British was Todd Andrews, who was sent to Mullingar, County Westmeath, with a paper signed by Dalton to meet the British Army major in charge of the local military barracks, to take over the building and its contents, except arms.[23] Andrews went on to County Cork to take over a number of other posts, in Bandon, Bantry, Ballineen and in Kinsale, the major base, Charles Fort. It was part of Andrews's role to arrange for the local IRA unit to occupy a facility after it had been handed over. As it happened, Andrews was destined to take the anti-Treaty side in the Civil War. (Dalton did not always send an emissary from Dublin to take over a facility – he might request a local divisional IRA command to deploy an officer to carry out this work, especially if it was a small facility at a considerable distance from Dublin.)

Dalton sought to enlist the services of a young officer based at Beggar's Bush Barracks, Andy Cooney, in taking over British military bases. Cooney was a medical student who had been active in the Volunteers during the War of Independence. He had taken part in the Squad's assassination of British officers in Dublin on Bloody Sunday. Cooney and Dalton's brother Charlie were part of a unit that attacked officers at 28 Upper Pembroke Street.

Dalton asked Cooney to drop in to see him at the Gresham and outlined the work that would be involved in taking over the bases. Cooney, whose sympathies were now firmly with the anti-Treaty side, inquired on whose behalf the bases were being taken over, and Dalton explained that it was on behalf of the Provisional Government. Cooney said he would be only interested in taking over the bases on behalf of the Republican Government, and that he wanted to explain his case to Chief of Staff, General O'Duffy.[24] Dalton give him a lift to Beggar's Bush Barracks where O'Duffy agreed to meet Cooney. O'Duffy heard Cooney's objections and said amicably if he did not wish to take over bases he would not be asked to do so. For Dalton, it was yet another ominous reminder of the divisions that were appearing in the ranks of the IRA. Cooney took the republican side in the Civil War, and briefly served as IRA Chief of Staff in 1925. There were other officers willing to assist with evacuation work and who Dalton knew he could trust – these were officers from the Dublin Guard, mainly men who had served in Michael Collins's Squad. They included Bill Stapleton and Tom Keogh who had both taken part in the attempted MacEoin prison rescue, as well as Ben Byrne and Jim Slattery. Stapleton stated that he and a number of other Dublin Guard officers took over RIC and military facilities in counties Limerick and Clare, including posts in Limerick city and the town of Ennis.[25]

Amid increasing tension with the anti-Treaty side, Dalton was eager to take over from the British, as soon as possible, military bases that would facilitate the training of National Army officers who could then be deployed in contentious areas where anti-Treaty elements posed a threat. He was frustrated at the delay by the British in handing over certain facilities where this training could be carried out. On 28 February he wrote about the problem to Lieutenant General J.J. O'Connell, Assistant Chief of Staff, who was now in charge of building up and organizing the regular army. Dalton explained that he was met with a 'blank refusal' by the British military on the question of getting possession of Naas barracks:

> They state that it is the express wish of the Commander-in-Chief to retain that barracks until the Curragh has been evacuated. However, I put the case very strongly before them, and indicated that the advantage would be enormous, because we would be in a position to send officers to be trained correctly, and in the right environment to take over the cantankerous areas. The British appreciate this of course, and I am sure they will endeavour in every way to help us.[26]

The situation in Limerick was particularly challenging, as the area came within the region covered by anti-Treaty militant Ernie O'Malley, commanding the IRA's Second Southern Division. The British had begun to withdraw in late February, and O'Malley wanted to ensure that his forces took over the bases. Owing to Limerick's strategic importance, the Provisional Government did not want this to happen, and deployed pro-Treaty forces into the area. There was a tense stand-off between O'Malley's forces and pro-Treaty forces. O'Malley was in a stronger military position and the Provisional Government forces had to come to a compromise agreement with the republicans, each side occupying certain garrisons. It appears that back in Dublin, Dalton was unhappy with the compromise. In his memoirs, General Macready told how he was anxious to evacuate his Limerick garrison. He thought his troops were vulnerable and wanted to pull them back closer to Dublin. Michael Collins was notified that the evacuation would take place on 11 March, but at Collins's urgent request it was postponed until 21 March. (No doubt

Collins wanted to prevent anti-Treaty forces occupying the vacated facilities.) The night before the scheduled withdrawal, an official at Dublin Castle phoned Macready to say that the Provisional Government wanted the troops to remain at Limerick. Macready decided to go ahead with the evacuation, as it was too late to change. Collins appealed over Macready's head to Winston Churchill in London, but apparently the War Office failed to forward his message to the general. On 21 March Collins sent Major General Dalton around to see Macready. According to Macready's account, Dalton explained that the trouble arose because he wanted to send certain men to occupy the barracks at Limerick, but his politicians would not agree, wanting to put local men who Dalton mistrusted into the barracks. Macready told Dalton that if he so desired, he could ask for a Royal Navy destroyer to sail up the Shannon and shell out the republicans if they gave trouble, but Dalton did not accept the offer. Macready noted that during the last week of March, all outlying British troops had been brought into Dublin, Cork or the Curragh.[27]

In Dublin, at the end of March, there was an incident which provided another reminder of mounting tension over the Treaty. A group of anti-Treaty republicans led by Rory O'Connor smashed the printing presses of the pro-Treaty *Freeman's Journal* (*FJ*). The voice of moderate nationalism, the *FJ* was probably the favourite newspaper of Emmet's father James F. Dalton. It was in the *FJ* that James had advertised his laundry business and his insurance business, and his name had been often mentioned in the newspaper's reports on Home Rule events, the activities of the Irish Parliamentary Party and matters to do with the National Volunteers. The *FJ* had given lavish coverage to the dinner at the Gresham Hotel in 1911 in James's honour. (In 1923, Emmet Dalton published in the *FJ* his first-hand account of the death of Michael Collins.) The attempt to silence the *FJ* was probably an 'own goal' for Rory O'Connor as it was one of the acts that helped to associate anti-Treaty republicanism with lack of respect for freedom of the press and freedom of expression.

As Chief Liaison representative, Emmet Dalton helped arrange the supply of war materiel from the British for the equipping of the National Army. Among the items on his wish list were bombs and grenades, which, as indicated below, the British were unwilling to supply. Meanwhile, anti-Treaty forces in Cork were making their own independent arrangements to get arms – on 29 March they pulled off a major coup when they hi-jacked a British freighter, the *Upnor*, off the County Cork coast and seized up to 400 rifles, as well as more than 700 revolvers, 33 Lewis guns and 29,000 rounds of ammunition. The incident, a major breach of the Truce, made British Colonial Secretary Winston Churchill more amenable to providing arms to the Provisional Government to counter the additional threat from republican forces. He authorized Alfred Cope to provide up to 6,000 rifles and 4,000 pistols to the Provisional Government straight away. However, Churchill baulked at supplying a large quantity of Mills bombs and rifle grenades that had been requested by Dalton. In a letter to Michael Collins on 5 April, Churchill wrote, 'I do not recommend you drawing, as requested by Dalton, 25,000 Mills Bombs, and 5,000 rifle grenades. These are the weapons far more of revolution than of government if they fall into the wrong hands.' Churchill said he was quite ready to supply a small quantity for the defence of particular posts, and he suggested that Collins talk the matter over with Cope the following day. Churchill added, 'You never know whom a bomb will kill; very likely a woman, probably a widow.'[28]

In Dublin, on 12 April, another important military base was taken over by the Provisional Government forces – Wellington Barracks, on the South Circular Road. Troops of the 2nd Eastern Division under Dalton's friend Commandant Tom Ennis formally took possession of the facility. Among the elements to be accommodated at the barracks, later renamed Griffith Barracks, would be army intelligence. Meanwhile, tension in Dublin between pro- and anti-Treaty elements continued to escalate. On 14 April, about 200 republicans loyal to the anti-Treaty IRA Executive occupied the Four Courts in central Dublin, showing defiance to the Provisional Government. Some of the most militant and ablest of the anti-Treaty republicans based themselves in the complex – such as Rory O'Connor, Liam Mellows and Ernie O'Malley. Andy Cooney, formerly of the Beggar's Bush Barracks, also joined the Four Courts garrison. Other buildings were seized in Dublin. The question arose – if the anti-Treaty republicans were unhappy with a majority decision of the Dáil, what was their alternative? Rory O'Connor, on being asked by a journalist if he favoured a military dictatorship, replied: 'You can take it that way if you like.' Commenting frankly in later years in his memoirs, Todd Andrews, who was part of the Four Courts garrison, claimed that the idea of 'military dictatorship' in itself did not have the frightening connotations in April 1922 that it eventually came to acquire; Mussolini was yet to march on Rome and the word 'Fascist', to the few who had ever heard of it, 'had no untoward significance'. According to Andrews, the words 'democratic process' would have fallen on uncomprehending ears in the Ireland of 1922.[29] Dalton, while he knew, liked and indeed respected some of the men who had gone over to the IRA Executive, had little tolerance for what he regarded as a 'mutiny', and favoured a hard-line stance against the 'mutineers'. In later years, he would state that so far as he was concerned, the Civil War effectively started with the seizure of the Four Courts and other buildings by the republicans.[30]

Shooting Incident

On 20 April 1922 the General Headquarters of the National Army, based in Beggar's Bush Barracks, issued a statement giving details of a number of incidents in which, it was claimed, shots had been fired at troops in various locations around Dublin. It was an indication of increasing tension in the city. In one incident it was stated that Major General Dalton, Chief Liaison Officer, was fired on at approximately 12.30 am as he was proceeding in a motor car along Parnell Square, Dublin, towards Findlater's Church. He was probably on his way home to Drumcondra. The shooting was said to have been carried out by three men standing in a laneway opposite the Rotunda. The statement went on: 'Maj.-Gen. Dalton's car pulled up and the attackers were called on to halt. Two of the men put up their hands. A third, who attempted to run away, was fired upon and wounded. He was taken to Jervis St. Hospital by Maj.-Gen. Dalton.'[31]

The IRA Executive in the Four Courts issued a statement about the incident giving an entirely different version of events:

> While two members of the IRA Executive Volunteer Guards were standing in Cavendish Row, at 12.30 a.m. last night, a touring car, containing Major-Gen. Dalton, C. Byrne, and other Free State IRA troops came on the scene. Volunteer [Denis] Fitzpatrick, one of the IRA Guards, who was armed with a revolver, ran down the lane; his comrade, who was unarmed, did not run. The officers in the car from Beggar's Bush immediately fired at Fitzpatrick. He was wounded, and he now lies in Jervis St. Hospital in a serious condition with a bullet lodged in his left lung. Witnesses can testify that the firing by the officers concerned was unprovoked and altogether unnecessary.[32]

It is difficult to reconcile the two accounts. As already indicated, the National Army provided details of a number of incidents in Dublin at this period in which it said its posts and vehicles were fired on, and it is difficult to see why Dalton's party would have launched an unprovoked attack.

Fitzpatrick claimed before a military service pension hearing in 1935 that Dalton shot him. 'A private car with six members of the national army in it opened fire. I made a run for another car. Before I got to the car I was hit.'[33] Some time before the incident, Fitzpatrick had resigned from the National Army at Beggar's Bush. The officer named Byrne referred to in the IRA Executive statement was probably Charlie Byrne, who had been a member of Michael Collins's Squad. It was the first time that Dalton had been personally caught up in a shooting incident involving rival elements of a formerly united republican movement and it was an ominous sign of further trouble to come.

A propaganda war was also getting under way. Somehow, the republicans managed to get their hands on a copy of the letter, written by Dalton to J.J. O'Connell in February (cited above), in which he expressed the view that the British would try to help the National Army by transferring facilities where officers could be trained. O'Connell stated later that the letter had been 'stolen' from his office.[34] On 21 April, the Director of Publicity of the IRA Executive at the Four Courts issued a statement which quoted the text of the letter, claiming that it 'proves conclusively that there was collaboration between the British troops and those of Beggar's Bush to train officers in the proper environment from their viewpoint'. The letter was quoted in a story in the *Irish Independent* and a British secret service collator thought the matter of sufficient interest to include a cutting of the article in the Dublin Castle intelligence file on Dalton.[35] It appears that Dalton took the philosophical view that accusations of collusion were an occupational hazard for those engaged in liaison work. Dalton observed that many of the latter were looked on as 'traitors' by their own side on account of their association with the British.[36]

Meanwhile, the evacuation of the many RIC barracks around the country was drawing to a close. On 24 April Dalton reported to the Department of Defence that the last RIC barracks in the provinces had been closed – Mullingar Barracks had been evacuated. Remaining members of the force were being discharged at Gormanston, County Meath and at 'centres at Collinstown Aerodrome, Ship Street Barracks in Dublin and the RIC depot in the Phoenix Park'.[37] During the War of Independence, hundreds of RIC men, most of them Irish Catholics, had lost their lives.

Abduction and Killing of British Officers

In late April there was a serious incident in West Cork which came close to wrecking the Truce. Three British officers and their driver disappeared on a visit to Macroom. At least two of the officers had an intelligence background and it was feared that all had been executed by the IRA. The men were Lieutenants George R.A. Dove, Kenneth Henderson and Ronald A. Hendy, and their driver Private J.R. Brooks of the Royal Army Service Corps.

In his memoirs, General Macready recalled that the matter of the missing men was raised with the liaison people in Cork, and he himself informed Michael Collins 'who at once ordered General Dalton to make inquiries'.[38] It appears that when Major Bernard Montgomery and a party of British military went to Macroom on 1 May to investigate the matter, they were accompanied by two IRA officers, from the pro- and anti-Treaty camps respectively.[39] This was an unusual development and was presumably arranged by the liaison authorities, possibly by Dalton himself.[40]

If the officers had been engaged on a covert intelligence mission, that would have been a breach of the Truce, but it was also a breach to execute them. Anti-Treaty IRA forces were based in Macroom Castle at the time and at one stage there was a confrontation between them and Major Montgomery and his men, which almost developed into a firefight. In his memoirs, General Macready said that to have given orders for an attack on Macroom Castle 'would have given me infinite satisfaction' but Winston Churchill vetoed any such action for political reasons.[41]

In December 1923 the Free State authorities found the decomposed remains of the missing men in a shallow grave at Clondrohid, some miles from Macroom. According to statements to the BMH by two men who had been in the anti-Treaty IRA, two of the officers had 'tortured and shot unarmed prisoners' and orders were received from Brigade HQ to execute all four.[42] Another former member of the anti-Treaty IRA told the BMH that the men were executed because they were engaged in 'intelligence work'.[43] There was an unconfirmed report that the officers pleaded for Private Brooks to be spared, pointing out that he was a Catholic.

Takeover of Baldonnel Aerodrome

In light of his previous involvement in aviation, Dalton took a particular interest in the takeover of Baldonnel aerodrome, near Dublin. The British handed over possession on 3 May. A military unit from Clonskeagh, Dublin was moved into the aerodrome later that day to function as a garrison. Baldonnel, like the sprawling Curragh camp in County Kildare, would remain firmly in pro-Treaty hands and the aerodrome would become the main base of the fledgling military air service of the National Army. On 16 June there was a memorable event when the first aircraft of the new service arrived at Baldonnel in a crate, having been transported by road and sea from England. This was the Martinsyde aircraft procured under Dalton's supervision during the Anglo-Irish Treaty negotiations. It was assembled and test flown four months later, on 13 October. Meanwhile, the new air service received other aircraft which enabled it to support the National Army during the Civil War.

As the evacuation of British forces proceeded, an issue arose as to a rather mundane matter – the removal by the British of fire appliances when they were pulling out. Defence Minister Mulcahy objected, and as so often happened in this period, the problem ended up on Dalton's desk.[44]

Quest for Army Unity and the Takeover of Portobello

On 4 May, talks began between pro and anti-Treaty elements of the IRA to restore unity. Truce terms between the two sides were drawn up by mid-May, and a joint announcement about the terms of the truce was made by National Army Chief of Staff Eoin O'Duffy and Liam Lynch, leader of the anti-Treaty IRA Executive. (Michael Collins had already been involved in a covert scheme with Lynch to send 'untraceable' rifles to Northern Ireland to support IRA operations in an area where, amid inter-communal strife, Catholics were under attack, and there were fears of a full-scale pogrom, although there was also a view that IRA attacks left Catholics more exposed than ever to reprisals.[45]) J.J. O'Connell was deeply suspicious of Lynch, an attitude that Dalton seemed to share. O'Connell regarded Lynch as a most formidable opponent who would eventually have to be fought, and believed others on the pro-Treaty side were too accommodating towards Lynch.

In an undated memorandum, O'Connell said that Lynch was a regular visitor to Beggar's Bush, and 'had very great influence' with certain members of GHQ at the barracks, while he himself, as Assistant Chief of Staff, and Emmet Dalton, the Director of Training 'had not any such influence at all'. He believed this could be explained 'on IRB grounds'.[46] (He may have been pointing to Eoin O'Duffy, who had become member of the Supreme Council of the Irish Republican Brotherhood, as had Liam Lynch.) If Dalton lacked influence at GHQ it may have been partly due to the fact that he was busy with his work in liaison and evacuation in his office at the Gresham Hotel, only going to Beggar's Bush for GHQ meetings.

According to the army unification proposals, Liam Lynch would serve in a reunified Army General Headquarters staff under Eoin O'Duffy. Lynch would assume O'Connell's job as Deputy Chief of Staff. Another senior Anti-Treaty officer from Cork, Liam Deasy, would replace Dalton as Director of Training. Defence Minister Mulcahy indicated later that he reluctantly went along with the compromise proposals for an army council and GHQ staff comprising representatives of both pro- and anti-Treaty sides.[47] In this re-organized GHQ, the only two officers with previous conventional military experience, O'Connell and Dalton, would have been left out, to make way for Lynch and Deasy respectively. One cannot imagine O'Connell or Dalton taking kindly to being sidelined in this way. Some republicans were unhappy with the idea of a pro-Treaty officer such as O'Duffy remaining on as Chief of Staff of a unified army, and talks on unity ultimately failed. The IRA Executive decided on 14 June to cease negotiations on army unification with Beggar's Bush, which helped to cause a split between its militant and more moderate wings, the latter led by Liam Lynch.

While the army unification talks were in progress, Dalton was anxious nothing should occur to disrupt the continued British withdrawal from their bases. Dalton wrote to Defence Minister Mulcahy on 10 May wanting to know if it would be possible to prolong the truce negotiations until 19 May, by which time he believed he could have the British 'cleared out of the Curragh, Cork and part of Dublin'. Meanwhile, Dalton pressed ahead with the process of taking over major bases from the British.[48]

The takeover of Portobello barracks in Rathmines, Dublin in mid-May was particularly significant. Dalton worked on the preparations, arranging for a number of officers from the National Army to liaise with the British on an inventory of relevant items. Portobello with its parade grounds and complex of two-storey redbrick barrack buildings and other facilities, was one of the most important military bases in the country, and later became the headquarters of the National Army. Michael Collins himself would take up residence there, and it was from Portobello that he would leave on his last, fateful journey to his native County Cork.

On 17 May 1922 a large crowd gathered outside the main gates of Portobello off the Lower Rathmines Road to witness the historic handover of the barracks. At 3 pm a car arrived carrying Commandant-General Tom Ennis and Colonel-Commandant Frank Thornton, both members of Collins's inner circle. On arrival in the main square, the officers were greeted by Major Clarke of the Worcestershire Regiment who remarked: 'This is your show now', and handed over possession of the base.[49] A party of about fifty Irish military police, followed by an armoured car, *The Custom House*, entered through the gates, to cheers from the crowds. Shortly afterwards General Eoin O'Duffy arrived with Emmet Dalton and Quartermaster-General Sean McMahon, followed by an armoured car, *The Big Fella*, flying the tricolour.

Dalton's friend Lieutenant Commandant Pat McCrea got down from *The Big Fella* and was asked pleasantly by a British officer if he had ever been in Portobello before. 'I was', replied McCrea with a smile. 'I was in here just a year ago, half an hour after I commandeered the armoured car at the abattoir and paid a visit to Mountjoy Jail'.[50] This was, of course, a reference to the MacEoin rescue attempt. As indicated previously, after the failed rescue operation, McCrea made grocery deliveries to Portobello. (The *Freeman's Journal* in reporting McCrea's remark also mentioned the role of Major General Dalton in the rescue attempt.)[51]

O'Duffy, Dalton and Ennis lined up just inside the main gates of Portobello as the skirl of the pipes heralded the arrival of the members of the new garrison under Commandant Paddy O'Daly. The three officers took the salute as 800 soldiers marched in their field-green uniforms with their rifles, and with a tricolour at their head, into the barrack square. The *Freeman's Journal* reporter recorded that a 'great demonstration of welcome from the crowds at the gate drowned the music of the band'.[52]

During May, British troops were withdrawn from bases in County Kildare – these included the sprawling Curragh complex, and the barracks at Kildare, Newbridge and Naas. The Curragh became a major training centre for the National Army, and Dalton posted there experienced military instructors with previous service in other armies, mainly the British Army. One of the officers assigned to the Curragh was Commandant Patrick Cronin from Chicago, one of the two former US Army officers who smuggled Thompson sub-machine guns into Ireland for the pre-Truce IRA.

In early June the Volunteers' publication, *An t-Óglach*, reported that Major General Dalton had 'resumed duty as Director of Training, and will proceed shortly to the Curragh, to direct the work of his department there'. (In Dalton's absence it appears that Dermott MacManus had been functioning as Director of Training from the previous month[53] – he came from a well-to-do family in County Mayo, was a Sandhurst-trained officer with the Royal Inniskilling Fusiliers in the Great War; was wounded at Gallipoli; later studied at Trinity College and joined the IRA.) The journal also noted that the Deputy Director of Training has been transferred from Beggar's Bush Barracks to the Curragh.[54] The news that Dalton was being sent to the Curragh alarmed General Macready, who feared that this meant there would be no Liaison Officer in Dublin that he could deal with. In his report to the War Office for the week ending 10 June, he expressed dissatisfaction with the situation and said that the Provisional Government 'has been approached on this point'.[55] However, a subsequent report by Macready, on 8 July, indicated that Dalton was still acting as Chief Liaison Officer.

Alfred Cope was in touch with Dalton in June seeking assistance in regard to a prominent Unionist and former British Army officer, Colonel John Pretyman Newman.[56] This wealthy Anglo-Irish landowner who was serving as a Conservative MP for an English constituency at the time, had a very fine ancestral home, Newberry Manor, near Mallow. The mansion, set on a big estate, had been burned down by the IRA in June 1921, apparently in reprisal for the destruction by crown forces of the home of an IRA officer, Paddy O'Brien. Newberry Manor was just one of many big houses in County Cork burned by the IRA during this period.

Intimidation of Former RIC Men

As the RIC disbanded, there were reports of intimidation of men who had served in the force and their families. Dalton was informed of a complaint from a former RIC Constable who said that there was a boycott on his family in County Mayo. Dalton wrote to the local Liaison Officer in Castlebar, stating, 'From the report I have received it would not appear that the boycott is justified, and I would be glad if you would make enquiries, and let me know the result.'[57] Dublin Castle official Norman Loughnane, in a letter to the Evacuation Office drew attention to RIC pensioners living at various locations around the country who had been intimidated and/or ordered to leave their homes. The letter listed the names and addresses of fourteen pensioners around the country who were said to have been targeted. Loughnane stated: 'I hope it will be possible for some action to be taken to enable these men and their families to remain in their homes unmolested, or to enable them to return to their homes if they have already been driven away.'[58]

As Dalton proceeded with his evacuation work, Dublin was a relatively easy area to deal with, in so far as the major bases being vacated by crown forces were occupied by pro-Treaty forces from the outset. Ensuring pro-Treaty control of evacuated facilities in the provinces could pose greater problems. A local unit of the IRA might take over a facility, with the majority of the personnel then going on to support or oppose the Treaty, as the case might be. Some facilities might remain in the possession of anti-Treaty forces until expelled by the National Army in the course of the Civil War. Many of the bases and facilities occupied by anti-Treaty forces were burned as they withdrew in the early weeks of the Civil War, as they reverted to guerrilla warfare.

After August 1922, republican forces mainly operated as a guerrilla force. Nevertheless, the question of which element occupied a town or a barracks or a post at any particular time would assume great importance for those traders and business people who had supplied goods or services on account. Dalton's evacuation work continued to have reverberations long after hostilities had ceased. Following the Civil War, military records indicate that when bills or invoices were sent to the National Army for goods or services supplied, a basic question would be asked – were these goods or services provided to the 'Irregulars' or to the National Army? If in doubt, the finance officers of the army or of the Department of Defence would ask for guidance from the Intelligence Department at army headquarters. In one case, an undertaker in Charleville, County Cork was refused payment for coffins for two National Army soldiers killed near Kilmallock because the coffins had been ordered by 'Irregulars'. A grocer in Clonaslee, County Laois was refused payment for the supply of 'foodstuffs and cigarettes' to a local commander called Lynch – he turned out to have been interned as an 'Irregular'. However, in Dundalk, it appears the benefit of the doubt was given to a trader who supplied goods to the local garrison as it had occurred before Frank Aiken formally broke with army headquarters in Beggar's Bush.[59]

Meanwhile, in the summer of 1922 in Dublin, tensions were coming to a head between the Provisional Government and anti-Treaty forces. On 16 June, following a pact between Michael Collins and de Valera, there was a general election that saw anti-Treaty candidates win only thirty-six of 128 seats. This indicated a strong public support for the parties and candidates that were pro-Treaty or were at least prepared to take their seats in the 'Free State' Dáil. This bolstered the sense of legitimacy of the Provisional Government and the National Army. Anti-Treaty IRA men still held out in the Four Courts and other buildings in Dublin, and despite the landslide vote against the anti-Treaty stance, they were unwilling to compromise on the issue of the republic. The historian Richard English commented on IRA thinking at this period: 'Many in the IRA saw their role as that of a vanguard protecting the prior rights of the Irish nation, an army that led rather than followed popular opinion.'[60]

Liam Deasy, a significant leader of anti-Treaty forces commented on republican attitudes in his book *Brother Against Brother*. He remarked that 'from the first by-election of 1917 we were never unduly influenced by election results'.[61] In addition, there was a famous quote attributed to republican figurehead Éamon de Valera: 'The majority have no right to do wrong.' Emmet Dalton and others would take a different view, placing more emphasis on the majority view of the country's parliament, the Dáil, although it could be said that there were some on the Free State side who were not exactly paragons of democratic virtue.

Dalton's father was a fervent constitutional nationalist. He had supported John Redmond's Irish Parliamentary Party, rather than physical force revolution. In a previous life in America, Dalton senior had also been an activist in the Democratic Party. This family background in constitutional politics may have influenced Emmet Dalton. In addition, he had a soldierly respect for what he considered was lawful authority. He was also a man of stubborn independence of thought, who would not have taken kindly to the idea of being told how to think and act by certain senior republicans who, in his view, did not have a democratic mandate. His instinctive reaction would have been to reject dictation from individuals who, to his mind, were in a minority and lacked the authority to impose their will or their ideas upon him. Events in the summer of 1922 soon brought about a crisis, and Major General Dalton would once again find himself immersed in an armed conflict.

CHAPTER SEVEN

Battle of the Four Courts

As Ireland drifted towards civil war in the latter part of June 1922, Emmet Dalton wrote a letter from his Evacuation Office to his opposite number in the British General Headquarters at Parkgate, Dublin. The letter dated 26 June had a significance that may not have been apparent immediately to his British counterpart. Dalton's letter informed the Deputy Quartermaster General, Colonel Evans, that he was authorizing Captain P. Mathews of his staff 'to sign on my behalf documents affecting this department'.[1] It seems that Major General Dalton was clearing his desk prior to taking up active military service again. Historian Michael Hopkinson believes that it may have been on this date that the Provisional Government virtually decided to make a definite move against the republicans occupying the Four Courts.[2] Emmet Dalton was going back to war.

The outbreak of civil war meant that Dalton would have to put an important personal matter on hold. He had been planning to marry his sweetheart Alice but in light of the developing drama in Dublin and London it would be some months before the pair could walk down the aisle. A crisis had been sparked on 22 June, when Field Marshal Sir Henry Wilson was shot dead outside his London home. Wilson was chief security adviser to the new Northern Ireland government, a passionate Unionist and a fervent supporter of Ulster resistance to Home Rule. The assassination shocked the British establishment. General Macready, the commander of the British forces in Ireland, was particularly stunned – he was a close friend of Wilson's. Two members of the London IRA were arrested almost immediately for the assassination, Reginald Dunne and Joseph O'Sullivan. Both had served in the British Army in the Great War and O'Sullivan had lost a leg at Ypres. They were later tried, and executed on the same scaffold at Wandsworth Prison.

The British government immediately blamed the republicans in the Four Courts for Wilson's killing – this assessment proved incorrect. The day after the assassination, Arthur Griffith, accompanied by Major General Dalton, met the senior British official Alfred Cope and two senior British Army officers in Dublin. Dalton was probably present in his role as Chief Liaison Officer. According to the *Manchester Guardian*, the purpose of the conference was to consider 'the continued occupation of the Four Courts by the Irregulars under General Rory O'Connor'.[3] Hopkinson believes that Griffith and Dalton discussed with the British the possibility of materiel being loaned to the Provisional Government forces to enable them to attack the Four Courts.[4]

At first, the British intended to use their own forces to attack the IRA garrison. Macready urgently sent his right-hand man Colonel Brind to London to warn the government that an attack by the British would only reunite republicans of all hues. The impetuous Winston Churchill pulled back from the brink, much to the relief of Macready. Instead, the British pressured Michael Collins to act against the Four Courts. The British had a trump card – they had withdrawn most of their troops from the twenty-six counties, and Collins was anxious that they continue the withdrawal. Any intervention by the British against the republicans could end the withdrawal process, the logistics of which had been overseen by Dalton. Even without British pressure, it may only have been a matter of time before the pro- and anti-Treaty sides came to blows, although there were many on both sides who clearly wanted to avoid civil war. It could be argued that Collins could not tolerate indefinitely the existence of a dissident military force that had taken up arms, occupied buildings, robbed banks and was refusing to accept the authority of the Provisional Government.

A great irony of the Wilson saga is that the IRA Executive in the Four Courts had nothing to do with the Wilson killing. The finger of suspicion has instead been pointed at Michael Collins himself. One theory is that Collins gave the order for Wilson's assassination during the War of Independence, and then forgot to rescind it; another theory proposes that he gave the go-ahead for the killing as a reprisal for attacks on Catholics in Northern Ireland. Emmet Dalton met Collins at Portobello a few days after the Wilson shooting, and he told the writer Meda Ryan that Collins was angry that the London IRA had taken such an irresponsible attitude. 'Collins had enough of problems around this period; he was hoping that army reunification was still a possibility.' Dalton did not believe that Collins ordered the killing of Wilson 'at this time' – any orders given for such an assassination during the War of Independence would have been revoked when the Truce came into operation.[5]

There were other incidents at this period which provoked the ire of the Provisional Government, especially the abduction by Ernie O'Malley of a senior National Army officer, J.J. 'Ginger' O'Connell, in retaliation for the arrest of a member of the Four Courts garrison who had tried to commandeer cars from a firm in Dublin. Meanwhile, Collins decided reluctantly to proceed against the Four Courts garrison. Emmet Dalton, who had assumed the role of Director of Operations of the fledgling National Army, attended discussions of the General

Staff as to how to oust the anti-Treaty forces occupying the Four Courts on the banks of the River Liffey in Dublin. Various suggestions emerged – one suggestion was that the Four Courts garrison might be deprived of water and food, that they be starved out. The problem with this option was that the republicans could probably get food anyway, and public sympathy could swing towards the garrison. Dalton did not favour the 'starving out' approach. He advocated the use of artillery to shell the building, an option adopted by the army leadership.[6] Dalton believed that the use of the guns would have a 'very demoralizing effect on a garrison unused to artillery fire'. But he also realized that the employment of the guns against the sturdy stone Four Courts buildings would be 'quite insignificant'.[7] It fell to Dalton, as Chief Liaison Officer, to procure the required eighteen-pounder field guns from the British.

Following the intervention of Alfred Cope, instructions arrived from London for General Macready to hand over two field guns to the Provisional Government, with a reasonable supply of ammunition. This enabled the attack on the Four Courts to proceed. Macready later wrote that in terms of artillery shells, they only had sufficient for their own needs on hand. As a result, only a limited quantity of shells was handed over. According to Macready, although the Provisional Government wanted the guns, the Irish were not sure their men could operate them. He also reflected that it was not to become known that the British government had loaned the guns until they were in action. In his view, General Dalton was the only one among Collins's officers familiar with field guns.[8] In fact Dalton, despite his military experience, had received no training whatever in artillery.

Nevertheless, it now fell to Dalton to collect the field guns and shells from a British artillery unit. In the dead of night Dalton drove via Kilmainham to the Phoenix Park with a party of troops and at a location there he collected the guns from 'resentful' British artillery men.[9] With him were Commandant General Tony Lawlor and Commandant Peadar McMahon (later the National Army Chief of Staff). Lawlor, who had served as an airman with the British forces in the Great War, had been training his men in Athlone on an old horse-drawn fifteen-pounder artillery piece left behind by the British. Lawlor and his men were summoned to Dublin by General O'Duffy for the attack on the Four Courts. At Beggar's Bush barracks, Dalton gave Lawlor a briefing on what had to be done.[10] Dalton and Lawlor knew each other well, as they had been students together in the Royal College of Science.

The troops who travelled to the Phoenix Park to collect the field guns included a young soldier called William Mullen. His son (also called William Mullen), would later recall an account his father gave him of the events of that night. Mullen senior and other soldiers were billeted at Wellington Barracks on the South Circular Road when, in the middle of the night, they were wakened by an officer and told to dress. They were put on lorries and proceeded to what is now the headquarters of the Ordnance Survey in the Phoenix Park.[11] The British brought out field guns and hitched them onto the back of the Lancia armoured lorries. They then placed straw on the floors of the lorries, on which they placed a number of shells.[12]

The field guns handed over were from the 17th Battery, Royal Field Artillery, in the charge of a tough, wiry Scot, Major Colin McVean Gubbins. A native of Stornoway in the Hebrides, he had fought at the Battle of the Somme and after the Great War had fought the Bosheviks in northern Russia before being sent to Ireland. Gubbins recorded in the Division's War Diary for June 1922 that the two eighteen-pounders were handed over to the Provisional Government on 27 June at 11.59 am.[13] This does not appear to tally with other accounts that the guns were handed over during the hours of darkness. Possibly the entry denotes the time when approval was given for the handover. Alternatively, he may have confused am with pm. Gubbins had Anglo-Irish family connections and it gave him no pleasure to hand over artillery to men who were essentially the successors of the pre-Truce IRA. The consolation for Gubbins would have been that the guns were to be used against the more extreme republicans in the Four Courts. (Drawing on experience in Ireland and other trouble spots, the Russian-speaking officer later became one of the British War Office's experts on insurgency. During the Second World War, Gubbins headed the Special Operations Executive which organized sabotage and subversion behind enemy lines.)

After collecting the guns, Dalton's party drove to the city quays, across the Liffey from the Four Courts. Dalton put the artillery in place and set about giving a crash course to his troops in how to operate the equipment.[14] Dalton himself may have been given some rudimentary instruction in how to fire the guns by the British – possibly by Gubbins himself. According to Gubbins's biographers, Gubbins 'took part in the attack' on the Four Courts.[15] It may be the case that Gubbins's 'participation' in the attack consisted of advising the Irish on how to fire the eighteen-pounders. According to a briefing given to British Cabinet Ministers, a Royal Artillery officer was giving information to the Provisional Government forces on the weapons. This may have been Gubbins.[16] The role of a British officer in assisting the troops manning the guns was not something which the Provisional Government would have wanted to advertise. It wished to emphasize the fact that it was its own army that was attacking the Four Courts, not the British Army.

A hand-written account by Lance Bombardier Percy Creek, in the Imperial War Museum archives, claiming that his Royal Field Artillery unit fired two shells at the Four Courts received much publicity in the Irish media in 2012, after being highlighted in a BBC documentary.[17] However, the account has not been corroborated – Creek wrote the note in old age and was under the impression that Black and Tans, not republicans were occupying the Four Courts.

A field gun that was to fire the first shells at the Four Courts was placed by Dalton at Winetavern Street, near the historic Christ Church Cathedral. The people living in tenements on the cobblestoned street soon became aware of the arrival of Dalton's men and their motor vehicles, and the unusual sight of an artillery piece being put in place. Soon, people were poking their heads out of windows, inquiring what was happening. The National Army took the precaution of parking Lancia vehicles in front of the gates of the courts complex, to prevent the republicans driving out in an armoured car to attack the gunners on the opposite side of the

Liffey. The republicans had earlier seized the Rolls Royce Whippet armoured car in County Tipperary, and with a touch of wry humour called it *The Mutineer*. They had it parked in the courts complex as well as a number of motor cars they had seized.

Several hundred National troops took up their positions between the hours of 2 am and 3 am. Details of their deployment were given in a memo written by the Chief of Staff, General Eoin O'Duffy.[18] A force described as the City Guard, 500-strong, occupied positions in the immediate vicinity of the Four Courts. Brigadier Paddy O'Daly commanded these forces posted at Chancery Place, the Bridewell and the Four Courts Hotel. Further out from the Four Courts, a cordon was formed by a 600-strong contingent from the 2nd Eastern Division under Divisional Commandant Tom Ennis, who retained control of the entire operations in the city. A section of men under Commandant Bolster was deployed to deal with the republican forces at Fowler Hall, on Parnell Square, which the IRA had seized from the Orange Order. At 3.20 am the officers in command of the different positions (presumably Dalton among them) reported to headquarters in Wellington barracks that all was ready. An ultimatum was sent to the men in the Four Courts that they evacuate the buildings by 4 am. It was rejected.

A few minutes after the 4 am ultimatum expired, the sound of gunfire rang out. Commandant General Dermott MacManus of the National Army believed he fired the first shot.[19] In the Four Courts, Ernie O'Malley heard a machine gun from outside echoing through the night.[20] O'Duffy claimed there was a fusillade of fire from the Four Courts at one of his armoured cars, putting it out of action – although he added it was not sufficiently damaged to prevent it being driven to headquarters.[21] At 4.15 on the morning of Wednesday, 28 June, Dalton's artillery opened fire, and a shell hit the Four Courts. Whatever the effect might have been on the republicans in the courts complex, there was pandemonium on Winetavern Street. Dalton would recall in later life how windows in the old buildings crashed out on to the street, with razors, shaving brushes, looking glasses and the like.[22] The men operating the field gun also got a shock – they were almost knocked out when the gun jumped back on being fired. Dalton admitted later that he had forgotten one basic rule of firing a field gun – to make allowance for the recoil. He was to reveal many years later that in instructing a team of four men how to load the eighteen-pounder, he had overlooked the fact that the team needed to put something under the tail of the gun to stop the recoil.[23] (Photographs of gun crews operating at the Four Courts and subsequently in the Sackville Street area during the 'battle of the hotels', show that a pickaxe formed part of their equipment – to make a hole in the road so the tail could be anchored, to deal with the recoil.) Nevertheless, the first shell fired was followed almost immediately by a second shell.

According to O'Duffy's memorandum, the besieged garrison replied with Lewis and Thompson gun fire and rifle fire. After fifteen minutes a third shell was fired, followed by a fourth. Then, after another fifteen minutes, the fifth shell was fired. According to O'Duffy, three of the shells had very little effect but two perforated the wall and lodged in the interior of the building. At this stage a second opportunity was given to the Four Courts to surrender. The answer was, 'Not d..n likely.' It was now about 6 am and Dalton reported to army headquarters at Portobello. Following a discussion, it was decided to move the field gun to another street corner, just down the quays at Bridge Street, close by the twelfth-century inn, the Brazen Head. As in the case of the Winetavern Street position, this location was on the south side of a bridge across the Liffey, and gunners could take shelter behind the buildings on the street corner. From Bridge Street, five further shells were fired into the Four Courts between the hours of 7 am and 8.30 am. According to O'Duffy's memo, these had the effect of 'shattering the entire front of the Four Courts, openings in the walls being as large as 7 foot square'. It is unclear how one can reconcile this version of events with Dalton's later account that the shells he was using were shrapnel shells that had little or no effect on the walls of the Four Courts. Meanwhile, at 8.30 am there was a conference at headquarters during which, according to O'Duffy's memo, Commandant O'Daly reported that the morale of his troops was good, and that with a few more bursts of artillery fire he expected to be in a position to rush the front block of the building. This would prove to be an over-optimistic assessment – the siege would go on over a three-day period. In the early morning air, the sound of the bombardment rang out over the sleeping city, rousing Dubliners from their slumber.[24]

O'Duffy considered there was little point in continuing to bombard the front of the Four Courts which, as far as could be seen, had been evacuated. It was decided that Dalton should move the artillery to a position north of the Liffey, a position at the junction of Chancery Place and Chancery Street. This time Dalton made sure that arrangements were made to dig up the cobblestones so that the tail of the gun could be fixed in place. At 10 am an attempt was made to entrench artillery here, but because of intense machine gun fire from the Four Courts, Dalton was compelled to withdraw, according to O'Duffy's memo. He reported that 'three of our medical service were wounded in the withdrawal'. O'Duffy wrote: 'I should state here that the position was made more untenable by the fact that armour-piercing bullets which perforated the fire screen on the gun were used, and that the Vickers gun on the armoured car, used as an auxiliary to the artillery failed – firing only one shot at a time.'[25] It is unclear what type of armour-piercing rounds the republicans would have possessed at this period – the screen may have been designed to protect against shrapnel rather than high-velocity rounds. O'Duffy reported that at a further conference it was agreed that the Chancery Place/Chancery Street position was the best possible location from which to bombard the Four Courts. Two armoured Lancia cars were placed in front of the field gun to protect their crews. O'Duffy remarked that this was being done as he wrote at 2.30 am, and he was not in a position to report the result. He expressed the view that with simultaneous fire from front and back the garrison will be forced to surrender 'in a few hours time' – a view that again proved to be over-optimistic.

During the first day, the National Army asked the British for two additional eighteen-pounders and these were supplied.[26] During the siege, field guns would be deployed at various positions. In addition to the three positions outlined above, artillery would also fire on the courts complex from Hammond Lane, located north of the river and to the west of the republican garrison. At one stage, Dalton had two field guns, shielded by two Lancia armoured lorries, firing on the Four Courts from Winetavern Street. Crowds gathered to observe the shelling – and troops strove to keep them at a safe distance.

In case the eighteen-pounder guns proved inadequate against the strong walls of the Four Courts, the British Government offered two sixty-pounder guns, and British gunners to handle them. Dalton was consulted on the offer, and told General Richard Mulcahy that he did not consider there was any point in accepting these guns. Mulcahy remarked that Dalton considered that these guns would do more damage to the street from which they were fired than to the building hit at close range. (Dalton had seen the impact of an eighteen-pounder gun on the windows of Winetavern Street.) Dalton added that with the guns he had, he should be able to take the Four Courts 'by tonight'. The offer of the two sixty-pounder guns was rejected by the Provisional Government.[27]

During the siege, National Army riflemen occupied various positions around the Four Courts and fire was constantly exchanged between the opposing forces. Although their armoured car was blocked into the courts complex, the republicans were able to deploy the Vickers machine gun in the vehicle to fire on the besieging soldiers. Dalton would say later that he had asked for high explosive shells but the forty shells the British provided were shrapnel shells, which could startle the occupants of the Four Courts but which he considered ineffective in making breaches in the walls to allow the National Army troops to effect an entry. He later explained how he felt 'deceived' by the British, and in his RTÉ interview with Cathal O'Shannon he remarked that firing shrapnel shells at the walls of the Four Courts was like 'throwing peaches' at them.

The celebrated writer and wit Brendan Behan once quipped that the first item on any Irish republican agenda was 'the split'. Indeed, in 1922, there was even a split for a short period in the anti-Treaty IRA after it had seceded from the pro-Treaty IRA. This was partly over the army unification proposals. Militants in the Four Courts rejected the peace plan, while Liam Lynch and his Munster officers supported it. During this temporary split among the republicans, Liam Lynch set up his headquarters in the Clarence Hotel, on the southern side of the Liffey quays, while his rivals held sway in the Four Courts across the river. After the attack on the Four Courts began, Lynch drew up a proclamation calling on all citizens to rally to the support of the Republic, 'and recognize that the resistance now being offered is but the continuance of the struggle that was suspended by the truce with the British'. Lynch, a native of County Limerick, was a tall, intense, rather ascetic figure, utterly devoted to the cause.

Emmet Dalton had set up his forward headquarters at the Dolphin Hotel, just off the southern side of the Liffey quays. The hotel was very close to the Clarence. Dalton was in his staff car in nearby Parliament Street with driver Pat McCrea and Liam Tobin when he spotted Liam Lynch and his party who were setting out for the country, having just sent their proclamation to the printers. Dalton, who was suspicious of Lynch's intentions, instructed Tobin to arrest Lynch and his colleagues and take them to Wellington Barracks, which he duly did.[28] Dalton then got on with the bombardment.

Lynch was questioned at Wellington Barracks by General Eoin O'Duffy, who allowed him to go on his way with his companions, who included Liam Deasy. Dalton was present when O'Duffy gave a report on his talk with Lynch to Mulcahy and Collins. According to Duffy's account as remembered by Dalton, Lynch had made it clear that he would not take up arms against the Provisional Government and that, as a member of the Irish Republican Brotherhood (IRB), he would not dissent from the decision of that body's Supreme Council in favour of the Treaty. Indeed, O'Duffy came across as annoyed that Lynch had even been arrested.[29] On his way south, there were suggestions that Lynch had also given his parole to officers serving with the National Army's Colonel Prout at Castlecomer. (This was strongly denied by Liam Deasy, who claimed in his book *Brother Against Brother* that after a pleasant meal with Free State officers, they were only asked to leave autographs on a piece of paper 'as a token of friendship'.) Lynch continued on to Mallow where he issued a proclamation saying he had re-assumed duty as Chief of Staff. He moved on to Limerick where he set up his anti-Treaty IRA headquarters, ready now to pursue the campaign 'for the Republic'. The pro-Treaty side accused him of deception. These accusations were strenuously denied. Liam Deasy branded the accusations as 'vile misrepresentations' and 'despicable'.[30] (It has been suggested that O'Duffy interpreted Lynch's expression of disappointment at the start of the war as an undertaking that he would not get involved.)

Meanwhile, a rather panicky Provisional Government was putting pressure on the British for more ammunition for the assault on the Four Courts. Macready sent a destroyer to Carrickfergus, County Antrim for some ammunition on 28 June, and also telegraphed to England for additional supplies of shells. In addition, he asked for more field guns for his own forces to replace the ones that had been handed over to the Provisional Government. Nothing had arrived by 28 June, and that evening, following the first day of bombardment, the National Army had exhausted its supply of artillery shells. Macready was getting 'frantic' phone calls from Dublin Castle official Alfred Cope, and also from General Eoin O'Duffy. Macready later recalled that when he told them they would have to wait till the next day for more high-explosive shell, 'they metaphorically turned their faces to the wall and gave up the enterprise as lost'.[31] There was clearly much concern among members of the Provisional Government about the lack of progress in expelling the republicans from the Four Courts. One obvious concern was that republican forces from other parts of the country could come to the aid of the garrison and that the newly-formed National Army would be unable to cope.

Macready told in his memoirs how, after his phone conversations with Cope and O'Duffy, he asked if Dalton could be sent to see him. An exhausted Dalton visited Macready at the latter's period residence at the Royal Hospital, Kilmainham. Macready, who seemed to like and respect Dalton, recalled: 'The poor man arrived about 9.30 pm, thoroughly worn out but full of fight.' He clearly needed a drink, and Macready obliged. Macready went on: 'After he had got outside a drink or two, he told me his story.' Having collected the field guns the previous night, Dalton put them in position in narrow streets about a hundred yards from the Four Courts. He set about training some men to load and fire the guns. After the bombardment began, two men were working one of the guns when one was hit by a sniper ensconced in a nearby house. The other soldier announced he was going home, and departed. Dalton was left to work the gun himself for three hours, as well as command the whole artillery attack, until he could collect another team.[32]

Macready stated that although Dalton agreed with him that the Four Courts could not be taken by artillery fire alone, he believed he could not get his men to risk their lives in an assault. In fact, National Army soldiers would show considerable bravery in storming the courts complex. Macready said Dalton told him that no arrangements had been made to provide rations to the men, and they had been 'without food all day'.[33] (Ultimately meals were prepared at various locations by members of the women's auxiliary group, Cumann na Saoirse. The meals service operated during the battle of the hotels which followed the Four Courts siege – but it may not have begun early enough to feed Dalton's gunners.)[34]

Before Dalton left, Macready agreed to give him fifty rounds of shrapnel 'which is all we had left' simply so that the guns could make a noise during the night. According to Macready, Dalton feared that if the guns stopped firing, his men would 'get disheartened and clear off'. During the night shrapnel shells continued to be fired at the Four Courts every quarter of an hour. They burst against the walls, and apparently caused much noise but little damage.

The following day, Macready and his staff were greatly alarmed when one of the shrapnel shells burst over the Royal Hospital where his headquarters was located. Dalton was at his headquarters in Portobello when he received an urgent phone call from Macready's staff officer, Colonel Brind, who was aghast at the thought of being shelled with their own guns. Brind asked Dalton to see Macready immediately. Dalton would describe in interviews in later years that just as he arrived at Macready's headquarters another shell landed, this time in the saddling paddock. Dalton then encountered an angry Macready who was standing with members of his staff on the steps of his headquarters. 'Did you see that?' asked a very agitated Macready. Macready indignantly pointed out that the field guns and artillery had been supplied on the basis that they would not be used against the British, and now the Royal Hospital was being shelled. Dalton was mystified. He assured Macready he would immediately find out why the shelling occurred and ensure that it stopped. He hurried back to the siege of the Four Courts. There, near Chancery Street he found one of his officers Ignatius O'Neill, 'a great character from County Clare'. O'Neill was using an eighteen-pounder like a rifle and had it canted up to hit a sniper in the dome of the Four Courts, and the shells were going right through the dome and landing at the Royal Hospital.[35] When Dalton was putting the gun in position, he accepted the affable O'Neill's offer to help with the operation. A native of Miltown Malbay, he had fought in the Great War with the Irish Guards. He was a notable IRA commander in County Clare during the War of Independence, and was twice wounded in firefights with crown forces. Dalton ensured that Captain O'Neill immediately ceased his practice of using the field gun for sniping purposes.

One of the guns firing on the Four Courts was under the control of Captain Johnny Doyle. He would later claim that as a result of firing the field gun at the Four Courts, he was the first artillery officer of the Irish Army.[36] Military archives show that the gun under Doyle's control, gun 10756 (eighteen-pounder, mark II) fired a sizeable total of 375 rounds during the Four Courts operation. (This tally may include rounds fired during the 'battle of the hotels' that followed the attack on the Four Courts.[37])

The crews manning the field guns continued to be the target of republican snipers and also of machine gunners operating from the Four Courts. While armoured Lancia lorries shielded the gun crews republican snipers sought to circumvent the armoured protection by trying to get bullets to ricochet upwards from the pavement and hit the gunners. Sandbags were placed under the Lancia trucks to prevent this happening and give extra security to the artillery men. Tony Lawlor later told the writer Calton Younger: 'Bullets hopped off the cobblestones, flying in all directions, and some of our men were scared.'[38] Lawlor, who suffered lacerations to the face from pavement splinters, recalled how Dalton reassured the men in his own inimitable way. Dalton beckoned him to follow him into the middle of the street, where they lit cigarettes and talked quietly for a while, before sauntering back. Lawlor recalled how Dalton was quite unconcerned by the danger. Lawlor himself thought it was a rather hazardous way of inspiring the men.[39] (Ironically, Dalton later described Lawlor as a 'first class soldier' but a bit inclined to deeds of 'too much daring'![40])

As the siege dragged on, additional military supplies from the British, including high-explosive shells, were delivered. Dalton and other senior officers decided that a significant breach would have to be made in the walls so that troops could enter and secure the complex. On the second day of the siege, 29 June, Tony Lawlor's artillery, operating from Bridge Street, made a breach in the western wall of the Four Courts, on Morgan Place. Paddy Daly asked him to widen the breach, and the gunners continued to pound away.[41]

That afternoon, as rain came down on the deserted streets, the National Army troops prepared to storm the Four Courts. Troops were preparing to come in from the Kingsbridge (western) side of the courts, and Dalton had instructed Lawlor to pull his artillery back from Bridge Street to Winetavern Street.[42] This was apparently because the field gun could not be used at Bridge Street for fear of hitting advancing troops. Artillery opened a barrage on the Four Courts, firing from south of the Liffey and from Hammond Lane to the west of the courts and this was followed by a fusillade of machine gun and rifle fire that raked the complex. A ceasefire signal was sounded and then National Army troops moved at the double to fight their way into the complex. They came from two bases – the Four Courts Hotel on the quays, and Hammond Lane to the west of the courts.[43] Brigadier General Paddy O'Daly and Commandant Joe Leonard led the sortie from the Four Courts

Hotel, while the attack from Hammond Lane was led by Commandants Padraig O'Connor and Jimmy McGuinness.

Joe Leonard (another veteran of the Sean MacEoin rescue attempt), was wounded along the quays in front of the courts complex as he moved to lead an assault party through the west wing.[44] He and his men came under heavy fire from a Lewis gun. The party continued on and got through a breach in the wall at Morgan Place, on the quays, breaking through barbed wire defences. The other party led by O'Connor and McGuinness stormed through a gap in the railings made by artillery fire and used wire-cutters to slice through barbed wire obstructions. As a senior officer in charge of the artillery, Dalton could probably have avoided actually entering the Four Courts but according to one version of events he was among the troops who battered their way into the complex.[45] The fighting raged on at close quarters. During the assault, three National Army soldiers were killed and fourteen wounded. By midnight, the National Army had occupied the greater part of the main building, including the Central Hall and library, and had taken more than thirty prisoners. The republicans had withdrawn to the eastern part of the rear building. Artillery fire continued into the following day.

Destruction of the Archives

In the latter stages of the siege there was a massive explosion in the central hall of the Four Courts. Then a fire and other explosions destroyed the munitions block. This was a free-standing building, in the northwest corner of the courts complex, which housed the Public Record Office. A priceless part of Ireland's historical archives going back to the twelfth century, comprising civil administration and ecclesiastical records, was destroyed. There have been conflicting theories and claims about the cause of the destruction.

The record office had been used as the republican garrison's munitions store and bomb factory.[46] The building had been shelled by the National Army, and Ernie O'Malley considered it was a weak post, insecurely held. O'Malley discussed the situation with Paddy O'Brien, commander of the garrison. O'Malley would tell later how it was decided to destroy the building which, he claimed, had suffered more than any other building from shellfire. O'Malley believed the broken mortar and rubble of the outer walls would be a fine defence and mines could be scattered through the building and used on attacking parties.[47] According to O'Malley's account, Paddy O'Brien sent Lieutenant Ned Kelleher to withdraw the orderlies from the munitions block and then to destroy the building. As it happened, the National Army troops had already broken into the court precincts, taken the orderlies prisoner, and Kelleher himself was captured before he could carry out the destruction.

There is a report that Dalton had targeted the munitions factory after receiving information that the garrison had placed mines in the factory and planned to blow them up when the troops stormed the building. An undated handwritten note by Minister of Defence Richard Mulcahy suggests Dalton used an eighteen-pounder to 'get' the munitions factory before the infantry rushed the buildings.[48] Nevertheless, the munitions block seems to have been relatively intact when occupied by National troops under Commandant Padraig O'Connor, and Free State artillery would have ceased firing on the building at that stage. In an account published in 2011, based on his notes and papers, O'Connor described finding what he considered to be signs of preparations for setting the building on fire, with large holes cut in each floor, and blankets draped down through the holes, to ensure that a fire, once started, 'would spread rapidly from floor to floor'.[49]

The republicans were still holding out in a section of the courts complex. O'Connor and a party of his men were lined up inside the record office, preparing to advance further with fixed bayonets. He proposed to move around a nearby block that was on fire. (This fire could have posed a threat to the munitions factory.) Then they were caught up in a massive explosion that left them stunned and bleeding.[50] His men staggered out of the building and were put lying on the path outside to receive Red Cross treatment, although O'Connor went back in to retrieve his great coat. The troops had been hit by the blast from a huge explosion in the central hall, now occupied by National troops, and which shook Dublin city centre. In his interview with Calton Younger, Emmet Dalton was convinced that a mine was detonated in order to kill as many Provisional Government troops as possible.[51] A statement by the National Army GHQ said that those who were in the hall of the Four Courts at the time of the explosion are 'well aware that it was a mine that exploded'. The statement said that other mines were laid 'with the intention of slaughtering our troops, but this was the only one which succeeded'. The statement added: 'Mr Ernest O'Malley assured Brigadier General O'Daly that the mine was exploded by Irregulars in the Four Courts. He also expressed regret that the casualties among the troops were not greater.' It was reported that about fifty National Army soldiers and five republicans were injured, though miraculously none was killed.[52]

Republicans denied that the explosion was caused by a mine set off by the garrison. They claimed that the explosion arose from the ignition of two tons of explosive material, either by shells or by flames from petrol stores that had caught fire.[53] An IRA memo in the Military Archives shows that on the second day of the siege, 29 June, an IRA commander, Oscar Traynor, who was outside the Four Courts, wrote that he had arranged a line of retreat for the Four Courts garrison and that he had asked them 'to blow their mines as a signal of their retirement'.[54] Liz Gillis, author of a study of the siege, says it is hard to see how the IRA Executive would have taken a decision to blow up the building although she considered it 'quite plausible' that a lone Volunteer caused the explosion.[55]

An *Irish Times* correspondent who was on the scene claimed that after the explosion the whole west wing of the main block was ablaze, 'and flaming brands from the explosion set on fire the adjoining Record Office, the Chancery Office wing of the block fronting on the river, and the Rolls Court'.[56] The correspondent saw the Record Office ablaze – 'flames were red in its heart, and the brisk wind blowing through the broken windows fanned them furiously'. He went on: 'Firemen were close on hand, and National troops were ready with a hose. But it was known that the building had been used by the occupants as a bomb factory, and it was considered too dangerous to approach close.' The correspondent reported two explosions at the Record Office at 2.15 pm and 2.16 pm which he attributed to 'two heavy mines'. The correspondent reflected, 'The Four Courts can be replaced, but the records in the Record Office are gone forever.' On the Friday evening of the siege, the garrison surrendered, although a few escaped from their captors shortly afterwards, including Paddy O'Brien, Ernie O'Malley and Sean Lemass.

Battle of the Hotels

After the seizure of the Four Courts, Dalton accompanied the Chief of Staff General O'Duffy on a tour of the captured complex. They interviewed a number of officers who had taken part in the bombardment and storming of the court buildings. Meanwhile, the 'battle of the hotels' which followed the Four Courts siege was already under way in the centre of Dublin. Republican forces had occupied a number of buildings on O'Connell Street, including hotels. Artillery that had been used against the Four Courts was now being deployed against republican positions. An item in the file on Dalton compiled by the British in Dublin Castle indicated that Dalton was also in charge of the artillery during this phase of the fighting. The entry stated that Dalton controlled the eighteen-pounders in the attack on 'Republican strongholds in and around Dublin'. The unnamed writer also appeared to believe that Dalton played a more significant role in the attack on the republican positions than had been generally acknowledged, commenting: 'Although it was stated that Dalton was assisting the Chief of Staff [Eoin O'Duffy], it is believed that he actually carried out the duties.'[57] Dalton's brother Charlie took part in the National Army's battle against the republicans in Dublin city centre – he was second-in-command of the military post at Amiens Street railway station.[58]

During the tour of the Four Courts by Dalton and O'Duffy, the latter's attention was reportedly drawn to a large number of unexploded mines, inside and outside the Four Courts. According to an *Irish Times* special correspondent, the place was 'literally a network of mine cables'. Only one mine had exploded when the complex was being rushed, and 'caused no serious injury to any of the National troops,' the correspondent observed.[59] O'Duffy also inspected the remains of a number of motor cars that the republicans had taken into the complex and which the National Army intelligence had been seeking for some time. O'Duffy and Dalton visited various National Army positions in the central city area, where the army was gradually gaining the upper hand on republican forces ensconced in hotels on Sackville Street (later O'Connell Street). The National Army positions visited included Brigade Headquarters at Amiens Street railway station, and posts at the Four Courts Hotel on the Liffey quays, and the Bolton Street Technical Schools. O'Duffy told the *Irish Times* correspondent that he was absolutely satisfied that the revolt had been broken in the city, and that remaining positions occupied by the Irregulars would be cleared of these 'very shortly'.

Ultimately the anti-Treaty forces were ousted from central Dublin. The Provisional Government forces had the benefit of considerable assistance from the British. In addition to field guns, armoured cars had been supplied. Two Rolls Royce Whippet armoured cars had been handed over on 27 June, with a further three being transferred early on 3 July. In addition, a 'considerably quantity' of arms and ammunition was also received.[60] One of the Whippets supplied was christened *Slievenamon* by the National forces and, would figure in the story of Emmet Dalton and Michael Collins.[61] It was estimated that more than sixty people, mainly civilians, died in the 'battle of the hotels'.[62] Among the fatalities on the anti-Treaty side were the prominent republican Cathal Brugha, described by Dalton as a 'lovable fanatic'[63] and Charles Malley, a younger brother of Ernie O'Malley. There was much destruction of major buildings in the city centre.

In an effort to counter allegations that the British had shelled the republican stronghold at the Four Courts, the National Army General Headquarters issued a statement on Sunday, 2 July, about the artillery bombardment in which the name of Emmet Dalton and his record in the War of Independence was emphasized.[64] The statement said:

> In view of the fact that fictitious stories are being circulated, it is necessary to state that the artillery used against the Four Courts was under the command of Major-General Dalton who, it will be remembered, entered Mountjoy Prison in the attempt to rescue Major-General Sean McKeon [MacEoin] last year...
>
> It is desired to contradict the allegations being made from certain quarters with regard to the use of artillery, and the public will clearly understand that the artillery was controlled, directed, and manned by officers and men of the regular I.R.A.
>
> The field pieces were used principally in order to effect breaches in the walls through which our troops could storm the building.
>
> No incendiary shells were used, and artillery fire was not the cause of the conflagration, which was really caused by the land mine exploded by Irregulars of the Four Courts garrison.

Ireland's Civil War was now well and truly under way, and it would last for close on a year. There would be examples of barbarity, as well as of magnanimity and bravery, on both sides. In some families, it would be a question literally of brother against brother. The war would have a lasting impact on Irish politics and Irish society, and leave a legacy of bitterness.

CHAPTER EIGHT

Fighting Spreads

Fresh from overseeing the bombardment of the Four Courts and pushing the republicans out of central Dublin, Emmet Dalton was sent on a troubleshooting mission to Dundalk where Frank Aiken was the local IRA commander. The County Louth town was situated in a strategic position close to the border with the new state of Northern Ireland, and it was important for the pro-Treaty military leadership to ensure that Aiken's 4th Northern Division stayed loyal to the Provisional Government. Aiken had taken over Dundalk Barracks in April 1922 when the British pulled out.

General Richard Mulcahy, Minister for Defence, had become concerned that Aiken, hitherto neutral, was now leaning to the anti-Treaty IRA Executive. It would be a major setback if Aiken brought his forces over to the anti-Treaty side. For Mulcahy, the omens were not good. Following the attack on the Four Courts, Aiken reproached Mulcahy in a letter dated 4 July. He asked if Mulcahy was prepared to carry on a war with his own people to enforce an oath of allegiance to England, while he had a splendid opportunity to unite the whole nation to fight against it?[1] Dalton was intervening in a highly sensitive situation, in which any troubleshooting skills he possessed would be tested to the full. For some weeks, Dalton, among other duties, would maintain a 'watching brief' over Dundalk.

Frank Aiken, a native of Camlough, County Armagh, was a particularly resourceful and active IRA leader. In 1919, during the War of Independence, crown forces burned his family home at Camlough as a reprisal, and he went on the run. Tall, with craggy features and an imposing presence, aged only in his twenties, he had considerable leadership qualities and much physical courage. One of his most audacious attacks was the derailment at Newry of a troop train carrying the cavalry guard of honour for King George V at the opening of the Northern Ireland parliament in June 1921.

The conflict along the border and in Northern Ireland involved inter-communal strife, with atrocities committed by both sides, although Catholics suffered a greater proportion of casualties, even though they were a minority in the new northern state. IRA attacks on the security forces brought heavy retaliation. The Special Constabulary developed a sinister reputation among nationalists for intimidation and worse. One of the most shocking atrocities against Catholics occurred in Belfast in April 1922 when five entirely innocent members of the McMahon family were murdered at their home by uniformed masked men believed to be police. The slaughter was apparently in retaliation for the deaths the day before of two policemen, shot dead by the IRA.

The following month, just before the shelling of the Four Courts, Aiken's men mounted an infamous attack north of the border, reportedly in reprisal for the murder of two Catholics by Special Constabulary and the sexual assault of a woman. Aiken's men attacked Protestant families in the small rural community of Altnaveigh in South Armagh and the incident is embedded in the local folk memory to this day. The IRA men raided a number of houses in the remote district, ordering families out of their homes and shooting people at close range. Six Protestants died, including a married couple; others were seriously injured and houses were destroyed. In this region, it was the biggest massacre of Protestants by republicans until the Kingsmill attack in South Armagh in 1976.

Writing an account for the BMH in 1955, Newry-born Patrick Casey told of the 'reprisals party' returning to Dundalk Barracks after the attack. 'Writing this, 35 years later, I still have the view that it was a horrible affair – nothing could justify such a killing of unarmed people and I was surprised at the time that Frank Aiken had planned and authorized this.'[2]

When the Civil War broke out at the end of June, all military operations were called off by 4th Northern Divisional staff in that part of Northern Ireland covered by the division.[3] The situation on the border was relatively quiet although extremely tense when Mulcahy sent Emmet Dalton to Dundalk 'to sort out any difficulties.'[4] As it happened, when Dalton arrived in Dundalk, Aiken was not there – he had gone to Limerick. Aiken favoured a truce, and in Limerick on 8 July he conferred with Liam Lynch, Chief of Staff of the anti-Treaty IRA and apparently told him that while he had moral right on his side, his strategy was bad.[5] Meanwhile according to his account to Calton Younger, Dalton decided to put National Army Commandant General Dan Hogan in charge at Dundalk. Hogan did not move into Dundalk immediately – as will be seen, a more subtle approach was clearly considered necessary. Hogan would have seemed a safer bet than Aiken. He was the commander of the neighbouring 5th Northern which included Cavan and Monaghan, and was regarded as a protégé of Eoin O'Duffy who was fully in support of the Treaty. He was a brother of Michael Hogan, captain of the Tipperary team who was among those shot dead by crown forces during a match at Croke Park on Bloody Sunday in November 1920.

Dalton returned to Dublin to prosecute the war in the Leinster counties closer to the capital. Aiken returned to Dundalk having moved even further away from the Provisional Government. He and his divisional officers decided that they would not support the government unless the Treaty oath was withdrawn. He also ordered that all war materiel held by the Division should be hidden away.[6] Then, early on the morning of 15 July, Hogan and his forces moved quietly into Dundalk, gaining access surreptitiously to the barracks. Aiken woke up to find a gun pointed at his head. Hogan's troops arrested Aiken and about 300 of his men. (It is unclear if this was all part of Dalton's plan. Historian Michael Hopkinson suggested Hogan acted on his own initiative.[7])

Aiken and other captives were detained in Dundalk Prison. When Hogan took over the barracks it was discovered that seventeen members of the Ulster Special Constabulary were being held as prisoners. They were released, taken to the railway station, and given tickets to return home.[8] Aiken's trusted comrade Jack McElhaw would later tell the BMH that at this stage they decided that they would abandon their neutrality and attack the pro-Treaty forces who had invaded their area. Just ten days after being arrested, Aiken was freed in a raid on Dundalk prison. On 14 August Aiken led a surprise attack, taking control of his old base, the army barracks – five National Army soldiers died in the assault. In the process, Aiken took control of Dundalk which he held for three days before evacuating the town as National Army forces closed in.

By the time of the Aiken jailbreak in the latter part of July, Dalton had become commander of Eastern Command. It now fell to him to investigate potentially disturbing reports of how Aiken and his men had been 'sprung' from prison. He instructed a promising young officer, Captain Michael Rynne, to go to Dundalk and carry out inquiries. Ultimately, the inquiry concluded that the escape occurred, not because of any fault of Hogan's, but because of 'laxity or possibly treachery of guards or warders in the prison.'[9]

Meanwhile, Dalton was busy on other fronts. Following the attack on the Four Courts, fighting flared in other parts of the country, and forces on both sides moved to occupy strategic positions. After returning from his brief mission to Dundalk, Dalton organized mobile columns of National Army troops to confront republican forces in south Leinster, around counties Wicklow, Wexford and Carlow.[10] He was based at army headquarters in Portobello and was one of a select number of senior officers to be given a personal telephone line.

One of the urgent tasks undertaken by Provisional Government forces was dealing with the republicans who had occupied the small County Wicklow town of Blessington, about eighteen miles from the capital. Roughly 100 republicans from South Tipperary under Mick Sheehan had moved into the town, occupying buildings and commandeering supplies. Other anti-Treaty elements joined the occupying forces. They included men who had been defeated in Dublin, such as Oscar Traynor, Ernie O'Malley, Sean Lemass and Harry Boland. It was originally planned that the republicans would use Blessington as a base from which to advance on Dublin. This plan was abandoned and O'Malley and some fighters moved on to County Wexford. Meanwhile, Provisional Government troops converged on Blessington, and seized the town on the night of 7/8 July. The troops were from the Curragh, under the command of one of Dalton's Irish-American training associates, Commandant Patrick Cronin. There was no major battle, one possible reason being that combatants at this early stage in the war were still reluctant to inflict heavy casualties on fellow Irishmen. Cronin reported that about twenty prisoners were taken, including senior republicans.[11]

Despite early successes against the republican forces in Dublin and in areas close to the capital, Dalton and other senior National Army officers were clearly worried about the situation in other parts of the country. As the forces of the Provisional Government and of the republican Executive competed for control in the provinces Dalton continued functioning as Chief Liaison Officer. He communicated his own bleak view of the situation to the British. In early July, he admitted to General Macready that the authority of the Provisional Government in Galway, Limerick and Cork was 'non-existent', although the IRA in County Clare was loyal to the government. Dalton, however, seemed to take some consolation from the conviction that most of the Irish people supported the government and the Treaty.[12]

There was an historic development on 5 July at Baldonnel aerodrome when Captain Charles F. Russell, who had been recruited by Dalton as a pilot during the Treaty talks, landed the first state aircraft at the air base. It was Bristol BF 1, one of three Bristol F2B fighters delivered in July from Britain's Royal Air Force (RAF). As the conflict developed, the Provisional Government was gradually building up its air capabilities, and Dalton, a committed believer in air power, sought to make full use of any air support facilities available to him.

Intelligence System

As fighting escalated, Dalton felt the National Army needed a more effective intelligence system, and in his usual assertive way, did not hesitate to make his views known. On 10 July, from his office at Eastern District Command headquarters, Portobello, he wrote a rather blunt letter to the Minister for Defence, General Mulcahy on this issue. It appears that Dalton at this stage held the post of Chief of Staff of Eastern Command. Drawing, perhaps, on his background as an Intelligence Officer with the 6th Leinsters in Palestine, he emphasized the need for a proper intelligence branch. He began: 'May I again draw your attention to the fact that we have NO intelligence system. The necessity for perfecting this branch is being made glaringly obvious each day.'

Showing an independence of spirit, Dalton went on to say that 'in the best interests' of the men under his command, he had decided to organize an intelligence service in the area of his command. He realized that this could not be done without causing trouble with officers who held army appointments for a service which was clearly not functioning. Dalton concluded his ultimatum on a slightly more conciliatory note: 'I will be glad to receive your advice and instructions before I take a step which might have serious results.'[13]

At this stage Dalton's brother Charlie was an intelligence officer with Eastern Command, also based at Portobello. Presumably, he was part of the new 'intelligence service' referred to by Emmet. Certainly Charlie had much experience of intelligence work, gained while working for Michael Collins in the War of Independence. (During the Truce period he was said to have been second-in-command at the Criminal Investigation Department, Oriel House, doing administrative work and apprehending bank robbers and other lawbreakers. He transferred to GHQ Intelligence during the Civil War, after serving in the 'battle of the hotels'.[14]) On the same day, 10 July, Charlie wrote to the Minister with an interesting file 'for your information and retention'. One of the documents captured at Blessington was a memo dated 4 July 1922 from C. O'Donovan, battalion Vice O/C to headquarters saying that Harry [Boland] has 'just arrived here' and giving details of a proposed attack on Naas. Dalton signed his name in Irish, 'C. Daltúin', and described himself as 'Captain on staff; acting intelligence officer, Eastern Command'.[15] By now a third Dalton brother, Martin J., half-brother of Charlie and Emmet, was also in the National Army. He joined as a Private at Portobello in June 1922, and was assigned to the Pay Corps. Probably in light of his superior educational qualifications, he was quickly advanced to 2nd Lieutenant, serving in Soldiers' Accounts Branch. He left the army after the Civil War, in late 1923.[16]

Conflict in County Wexford

In County Wexford in early July 1922, a republican force led by Ernie O'Malley captured the town of Enniscorthy after a firefight with Provisional Government troops. During the fighting, O'Malley's comrade and friend, Paddy O'Brien was critically wounded. As earlier mentioned, O'Brien, O'Malley and Sean Lemass were among the republican prisoners who escaped after the Four Courts siege. O'Malley and Lemass visited O'Brien as he lay dying in a local hospital. Wounded Free State soldiers were also in the ward, and O'Malley in his memoir *The Singing Flame* recalled how they shook hands with himself and Lemass in sympathy. As they left their dying friend, O'Malley gave him a farewell kiss and remarked bitterly to Lemass that the capture of Enniscorthy was never worth the loss of such a man. Lemass agreed, and said he wished they had 'never come near the damn place'.[17] The republicans were soon forced out of Enniscorthy and other towns in County Wexford by the arrival of a major National Army column, which set off from Dublin on 8 July.

This was one of a number of columns that moved out from the capital after the fall of the Four Courts organized under Emmet Dalton's command, even though Dalton does not appear to have taken over formal control of the National Army's Eastern Command until later in the month.[18] The Wexford column's mission was to clear republican forces from towns in County Wexford. The column moved down through County Wicklow in considerable strength – it comprised 230 men and sixteen officers in a convoy of lorries supported by two armoured cars, artillery and four Lewis guns. It was led by Brigadier General Niall MacNeill, son of Eoin MacNeill, a Minister in the Provisional Government, with the support of some prominent officers, including Paddy Slattery, Tom Keogh and Joe Vize.[19] The republican defenders in Ferns had blown up a bridge but a National Army armoured car found a way through the fields and opened fire on some of the unsuspecting republicans – a lookout had failed to warn them of the convoy's approach. The column took some dozens of prisoners at this stage. National Army posts were set up in Enniscorthy and Wexford town after the republicans pulled out; a post was also established in New Ross. Ernie O'Malley was on the move yet again.

Back in Dublin, the family of Paddy O'Brien were anxious that his brother Donnchadha, who was interned at Mountjoy Prison after being captured at the Four Courts, should be freed to attend his funeral. A family friend, Sean M. O'Duffy, approached the authorities to have Donnchadha released on parole. O'Duffy stated that he approached Joe McGrath, a member of the Provisional Government, at Portobello barracks but the request was refused. Paddy O'Brien's sister suggested that he make another effort by contacting General Dalton, and he did so. Dalton, through his role as Director of Training at IRA GHQ, had known Paddy O'Brien in 1921 when O'Brien was an assistant under Dalton at a training camp in Glenasmole, in the Dublin Mountains.

On hearing the request for parole, Dalton showed magnanimity and immediately wrote a letter to the Governor of Mountjoy with an order that Donnchadha O'Brien be released for the funeral. O'Duffy, glancing at the letter, noticed that Dalton stated: 'I have got Government sanction for this...' On this point, Dalton may have been exaggerating. Dalton asked O'Duffy if the family would accept a letter of sympathy and O'Duffy said he believed the family would accept it in the spirit in which it was given. The letter, addressed to O'Brien's sister, was published in the *Irish Press*[20] just after Dalton's death in 1978, as part of an interview with Mr O'Duffy:

> 12th July 1922
> Miss O'Brien, A Chara,
> I have heard with great regret of the death of your brother, Patrick. He was an officer for whom I had the highest admiration and in expressing my sympathy with you and the remainder of his family, I am very sincere.
>
> I wish to God that the circumstances which have brought about the death of this great patriot and soldier had never occurred.
>
> It will be some little comfort to you to know that your brother was held in the highest esteem by every Irish man and soldier who knew him, apart from his political views.
>
> Mise le meas,
> J.E. Dalton

Tragically, Donnchadha O'Brien also met a violent death. Known as Denis or 'Dinny', he was one of the many republicans who followed Éamon de Valera and his Fianna Fáil party into constitutional politics after the Civil War. As a garda detective under a de Valera government he was now working against the IRA. In September 1942 Detective Sergeant Denis O'Brien was shot by IRA gunmen outside his home at Ballyboden, County Dublin, dying in the arms of his wife Annie. IRA leader Charlie Kerins was later hanged for the murder.

As head of the Eastern Command, Emmet Dalton received a constant stream of instructions, especially in regard to safeguarding the railway system that had been targeted by republicans. He was also asked to ensure that roads were clear and bridges were repaired or protected. From his base in Portobello, Dalton had a big area to cover – from the border county of Louth in the north to the furthest regions of County Wexford in the south. On 14 July, Defence Minister, Richard Mulcahy sent Dalton a memo urging the immediate repair of a bridge between County Monaghan and County Armagh. He believed the local commander Dan Hogan 'should be in a position to fully control this area'. The Minister was also anxious about a bridge at New Ross.[21] The following day the Minister sent another memo to Dalton stating that the railway bridge on the Waterford-Rosslare line and the railway bridge above New Ross 'should be specially guarded'. This was a demanding task, but essential to keeping the economy functioning.

Capture of Baltinglass

Dalton's forces had made considerable progress as they fanned out of Dublin. They strengthened their hold on an area that encompassed south County Wicklow, parts of Counties Wexford and Carlow, as well as parts of Counties Kilkenny and Kildare. Dalton had heard that Ernie O'Malley was leading a group of 'Irregulars' in Baltinglass in south County Wicklow near the border with County Carlow so that town became a particular target.[22] By the time that Dalton mounted his expedition in mid-July, the elusive O'Malley had moved on, but there was still a republican garrison in Baltinglass, mounting patrols and guarding various locations. The ancient town is pleasantly situated by the banks of the River Slaney about thirty-seven miles from Dublin.

The republican forces occupied Baltinglass on 2 July after seven National Army soldiers in the local barracks were reported to have surrendered after their ammunition ran out.[23] The republicans were billeted with local families. During the period that the anti-Treaty forces held Baltinglass, the town was visited by a republican contingent that included Ernie O'Malley, the IRA Acting Assistant Chief of Staff; Sean Lemass and Tom Derrig. O'Malley recalled in his memoirs that the inhabitants were 'not friendly'. He also told how the priest at Mass the next day preached a sermon against the anti-Treaty forces, branding them as 'looters, robbers, murderers', and urging local people not to have anything to do with them. Some of his officers stood up to walk out but O'Malley motioned to them to stay.[24]

Dalton drew up an operational plan deploying hundreds of troops to confront the republican forces in Baltinglass and in the County Carlow towns of Tullow and Myshall, and in Newtownbarry (now Bunclody), County Wexford, and places in between these locations. The plan also involved troop movements in other parts of these counties as well as Counties Kildare and Kilkenny to secure or rein- force various positions. As part of the operation, troops would occupy crucial cross roads, and garrison towns and villages. It appears Dalton had a number of objectives – to round up republican fighters or to at least impede their movements, and to ensure that they did not retain control of any local towns or villages. Aerial reconnaissance by the fledgling Military Air Service would also form part of the operation. Dalton had estimates of the strength of 'Irregular' forces in various locations – there was no indication as to how he had obtained this intelligence. He believed that there were about 100 in Baltinglass on the night of 16 July, with another sizeable contingent occupying Tullow. He estimated that about 200 of the enemy evacuated Newtownbarry on the morning of 16 July. He observed that Myshall, County Carlow was said to be occupied by seventy-five men.[25]

Dalton's forces began moving out on the night of the 15th. For the assault on Baltinglass, it would appear that he devised a pincer movement. Among the forces deployed were 200 men from the 2nd Brigade, 2nd Eastern Division. They moved out from Tallaght, passing through Blessington and then detouring off the main road through a mountainous area through Donard and then on to Spinans cross roads where they took up position, a few miles from Baltinglass. Another 100 men left Naas, to approach Baltinglass from a different direction, via Dunlavin and Grangecon.

To boost the security of the wider region around the area occupied by republicans, Dalton was eager to reinforce Carlow command. He arranged for 250 men from the Curragh camp to proceed by rail to Athy, County Kildare; 100 of the men detrained here, and proceeded to Castledermot. The remaining 150 went on to Carlow to provide extra support to the Carlow command. This gave the local commander Brigadier Stack 300 men with whom to operate. According to Dalton, Stack occupied a range of positions, including Bagenalstown, Leighlinbridge, Palatine, Millford and Killerick cross roads.

Dalton also deployed mobile units which he called 'flying columns', a term used by the pre-Truce IRA. In his report to headquarters, he referred to the 'Wexford flying column' leaving Wexford town, passing through New Ross where they left thirty men to guard the bridge head. (As indicated above, Dalton had been under pressure to secure bridges and rail facilities in the New Ross area.) The rest of the column took up a position at Borris and established an outpost to cover Goresbridge and another to make contact with Bagenalstown. Another National Army contingent, 200-strong, from the Dublin Brigade, 2nd Eastern Command, departed from Dun Laoghaire, travelled by rail to Arklow and then through Aughrim to Tinahely. Here the force split into two 100-strong units, one proceeding to Hacketstown to occupy Rathvilly and Fortgranite House; the other unit moved through Kilquighen to occupy Knocklaw and Rathglass Bridge.[26] (Fortgranite House is a granite, square country mansion built around 1730, located south east of Baltinglass.)

Dalton's organizational ability is underlined by the deft deployment of up to 1,000 men in a series of movements to occupy a complex range of positions, in a short space of time, in order to secure south Leinster. When the groundwork had been laid he turned his attention to the enemy forces in Baltinglass. As a senior officer he could have safely directed operations from his base in Portobello barracks in Dublin, but he clearly preferred to be where the action was, and he personally led the assault. On Sunday, 16 July, the day before Dalton's advance on Baltinglass,

Dalton's airman friend Commandant General W.J. McSweeney, head of the Military Air Service, flew over the town in an army aircraft to carry out reconnaissance. It is likely that Dalton, with his emphasis on operational intelligence, had requested such reconnaissance to establish the dispositions of the rebel forces, the location of outposts, the possible strength of the enemy and to check if roads had been cut or bridges destroyed.

In his report to the Adjutant General, McSweeney said that at 3.45 pm on Sunday, 16 July, he left Baldonnel with Lieutenant Nolan.[27] 'I flew over all roads between Naas to Tullow at height of 600 feet looking for road obstructions and movements of troops. On arriving at Baltinglass I remained over the town for about 10 minutes and noticed nothing unusual.' He then flew on to Tullow. The town was full of men but they were only standing around. There appeared to be no activity of a military nature. He noted that each entrance to the town was blocked by a stone barrier half way across the road, with sufficient space to allow carts to pass. There were no sentries on these barriers and no activity in the barracks in the centre of the town. On his way back to Baldonnel, the engine of the aircraft cut out and McSweeney had to land in a field near Naas. The aircraft overturned in a ditch and Lieutenant Nolan was knocked unconscious. It was the first crash landing of the new military air service. Nolan was unable to contribute his observer's reconnaissance report so clearly McSweeney had to make do with supplying a 'recon' report based on his own impressions.

McSweeney put on record that he should have two more machines as soon as possible, and if these were to be handed over by the British, new material should be demanded, 'not the oldest machines in their establishment'. According to McSweeney, both machines handed over the previous week were old. 'One has crashed and the other is giving trouble.' An aircraft which crash-landed was a matter of great curiosity and it was said that hundreds of onlookers turned up to view the spectacle. A military guard was placed on the aircraft overnight until it could be towed by a Crossley tender to Baldonnel for repairs. A local newspaper described the aircraft as a Bristol bi-plane with Irish tricolour markings on both sides.[28]

Early on the morning of 17 July, yet another aircraft circled over Baltinglass and was noticed by the locals – and by the republicans.[29] Military records show that it was flown by another of Dalton's aviator friends Captain Charles Russell. The pilot's observer was Captain Bill Stapleton, yet another veteran of the Sean MacEoin attempted prison rescue. As Russell flew over Baltinglass, anti-Treaty fighters opened fire on Russell's plane. In his reconnaissance report, Russell told how he took off from Baldonnel at 7 am with Captain Stapleton, arrived at Tullow at 7.40 am and found the town asleep, no movement whatsoever.[30] He noted a stone barricade on the road a half mile south of the town, and two trees across the road about two miles north of the town, but did not see anything of an unusual nature. He noted that he failed to pick up 'any of our troops'. He arrived at Baltinglass on the return journey at 8 am. There were a good number of people around the street. Bridges were intact and roads appeared to be clear. The weather was bad and he flew low. While over Baltinglass, eight rifle shots at irregular intervals were fired at the plane. One round appeared to have hit the machine, but damage on first inspection appeared to be negligible. Russell noted that the shots were fired from three different points but he was unable to locate the snipers due to mist, and did not return the fire. (It is likely that the aircraft would have been equipped with a Lewis gun.) He returned to Baldonnel at 8.45 am.

Two aircraft had now been seen on successive days over Baltinglass, and this may have alerted the republicans to the imminent Free State assault. Nevertheless, Dalton by now knew the situation in Baltinglass. While roads were clear and bridges intact, anti-Treaty forces seemed on the alert and there were snipers who could pose a threat, as Dalton would discover. He advanced on Baltinglass, accompanied by his trusted comrades Commandant General Tom Ennis and Commandant Pat McCrea. As National Army forces converged on Baltinglass, they encountered 'machine gun resistance' north west of the town, and also north east, according to Dalton's later report. Some elements moved more slowly than others so Dalton decided to advance into the town himself. He was in a touring car with Ennis, and McCrea, supported by an armoured car. According to Dalton's account to Calton Younger, they took some prisoners as they went in, while other elements of their force came down from the hills. This was probably a reference to the troops who had detoured through Donard, who had circled around, and who would now have been moving in from the southeast. Dalton's party came under fire from different locations as they crossed a bridge. In Dalton's laconic account to Younger: 'We had a little bit of a battle, an exchange of shots, if you like.'[31]

A local newspaper reported that republican snipers were operating from the tower of the local Catholic church, and from the ancient ruins of the Cistercian monastery.[32] It was an occasion when Dalton came close to serious injury. With a well-aimed shot, a sniper hit the car in which Dalton was travelling, obviously hoping to disable the driver and his vehicle. Dalton told Calton Younger that McCrea was driving, and that the round shattered the steering wheel in McCrea's hands, wounding him on the wrist, while fragments hit Dalton in the face.[33] The interview took place decades after the event and Dalton's memory may not have been quite accurate as to who was driving. In Dalton's report to the military authorities written on the day of the capture of Baltinglass, he recorded that he himself was at the wheel. He reported that he was attacking the southern side of the town to which the enemy, about 100-strong, had retreated, when a shot hit his car: 'I was driving my touring car and a sniper blew the steering wheel out of my hands. Commandant McCrea was wounded in the wrist by the same sniper.'[34] Being at the wheel would, in effect, have made Dalton a more attractive target for the sniper.

After about three hours, the fighting came to an end. Dalton observed in his report to headquarters that the advance left one line of retreat for the Irregulars, directly towards Tullow. Presumably Dalton could have cut this escape route – a force could, for instance, have been sent across from Carlow to carry out this function. The question arises – did he leave it open as a 'safety valve' to avoid serious bloodshed? Those republicans who did not manage to slip away, surrendered. In his report to the Adjutant General, Dalton noted that the town was in their hands at 2 pm; his forces had one casualty and the enemy suffered none, 'owing to the fact that they fired first and then surrendered'. They took twenty-five prisoners and forty rifles, six revolvers and some hundreds of rounds of ammunition and bombs.[35] It can be presumed that the single casualty referred to by Dalton was McCrea. However, a local newspaper, the *Kildare Observer*, reported that a National soldier, Private Smith, was shot dead and two others were slightly wounded, including Lieutenant Keane who was 'injured in the head'.[36] The newspaper said that during the attack, a priest from Baltinglass came out and praised the National soldiers and 'gave them Absolution'. (This may well have been the same priest who annoyed Ernie O'Malley by denouncing the anti-Treaty forces from the altar.) The story also stated that in the course of operations 'five Irish military aeroplanes hovered over the town'. The newspaper reported that the anti-Treaty forces retreated towards Tullow, which tallied with Dalton's version of events. The *Kildare Observer* referred also to the warm welcome given to the National troops. 'Everywhere the people received them with joy.' Also on 17 July, Dalton's forces moved into Tullow, south of Baltinglass, at about 1 pm and occupied the town without any resistance. Dalton said in his report to the Adjutant General that he received information that the anti-Treaty forces had departed from Tullow on the night of the 16th in the direction of Bagenalstown, County Carlow. About 1.15 pm Dalton's forces occupied Newtownbarry, under the command of Tom Kilcoyne, who would play an important role when Dalton's forces landed in County Cork the following month.

Following the entry of the Free State forces into Baltinglass, Tullow and Newtownbarry, General Headquarters of the National Army issued a statement announcing the occupation of the towns by National troops. The statement recorded the fact that Commandant McCrea was wounded in the wrist. The statement continued: 'A doctor and three ladies in charge of a Red Cross station belonging to the Irregulars in the town gave their word of honour that no arms or ammunition were concealed in the building. When searched however, a bag of grenades was found by the troops on the premises. In consequence of this abuse a more thorough search of persons displaying the Red Cross was made. One of the women wearing the Red Cross badge carried papers belonging to a leader of the Irregulars in a dispatch case. Another woman, also wearing the Red Cross badge, when examined by women searchers, was found to have ammunition concealed in her clothes. The ammunition found on the prisoners was nearly all dum-dum. When interrogated as to how they came to have such ammunition in their possession, several of the prisoners blamed those responsible for issuing their supplies.' In his report to the Adjutant General, Dalton said that the prisoners 'apologized' for having dum-dum ammunition.

One of the women detained was Madge Clifford, a committed republican activist. In happier times, the previous December, she and Dalton had each attended the Squad dance at Howth Summit. (See Chapter Five.) A native of Ballybane, Firies, County Kerry, she came to Dublin as secretary to Austin Stack when he became Minister of Home Affairs. She went on to work for a range of other senior figures in the movement. An attractive young woman, she found that her feminine wiles came in useful on at least one occasion. She was working for Diarmuid Hegarty, secretary of the Dáil Éireann Cabinet at an office in a building in Lower Abbey Street, Dublin when a group of Auxiliaries came in on a raid. She flirted with an Auxiliary and successfully managed to divert attention from sensitive Dáil files.[37] She carried out secretarial work for Éamon de Valera, and took the minutes of Cabinet meetings. She took the republican side in the Civil War, and worked as a secretary for Ernie O'Malley and also Liam Lynch. She was in the Four Courts using a typewriter when, it was said, one of the first shells fired by Dalton's gunners hit the building close to where she was working, 'but failed to explode'.[38] The republican Todd Andrews was highly impressed by Clifford. Watching her in action, he had a remarkable moment of epiphany – he described how he realized for the first time that 'women had a role outside the home'.[39] She was not arrested at the surrender of the Four Courts, and apparently was only temporarily detained when Baltinglass was captured.

Following a statement from the National Army accusing her of wearing a Red Cross armband and carrying illegal dum-dum ammunition, she sent a letter to the *Irish Times* angrily denying this claim. The National Army replied in a further statement naming three local witnesses saying that they saw Miss Clifford in Baltinglass wearing a black waterproof coat and carrying a revolver. It was claimed she was with a gentleman and two ladies who were later seen wearing Red Cross armlets. The statement included testimony from a Mrs Butler saying that at the request of an Irish Army officer she searched three ladies, 'all of whom were wearing Red Cross armlets'. Mrs Butler went on: 'During my search I took from the hand of Miss Madge Clifford a despatch case', in which she found dum-dum ammunition and some ladies' underclothing. In his report to the Adjutant General, Dalton referred derisively to Madge Clifford as an 'alleged nurse', saying that abuses of the Red Cross 'prove once more and conclusively that honour does not exist in the ranks of our enemies'.

Following the occupation of Baltinglass, Tullow and Newtowbarry, Dalton informed headquarters that the only position that had been occupied by the anti-Treaty forces, and that his forces had not yet entered was Myshall, a small village on the northern edge of the Blackstairs Mountains. He believed that there were large numbers of the enemy still in the area, but they had split up into groups of twos and threes and temporarily hidden their weapons. To round them up, he garrisoned towns in the region. Apart from these static deployments, he also deployed 'flying columns' operating from some of the main garrisons. One column was operating in a southerly direction from Baltinglass; three columns, each fifty-strong, were operating from Tullow; two columns of similar strength were operating from Newtownbarry, towards Myshall; two columns were operating from Carlow, one northwards and the other southwards.[40] Effectively any republicans remaining in Myshall were surrounded. Dalton added that in his absence, the officer commanding the operation was Commandant General Ennis. In his report Dalton referred to the total number of prisoners taken as thirty, and casualties as one Irregular dead, one officer (National Army) wounded, and one civilian injured by a splinter. The communication did not contain any information to corroborate the report by the *Kildare Observer* that a Private Smith had been killed and two other National Army personnel wounded in the assault on Baltinglass.

On 19 July Dalton was busily engaged in paperwork back at his office in Portobello, writing up a report on the capture of Baltinglass. That same day, the Minister for Defence General Mulcahy wrote to Dalton drawing his attention to a letter complaining about the behaviour of some National troops in Wexford. It was claimed, inter alia, that some of them 'fire shots now and then for sport'.[41] The complaint came from a nun at the Loreto Convent, and for Mulcahy, who was very devout, this may have added weight to the complaint. Dalton drew up a manifesto for all troops of Eastern Command stating that during times of war, the confidence of the people was placed in the army, and in order that this confidence should not be shaken, it was essential that all troops carried out their operations and duties 'with characteristic bravery'. He continued, 'Their actions should be thorough and firm, at the same time being polite and dignified.'

Dalton emphasized that should it be necessary to search civilians, 'it should be remembered that the vast majority of the civilian population is friendly', and that discourteous treatment 'is likely to alienate their sympathy and friendship'. He said it was necessary 'to display discipline through our actions and smartness of dress'. As regards the latter point, Dalton was always well turned out, and clearly he wanted to impress on his men the importance of a smart, neat appearance.

On 28 July yet another problem landed on Dalton's desk. Michael Collins, who by now had taken over as Commander-in-Chief of the National Army, was furious when he read two Military Orders on the front page of the *Irish Independent*, signed by Commandant General T. Ennis, HQ, 2nd Eastern Division, Wellington Barracks. One order warned that the proprietors of Licensed Houses in Dublin City and County were prohibited from supplying members of the Irish Army in uniform with intoxicating liquor: 'Where a member of the Irish Forces is found under the influence of drink in a licensed premises the licence of such will be immediately cancelled and a fine imposed.' In the second Military Order, Ennis directed that all Licensed Houses remain open only between the hours of 9 am and 9.30 pm on week-days and between the hours of 2 pm and 5 pm on Sundays. Collins requested an explanation from Major General Dalton 'as to the circumstances in which these advertisements came to be inserted in the press, and whether Commandant General Ennis acted on his own initiative'. Collins emphasized that it must be impressed on officers that they had no authority to issue such orders without the sanction of Government.[42]

As Collins settled into his role as Commander-in-Chief, he quickly made his presence felt among senior officers by demanding swift action on any reports of 'Irregular' activity. On 3 August Collins sought a report from Dalton on incidents that had occurred in his Eastern Command area in places as disparate as Drogheda, Naas, New Ross and Waterford. Dalton was also asked what arrangements were being made 'to deal with such activities'.[43] Meanwhile, Dalton was busy overseeing a major security operation in Dublin on 3 August in which troops, supported by armoured cars and in cooperation with members of the Dublin Metropolitan Police, erected barricades, organized vehicle checkpoints and carried out patrols.[44] Some of these troops were involved in the arrest of more than 100 republicans after the National Army learned of a plot to isolate Dublin on the night of 5 August by destroying bridges, cutting railway lines and disrupting communications.[45]

Recruiting Military Specialists

In the campaign to defeat the republicans, the Provisional Government forces received major assistance from Britain which supplied arms, ammunition and equipment, as well as aircraft. Apart from being better armed than their opponents, the National Army also had greater mobility. By early July the British Government had handed over 355 vehicles to the Provisional Government, including 81 with armoured plating.[46] It was also essential to quickly expand the strength of the National Army, and as the Civil War got under way a recruiting drive was launched. During the battle of the Four Courts, the opposing sides were composed essentially of men who had been in the pre-Truce IRA. Now the pro-Treaty IRA had evolved into the National Army. This latter force which was previously comprised of Volunteers who had served in the IRA against the British, now rapidly expanded, taking in new recruits, including Great War veterans who had served in the British Army.

As the National Army rapidly expanded, Dalton and Commander-in-Chief Michael Collins wanted to boost the capabilities of the army by recruiting men with previous military service who had specialist skills or who could act as instructors. Irishmen who had served in the British Army in the Great War had such skills, and were available, and were probably desperate for work at a time of unemployment. As part of this recruitment drive, Collins was in touch during July with M.R. Walker, Chairman of the Legion of Irish Ex-Servicemen, and he arranged for Dalton to liaise with Walker, who was a very active campaigner for the rights of demobilized Irishmen. Walker was demanding that the British Government give a better deal, especially in the area of housing, to the Irish who had served the empire during the Great War. The opportunity of serving in a new Irish army must have appeared most attractive to unemployed ex-soldiers, and Walker seemed eager that members of his own organization would be chosen, and perhaps even get preference.

On 4 August Dalton met with Walker, who worked from an office at 3 Molesworth Street, not far from Government Buildings. Dalton reported to Collins that he had outlined the list of special services men they required in the various categories and specialities – training instructors; artillery; machine gunners; engineers; Lewis gunners; military police; motor drivers; army medical corps; armourers; aeroplane riggers and aeroplane fitters. Dalton quoted Walker as saying that he believed that numbers of these men could be supplied in a couple of weeks' time but he was anxious to receive details of the terms of employment. Dalton reported that he had been told by Walker that 'large numbers of ex-Servicemen whom we have taken on under the recruiting scheme are unsatisfactory and quite liable to give dissatisfaction'. Dalton said that Walker informed him that large numbers of first-class ex-Servicemen had remained intact in Cork and Southern Ireland: 'He believes it would be possible to engage these men under our new scheme.' Dalton added that Walker struck him as 'quite a capable fellow'.[47]

In a follow-up letter to Dalton, Walker said he had taken the necessary steps to obtain the services of twenty instructors. He asked about the possibility of arranging railway warrants to enable men to travel to Dublin for interview. He mentioned also that it might be necessary for him to visit centres in the country where branches were cut off from mail services, and thought it would be advisable for him to have a permit for a revolver – a reminder of the turbulent times in which the letter was written.[48] Meanwhile, Collins, accompanied by Dalton, went on a tour of inspection of the Curragh camp, which was destined to become a major training base for the National Army. A photograph survives of Collins and Dalton taken at the conclusion of a visit to Beresford Barracks at the Curragh. Also in the photograph are Colonel Dunphy, Commandant General Peadar McMahon and Commandant General Diarmuid O'Hegarty. According to the British intelligence file on Dalton, during this period he was playing an important role in selecting officers and Non-Commissioned Officers (NCOs) for the army.[49] Dalton would later state that he recruited a number of Irishmen who had served as officers in the British Army. With them he was able to organize a training schedule for the different areas, especially at the Curragh.[50]

Unfortunately for Walker, some of those whom he had recommended as NCO instructors were rejected when they arrived at the Curragh. Walker complained about the rejection, expressing the personal opinion that the fact that the men were not all late Royal Dublin Fusiliers 'had something to do with it'.[51] As regards ex-servicemen in the south, Dalton would go on to recruit some of these men in the Cork region, but first he had to seize Cork city and expel the republican forces from their Munster stronghold. He would achieve this objective by a daring seaborne offensive.

CHAPTER NINE

The Landings

D alton was a strong advocate of seaborne landings by troops to overcome resistance by republican forces. The Free State approach from the sea was to prove of particular importance in Munster, large parts of which were under the control of anti-Treaty forces, especially Cork city and county. The republicans had cut roads, destroyed bridges and blocked railway lines, making military advances by land difficult.[1] Dalton had talks with Collins and Mulcahy, and it was finally decided that the best way to attack was by sea, and that Dalton would personally lead one of the major landing operations in Cork. He firmly believed in the element of surprise so he intended to steam up the River Lee by night, and then 'capture Cork while they [the enemy] were asleep'.[2] However, this plan would not prove as straightforward as Dalton might have hoped.

There were risks involved in landing troops at various points around the coast as the Civil War got under way. The main ships deployed were not naval vessels protected by armoured plating and equipped with naval guns, as the new National Army had little in the way of a naval element. Instead the army used mainly passenger ferries or cargo vessels that had been commandeered and pressed into service by the Provisional Government, and on 15th July 1922 Collins received a letter from Mulcahy outlining a 'list of vessels which can be made available as troop transports…' Details were then given of ten vessels, their gross tonnage, dimensions, draft and the numbers of troops that could be accommodated on each ship.[3]

Apart from ships that could be commandeered, the National Army was also deploying a fishery protection vessel, the *Helga*, a former British gunboat which had been handed over to the Provisional Government. It would land some of Dalton's troops during the landings in County Cork, and was later used for patrolling and transport purposes. During the Easter Rising in 1916 the *Helga* famously sailed up the Liffey and used her war-time twelve-pounder ordnance to bombard Liberty Hall.

The *Helga* (re-named *Muirchú* in late 1923) was intended to carry out fishery protection duties for the Department of Agriculture of the new Irish state. However, as conflict developed, she was taken over by the National Army, forming the foundation of a future naval service. While the ship continued to be operated by a civilian crew, an army officer and soldiers (seconded by the army's Marine Investigation Department) provided the military element, armed with the ship's Hotchkiss three-pounder gun and assorted Vickers and Lewis machine guns.[4] It would patrol coastal waters to block any attempt to land arms for the anti-Treaty forces and crucially it provided the National Army with an alternative to the rail and road networks which were vulnerable to republican disruption.

Early in the Civil War, the *Helga* had been deployed as part of General John T. Prout's operation to take Waterford, landing reinforcements and vital supplies of arms and ammunition[5] and she was also used to deliver a field gun and armoured cars to the troops at Buncrana, County Donegal in mid-July 1922. In an important development, the ship *Menevia* was also deployed in July for a crucial seaborne landing at Westport, County Mayo, where it delivered 400 National Army troops, a Whippet armoured car and an eighteen-pounder field gun. Buoyed up by the success of the Mayo operation, the next area targeted for sea-borne invasion was County Kerry. About 450 men of the Dublin Guard, under the command of Brigadier General Paddy O'Daly, with an armoured car and an eighteen-pounder field gun, sailed from the North Wall of Dublin port aboard the Lady Wicklow early on the morning of 1 August, and landed at Fenit. From there the troops took the town of Tralee, and in a supporting operation the following day, National Army forces used three fishing boats to ferry about 300 men across the Shannon, taking control of the County Kerry harbour of Tarbert.

Landings in County Cork

In early August, the big prize of Cork city was now firmly in the sights of the National Army. It was the main stronghold of the anti-Treaty forces and seen as the *de facto* capital of what remained of the 'Munster republic'. With its various facilities, the city would also be an important, central base for the southern command of the National Army. Originally the republicans had sought to hold a defensive line protecting the Munster region, running from Limerick in the northwest to Waterford in the southeast. By early August Limerick was in the hands of the Free Staters under General Eoin O'Duffy, who had opposed seaborne landings in Cork and Kerry as too dangerous. Waterford was firmly under the control of General Prout. Paddy O'Daly's men were ensconced in County Kerry. Kilmallock in south County Limerick, in the northern sector of the 'Munster republic' had fallen to the National Army after heavy fighting in late July and early August, and National troops were now in a position to push southwards overland towards Cork.

Dalton would recall in later life how Collins told him of the necessity of capturing Cork. With road and rail links disrupted, anti-Treaty forces were in full control. Collins had been told by various sources, including family members in the region, that if a National Army force arrived it would be well received by the citizens who were anxious to be relieved from the 'oppressions of rule' by the 'Irregulars'.[6] In mentioning 'family members', Dalton was probably referring to Collins's sister, the feisty Mary Collins-Powell. She had travelled in early August via a circuitous route from Cork to Dublin with the message that there were up to 500 men ready to join the Free State forces whenever the National Army moved into Cork. Having avoided the potential disruption of road and rail travel by sailing to Waterford on a yacht, the *Gull*, she then took a taxi to Rosslare, boarded a train to Dublin, and reached Portobello in time to see Collins before he left the barracks.[7] However, it appears she failed to arrive in time to give a briefing to Dalton before he sailed for Cork. Dalton planned to recruit additional troops on arrival and he would later indicate that he was unaware of the full extent of the considerable numbers waiting to join his forces. The Provisional Government also received some limited intelligence on republican activity in the Cork region from the senior British official at Dublin Castle, Alfred Cope, who was in touch by wireless with the Royal Navy at Haulbowline in Cork Harbour. In early July, Cope passed on information from Haulbowline that republicans were seizing all motor boats and vehicles, other than medical ones; that they were commandeering clothes, boots and provisions in Queenstown, Cork and Crosshaven; that they were forcing civilian employees from the dockyard to dig trenches and that they appeared to have placed examination boats in the channel at Little Island.[8]

In coming in from the 'back door', i.e. the sea, Dalton was hoping to undermine any republican land-based defensive line across Munster. The republicans were no fools – they were fully aware that the Provisional Government forces might mount a ship-borne invasion. They had taken precautions for such an eventuality, as underlined by Alfred Cope. The anti-Treatyites had placed garrisons at possible landing points, were monitoring the channel to Cork city with a view to blocking it if necessary, and making certain piers unusable. However, they had a long coastline to defend, with limited resources, and it was difficult to predict when or where the Free Staters might come storming ashore.

Major General Dalton drew up an operational plan to take Cork city and county. It involved a three-pronged assault from the sea, with the main force landing at or near Cork city, with two other landings, one to the east at Youghal and another to the west, at Union Hall in Glandore Harbour, between Skibbereen and Rosscarbery. The main force, which he termed Party A, had a strength of about 450 men; Party B, to land at Youghal, had a strength of about 200, while Party C, to land at Union Hall, had about 150 men.[9] Heavy equipment, including armoured cars, Lancia armoured lorries and field guns, would also be landed. It was planned that each contingent would rapidly expand its strength after landing by recruiting local Volunteers of the pro-Treaty IRA who were keeping a low profile, and also ex-members of the British Army who had military experience. Hundreds of additional rifles would be carried with the convoy to arm those who would be recruited.

After landing, each contingent would consolidate its position and advance into surrounding areas, taking control of local towns. They would also coordinate with neighbouring commands, such as Paddy O'Daly's forces to the west in Kerry;

the forces of General Eoin O'Duffy who was based to the northwest in Limerick, and the forces of General Prout to the east. The intention was to squeeze the republican fighters from every direction. For the crucial landings to take Cork city, the Provisional Government commandeered the ferries, *Arvonia*, operated by the London and North Western Railway, and the *Lady Wicklow*, operated by the British and Irish Steam Packet Company (B & I). Dalton would personally lead the expedition, with his close comrade-in-arms 27-year-old General Tom Ennis. Dalton marched his troops aboard at the North Wall in Dublin port. *Lady Wicklow* was fresh from her adventure landing troops in County Kerry, and had returned to Dublin port with a sombre cargo – nine coffins containing the remains of soldiers killed in the fighting. Most of the troops travelled on the *Arvonia* and Dalton established his maritime headquarters on the ship for the voyage to the south. A smaller number of soldiers travelled on the *Lady Wicklow* – it was initially intended that the ship would carry out a scouting role, sailing ahead of the *Arvonia*.

Some of the 450-strong contingent were from the Second Battalion of the Dublin Brigade and there were also about 150 fresh recruits of the new National Army who had only been supplied with uniforms and rifles a week before. An eighteen-pounder field gun and armoured vehicles were also being transported to Cork. During the sea voyage the new recruits were trained in how to handle their rifles. As regard the vessels that were to be deployed for separate landings in County Cork, it was decided that the *Helga* would land the troops and equipment at Youghal while another vessel, the *Alexandria*, would land men and equipment at Union Hall. The equipment to be landed at these two locations included an armoured car, an eighteen-pounder field gun and Lancia armoured vehicles.

Collins had taken a personal interest in the arrangements for the landings, even to the extent of checking out the draft of ships that could land at Union Hall, in his native region of West Cork. Collins also arranged for aerial reconnaissance to be carried out by the new Military Air Service in advance of the landings.[10]

Dalton was conscious that many of his troops were inexperienced, yet he must have been encouraged by the presence of a hard core of reliable officers, such as General Tom Ennis, his second-in-command. Ennis was a charismatic, brave officer who had not only taken part in the Easter Rising in 1916 and the subsequent War of Independence, but also played a crucial role in storming the anti-Treaty garrison at the Four Courts. Then there were Liam Tobin, Pat McCrea, Ben Byrne and Tom Kilcoyne, who were trusted members of Michael Collins's Squad, fearless men who would not be found wanting in a firefight.

Dalton had some personal knowledge of the lie of the land – it will be recalled that he was shown around the Cork region by Tom Barry during the Truce. Nevertheless, he needed back-up from somebody with more detailed local knowledge. This vital expertise was supplied by another of his officers, Frank O'Friel – he had spent his childhood in the Cork Harbour area where his father worked as a lighthouse keeper. A particularly valuable addition to Dalton's force was Peadar Conlon, who had served in the British Army during the Great War and then took part in the War of Independence, fighting under General Sean MacEoin.

A particularly resilient and resourceful fighter, he came from Ballinalee, where MacEoin also had his origins. When the split in the movement came about, Conlon took the pro-Treaty side like MacEoin.[11]

The ships set sail on the afternoon of Monday, 7 August 1922, a bank holiday. The departure was timed so that the ships would arrive under cover of darkness. There seems to have been little or no secrecy surrounding the departure of the troops from the North Wall. A photograph taken by cameraman W.D. Hogan on the day shows that a sizeable crowd of relatives and well-wishers had assembled on the quayside to see off the troops on the expedition. It was an uneventful voyage. There was a festive air among the young soldiers. For some, it may have been their first time on a ship, their first time on a trip to Munster. They played games, they sang, they danced on deck, waltzing with each other to the music of a melodeon.[12] Some of the soldiers were very young – they included two teenaged brothers, Private Frederick McKenna (18) and Private Gerald McKenna (17) with an address at Phibsboro, Dublin.

It was dark as *Arvonia* and *Lady Wicklow* approached the County Cork coast, reaching Roche's Point at the entrance to Cork Harbour about midnight. With moonlight reflecting on the dark sea, the ships moved north into the sheltered bay, one of the biggest deepwater harbours in the world. They steamed towards Cork city, located about eleven miles upstream on the River Lee in the northwest area of the harbour. By Queenstown harbour (now Cobh) the *Arvonia* was challenged and searchlights were directed onto the ship. It turned out that the challenge came from a British Royal Navy vessel – Queenstown was one of the 'Treaty ports' that remained in British hands following the Treaty and the withdrawal of most British forces. The captain of the *Arvonia* was ordered to heave to, explain who he was and state where he was bound for. The captain was unsure how to handle the situation. Dalton told him to tell the British that he (Dalton) was on an expedition to Cork to re-capture the city for the Provisional Government and that he would be grateful if they did not interfere in any way. According to Dalton in his RTÉ interview with Cathal O'Shannon, the British said, 'Good Luck', and stayed out of the way.

The Royal Navy seems to have been taken by surprise by the arrival of Dalton's seaborne forces. Apparently the Provisional Government had not informed the British in advance of the intention to take Cork. Days before Dalton mounted his offensive, there had been an attempt by Michael Collins to get Prime Minister Lloyd George and Winston Churchill to agree to the handover of at least one of the forts still held by the British in Cork harbour. This request was refused, and the British military headquarters in Dublin reported back to London that General Dalton had hinted that Collins 'would give no plan for occupation of Cork via Queenstown if loan of fort was refused'.[14]

In an exchange of signals, the British advised the captain of *Arvonia* that he needed a pilot to take them further up the Lee closer to Cork. A pilot was summoned at Cobh and duly went aboard. The troops were hidden below decks but Dalton was in his uniform and on the bridge. The pilot, startled by the presence of an armed military officer, asked what was going on. The captain said they were just sailing the ship – in other words, don't ask me, ask the military man. When Dalton informed the pilot that his help was required to guide the ship up the Lee, the pilot protested that he could not take them up the river as he was a deep-sea pilot not a river pilot. Also, there were obstructions in the river.

According to Dalton in various interviews he gave in later life, he drew his revolver and instructed the pilot to take the ship as far up the river as he could: 'You are taking us up the river whether you like it or not.' If he refused, he would be shot. Dalton told the man he could not believe that he had spent twenty years as a pilot without getting to know the river. The pilot told Dalton that if he made a mistake, it would be Dalton's fault. 'So be it,' snapped Dalton.[15] Dalton had hoped to land at Ford's wharf in Cork City, but the pilot informed him that the river was blocked beyond Passage West. The republicans had placed two vessels at a narrow point in the channel.

Dalton considered landing at Cobh instead but his orderly officer, Commandant O'Friel, would recall later that he warned Dalton that Cobh was located on an island, Great Island, and that their advance across the bridge at Belvelly to the mainland could be easily blocked by opposing forces with a few machine guns.[16] It later emerged that the republicans had taken precautions here to block any advance from Cobh, erecting barricades and digging trenches on the Cork side of Belvelly bridge, and preparing mines to blow up the road bridge at Belvelly and the Fota railway bridge linking Cobh to Cork.[17]

The writer Eoin Neeson, in his account, states that when Dalton's ship first appeared off Cobh none of the anti-Treatyites ashore could identify her. The Cobh OC sent a small boat out to investigate but failed to make contact. Republicans in three cars with Lewis guns mounted on them tracked the ship, driving along the road to Rushbrooke. At one stage, warning shots were fired by the republicans, and an answering burst came, but it was unclear where it came from.[18]

The pilot guided the ship, sailing without lights, towards a landing place at the small harbour of Passage West in the Lee estuary, about seven miles from Cork City. It was about two o'clock on the morning of Tuesday, 8 August. Before *Arvonia* moved into a berth at the shipbuilding and engineering docks, Dalton ordered Frank O'Friel to take about twenty men in a boat and go ashore. They were accompanied by General Liam Tobin. The republicans were aware of the threat from seaborne landings and had a small garrison in a granary at the dock. There were some warning shots fired from shore as the ship approached the landing stage. As it came closer, a man came forward cautiously with a lamp to apologize for firing on what appeared now to be a friendly ship – apparently he mistook it for the *Classic* that had earlier sailed for Fishguard. Clearly, there was at least one advantage in using a civilian vessel as a troopship – it was not immediately recognized as a threat by the republicans, and helped Dalton to maintain an element of surprise. The captain of *Arvonia* helped to push out the gangway while some of the ship's officers jumped onto the quay in order to tie up the vessel to the harbour wall. Suddenly there was activity on the ship as uniformed soldiers began to emerge noiselessly from below decks in the darkness. Dalton was well on the way to establishing a vital bridgehead. Some of the troops went on to the quay and took a number of prisoners, one of whom was wounded after troops opened fire. The ship was fired on from Great Island on the opposite bank of the channel. The sniping continued during the night and the following day.[19] Troops, shielded by sandbags on the decks of *Arvonia*, replied to the fire from the Cobh anti-Treaty riflemen with rifle and machine gun fire.

Meanwhile, O'Friel and Tobin entered the granary that had been used as a base for the republicans, and found signs of a swift evacuation. While Tobin was in the building the telephone rang and Tobin picked it up. It was the Cork City Headquarters of the IRA at Union Quay barracks. Some firing had been heard and the caller wanted to know what the shooting was about. Tobin, who came originally from Cork before settling in Dublin, passed himself off as one of the garrison and said in his best Cork accent that it was nothing – 'just an incident on the river'.[20] That seemed to mollify the caller. The republicans, in their hasty retreat, left behind some motor launches which were taken over by the National troops, who also reportedly collected a number of rifles and revolvers that had been abandoned.[21]

Elsewhere along the coast, late on the Monday night or early the following morning, the *Helga* landed the troops at Youghal, while troops under Captain Larry Finnegan and Captain Paddy Kelly landed from *Alexandria* at Union Hall. A later bulletin from the Publicity Department, Field General Headquarters, South-Western Command, stated that the landing at Passage West was effected without resistance. The bulletin stated that the landing at Youghal met with no resistance – however, a newspaper story on the first anniversary of the landing claimed that *Helga* had come under fire from Irregulars after the vessel 'rushed' into the harbour at 6 am, berthing at the Pier Head. According to the story, Dublin troops under Captain Hancock captured the former RIC barracks and its occupants. The troops divided, and made for the military barracks and the Strand outpost, 'which were hurriedly evacuated'.[22]

There was some resistance as the troops landed at Union Hall, the first party of troops going ashore in two lifeboats from *Alexandria*. There was an exchange of fire with anti-Treaty forces, with troops on *Alexandria* reportedly firing a machine gun to suppress the fire from the republicans. The *Freeman's Journal* reported that the pier which had been in the possession of the 'Mutineers' for some time, was destroyed in two places, but the vessel carrying the troops came in at high tide almost to the shore, and the troops disembarked in small boats. Anti-Treaty forces occupying the Coastguard Station and the local school fired on the first party of troops to land in the two boats. However, the troops came ashore, occupied positions and returned fire. The anti-Treaty forces were driven out and the landing of the troops was completed.[23] When word reached the republicans in nearby Skibbereen that National Army troops had landed at Union Hall, they decided to vacate their barracks and set it on fire – this was on Tuesday, 8 August. The retreating republicans also burned down two fine mansions, Glencurragh House and Clover Hill, in case they might be of use to the Free State forces. Early the following morning, the Free State troops marched into town.[24]

At dawn on the Tuesday, heavier equipment was landed at Passage West. In the operations over the following days, in addition to an eighteen-pounder field gun,

Dalton also deployed two armoured cars – a Rolls Royce Whippet known as *The Manager*, equipped with the usual Vickers machine gun, and a Peerless, a much heavier vehicle, with twin Hotchkiss machine guns. There was a delay in getting the Peerless off the ship. The heavy crane at Dublin port could lift the vehicle onto the ship, but the lighter crane at Passage West was unable to transfer it onto the dock. The soldiers had to wait until the tide raised the ship to the level of the quay, and the Peerless, weighing about six tons, was then taken onto the quay, across heavy planks. It was just one of the ways in which Dalton and his forces had to improvise as they went along. At least one armoured Lancia lorry was also landed – apart from its role as a troop transport and armoured vehicle equipped with a Lewis gun, it appears to have had the task of towing the field gun. The Lancia personnel would also have had the role of protecting the eighteen-pounder and crew, and ensuring it did not fall into enemy hands.

Dalton's troops were at their most vulnerable when they were going ashore. As an extra precautionary measure, Dalton deployed about 150 men, divided into three parties led by Tom Ennis, Tom Kilcoyne and Peadar Conlon, to fan out and form a protective screen about a half mile inland while the main body of troops gained a foothold on dry land.[25] Ennis, carrying a Thompson sub-machine gun, looked relaxed and at ease when he was photographed along with Pat McCrea on the quayside at Passage West by W.D. Hogan.

The National Army forces quickly consolidated their position in Passage West. Troops were deployed at strategic positions to secure the town and an improvised barracks was set up in a four-storey building formerly used as a mill. At the dockside, troops lined up with their rifles and the march on Cork began, across a two-mile front. One element set off to advance along the main road by the Lough Mahon shore towards Rochestown. With Dalton coordinating operations from Passage West, Tom Ennis commanded the advancing troops. Dalton had worked out a plan as to how the advance would proceed, with troops moving forward in coordinated waves, with armoured car and artillery support, and carrying out flanking movements. Dalton was using infantry manoeuvre tactics he had learned in the British Army – it will be recalled that he drew up 'Operation Orders' for his company as part of an exercise involving an advance on a town by a force of battalion strength while with the 2nd Leinsters in Germany in early 1919.

Meanwhile, word had spread among the republicans that the Free Staters had landed, and there was consternation in the anti-Treaty IRA headquarters in Cork. Forces were quickly assembled to stop Dalton's advance towards the city, with reinforcements drawn from as far away as Kerry and Limerick. Special trains were pressed into service in areas still controlled by the republicans. Some of the IRA in Cork – it is unclear how many – decided they did not want to fight other Irishmen, so they dropped out.

The Advance on Cork

Some of the republicans who had pulled out of Passage West staged resistance for a period at Clarke's Field, outside the town, delaying Dalton's advance. Meanwhile republicans hastily moved into unprepared positions at Rochestown, occupying high ground overlooking the road, taking advantage of the cover provided by wooded glens, moving into houses which offered good fields of fire, and blowing up the road bridge leading into the town. The railway bridge at Rochestown was among other bridges destroyed, to impede or delay the movements of the National Army. It gave time to the IRA back in Cork to destroy buildings and facilities that might be of value to the invading forces, prior to retreating to rural West Cork. For Dalton, the element of surprise was now gone. He and his men encountered stiff resistance from the republican fighters in Rochestown and Douglas on the advance towards Cork city, which lay about seven miles away.

As a unit of republicans moved into position around Rochestown, they came into contact with the National Army troops. Both sides seemed to have been taken by surprise by this encounter. There was a skirmish and according to one account, a man on both sides was killed. Peadar Conlon had the tips of three fingers blown off – he wrapped them up and continued to fight on. He managed to have his wounds properly dressed a couple of days later.[26] Meanwhile the *Lady Wicklow* returned to Dublin, with the body of the first soldier in Dalton's contingent to have been killed. The ship would return with reinforcements and supplies on 11 August.

The anti-Treaty forces had some experienced fighters, such as Cork No. 1 Brigade training officer, Sean Murray, who had served in the Irish Guards during the Great War. Some of the anti-Treaty fighters were armed only with shotguns, no match for the longer range and accuracy of the Lee Enfield .303 rifles of the National Army soldiers. The republicans, of course, also had rifles, although limited in number. Crucially, they had a number of Lewis machine guns, which were to inflict serious casualties on the Free State troops. The advancing soldiers, for their part, had the vital advantage of armoured car and artillery support. An eighteen-pounder field gun which had been deployed the previous month for the shelling of the Four Courts (and later during fighting at Drogheda), supplied vital firepower. There were positions that republicans could hold against enemy riflemen but not against artillery shells. Records show that during the Free State advance from Passage the artillery piece was relatively busy, firing twenty-five rounds.[27] Early on in the fighting, the field gun went into action, hitting a cottage which republicans had occupied – they apparently evacuated the building when they spotted the gun being wheeled into position for firing.[28] The gunners scored a direct hit from about 1,000 yards, presumably after some initial ranging shells, suggesting that lessons had been learned from experience at the Four Courts and Drogheda.

There were to be many close encounters between the opposing sides as the fighting raged on in the fields and woods and along the roads. In one hand-to-hand encounter a young National Army non-commissioned officer called Michael Collins, a relative of the Commander-in-Chief, attacked a machine gunner and tried to shoot him but his automatic pistol jammed. As they struggled the republican managed to fire the machine gun and Collins was seriously injured in the groin. He died later in hospital.[29] During the day republican reinforcements arrived from Cork to bolster resistance, with lorry-loads of fighters being transported into the area.[30]

However, under pressure from the Free Staters, the republicans pulled back towards Old Court woods, using felled trees to block roads to further obstruct the advance. Mines were laid along the route that the National Army troops were to take but none exploded and they were made safe by the troops. By 9 o'clock that night the Free State forces had advanced about three miles along the main road from Passage West to occupy Rochestown and the railway station. They set up headquarters in Kelleher's pub in the village. They were almost half way on the advance to Cork city. The troops proceeded to fortify positions, to clear obstacles and to attempt some hasty repairs to the road bridge that had been blown up. During the night there was sporadic firing between the two sides.

After he arrived in Passage West, Dalton received some discreet assistance from Britain's Royal Navy. Captain Hugh Somerville, Senior Naval Officer commanding the British naval forces in Haulbowline, personally helped to clear an obstruction placed by republicans further up the River Lee channel leading to Cork. Somerville had good local knowledge, as he came from an Anglo-Irish background in West Cork – his sister was the writer Edith Somerville who lived at Castletownshend. Somerville enlisted the support of another officer who was well-used to dangerous escapades, Captain Alfred Carpenter who won the Victoria Cross for his role in the Zeebrugge raid during the Great War. In a motor launch, Somerville and Carpenter proceeded up the river on Tuesday, 8 August, and went aboard a dredger, *Owenabuee*, that had been moored to block the channel. The officers cast off the stern anchor, so that the vessel could swing with the tide, clearing the channel. They also disconnected a cable linked to a mine below deck. The two officers then returned via Passage West, where they informed Dalton that the passage was clear to Cork.[31] In addition, Somerville said he assisted Dalton by informing him of the position of mines planted by the republicans.[32] In addition to deploying *Owenabuee*, the republicans had sunk a dredging barge which failed to fully block the channel to Cork and on the Wednesday they sank a steamer in the channel, *SS Gorilla*, but the tide pushed it to one side. Although the channel was open to Cork, there were obstacles that would have to be avoided. At one stage W.D. Hogan took a photograph of Dalton on board one of the landing ships at Passage West using a loudhailer to warn a ship that had just arrived of 'danger' – probably a reference to obstacles upriver and the threat from snipers.[33]

On the Wednesday, 9 August, there was intense fighting all day in the hills and the woods as the National Army troops sought to push towards the next village of Douglas, which lay on the outskirts of Cork city. The republicans deployed their own home-made armoured car, *River Lee*, an unwieldy, slow-moving armour-plated lorry. It helped to impede the Free State advance. It was taken on by the National Army's armoured car, *The Manager*. At one stage, the Free State artillery bombarded anti-Treaty fighters who were operating on the north side of the channel at Fota island.

In the face of strong IRA resistance, Dalton had to move forward reserves from Passage West, where he maintained a body of troops to guard the forces' rear area and the landing point. He organized two parties to carry out a pincer movement.

One, to take the right flank, was headed by Frank O'Friel while the other, led by Tom Kilcoyne, was to take the left flank. The idea was that Kilcoyne's group would circle around the republican positions and attack from the south and west. Much to Dalton's frustration, the left flank failed to close the circle in time, and enfilade the republican positions. O'Friel lost a number of men as he advanced through a field, not realizing it was covered by republicans with a Lewis gun. For a time, the tide of battle seemed to turn in favour of the republicans, and some of the National troops began to waver. Eventually Kilcoyne's party came up to threaten the IRA flank, while O'Friel's party, backed up by Conlon's unit kept on the offensive, and the republicans began to fall back.

Three republicans held out in Cronin's cottage, covering the retreat of their comrades, and kept up a steady fire on the Free Staters. Courageous as ever, Peadar Conlon led a party of soldiers in an attempt to storm the house. He called on the occupants to surrender and was injured by a shotgun blast, his face peppered with pellets. One of the men in Cronin's cottage was an unusual member of the IRA. He was a tall young Scot, Ian Mackenzie-Kennedy, known as Scottie.[34] Born in 1899, it was said that he came from a distinguished military family at Lochaber in Inverness-shire in the Scottish Highlands, and that he had been brought to Ireland in 1916 by his mother, who had lost a son in the Great War and did not want to lose Ian as well. He settled in Ballingeary, in the West Cork Gaeltacht and learned Irish. He was a rather eccentric figure, liked to wear a kilt, and was popular with the local people.

Eventually Mackenzie-Kennedy and another republican James Moloney emerged from Cronin's cottage, and were shot down. There were differing reports as to the circumstances. There was a republican claim that the two men were shot while surrendering, with their hands up. The Free State side insisted there was no surrender. That version was supported by one particular republican who was present on the day and who was interviewed by Father Patrick Twohig. Jamie Moynihan stated that Scottie had jumped up to re-attack across a roadway and was hit by a stream of tracer bullets from a machine gun.[35] Many years later, in his RTÉ interview with Cathal O'Shannon, Dalton paid tribute to the courage of the young Scotsman: 'He wouldn't give in. Wouldn't surrender. So he died.' Dalton added: 'I salute bravery wherever I see it.' Other republicans killed on the day were Jack Hourihane, and Christy Olden of Cork city.

On Thursday, 10 August, Dalton's forces used the high ground they had captured to open up the offensive again on the republicans, using artillery and machine gun fire. The Free State troops, with armoured car support, moved into Douglas from several points. The republicans fell back into Cork and from there retreated to West Cork. Dalton moved up the road from Passage West and among those he encountered was the local dispensary medical officer, Dr. James Lynch. The doctor and his family were truly heroic in providing medical and nursing aid to the wounded and the dying from both sides. It was a frightening time for Lynch, his wife and children – the fighting raged right around their home at Garryduff. In and around the house the wounded and the dying were given medical aid, and food provided to scores of famished men. At some stages there were dead bodies and injured men as well as exhausted soldiers all around the house. Dr. Lynch recounted how, after snatching some badly-needed sleep, he was awakened at daylight by a loud knocking on the door. In his dressing gown he opened the door and angrily demanded of the callers what they meant by this. In a gentle voice Major General Dalton apologized, introduced himself and General Ennis, adding that he had to see the officers in the house – an exhausted and battered Peadar Conlon had spent the night on the sofa in the Lynch home. Dalton, who had seen so much bloodshed at the Somme, is said to have been astounded by the sight that greeted him – dead bodies as yet uncovered, and wounded men writhing in pain.[36]

Other medical assistance was also provided. The *Irish Times* correspondent reported that 14 of the wounded from both sides, but mainly 'Irregular', were taken back to *Arvonia* where they received medical treatment in the saloon from military medical personnel attached to the National Army, the more serious cases being transferred to hospital.[37] A *Cork Examiner* journalist reported that in the early hours of Thursday morning National soldiers temporarily took over Moorsfield House, the home of Mr. W.P. Clarke at Rochestown, and turned it into a Red Cross Hospital where about thirty wounded men on both sides were treated until they could be transferred elsewhere. The correspondent noted that on the Thursday doctors arrived from Cork and Dublin, and some of the wounded were removed by ship to Dublin.[38]

In a message to the Commander-in-Chief, Dalton would later give his casualty figures as ten dead, twelve wounded, while the figures for the enemy were twenty-five dead, thirty-five wounded. In calculating his figures for wounded, Dalton may only have taken into account the more serious cases requiring hospital treatment, and he may have over-estimated the figure for the republican dead. (Other estimates for the latter range from seven or eight upwards.[39]) In comparison with the massive casualties that would have been sustained in a single day during the Great War at the Somme, the figures were miniscule. However, by the standards of the Irish Civil War, the casualties were considerable. Still, there were those such as the British commander General Macready, who had expected a much bigger battle for Cork.

Air Support

Dalton had some limited air support in the campaign to take Cork. His friend Colonel Commandant Charles Russell, with Captain Bill Stapleton as observer, flew a mission on Thursday, 10 August as Dalton's forces moved closer to Cork.[40] Russell took off at 4.10 pm from Waterford, where the racecourse was used as an airfield. This was in the area controlled by the forces of Commandant General John T. Prout. Russell's superior, Commandant General Jack McSweeney had already reported to Michael Collins on 30 July about the preparations for air operations.

Russell, flying a Bristol fighter equipped with a machine gun, had a number of tasks. One was to observe conditions on the ground from Waterford to two miles west of Cork city. He would have been keeping a watch for the location of republican forces, and for any disruption to road or rail communications, such as the destruction of bridges that might disrupt the movement of Dalton's troops. He was also required to distribute (i.e. to drop from the air) 4,000 copies of the Provisional Government's publication *An t-Óglach*. He was tasked with providing machine gun support, if required, to the ground troops. However, as he lacked direct wireless communication from the air with the land forces, coordinating such support (what would nowadays be termed 'close air support') could prove difficult.

Finally, he had the task of delivering an important message to Major General Dalton. The message was to confirm to Dalton that his wireless communications were being received at headquarters in Dublin, and that part of the facilities he had asked for would be sent to him 'immediately' – Dalton felt in dire need of reinforcements and other support, so this message would have given him some reassurance. Dalton had been able to send wireless messages from *Arvonia* back to headquarters, but possibly due to damage caused by gunfire from the republicans, the ship's wireless operator had lost the ability to receive messages.

Russell flew over Kilmacthomas, and observed that all was quiet, 'awaiting occupation by our troops'. He continued on over Youghal, where Dalton's forces had landed from the *Helga*, and observed that all was quiet here also, with National troops moving around the town freely. At Passage West, he noted two ships drawn up at the landing stage, with a number of troops on board. All was quiet in the vicinity of the ships, with people moving freely around the streets of the town. The only way that Russell had of delivering a message to Dalton was to drop it in a container, and this he did at Passage West. Unfortunately, he seemed unaware that the message drifted into the sea and could not be retrieved, to the great consternation of troops on the ground. Minutes later, just a half hour after leaving Waterford, Russell was over Cork city. The weather was fair but the visibility was poor. At first, it seemed like the whole city was enveloped in flames. Closer scrutiny showed that all the barracks, police and military, were on fire. Victoria Barracks, despite the fire and the smoke, was a hive of activity, with large numbers of people milling around 'in a very excited manner'. The republicans were in full retreat and about to complete their withdrawal from Cork. Russell had a bird's eye view of the hurried evacuation. Russell did not have an opportunity to use his machine gun in support of Dalton's forces, but on the way back to Waterford, he was fired on at Midleton and circled over the town, returning the fire. It was one of the last shows of defiance by the republican forces in the town – they pulled out of Midleton that night, burning the barracks they had occupied.

Advance from Douglas to Cork

When the three companies of soldiers which had done much of the fighting assembled in Douglas on the Thursday afternoon, Dalton considered halting for the night in the area prior to advancing into Cork the next day. He was conscious of the pressure they had been under during days of hard combat and thought they needed a rest. He also feared they might have a tough fight on their hands to take Cork city. However, his officers were elated at their progress so far and wanted to push on. Dalton readily agreed.[41] As it happened, there would be no resistance in

Cork city itself – the republicans had pulled out. In recognition of their bravery and the contribution they had made to the campaign, Dalton gave 'promotions in the field' to Conlon and O'Friel, elevating them from Captain to Commandant.[42]

One of Dalton's officers who signed himself 'Liam', almost certainly Liam Tobin, sent a hurried message to Collins, dated 10 August, written at 8 pm in Douglas. He starts the message with the words, 'Excuse hurried note and pencil'. He records that Douglas was taken at mid-day, and they were now moving on Cork city. 'The enemy have retired everywhere towards city. I think the Irregulars are making for West Cork. They are using B [bloody] awful "stuff" as can be seen by wounds caused. Going towards Douglas today we came across one of our lads dead with his arms stretched above his head. From the city, we should be able to organize our friends through the county.' The officer set out the urgent requirements of the expeditionary force – arms, ammunition, reinforcements, transport, armoured cars. 'Dalton will send full report tomorrow.' He ends on a personal note, 'Hope you are ok, Liam.'[43]

Meanwhile, Dalton had some sombre duties to perform – arrangements had to be made for the remains of his men killed in the fighting to be taken by ship back to Dublin. The National Army had taken dozens of prisoners, and these also had to be shipped out. The *Sunday Independent* published a photograph of prisoners on board a ship (probably *Alexandria*), talking to relatives on the quay at Passage West, before being transported out of the combat zone. The newspaper also ran a photograph of beaming National Army troops being entertained to tea by smiling locals outside a house in Passage West in bright sunshine.[44]

Alexandria, which had landed the troops at Union Hall, then returned to Dublin port, reaching the North Wall at 11.30 pm on Wednesday, 9 August. The ship set sail again with a contingent of troops for Passage West at 1 o'clock the following morning. Despite the advances made by Dalton's forces, the anti-Treaty IRA were still active, as the troops aboard *Alexandria* would discover. One of the officers, Captain P. Dalton, recorded that they had an uneventful voyage until passing Queenstown [Cobh] 'when we were fired on – about 30 shots'.[45] Immediately after the ship berthed at Passage West, heavy fire was opened from five houses on the opposite shore. Said Dalton: 'We replied with Lewis guns and rifles. After a heavy fire, enemy was silenced and withdrew after night fall.' Captain Dalton moved up the road to the Capuchin monastery at Rochestown, about three miles from Passage West, and there met Major General Dalton. The Capuchins helped to look after men wounded in the fighting and to render spiritual assistance to the dying.

Emmet Dalton appears to have used the friary, set in secluded woodlands, as a temporary base en route into Cork City. When they met at the monastery, Major General Dalton instructed Captain Dalton to send up all his escort except six men, and return to Dublin with 'the bodies of eight of our men, as well as 36 prisoners'.

The two teenage brothers, Gerald and Frederick McKenna, mentioned above, were among the dead. They were both recorded as being killed on 8 August, the first day of the fighting. There was a Requiem Mass at Portobello on 14 August for the two youths and other soldiers killed in the battle. The lids of the coffins were removed for a period so that relatives could have one last look at their loved ones. The other dead soldiers were named as Private Patrick Perry (24) from Blackrock, County Dublin; Private William Nevin (38), Marietta Lodge, Sandycove; Private T. Lynch and Private Christopher O'Toole, both of the Dublin Guards Reserve, and Private Terence Maguire, Sligo. After Mass, the funeral was to Glasnevin Cemetery where the soldiers were buried with full military honours. (Procedures for identifying the dead seem to have been imperfect. Some time after the fighting, a distraught couple, Henry and Esther Quinn from 43 Wellington Street, Dublin, who had not heard from their soldier son, Private Henry Quinn, were in touch with the army authorities. An inquiry was carried out and it emerged that the soldier buried as T. Lynch was, in fact, their son who had been listed as 'missing' – he had apparently been killed at Rochestown and had suffered severe facial injuries, causing identification problems.[46])

From Douglas, Dalton's troops advanced into Cork on Thursday evening. Peadar Conlon led an advance guard into the city, followed by Tom Ennis in the armoured car *The Manager*, about 7.30 pm. A number of riflemen crowded onto the outside of the armoured car, staying on the alert and keeping a lookout in every direction. Another party of troops travelled in a Lancia armoured lorry, with Lewis guns poking out the side. They proceeded along Douglas Road, Southern Road and Anglesea Street, and were warmly welcomed by dense crowds who lined the streets. The *Irish Times* reported that people 'waved handkerchiefs, cheered to the echo and were delirious with joy'.[47] About a half hour after the advance guard, another party of troops entered the city centre, and they also received a tumultuous welcome. A journalist with the *Irish Independent*, Frank Geary, witnessed the arrival of the National troops and wrote a vivid account for his newspaper. He described the troops as tired, unshaven, mud-stained, and all wearing badges of the Sacred Heart in their caps and on their coats. 'The people are almost frantic with delight; they cheer and shout and wave handkerchiefs.'[48]

Some of the soldiers moved into the Albert Quay terminus of the Bandon railway, while others found accommodation in other buildings such as schools and halls in the city. General Macready commented in one of his regular reports to the War Office: 'It is reported that the Provisional Government troops received a very warm welcome entering the town, especially from the young ladies, whose embraces considerably delayed the pursuit of the enemy...'[49]

In London, *The Times* hailed the landings by the National Army troops at Passage West, Youghal and Union Hall as 'the most daring stroke of the whole campaign against the Irregulars...' Under a headline, 'Irish Nationalists' Coup', the newspaper published a photograph of Emmet Dalton aboard a ship, with sailors in the background.[50]

Before they retreated from the city, republicans burned facilities such as Victoria Barracks that might be of use to the incoming National Army forces. Republican leader Tom Barry would later express the opinion that it was a mistake to burn the barracks. Instead of keeping pro-Treaty forces in one place where they could be got at easily, the forces were scattered around in ten or twelve places.[51] In a communication to army headquarters in Dublin, Dalton reported: 'It is hard to credit the extent of the disorder and disorganization that was displayed in the retreat. The amount of damage done to the city by mines and fires is not really as bad as it seems, because most of the positions that were destroyed have little value other than as military positions.'[52]

Dalton's own arrival in Cork seems to have been low-key. With military and police barracks in Cork burned out, he initially set up his headquarters in a railway carriage at the Albert Road railway station before moving a few days later into more spacious accommodation when he set up his headquarters at the exclusive Imperial Hotel on South Mall.[53] Living and working in the Imperial sent out the message that he was representing the state with all its power and prestige. The Imperial was a place where Dalton could receive, with some dignity, visiting notables such as bishops and politicians. Meanwhile, some of Dalton's troops moved into the burned out Victoria Barracks and sought to make it habitable, initially sleeping in billets protected by canvas canopies.[54]

Dalton's Forces Take Towns in County Cork

After his success in Cork, Dalton began taking on new recruits and he organized his forces to advance and capture other towns in county Cork, as far east as County Waterford and towards County Kerry in the west. Dalton's forces quickly linked up with the contingents that had landed at Youghal and Union Hall. Dalton organized three simultaneous drives, taking Fermoy, Macroom and Bantry. His forces followed this up by taking Clonakilty, Bandon and Kinsale. Then he managed to find enough men to take Dunmanway. Dalton's progress was greatly assisted by local pro-Treaty IRA leaders such as Sean Hales who deployed their own forces in support of the National Army and who assisted in taking control of various towns. Dalton accepted that the decision of the republicans to pull out of Cork city was probably well-intended on their part, as they did not want to see their city despoiled.[55] The republicans sought to disrupt the movements of the Free State troops by destroying bridges, disrupting the rail system and blocking roads – measures that did not make them popular with local people. In some cases, with motor transport in short supply and road travel disrupted, the National troops simply marched long distances to their objectives. Sea transport was also used. As the National troops approached, the republican forces normally melted away, to fight another day, burning buildings they had occupied so they would not be of use to the incoming Free Staters.

Despite his progress, Dalton was still deeply concerned about his military position. On Friday, 11 August, Dalton appealed urgently to Collins for reinforcements – he needed hundreds of extra men: 'I am at a standstill,' he said bluntly. He anticipated the republicans would respond with guerilla warfare. More troops would arrive by sea in the following days. The *Lady Wicklow* had sailed about 1 am from Dublin on 11 August with 200 men and six officers, an eighteen-pounder field gun; 100 shells of high explosive and shrapnel; two Lancias, six Lewis guns as well as ammunition and rations.[56] At this stage, Dalton was faring better in terms of supplies of equipment than General O'Duffy in Limerick, who was feeling distinctly neglected.[57]

A Severe Blow to Republican Morale

Dalton's capture of Cork was a severe blow to the morale of the republican forces. Cork was the last bastion of the anti-Treaty movement and now their forces had been pushed ignominiously out of the city. In one of his initial reports to Commander-in-Chief Collins after taking Cork, Dalton declared that the morale of the enemy was 'practically broken'. A senior anti-Treaty commander, Liam Deasy, would later describe how republicans had been 'taken by surprise' when the Free Staters began landing troops at strategic points around the Irish coast: 'The greatest blow of all was the landing at Passage West on 8 August.'[58]

Deasy, who was O.C. of the IRA's First Southern Division, recalled that when part of their forces eventually reached Ballincollig, to the west of Cork City, a further order was given to continue on to Macroom. However, many of the men 'just returned to their homes'. The anti-Treaty IRA was a volunteer force, and some men dropped out, or were allowed to drop out, when it seemed pointless to continue, or when they could not be armed, fed or billeted. Dalton's forces, on the other hand, were part of a regular, conventional army. Dropping out and returning home was not an option for troops who had signed on for a specific period of service.

Deasy also noted that when Liam Lynch heard of the landings he evacuated the two barracks in Fermoy and ordered them to be burned on 11 August. (As the flames went up, it was said that one of Lynch's men, Dan Mulvihill, burst into an operatic aria, the appropriately titled *Home To Our Mountains* from Verdi's *Il Trovatore*.[59]) Deasy reflected that these events marked the 'bitter end' of the first phase of the Civil War: 'The solid south, in which we had so much confidence, was completely broken.' Deasy came to realize some bitter truths. The people were no longer with them 'as in the earlier fights', i.e. the War of Independence. Also, the Volunteers seemed to have lost the heart for the fight. The knowledge that they were fighting against 'kith and kin', must also have 'influenced them very much', Deasy reckoned.[60]

Dalton Enlists Aid of Professor Alfred O'Rahilly

After setting up his headquarters in Cork, Dalton drove out to University College Cork (UCC) to see the feisty Professor Alfred O'Rahilly, the Registrar of the university.[61] Having come through a firefight, perhaps Dalton felt he now needed another type of firepower – intellectual firepower. O'Rahilly is best summed up by Professor John A. Murphy: 'He was a volatile and bristling polymath of inexhaustible energy; the vast range of his scholarly interests – politics, sociology, Christology, mathematical physics, history – aroused astonishment and envy.'[62]

O'Rahilly advised the youthful general on the wording of a proclamation to be issued to the people, assuring the public that the National forces had entered Cork city in order to ensure their rights and liberties. O'Rahilly drafted the proclamation in his own handwriting, and it was signed by Dalton.[63] O'Rahilly also provided

Dalton with a shortened version of the proclamation written in Irish. O'Rahilly maintained contact with Dalton and with other key players in an effort to bring about an end to hostilities.

Dalton's proclamation was given to the *Cork Examiner* for immediate publication. The departing republicans had, at gunpoint, smashed the printing presses with sledge hammers; they also destroyed the printing presses of the other local newspaper, the *Cork Constitution* which had a Unionist policy and was read by members of the local Protestant community. Nevertheless, the owners of the *Cork Examiner*, the Crosbies, with their remarkable entrepreneurial ability, found a way to get the newspaper onto the streets. Dalton's proclamation was published on the front page of the *Cork Examiner* on Saturday, 12 August. It read as follows:

> Proclamation
> The National troops have entered the City of Cork in order to restore and preserve the rights and liberties of the citizens. They have no desire to interfere unnecessarily with the normal civilian activities of the community. It is for the Citizens of Cork to organise and administer their own affairs. The National forces, so far as is consistent with their military duties, will assist and co-operate with the Civilian representatives.
>
> All arms, munitions, equipment and uniforms in possession of civilians must be immediately delivered to the Military Authorities. Also all stolen property by whomsoever held, including unlawfully commandeered motor cars and illegally seized money, must be forthwith handed to the police or military authorities.
>
> Civilians are expected in their own interests to co-operate with the military by returning information concerning sniping positions, ambushes, road mines and plans for destroying property.
>
> Signed
> J.E. Dalton, Major-General
> General Officer Commanding,
> 11 August 1922.

Death of Arthur Griffith

On 12 August, as Dalton tightened his grip on County Cork, Arthur Griffith, President of Dáil Éireann, died suddenly in Dublin. Dalton had come to know Griffith well during the Treaty talks in London and afterwards, and had much respect for him. Obviously it was a funeral Dalton would have attended had it been feasible but he had to remain at his post. Collins had embarked on an inspection tour of Tipperary, Limerick and Kerry and when word reached him in Tralee about Griffith's death he made immediate arrangements to return to Dublin for the state funeral which was to be held on 16 August. The Commander-in-Chief was clearly anxious to monitor the war situation generally in the south, especially Dalton's strategically vital operations to secure the Cork region. Even as he was departing Limerick for Dublin he was demanding details about the situation in Cork.[64]

The Taking of Cobh

Dalton was eager to secure strategic locations in the immediate vicinity of Cork city, and one of his priorities was to take control of Cobh, with its deep-water anchorage and its command of the channel in Cork Harbour leading to Cork City itself. On Saturday evening, 12 August, a contingent of troops boarded the *Lady Wicklow* at the Custom House Quay in Cork for the short voyage to Cobh. The soldiers were almost all young men, but a *Cork Examiner* special correspondent who travelled with the troops noted the presence among them of an older, grey-haired man who had served as a Major in the European war, and who had lost his home and everything he possessed 'through destruction by Irregulars'. He considered it his duty to join up as a private in the National Army. 'His aged appearance was in striking contrast to his comrades,' the correspondent commented.[65]

The troops duly landed at Cobh with no resistance. They received an enthusiastic reception from the local people. Before the republicans pulled out, they set fire to Admiralty House and other buildings, including the military hospital. A well-known anti-Treaty republican, Robert Briscoe, was lying low in a hotel in Cobh when the Free Staters came in. He had run guns from Germany for the pre-Truce IRA and would go on to become a Fianna Fáil TD, an active Zionist and the first Jewish Lord Mayor of Dublin. In his memoirs he relates how he got word that 'General Dalton had ordered a search' for him, and he knew he had to move fast.[66] As he was leaving his hotel room two soldiers with pistols held him up. They said they were looking for Briscoe. He denied he was Briscoe. One said, 'Come along and tell it to the general.' Then one of the soldiers looked at Briscoe more closely and asked if he was a 'Jewman'. Briscoe confirmed he was, indeed, Jewish. The soldier said to his comrade: 'He's only a Jewman, we'd be wasting our bloody time with him.' Briscoe continued on his journey to England and then America.

Dignitaries Welcome Dalton to Cork

The Catholic Bishop of Cork, Dr. Cohalan, an outspoken critic of the anti-Treaty republicans, paid a visit to Dalton and welcomed the National Army troops to Cork. Canon Flewett, acting on behalf of the Church of Ireland Bishop of Cork, Cloyne and Ross, also called on Dalton, to welcome him to the city and 'to assure him of the loyal cooperation of the clergy and members of the Church of Ireland'.[67] As he sought to restore normal life to Cork, Dalton, in effect, assumed the temporary role of *de facto* civil governor of the city, but was concerned that this was distracting him from his urgent military commitments. In a message to Collins on 12 August, Dalton expressed frustration at having to spend so much time meeting dignitaries and dealing with civil matters, believing it seriously interfered with his military duties.[68] He told how he had been called upon by 'hundreds' of prominent citizens who, apparently, had 'nothing better to do' than to wait hours to congratulate him. He also had to receive deputations from all representative bodies in the city, 'covering practically every branch of life'. He referred to unemployment as one of the 'greatest difficulties' that presents itself, and said the entire economic situation required immediate attention. He suggested that a representative from each of the government departments be sent down who could cope with the situation. He had interviewed all the big manufacturers and instructed them to get their factories going as quickly as possible.

In his message to Collins, he told how starvation was staring a great many people in the face. He had been in touch with a Capuchin priest, Father Thomas Dowling. He assured the priest that he had notified the government of the situation. As a sign of good faith, he gave £200 to the St. Vincent de Paul Society immediately in order to ensure some little relief.

In his communication with Collins, Dalton said he was considering fielding an unarmed police force to operate on the streets of Cork, and this idea would be quickly implemented. Dalton had already met a deputation from the Cork Corporation and Chamber of Commerce who asked him to set up a civilian police force for the city. On 14 August interviews for the Cork Civic Patrol (CCP), also known as the Cork Civic Police, were held at the Cork Courthouse, and more than 100 men were recruited. They were unarmed but had support from the National Army in carrying out their duties, which included conducting traffic; supervising public house closing hours, and preventing looting. Offenders arrested by the CCP were taken to the local prison, while looters were detained at Moore's Hotel.[69] The Cork Civic Patrol operated for the next three months, until a contingent of the state's new police force, the Civic Guard, to be known as An Garda Síochána, arrived in Cork on 9 November. As he strengthened his authority in Cork, it appears that Dalton became concerned about the loyalty of some of the telegraphic staff in the city, and suspended them from duty. A question was asked in the Dáil about the suspension 'by the Officer Commanding, Cork' of five staff members. The Postmaster General, J.J. Walsh said that he was informed that the officers 'co-operated with the Irregular forces who were occupying the Cork Post Office, to a degree that was incompatible with their duties as Civil Servants'. He added: 'An opportunity of meeting the charges will be offered to them in due course.'[70]

Recruitment Drive

As Dalton worked to increase the strength of his forces in the Cork region, he found no shortage of men willing to join up.[71] He reported that there were about 200 National Army men who had been captured at various locations by the anti-Treaty forces and held prisoner. These men had been released as their captors fled and had linked up with Dalton. They included what he described as forty of 'Ireland's best fighting men', the Dublin Guards. Dalton was in touch with the Legion of Ex-Servicemen. He was impressed by their leaders but decided that many of the ex-British Army soldiers were not of the type that he required. He temporarily accepted 200 'of the thousands' he was offered, and armed 100 of these.[72] Dalton was also in touch with local pro-Treaty IRA Volunteers. He put General Liam Tobin in charge of organizing them as part of the National Army. A local force of about 250 Volunteers had been organized in Cork prior to Dalton's arrival. After the landing of the National troops, the commanders of this local force, Commandant Paddy Scott and Captain John Kingston, who was related to Michael Collins, made contact with Dalton to request access to the rifles he had transported from Dublin. With these they armed their men. Dalton was very pleased to get the support of this contingent, which he named the 1st Cork Reserve. He considered that they were of considerable assistance to his campaign, giving a very good account of themselves in subsequent fighting.[73] Dalton informed Collins that he was receiving 'admirable intelligence' from the citizens of Cork, 'but owing to the limited nature of officers at my disposal, I find it quite impossible to put much attention to this branch'.[74]

On 14 August the *Alexandria* sailed from Dublin with stores for the troops and also a number of government officials to assist with relief and reconstruction, and the development of a civil administration, as urgently requested by Dalton.[75] One of the officials was the remarkable Joseph Brennan, a senior civil servant with the Ministry of Finance who had previously served in Dublin Castle under British rule, and was now working for the new Provisional Government. He had been authorized by Michael Collins to travel to Cork to deal with the situation arising out of the 'expropriation' of funds from the banks by republicans, and the seizure of government revenue. Brennan was to spend about a week in Cork compiling information and then travelled on to London 'to straighten things out on that side'.[76] (Brennan went on to become Secretary of the Free State's Department of Finance and in 1943, the first Governor of Ireland's Central Bank.[77])

Reinforcements from Limerick

Among the badly-needed reinforcements sent urgently to bolster Dalton's invasion forces was a contingent which arrived by sea from Limerick on 16 August. This group was estimated to number more than 200 troops, including members of the Dublin Guard. They sailed up the Lee into Cork city aboard the commandeered Limerick Steamship Company vessel *Luimneach*.

Tom Daly, from Newmarket-on-Fergus, County Clare, was one of the soldiers on board, having joined up in a recruiting station in nearby Ennis. In old age he gave an account of his experiences to Father Patrick Twohig. He recalled that only some of the men had uniforms, but they all had Lee Enfield rifles. On arrival in Cork, they slept on the floor in rooms at the quay – no beds. The following day they set off to march to Macroom, about twenty-two miles away. All the bridges along the way were blown and it took them two days to get there. The first place they got food was Coachford, where they were sent to different houses for meals. In Macroom, they were accommodated in the old workhouse building, the 'Union', where they did not even have knives, forks or spoons.[78] Daly's account underlines the strains under which the army was operating as it quickly expanded – lack of uniforms, lack of motor transport and even dining utensils in short supply. It also explains Dalton's constant lobbying for better logistical support for his troops from general headquarters in Dublin.

National troops under General Liam Tobin moved into the important town of Fermoy about one o'clock in the morning on Thursday, 16 August. As Provisional Government forces advanced to seize towns in the region, Dalton co-ordinated operations with Limerick-based General Eoin O'Duffy. His forces were advancing into north County Cork following the defeat of the republicans in heavy fighting around Kilmallock. Communicating by wireless, Dalton wagered O'Duffy £5 his forces would be the first to arrive in Macroom.[79] Dalton won the bet which O'Duffy presumably honoured. The friendly rivalry between Dalton and O'Duffy would later give way to friction between the two over the conduct of the campaign.

The question of taking Lismore Castle, in County Waterford, which was occupied by republican forces, was raised by army headquarters with Dalton a week after he entered Cork city. On 19 August General Mulcahy sent a message to Dalton to ask him to consider carefully how the castle could be captured without its being destroyed.[80] The castle, originally built by King John in 1185 was transformed over the centuries into a magnificent stately home. Mulcahy pointed out that the castle was owned by the Duke of Devonshire, 'a very powerful and influential figure' and contained valuable Irish manuscripts, including the Book of Lismore and a crozier 'supposed to belong to St Carthage'. After the destruction of precious historical documents during the battle of the Four Courts, and the burning of important buildings during the revolutionary period, Mulcahy was apparently conscious of the need to avoid further damage to the national heritage. Mulcahy invited Dalton to give consideration as to how the castle could be taken intact. The following month Dalton's forces took possession of the castle as the republicans pulled out.

Additional Recruits, Garrisons in Towns, and Columns

Dalton provided details to headquarters of the towns his forces had occupied and the strength of each garrison. In his 11 September report, Dalton noted that 'A' Party had reinforced Cork City positions and had also occupied Cobh, Douglas and Blarney; 'B' Party occupied Youghal, Killeagh, Carrigtwohill, Midleton, Castlemartyr 'and gained touch with Cork City'; 'C' Party occupied Skibbereen and Rosscarbery.[81] These appear to be references to the towns taken over by troops in the immediate aftermath of the landings. He also provided a much longer list of towns throughout County Cork, and into neighbouring County Waterford, in which garrisons had been established, and the strength of each garrison. Cork City, 600; Fermoy, 100; Lismore (County Waterford), 40; Cappoquin (County Waterford), 30; Kilworth, 40; Youghal, 80, Midleton, 50, Carrigtwohill, 30; Castlemartyr, 30; Killeigh, 20; Kinsale, 50; Passage, 30; Waterfall, 50; Bantry, 100; Skibbereen, 60; Rosscarbery, 50; Clonakilty, 50; Bandon, 60; Dunmanway, 50; Macroom, 100. In addition he gave details of mobile 'columns' based in Cork city, Lismore, Carrigtwohill, Passage West, Skibbereen, Bandon and Macroom, with strengths varying from 60 (Lismore and Carrigtwohill) to 150 (Macroom).

As he consolidated army control of part of County Cork region, Dalton needed to find new bases for his forces, if necessary by commandeering premises. At one stage, in order to establish a garrison in the East Cork town of Midleton, it was

1. Emmet Dalton in his youth. Image courtesy of Audrey Dalton Simenz.

2. Emmet Dalton in British Army uniform with unidentified young man - possibly his half-brother Martin. Image courtesy of Audrey Dalton Simenz.

Sgt O'NEILL. V.C, M.M, F.M.M, ⚔ Pte MOFFAT. V.C

3. Members of D Coy 2nd Leinsters decorated for bravery, front row from left, Emmet Dalton MC, Sgt O'Neill VC, Capt Moran MC and Pte Moffat VC. At right, Lt Dorgan. Dhunn, Germany 9 Jan 1919. Image courtesy of Audrey Dalton Simenz.

4. Emmet Dalton and Michael Collins in London in 1921 during the Anglo-Irish Treaty talks. Image courtesy of Private Collection/Bridgeman Images.

5. Emmet and Charles Dalton in National Army uniform with their parents, James F. and Katherine Dalton and other siblings, from left, Nuala, Deirdre, Dermot and Brendan. Image courtesy of Audrey Dalton Simenz.

6. Shelling of Four Courts, Dublin, 1922 with artillery under command of Major General Emmet Dalton. Image courtesy of the National Library of Ireland.

7. Michael Collins, Commander-in-Chief, National Army (second from left) with Major General Emmet Dalton (third left) at Curragh Camp, August 1922. Also in photo, from left, Colonel Dunphy, Comdt. General Peadar MacMahon and Comdt. General Diarmuid O'Hegarty. Image courtesy of Getty Images.

8. Major General Emmet Dalton (left) with General Tom Ennis, and ship's officers, aboard one of the ships deployed for the Passage West landings. Image courtesy of the National Library of Ireland.

9. Emmet Dalton (front row, right) at funeral of Michael Collins, with General Richard Mulcahy (left) and Adjutant General Gearóid O'Sullivan (centre). Image courtesy of the National Library of Ireland.

10. Wedding of Major General Emmet Dalton and Alice Shannon at Imperial Hotel, Cork, 9 October 1922. Image courtesy of the National Library of Ireland.

11. Emmet Dalton and bride Alice on their wedding day. Image courtesy of the National Library of Ireland.

12. Emmet Dalton and children, from left, Richard, Nuala and Audrey, in the back garden of their home at Iona Road, Dublin. Image courtesy of Audrey Dalton Simenz.

13. Emmet Dalton, smoking a cigarette as he finishes a golf swing. Image courtesy of Audrey Dalton Simenz

14. Dermot Dalton, in US Army uniform, with brothers Charles and Emmet at Leopardstown races, October 1945. Image courtesy of Audrey Dalton Simenz.

15. Emmet and Alice Dalton and family, 1945/46, in front row Nuala and Richard, at back from left, Sybil, Emmet Michael and Audrey. Image courtesy of Audrey Dalton Simenz.

16. Emmet and Alice Dalton at a film premiere in London. Image courtesy of Audrey Dalton Simenz.

proposed to take over Midleton College, a Church of Ireland school. The prospect horrified the local rector, Rev. W.E. Flewett, who feared it would spell the end for the school. He went to Cork with the headmaster and met Dalton who, he recalled, 'had a big revolver on the table beside him'. To their great relief, Dalton countermanded the order to occupy the school.[82] The presence of the revolver on the table, even within the well-secured sanctum of his headquarters, would suggest that Dalton was taking no chances with his personal security. (After lobbying by Lord Midleton, General Mulcahy had also asked Dalton to assist the school authorities, if possible.[83])

The conventional phase of the war in Munster had ended, giving way to a guerrilla campaign waged by the republican forces who were far more effective in this type of fighting than in conventional warfare. Dalton was all too well aware that although his forces had captured towns, many republican fighters were still at large, and armed. While many republican guerrillas had withdrawn from Cork city to West Cork, it was believed that some stayed behind 'under cover' or slipped back surreptitiously into the city, and soon there were reports of sniper attacks on the Free Staters in Cork. Troops outside Cork city were also under threat. A general report on 22 August (the day of Collins' death) warned that the Irregulars in Cork and Kerry were still more or less intact, that the present disposition of National forces left them vulnerable to attack, and that it was easy 'to isolate our posts'.[84]

Following the landings, the British commander General Macready recorded that Dalton and others had predicted that the republicans would 'really offer battle' in West Cork but that these predictions had not been fulfilled.[85] However, Macready predicted the revival by the republican forces of guerrilla warfare as had been carried on during the War of Independence in 1921.

Peace Moves

As Dalton took control of County Cork, efforts were being made to bring about a cessation of hostilities and Professor Alfred O'Rahilly was particularly active in this regard. He maintained contact with Dalton and worked with an *ad hoc* committee of prominent citizens seeking to bring about an end to the fighting. According to O'Rahilly's biographer J. Anthony Gaughan, O'Rahilly, along with other members of the committee and with the assistance of the 'neutral IRA', made contact with representatives of the Cork No. 1 Brigade of the IRA and then drafted proposals which he believed would be generally acceptable to both sides and bring about an end to the fighting. Among the committee members involved in drawing up the proposals were Thomas P. Dowdall, Barry Egan, F.J. Daly and Liam de Róiste TD.[86]

The proposals involved an immediate one-week truce, which would allow republican military and political leaders to negotiate peace terms. These terms included the concept that henceforth republican opposition to the government and parliament would be conducted on constitutional lines. Those members of the republican forces who wished to return to civil life would be allowed to do so, 'without molestation or penalisation'. Members of the republican forces who wished to join the National Army would be received therein 'with due recognition of rank and service'. Arms and munitions in the possession of republican forces would be handed over to a committee to be mutually agreed upon. There would be a 'general amnesty for all political prisoners'.

O'Rahilly passed on these proposals to Dalton, who forwarded them by wireless to Michael Collins at Portobello on 18 August. The following day Collins sent a wireless message back to Dalton:

> Government offer published in the press 5th June, and conveyed to the Peoples Rights Association, Cork, stands. For your guidance the terms are: 1) Transfer into the National Army of all war materials; 2) Restoration, without exception, of all seized property and money; 3) Particulars to be furnished of bridges, railways, roads which are or have been mined or rendered otherwise unsafe.

Publicity and Press Relations

Dalton's successful expedition to County Cork received much positive publicity at home and abroad. Dalton's own name featured prominently in press reports, although he does not appear to have given any on-the-record press interviews. The Provisional Government operated a military censorship system, instructing newspapers to use terms such as 'Irregulars' to describe republican fighters. However, it also believed in facilitating members of the media, so long as they did not interfere with military operations and looked after their own accommodation. Piaras Béaslaí, a member of Michael Collins's inner circle, was the National Army's Publicity Director, and press officers were appointed at local command level.[87]

Correspondents were facilitated in travelling on ships with National Army troops or with road convoys. A well-known photographer, W.D. Hogan, who had studios at Henry Street, Dublin, took photographs of Dalton's expedition to Cork. From early in the Civil War, Michael Collins himself realized the value of good publicity, including photographic coverage. In a communication from Collins, Commander-in-Chief, Portobello to Chief of the General Staff, dated 15 July 1922, Collins stated that photographers such as Mr Gordon Lewis, Mr W.D. Hogan and Mr W.W. Gore 'may be allowed to photograph at the discretion of the officer commanding operations in any particular area. They will, of course, be asked to undertake that they obey censorship rules issued or to be issued.'[88] In Dalton's own command area, a young officer, Lieutenant Barry, was appointed to his staff as publicity officer. Barry's role included issuing statements to the press; organizing 'photo opportunities' for press cameramen; sending reports to the publicity department at General Headquarters, and producing a magazine called *The Cap Badge*.[89]

Dalton seems to have had respect for the *Cork Examiner* and the quality of its reporting. In sending a report to Michael Collins on the landings and the fight for Cork, he included a copy of the newspaper's detailed report on these events, saying that while inaccurate in some details, it was mainly correct.[90] Dalton would remain extremely proud of his forces' achievement in capturing Munster's main city, but he was facing into one of the most traumatic and difficult periods in his military career.

CHAPTER TEN

Death at Bealnablath

Commandant Charlie Dalton was in his room at the National Army's sprawling Portobello barracks complex early in the morning of Sunday, 20 August 1922 when the Commander-in-Chief himself, Michael Collins called in to say goodbye. Collins was setting off with a convoy for a whirlwind tour of the south. He had been on a previous tour but cut it short to return to Dublin for the funeral of Arthur Griffith. Now he would resume his inspection which would take him to turbulent areas of his native County Cork and a rendezvous with Charlie's brother Emmet. With his successful invasion of the south, Emmet was the man of the moment. Charlie probably basked a little in Emmet's reflected glory.

Collins had taken up residence at Portobello. He was surrounded and protected by men who were utterly loyal and devoted to him, and who had been active in the Squad or his intelligence apparatus during the War of Independence. One can imagine the 'boy's club' atmosphere that prevailed. On the floor below Collins, Charlie Dalton shared a room with his friend, Captain James Conroy Jr. Conroy had been active in the Squad, and had fought in the Easter Rising with his father, James Conroy senior, who went on to serve with the anti-Treaty forces.[1] The personable and good-humoured James Conroy junior was a formidable gunman who had been involved in a number of killings and assassinations, as well as the MacEoin Mountjoy escape attempt.[2] Conroy had been selected to accompany Collins on his trip to the South. Charlie Dalton later recalled how Collins, 'looking hale and hearty' stuck his head into their room early in the morning before departing for his inspection tour.[3]

The officers accompanying Collins were specially trusted and loyal. Commandant Sean O'Connell, who had been a member of Collins's Squad, was in charge of the convoy. The tall, strikingly handsome man from Doora, County Clare was very discreet and security-conscious. While working as a railway clerk in Dublin he had played an important role in Collins's secret communications system, ensuring the delivery of messages to and from contacts in the provinces via the rail network.

The convoy included a Crossley tender with troops, and a Rolls Royce Whippet armoured car, *Slievenamon*. A young officer, Peter Gough, from Baldoyle, County Dublin, who had been a machine gunner in the British Army in the Great War before joining the Volunteers, travelled in *Slievenamon* to assist with the Vickers machine gun. He was yet another past participant in the MacEoin escape attempt. On the Collins trip to the south, Gough was working with the gunner John 'Jock' McPeak, a Scotsman who had also served as a machine gunner in the British Army during the Great War. Collins himself was travelling in a touring car, a Leyland Thomas, with two drivers. This fine vehicle with yellow bodywork suited the prestige of his position as Commander-in-Chief.

On the eve of Collins's departure, the evening of the 19th, he met Pat Moylett who had called to Portobello to get a permit for 1,000 gallons of petrol. This was the same Pat Moylett to whom Emmet Dalton had delivered rifles in Mayo in 1914. Collins told Moylett that he was going to do a circuit of the country, and that he intended to speak to 'the boys' – his anti-Treaty opponents. Collins said he knew them all personally and he would explain to them the foolishness of their action. He would tell them that if they continued their activities, he would use force and 'repressive measures' to stop them.[4]

Some in Collins's inner circle were horrified that he was travelling to such a volatile part of the country where republicans were still active. Joe McGrath in particular tried to persuade him not to go, but Collins was not for turning on the issue. It was said that among those seeing Collins off was his new private secretary Frank Duff, who founded the worldwide Catholic action group, the Legion of Mary.[5] In Limerick, en route to Cork, the convoy picked up another trusted officer from Collins's Squad, Joe Dolan. After the formation of the National Army, Dolan worked in military intelligence and was based for a period with the Criminal Investigation Department (CID).

In Limerick, Collins spoke with General Eoin O'Duffy, and anxiously monitored Dalton's progress in Cork. O'Duffy related how Dalton had reported some days previously, on 12 August, that Cork was 'entirely in his hands', only he thought there might be 'ambushing and sniping in a few days' time'.[6] Dalton was to be proven correct in the latter assessment.

Dalton had not been told in advance of Collins's intended visit to Cork. Collins may not have been entirely clear about his schedule when he set out – much might depend on events and whether roads were passable. According to accounts he gave in later life, Dalton was pleased to see Collins when the Big Fellow strode into the Imperial Hotel at about 8.30 pm on the Sunday night, but concerned that he was making the journey while conditions were still hazardous.[7] Collins checked into the Imperial and immediately held talks on the military situation with Dalton and other officers, including Tom Ennis.

Collins could be a hard taskmaster but also most generous in his praise. He congratulated Dalton on his great achievement in capturing Cork. According to the special correspondent of the *Irish Times*, Collins was stated to have expressed satisfaction with the 'rapid progress' made by the troops since their first landing less than a fortnight before, and with the 'effective consolidation' of the important positions they held throughout the county.[8] However, the correspondent also noted that with its main railway paralyzed and main roads seriously damaged, Cork was still suffering economically. Were it not for the use of the port facilities, the city would have been 'entirely isolated'.

A young army officer serving under Dalton, D.V. Horgan, told later of being present as Collins conferred with senior officers. Collins was planning a tour of West Cork and Dalton was concerned about this. Dalton 'tried to persuade him not to go,' Horgan stated. Collins replied, 'Nobody will shoot me in West Cork.'[9] In his interview with Cathal O'Shannon, Dalton told a similar story. He said he told Collins that being in the region was an 'unnecessary risk'. Collins replied jocosely: 'Surely they won't shoot me in my own county?'[10] It was just over a week after Dalton's forces had seized Cork. With the republicans already sabotaging roads and destroying bridges, Dalton was facing a major threat from republican guerrilla tactics, and he was feeling militarily vulnerable. On a positive note, the tour of military posts with Collins would impress on the Commander-in-Chief the requirements of the National Army in the region in terms of equipment, transport, manpower and logistical support. Collins could cut through red tape in order to assist Dalton with his urgent requirements.

As outlined in greater detail below, Dalton was particularly anxious to get the new Military Air Service to carry out reconnaissance of areas in which the anti-Treaty forces were active. At Dalton's urging, Collins took immediate action to ensure the reconnaissance was carried out. The tour of military posts with Collins also gave Dalton an opportunity to confer with his officers in various locations. Some of these officers, such as Peadar Conlon, the commander at Macroom, had accompanied Dalton from Dublin for the landings on the County Cork coast. Others were local men who may not have been as well known to Dalton – pro-Treaty IRA Volunteers who had followed Collins and local leaders like Sean Hales, and had emerged from the shadows to support Dalton's forces after they arrived.

According to Dalton's account of Collins's last trip to the south, which he wrote in November 1922 and was later published in the *Freeman's Journal*, Collins had two main objectives in visiting the Cork region. His first objective was to inspect the local military organization, to appreciate the difficulties faced by the military, to give advice, and to gather the information needed to secure assistance from General Headquarters. The second objective was to trace and recover money that had been taken from state funds by the republicans. Dalton estimated that the amount involved was £120,000, mainly excise duties belonging to the Customs and Excise Department. According to Dalton, the anti-Treaty forces had extorted this money by 'capturing the official collector, and under threat of death, making him sign the cheques which, of course, the banks honoured and paid'.[11]

Some writers believe that Collins was seeking to explore ways of ending the Civil War. According to Dalton, while Collins hoped that the republicans would 'throw in their hand', he had no intention of offering concessions – Collins was bitter and disappointed 'to the verge of illness' by de Valera's 'adamantine insistence on the dogma of republicanism and his ungenerous refusal to recognize the achievement of Irish freedom'.[12] After talks with Dalton and other senior officers, Collins dashed off messages to headquarters in Dublin seeking action on various matters. These included instructions to send court officials to Cork to establish a judicial system.[13]

Over the next couple of days Dalton spent most of his time accompanying Collins, as the hard-working Commander-in-Chief crammed in as much activity as possible. On Monday, 21 August, Dalton and Collins visited various army posts in the city. On the way to inspect Dalton's troops in Victoria Barracks, Collins stopped and got out of his car to shake hands with local people. Dalton accompanied Collins when he went to see Mr Crosbie, proprietor of the *Cork Examiner*. When the newspaper had been under republican control the stories reflected the republican point of view. Now the newspaper was taking a strongly pro-Treaty stance. Collins discussed with Crosbie the general army position on publicity.[14] During his time in charge of Cork command, Dalton made use of the *Cork Examiner* for issuing statements or proclamations – it was a very valuable media outlet.

Seizing the Money

Dalton was also with Collins when he went to visit a number of local banks as part of the mission to recover funds, mainly excise duties, that had been collected by the republicans and salted away in bank accounts. It would appear that an early form of 'money laundering' had been used to hide the source of the funds, and that republicans had instructed local sympathizers to lodge sizeable sums in their own names on behalf of the movement. Dalton recalled later that in accordance with Collins's instructions, he ordered the managers of local banks to attend a meeting at his headquarters. He demanded a list of those who had recently deposited sums of more than £500. The banks were reluctant to supply this information and it was a stormy meeting. Dalton threatened to close the banks if they did not comply. He got the information he needed and recovered £90,000 of the money that had gone astray.[15] It would appear that the process of recovering the money was not completed by Dalton until some time after Collins's death.

Dalton also told writer Meda Ryan of receiving a tip-off about money hidden in a church. Dalton and Collins went to see the priest who 'after some persuasion', unlocked the tabernacle where £3,000 had been hidden away. It must have shocked Dalton, a devout Catholic, to find that such a sacred place was being used to hide something as vulgar as money. When he told Ms Ryan about the incident in an interview on 2 April 1974, his voice was almost in a whisper. Then he appeared to regret having given the information, remarking: 'Maybe I shouldn't have told you, as I never told that to anybody.'[16]

After lunch at the Imperial Hotel, Collins and his convoy set out for Cobh to inspect National Army posts. Also on the Monday, Dalton accompanied Collins to Macroom about 30 miles from Cork. The *Slievenamon* armoured car was withdrawn for servicing, and was replaced on this journey by another armoured car, known as *Dublin Liz*. Collins inspected military posts, and had talks with one of the neutral IRA officers in the Civil War, Florrie O'Donoghue. This later gave rise to speculation that Collins sought a meeting with the anti-Treaty forces to bring an end to the conflict. In fact, the meeting with O'Donoghue appears to have been entirely by chance.[17]

Dalton was present as Collins conferred with the remarkable Peadar Conlon, one of Dalton's most trusted officers who had been in the thick of the fighting after the landings at Passage West, and who was now in command of the embattled garrison at Macroom. Conlon felt under great pressure because of attacks by anti-Treaty forces and badly needed a machine gun to bolster defences. Collins assured him that this would be supplied.

Despite the threat from republican forces, there was an air of festivity about the visit of Collins and Dalton to Macroom. Mr A.J.S. [Stephen] Brady, son of the local Church of Ireland rector, remembered that day.[18] He told how he saw a Leyland touring car and an armoured car drawn up beside Williams's Hotel, surrounded by a crowd of soldiers and civilians. The bar at the rear of the hotel was packed with military men standing at ease in groups, taking drinks at the long counter. At the head of the counter was the impressive, uniformed figure of Collins, his leggings well-polished and cap lying crown downwards on the counter, and with him Emmet Dalton. Somebody said, 'What are you having, Mick?' Collins replied with a smile: 'For once in my life I'll let the old country down – a drop of the Scotch for me.' Collins was in high spirits, and at one stage picked up the young barmaid, Aileen Baker, and to the clapping and cheering of those present, ran up the stairs still carrying her and deposited her on the landing. Nevertheless, in the midst of the festivities, Brady noted that Collins seemed to be wary and on guard. He was glancing constantly around him, as if he still had the 'alertness inherent in a fugitive'. Collins and his party were cheered by the crowd as they left the hotel to continue on their way. Collins appeared encouraged by his tour, to judge from the last entry in his diary. 'The people here want no compromise with the Irregulars… Civil administration urgent everywhere in the south. The people are splendid.'[19]

The Big Fellow's Last Day

At 6.15 am on 22 August, Dalton accompanied Michael Collins as the Commander-in-Chief made an early departure from the Imperial Hotel. Dalton was up and about in plenty of time and ready to go – there is an account of him pacing up and down outside the Imperial before the convoy set off. The convoy consisted of a motor cycle scout; an open Crossley tender with troops; an open touring car, the impressive yellow Leyland Thomas, in which Dalton and Collins travelled with two drivers, and the Rolls Royce Whippet armoured car, *Slievenamon*, fresh from its service, bringing up the rear.

Collins and Dalton again travelled to Macroom, sitting in the back of the touring car almost as if they were back in London during the Treaty negotiations. As Collins had promised, he delivered a Lewis gun to Commandant Conlon, as well as rifles and extra ammunition. The convoy then set off for Bandon. The main road was impassable because bridges had been destroyed, so a Macroom hackney driver, Tim Kelleher was instructed to board the Crossley tender to guide them along the way. At the foot of Ballymichael Hill, the armoured car ran into difficulties climbing the steep hill. A local couple saw the soldiers dismount from the tender and help push the armoured car up the hill.[20] At Farran hill the soldiers again had to push *Slievenamon* up the hill. It was not a good omen.

Dalton admitted later that the escort was totally inadequate. Collins was visiting an area where the republicans were in operation in the countryside, blocking roads by digging trenches across them or felling trees, and destroying bridges. In his RTÉ interview with Cathal O'Shannon, Dalton said he made his views known to Collins. Dalton said he would never have permitted the situation for one second had he been in Dublin. Dalton's stated case is that essentially he was presented with a *fait accompli*, and that it was impossible to dissuade Collins from making the tour. Could Dalton have insisted on a bigger convoy? Perhaps, on this occasion, the normally forceful Dalton decided to yield to the judgement of an even more forceful figure, his Commander-in-Chief. Collins had obviously decided that the protection afforded by the convoy was adequate. This convoy had been organized in Dublin and apparently came up to Collins's requirements. As for Dalton, his resources in Cork were stretched to the limit, and he would later complain bitterly to headquarters in Dublin about the lack of transport facilities for his forces. It appears Dalton was essentially a VIP guest on Collins's convoy.

Travelling to Bandon, the convoy stopped in the tiny crossroads hamlet of Bealnablath to inquire as to the correct route. A man called Denny Long was standing outside Long's public house and he obligingly pointed the way. Members of the convoy would not have realized that Long was an IRA sentry who had just put down his rifle close by. He was on guard duty because an important meeting of senior IRA officers from Cork No. 3 Brigade and First Southern Division was being held at Murray's farmhouse on the hill above the pub. Some of the IRA officers were billeted in the pub itself. The meeting had attracted senior anti-Treaty figures to the area, including Éamon de Valera, Tom Hales and Liam Deasy. The presence of these leaders could help explain why so many roads in the area had been obstructed. Denny Long recognized Collins in the back of the touring car and quickly reported the fact to the IRA leaders. Long had also gained another piece of useful intelligence – the Collins convoy was bound for Bandon.

It was decided to organize an ambush in the valley of Bealnablath on the basis that there was a good chance that the convoy might return along the same route. Even without the presence of a VIP, the military convoy would have made a good prospect for an ambush. The fact that the enemy's Commander-in-Chief was travelling in the convoy must surely have made it even more attractive as a target. The republicans had been suffering a series of devastating reverses – they had been driven out of Waterford and Cork and had to pull out of other locations such as Limerick and Kilmallock. They could do with a victory to emphasize they were still in business as a fighting force.

In 1964, Florence O'Donoghue held a meeting at the Metropole Hotel in Cork with six surviving republicans who had taken part in the Bealnablath engagement. The purpose of the meeting was to establish a record of what happened on the day. The document he drew up has since come into the public domain and is in O'Donoghue's papers in the National Library of Ireland.[21] Those present at the meeting in the Metropole were Liam Deasy, who was O.C. First Southern Division; Tom Kelleher, O.C. Fifth Battalion Cork No. 3; Jim Hurley, Brigade Commandant Cork No. 3; Dan Holland, O.C. 1st Battalion Cork No. 3; Pete Kearney, O.C. 3rd Battalion, and Tom Crofts, Adjutant 1st Southern Division.

In his report, O'Donoghue confirmed that the first information the republican officers received about the presence of Collins in the area came from Denis Long who saw the Free State convoy pass through in the direction of Bandon and reported it. A decision was made 'on Divisional initiative' to lay an ambush 400 yards south of Bealnablath cross roads for the Free State convoy on the assumption that it would probably return later in the day by the same route. The use of the term 'Divisional initiative' suggests that the senior IRA officer in Bealnablath on the day, Liam Deasy, commander of the First Southern Division, played a key role in the decision to set up an ambush.

Liam Deasy has also left his own personal account of the events of the day, in his book *Brother Against Brother*. According to Deasy, after receiving the intelligence that Collins had passed through in a convoy, de Valera asked him what was likely to happen. Deasy replied that the men billeted in the area included men who had been forced to retreat from Limerick, Kilmallock and Buttevant, and that in their present frame of mind they would consider that this incursion into their republican area was a challenge which they could not refuse to meet: 'I felt an ambush would be prepared in case the convoy returned.'[22] Despite his senior position, Deasy in this remark seemed to distance himself from the decision to attack the convoy, suggesting that it was inevitable that the men would want to mount an ambush. According to Deasy, de Valera remarked that it would be a pity if Collins were killed, because he might be succeeded by a weaker man. De Valera then departed to join Liam Lynch in north Cork.

Brigade Commandant Tom Hales and a group of men set about arranging the ambush. (Ironically, Michael Collins had once been very close to Tom Hales – during the Treaty talks in London, Collins had made sure to visit Hales who was being held in Pentonville prison.) The site chosen for the attack allowed the ambush party good cover in an elevated position to the west of the road. They had good fields of fire and easy access to routes that would facilitate a quick getaway. According to O'Donoghue, the ambush party numbered between twenty and twenty-five, and included Liam Deasy, Tom Kelleher, Jim Hurley, Pete Kearney, Dan Holland, Tom Hales, Tom Crofts, Con Lucey, Sean Culhane, John Lordan, Bill Desmond, Dan Corcoran, C. O'Donoghue, John O'Callaghan, Sonny O'Neill, Paddy Walsh, Sonny Donovan, Jim Crowley, Tady O'Sullivan and Jerh Mahony. (A contemporary IRA report gives a higher figure for the strength of the ambush party. The report dated 24 August 1922 to IRA Chief of Staff Liam Lynch from the Adjutant of the 1st Southern Division [Tom Crofts] placed the ambush party strength at 32, though additional members' names have not come to light.[23])

The O'Donoghue report says that a mine was laid and a commandeered horse-drawn cart with one wheel removed was used as a road block. 'A farm butt was also placed as a roadblock on the bohereen running almost parallel to the road on the eastern side'. (One wonders if this should have read 'western side' – it seems to be a reference to the bohereen located roughly parallel to the west of the road.) The ambush party remained in position during the day. It appears that the mine consisted of several pounds of explosive, with a command cable linked to a plunger on higher ground. The IRA did not have anti-armour equipment so they would have been relying on the mine to destroy or disable the Whippet armoured car which, with its Vickers machine gun, posed a particular threat to the ambush party. The Whippet was not armoured underneath and was thus vulnerable to a road mine. Were the convoy to halt in front of the barricade, with vehicles bunched up close together instead of being spread out, the tender and the touring car could also be hit when the mine was set off.

Meanwhile, after passing through Bealnablath, Collins's convoy had a brief stop in Bandon, at the Devonshire Arms Hotel, one of the buildings that had been occupied by National Army troops when they took the town some days earlier. The convoy then set off for Clonakilty, Collins's home town. About three miles from the town, the convoy found that the road had been blocked by a felled tree. Collins helped with clearing the obstacle. In Clonakilty, Collins interviewed the local garrison commander and took the opportunity to meet friends. Dalton was impressed by the warm welcome given to the Big Fellow.[24] One gets a sense of Collins returning to his native place as the 'local boy made good'. He was now the chief of the National Army, and had the trappings of power, including a magnificent motor car and a military escort. Dalton and Collins had lunch at the home of Maurice Collins, a cousin, and the convoy set off for Rosscarbery.

Along the way, Collins stopped in his home area of Woodfield and at nearby Sam's Cross, getting a warm reception from family, friends and neighbours. At the local pub, The Four Alls, he bought pints of 'Clonakilty Wrastler' for members of the convoy. Decades later, John McPeak, the machine gunner in the armoured car, would recall how Collins 'stood' drinks at the pub but he added, 'There was no serious drinking on that trip'.[25] The drinking that occurred on the day has given rise to speculation as to the level of sobriety that prevailed among the convoy members. In later life Dalton hotly refuted any suggestion that convoy members were drunk. 'That is a lie', he retorted in reply to a question from an interviewer.[26]

The convoy moved on to Rosscarbery and Skibbereen where National Army posts were inspected. At Skibbereen there was much excitement at Collins's visit, with a crowd gathering to catch a glimpse of the Big Fellow. Among the crowd was the writer Edith Somerville, whose brother, Captain Hugh Somerville, had given discreet assistance to Dalton during the landings at Passage West. The original plan had been to travel to Bantry, but as it was now getting late, it was decided to return to Cork. At the Eldon Hotel in Skibbereen, Dalton was with Collins as the Commander-in-Chief had what would turn out to be his last meal. The convoy moved off to Bandon, where the officer in command of the pro-Treaty forces was

Major General Sean Hales, who was also a member of the Dáil. Collins and Dalton met with Hales at Lee's Hotel. Just a few miles away, in the Bealnablath area, Sean's brother Tom Hales was in charge of preparations to ambush the convoy on the home journey. Another important officer who met Collins and Dalton was John L. O'Sullivan, who had been deployed by Hales to lead the Free State advance into a number of towns in West Cork.

Apparently, during the talks at Lee's Hotel, National Army officers warned Collins of the danger from 'Irregulars' that could lie along the route to Cork. Dalton was also concerned about the possible threat, and he would later say that he advised against returning by the same route by which they had come west, but his advice 'was not acted on.'[27] If Dalton was overruled it was presumably by Collins himself. In another comment in later life, Dalton said that while he was reluctant to return the same way, trees had been felled on alternative routes and they had to go via Bealnablath.[28]

Last Farewells

An excited crowd had gathered as Collins and Dalton emerged from Lee's Hotel and took their seats in the back of the touring car that had been parked directly outside the front door. Somebody snapped what would be the last photograph taken in life of Michael Collins. In the grainy image, Collins appeared to be wearing a greatcoat, as he sat in the back of the open-topped car. Dalton sat beside him, to his right, directly behind the driver. Dalton was studying a map – possibly an indication of concern about the route they were to take back to Cork. After they drove off from Bandon, Collins may have been mindful of the warning about the threat from the enemy when he remarked to Dalton, 'If we run into an ambush along the way we will stand and fight them.'[29] Instead of travelling in the open-topped touring car where he was vulnerable, it would have been safer for the Commander-in-Chief to have squeezed into the armoured car, where he could be protected. The *Slievenamon* machine gunner, John McPeak, would later state that at no stage in the journey did Collins indicate any desire to travel in the armoured car.[30]

In Bealnablath, as twilight approached, it appeared to members of the ambush party that the convoy was not going to appear. According to Liam Deasy, after attending a meeting at Gurranereagh, he walked back to Bealnablath with Tom Crofts, arriving about 7 pm. They were told by Jerh Long that the column was in ambush position and Deasy walked down towards that position. He met Tom Hales standing in the middle of the road. Hales told him that since the convoy was unlikely to return the same way, and as the ambush party had been in such an uncomfortable position all day, he was giving the order to withdraw.[31] Some rain had begun to fall – another possible reason for the decision to withdraw.[32]

During the day, the republicans sought to discreetly monitor Collins's movements, although there was a delay in intelligence reaching the ambush party in Bealnablath. The Crofts report notes that at 6 pm they got 'definite information from Bandon' that the Collins party had gone on to Clonakilty. According to Crofts, it was at 7.45 pm they 'gave up hopes of anything' and decided to 'withdraw for the night'.[33] The report noted that during the journey 'Michael Collins travelled in the touring car and made himself very prominent'. There was no mention of Collins's travelling companion, Major General Dalton, indicating that Dalton may not have been identified by the republicans.

The process began of lifting the mine and clearing the barricade. A rearguard stayed behind while other members of the ambush party walked north along the road to Bealnablath. According to the O'Donoghue report, the rearguard consisted of men from the Cork No. 3 Brigade – Tom Hales, Jim Hurley, Dan Holland, Tom Kelleher, Sonny O'Neill, Paddy Walsh, John O'Callaghan, Sonny Donovan, Bill Desmond and Dan Corcoran. Then there was a dramatic development that must have sparked something close to panic among the members of the IRA rearguard. In the still evening air, they heard the ominous sound of the motor cycle and the Collins convoy vehicles approaching. By now the land mine had either been lifted or disconnected. The IRA rearguard men realized that their comrades walking north towards Bealnablath crossroads would be in danger – it was feared the convoy would overtake these armed men in a ravine before they could reach their destination, and they would be extremely vulnerable. O'Donoghue states that seven or eight members of the Cork No. 3 section hurried to take up positions on the bohereen on the high ground to the west of the road, and opened fire. Apart from disrupting or delaying the convoy, the riflemen would also have been trying to warn their comrades further north along the road to the crossroads.

According to the Crofts report, some of the original ambush party had got as far as the cross roads at Bealnablath when a messenger came on 'post haste' to say that the convoy had arrived and was held up by the barricade. Fortunately, according to Crofts, six men had not left their positions and three more managed to get back. This section opened fire on the enemy. The rest tried to get back to help their comrades but were never in a position to render any real assistance. The firing from the enemy machine guns was 'terrific'.[34]

According to the O'Donoghue statement, Jim Hurley fired at the motor cyclist and 'missed him'. However, the motorcyclist, Lieutenant John Joseph Smith, stated that a bullet hit the handle bar of his motor bike and injured his left hand.[35] Another IRA Volunteer, Tom Kelleher, fired at the 'following vehicle' – obviously the Crossley tender. Further back in the convoy, Collins's touring car came under fire. Lieutenant Smith, aged in his mid-twenties and a native of Enniscorthy, County Wexford had served in the British Army and probably had practical experience of dodging enemy bullets. He would later tell in an interview how, after coming under fire, he immediately put on full speed, and rode through for about 300 yards.[36] He saw a barricade across the road, consisting of a large cart with a wheel off. He dismounted from the motor cycle, took shelter in the ditch, and crept back along the road to check on the other members of the convoy. The Crossley tender drove up and stopped. Commandant Sean O'Connell was the senior officer travelling on the tender. Captain Jimmy Conroy was apparently in the armoured car when the ambush occurred. Lt Smith called to the men in the tender to take cover. The soldiers divided into two parties – one party worked on dismantling the barricade while the other party began to reply to the ambush party's fire, with rifles and a Lewis gun. Members of this group covered their comrades who were clearing the obstacle in the road. One of the soldiers in the tender, Private John O'Connell, who had joined the convoy at Mallow as a guide, recalled that apart from the four-wheel dray 'full of porter bottles', there was also 'a lot of porter bottles that had been broken and strewn around the road'.[37] According to the Crofts report, the ambush party was too far away to cover this point with their fire.[38]

'Drive Like Hell'

Further back in the convoy, a bullet shattered the windscreen of the touring car carrying Dalton and Collins. Dalton believed they were being attacked with machine gun fire but this was not the case – the IRA rearguard men were armed with rifles and probably handguns. Dalton, as it has often been reported, shouted to the driver: 'Drive like hell'.[39] No doubt Dalton figured it was unwise to make a stand in a location that had been specially chosen by the enemy. (The very fact that the republicans were firing from higher ground gave them a tactical advantage.) Collins took a different view. According to Dalton's account, Collins put his hand on the driver's shoulder and declared: 'Stop, we'll fight them.'[40] In retrospect, it could be argued that Dalton should have insisted on the convoy moving at full speed ahead, but then Collins had a very forceful personality, and he did hold the position of Commander-in-Chief. It may be the case that Dalton's training in the British Army had conditioned him not to challenge an order from the commander of the army in which he served.

Joe Dolan, who was travelling in the back of the armoured car, would greatly regret in later years that it was not one of Collins's own regular drivers who was at the wheel of the touring car – Joe Hyland or his brother Batty. Dolan told the author Margery Forester that the Hyland brothers knew their impetuous Chief, and on hearing the command from Dalton would have obeyed the order and driven at full speed away.[41] Decades after the attack, the machine-gunner John McPeak told the *Irish Independent* that he believed it was silly to stand and fight: 'There was no need to do so.' He believed the convoy could have gone around the cart that had been placed across the road. 'I will never understand why we had to halt.'[42]

Dalton, Collins and the two drivers, Privates Michael Corry and Michael Quinn, quickly dismounted from the touring car. According to Corry's later account, Collins walked back the road for some fifty yards, followed by Dalton and the two drivers. The four took cover behind a hedge or ditch, about two feet high.[43] Dalton observed the enemy fire. It seemed to Dalton that most of the fire was coming from a concealed roadway on a small hill to their left, i.e. to the west. Some firing also came from the high ground to the east and north of the convoy. A number of IRA men, including Liam Deasy and Tom Hales, who were in Long's pub and who were alerted by the sound of the gunfire, had converged on this area, perhaps hoping to out-flank the convoy. Meanwhile, the armoured car backed up and the gunner, John McPeak, opened fire with the Vickers machine gun on the hidden members of the ambush party. At one stage the machine gun stopped firing and Corry, one of the touring car drivers, would later recall that Dalton called out to the gunner, asking why the Vickers was not in operation. 'The gun is jammed, sir,' McPeak replied.[44]

Dalton later told how Collins and he were lying within an arm's length of each other as the two opened 'rapid rifle fire' on their 'seldom visible enemies'. About fifty or sixty yards down the road, and around a bend, they could hear that the convoy's machine gunners and riflemen 'were also heavily engaged'.[45] Apart from the Vickers machine gun in the armoured car, the troops in the Crossley tender, as indicated above, had a Lewis gun. Dalton's memory of events was that the firefight continued for about twenty minutes, and then there was a noticeable lull in the enemy's attack. Collins jumped to his feet and walked over behind the armoured car, clearly trying to get a better view of the enemy's position. Dalton heard him shout: 'There they are, running up the road.' When Dalton next turned around, Collins had run about fifteen yards south along the road beyond the armoured car, and dropped into a prone position to open fire on the retreating enemy. Collins would now have been at the extreme southern end of the series of positions occupied by convoy members, and the most isolated.

Sean O'Connell, under fire, came running along the road from the other direction, and dropped down beside Dalton, telling him that the enemy had retreated from in front of them, and that the obstacle in the road had been removed. Then O'Connell asked: 'Where's the Big Fella?' Dalton replied: 'He's all right. He's gone a few yards up the road... I hear him firing away.' Then Dalton believed he heard a faint cry: 'Emmet, I'm hit.' Dalton and O'Connell ran to the spot and found Collins lying motionless in the firing position, 'firmly gripping his rifle, across which his head was resting'. Behind Collins's right ear, there was a big gaping wound, at the base of his skull. Collins could not speak and seemed to be dying. Dalton and O'Connell knelt beside him. O'Connell recited into Collins's ear the words of the Act of Contrition. Joe Dolan was also on the road. He heard somebody say that the Commander-in-Chief was hit. 'I did not know how bad it was until I saw Sean O'Connell whisper an Act of Contrition close to his head.'[46] One theory is that the stoppage in the fire from the *Slievenamon* machine gun may have given an opportunity to one or more members of the ambush party to break cover and open fire on the convoy, with a round or a ricochet hitting Collins.

Dalton provided covering fire with rapid bursts from his rifle, and ordered other members of the convoy to do likewise, as O'Connell dragged Collins across the road and behind the shelter of the armoured car. Then Dalton ran to Collins and raised the Commander-in-Chief's head on his knee, propping him up also against the mudguard of the *Slievenamon*, and tried to bandage the wound, but it proved difficult to apply the field dressing because of the size of the injury. He knew at this stage that Collins was dying, if not already dead. Collins's eyes closed and in Dalton's words, 'the cold pallor of death overspread the General's face'. Dalton told of his heart being broken and his mind numbed at the shooting of Collins. O'Connell was also stunned and in tears. Dalton recalled: 'I think that the weight of the blow must have caused the loss of my reason, had I not abruptly observed the tear-stained face of O'Connell, now distorted with anguish, and calling also for my sympathy and support.'[47] Corry, the touring car driver, recalled that Dalton remarked to him: 'The General is finished.'[48] According to his later account, McPeak heard somebody in the armoured car saying, 'Collins has been hit.'

Meanwhile Lieutenant Smith, who had observed enemy fire coming at one period from the hills on both sides of the road, made his way carefully on foot southwards, back towards the rest of the convoy. It was by now almost dusk. He encountered the Leyland touring car with nobody in it, and about 200 or 300 yards beyond that, he could see the armoured car in action. Because the firefight was still going on, he crawled along until he reached the armoured car. He saw Dalton and O'Connell with the stricken Collins, and attempts being made to bandage his head. Dalton called over Smith and another member of the convoy to get Collins into the armoured car.

As he was helping Dalton and O'Connell to lift the body of the Big Fellow a shot rang out and Smith was hit in the neck but only grazed. He remained on his feet and continued to assist. The armoured car moved slowly along the road with Collins's body. Dalton and some of his comrades used the car as cover as they moved along the road on foot, keeping the vehicle between themselves and the riflemen on the hill to their left. Now there was another problem, according to Smith's account – the Leyland tourer failed to start.[49] The armoured car pushed the Leyland in front of it, and after a while the driver managed to start the engine. They moved to where the tender was halted, and according to Smith's account, the armoured car was firing all the time. If this is correct, McPeak must have dealt with the earlier stoppage in the Vickers machine gun and was now providing covering fire, to deter any of the attacking riflemen from raising their heads to discharge another round at the convoy.

The body of the dead Commander-in-Chief was moved into the rear seating area of the Leyland car. Corry recalled how he lifted Collins by the top part of his body while Dalton lifted him by the feet.[50] Dalton got into the back of the car, holding Collins's body. Smith, now nursing a nasty neck wound, moved into the front seat next to the driver, as he had to abandon his motor cycle. As the shocked convoy set off for Cork, Dalton sat in the back of the car with his arm around the lifeless body of Collins and with the Big Fellow's head resting on his shoulder. In his memoir *Brother Against Brother*, Deasy said he could see very little of the convoy from his position. 'We had fired a few shots when suddenly the whole convoy moved off.'[51]

As the convoy approached Crookstown village, members of the group stopped a local man, Ted Murphy, and instructed him to guide them to the nearest priest. They wanted Collins to get the Last Rites. Murphy went aboard the tender and guided the convoy to Cloughduv church, where the curate was Father Timothy Murphy. The priest later explained what happened.[52] There was a knock on his door, which the housekeeper answered. She called the priest and said he was wanted outside. It was dark. A soldier and a local man, Ted Murphy, were standing at the door. The soldier, carrying a carbide lamp, asked the priest to come outside as a soldier had been shot. The priest walked out to the convoy which had stopped on the road and saw a soldier lying flat with his head on the lap of a young officer, who was sobbing and crying and did not speak. (The young officer was obviously Emmet Dalton.) The priest saw blood on the side of the dead man's face. He said an Act of Contrition and other prayers and made the Sign of the Cross. He told an officer to wait until he had got the Holy Oils: 'I went to the house but when I returned the convoy had gone.'

When asked about the incident decades later, Dalton's memory of the event was that the priest came out as far as the church railings, looked at the body of Collins lying on his (Dalton's) shoulder in the back of the car, then turned on his heel and walked back in. The impression was that the priest did not want to give the Last Rites. The officers were shocked, and perhaps believed that the priest had refused the Last Rites because of sympathy with the 'Irregulars'. According to Dalton, Sean O'Connell raised his rifle to shoot the priest and only that Dalton struck up the barrel the priest would have been shot: 'The bullet was actually discharged.'[53] Upset and angry over what he thought was the priest's refusal to anoint Collins, Dalton said he complained to Rev. Dr. Scannell, the National Army's unofficial chaplain in Cork.[54] More than sixty years later, when writer Meda Ryan informed Dalton that the priest had simply gone into the house for the Holy Oils in order to anoint Collins, and that he fully intended to give the Last Rites, Dalton became very emotional. With tears in his eyes and in a trembling voice he said he wished he had known all these years: 'I was so shaken at the time he turned his back, it hurt, it hurt me deeply.'[55]

During the nightmarish trip back to Cork with the body of Collins, the convoy came to Ovens Bridge on the main Macroom-Cork road and found that it had been blown up by anti-Treaty forces. The convoy took to smaller roads but became lost and drove through fields, the vehicles bogging down in the mud. The armoured car became stuck, and the Leyland touring car would not start. The darkness probably obstructed the drivers' efforts to get the engine back into operation. The car had to be left behind, to be recovered later. According to Private John O'Connell, the armoured car also had to be temporarily left behind.[56] If his memory is correct on this point, it is presumed that the armoured car was kept under guard through the night, until it could be recovered the following day.

In the darkness, there was a macabre scene as Collins's body was carried to the Crossley tender. Members of the convoy went to a nearby public house to see if they could use a telephone. Mrs Ciss Forde, a member of Cumann na mBan, ran the pub at Killumney, near Ovens, with her brother Danjo Walsh, later to be a Fine Gael county councillor. She remembered how soldiers came to her home in the middle of the night, clearly distressed and wary about the possible presence of anti-Treaty forces in the village. At gunpoint, they demanded to use her telephone.[57] They were obviously hoping to get through to the army headquarters in the Imperial Hotel in Cork. It is unlikely that they managed to make contact. Ultimately, the demoralized group of soldiers departed in the Crossley tender with the corpse of their Commander-in-Chief.

The next morning, Mrs Forde examined the abandoned touring car in the field beside the pub, and found a fully-loaded Webley revolver, in its brown leather holster, in the back compartment of the car, where Dalton had held Collins' lifeless body on the way back from Bealnablath. She hid the weapon in the attic of the house and it remained there until the premises were sold in 1976.[58] (The revolver was auctioned in 2009 and sold for €85,000.)

The Crossley tender carrying Collins's body had to negotiate further obstacles and make further detours on its journey towards Cork. Finally the party reached Ballincollig on the outskirts of Cork. As a devout Catholic, there was something preying on Dalton's mind – he was haunted by the fact that Collins had not yet received the Last Rites. Traditional Catholic practice was that the Last Rites could be administered within three hours of a person dying since it was not known exactly when the soul left the body. Dalton did not want the soul of the Big Fellow to pass into eternity without the consolation of the church's last blessing. Dalton ordered a stop at the Sacred Heart Mission, at Victoria Cross, Western Road. A priest was summoned and a Father O'Brien came out with the sacred oils and administered the Last Rites.[59] The lorry continued on to army headquarters at the Imperial Hotel.

After the convoy reached Cork with Collins's body, it was noticed that Dalton's uniform was smeared with blood. This created the impression that Dalton had been wounded, the *Freeman's Journal* reported. In fact, the stains were the blood of his leader.[60] (An early news agency story carried as far away as Australia reported that Major General Dalton had been wounded.[61]) One of Dalton's officers, Commandant Frank O'Friel, who had played an important part in the Passage West landings, accompanied the body of Collins in an ambulance to Shanakiel Hospital. Part of the hospital was used by the British Ministry of Pensions as a convalescent home for ex-soldiers wounded in the Great War. Another part of the hospital was used for the treatment of National Army soldiers who had been wounded in Dalton's capture of Cork.[62] Meanwhile, Lt Smith received medical treatment. He was also taken to hospital and the *Irish Times* reported a couple of days later that he was 'progressing favourably'.[63]

Before the body of Collins was transferred to Shanakiel Hospital, Dalton had a particular duty to perform. He knew about a key that Collins carried with him that had been given to him by the prominent Dublin surgeon and literary figure, Oliver St. John Gogarty, during the War of Independence. The key was to Gogarty's house at 15 Ely Place, Dublin. The stately Georgian house was situated in a cul-de-sac, but through Gogarty's garden there was a 'secret' route across a wall, then along a passage and through a wicket gate into nearby St. Stephen's Green. The idea was that Collins could use the Gogarty property as an escape route if he was being pursued. Gogarty had some cans of petrol placed beside the wall under an ash tree so as to facilitate the Big Fellow in crossing the wall in an emergency. After Collins' death, it fell to Dalton to retrieve the key to this secret getaway route from a pocket in Collins's tunic, according to Gogarty.[64] Some weeks later, Dalton returned the key to the eminent surgeon and poet.[65]

Dalton was faced with the onerous task of communicating the shocking message to the National Army headquarters in Dublin that the Commander-in-Chief was dead. When he reached his headquarters in the Imperial Hotel that was his priority. Telephone links to Dublin were not functioning and there are varying accounts as to how the message was transmitted. Decades later, Dalton recalled that there was a wireless link between his GHQ in the hotel and the Cable Station on Valentia Island in County Kerry. His memory was that he used this connection to send a message to New York, from where it was relayed to Dublin via London. In an interview, he described his outrage when, later that morning, he received a cablegram addressed to the Officer in Command, Cork from Hearst Newspapers in New York offering 1,000 dollars for the story of Collins' death in the ambush.[66] According to another account, a radio officer, Matt Quigley, had managed to set up a radio station in one of the buildings left intact at Victoria Barracks. He was sent to the Imperial Hotel to meet Dalton, who was sitting on a couch with the chaplain, Rev. Dr. Scannell. Dalton gave him a message to the effect that the Commander-in-Chief had been killed in an ambush at Bealnablath and instructed him to send it immediately to General Mulcahy. According to Quigley's account, he sent the message 'clear' rather than in code at about 1 or 1.30 am and had a reply about 3 am.[67] In fact Dalton probably sent more than one message, using different means of transmission. It was vital that this important message got through to Dublin as quickly as possible, and that nothing was left to chance.

Béaslaí Told of Dalton's Telegram

Piaras Béaslaí, the National Army's press censor and publicity director, was one of the first to learn of a communication from Dalton that Collins had been killed. He was in his office at the police barracks on Great Brunswick Street, Dublin (now Pearse Street) when he received a telephone call from a member of his staff, a clerk based at the Central Telegraph Office on Amiens Street, which was under military control. The clerk said he had just passed on a telegram from General Dalton to General Headquarters. The clerk read out the message stating that the Commander-in-Chief had been shot dead. According to Béaslaí's later account, Dalton added an agonized question: 'What in Heaven's name am I to do?'[68] (One has to question the accuracy of Béaslaí's memory on this point – in an urgent military message such as this, Dalton would have been anxious to convey the core message as briefly and as clearly as possible with no superfluous rhetoric.) Béaslaí went to a room where journalists, including pressmen from abroad, were waiting for one of his regular briefings on latest developments. The journalists asked if there was any news? This night, there was certainly news, and it would spread like wildfire all over the world. Béaslaí sat down at his desk, covered his face in his hands, and burst into tears. When he recovered his composure, he told the international press that Michael Collins was dead.[69] Some of the stories published over the following days attributed some rather fanciful quotes to the dying Collins: 'Forgive them … Let the Dublin Brigade bury me.' However, Dalton's eye witness account indicates that Collins died almost immediately and would have been unable to make such comments.

There were some tough-minded men based at Portobello – nevertheless there was shock, grief and weeping when word spread through the barracks about Collins's death. Charles Dalton was about to retire to bed at his room in the barracks when suddenly the door swung open and in walked Adjutant-General Gearóid O'Sullivan. He looked stunned and did not give his normal greeting. He stood in silence for some seconds and then broke down in tears, saying, 'Charlie, the Big Fella is dead.'[70] Dalton, like all the others who were to receive the news that night in Portobello, was dumbfounded.

Dalton described breaking the news to two of Collins' close friends who slept nearby. Then he and O'Sullivan told Joe O'Reilly, Collins' ever-faithful personal assistant and courier, who had since 1916 devoted his life to serving the Big Fellow. Then other members of the Collins inner circle at Portobello had to be told. A shocked O'Reilly accompanied Dalton and O'Sullivan to Tom Cullen's room. Cullen did not have electric light in his room. In the flickering light of a candle, and with a sense of foreboding, he scanned the sombre faces of the men who had come to see him. Before anyone could say anything, he said he knew that something terrible had happened. He had been dreaming of Collins and he knew what they were going to tell him: 'The Big Fellow is dead.'[71]

Among the National Army personnel in Cork there was shock and grief when word spread of Collins's death – and also anger. It would appear that some wanted revenge. Dalton received an urgent phone call from the prison to say that some officers wanted to enter the jail. Dalton went over to the prison and confronted the men who, it appeared, wanted to carry out reprisal attacks on republican prisoners. Dalton produced a gun, and managed to reason with the officers, persuading them to go away.[72] (Decades later, after Dalton's death, a local newspaper columnist told of how one of the prisoners in the jail at the time described how Dalton 'gun in hand' had saved their lives.[73])

The morning after Collins was killed, Dalton sent another message to army headquarters in Dublin to say that a vessel carrying the remains of the Commander-in-Chief would be leaving Cork for Dublin at noon. Dalton repeated details about Collins's death in the message which read: 'Commander-in-Chief shot dead in ambush at Bealnablath near Bandon 6.30 Tuesday evening with me. One man wounded. Remains leaving by Classic for Dublin today Wednesday noon. Arrange to meet. Reply. (signed) Dalton.'[74]

Meanwhile, according to an account he would later give to historian Calton Younger, Dalton heard that Éamon de Valera was in Fermoy. He gave orders for a search to be carried out but there was no sign of the elusive Long Fellow, as de Valera was often called.[75] Clearly, Dalton would have wished to ensure that de Valera was in custody. Dalton had shared in Michael Collins's frustration at the opposition mounted by de Valera to the Treaty. That frustration most likely turned to anger following Collins's death. Even though Dev had little influence with the men who were directing the military campaign of the anti-Treaty forces, he was commonly regarded by Free Staters as the man who had fomented the Civil War – Dalton would continue to take that view in later life.

In Dublin, General Richard Mulcahy, who would succeed Collins as Commander-in-Chief, issued an eloquent call for calm and restraint to members of the National Army in the wake of Collins's death. His proclamation began: 'To the Men of the Army: Stand calmly by your posts. Bend bravely and undaunted to your work. Let no cruel act of reprisal blemish your bright honour…'[76] The majority of army members probably did exercise restraint but there were elements who took the law into their own hands. On 26 August, in the Dublin area, three anti-Treaty republicans were found shot dead – Sean Cole, Alfred Colley and Bernard Daly. Extra-judicial killings would continue – in Dublin they were often attributed to elements in the Oriel House/military intelligence state security apparatus. However, Emmet Dalton expressed the belief in later life that Mulcahy's call for restraint did a great deal to calm highly-strung emotions, and possibly prevented 'terrible bloodshed'.[77]

Cork Bids Farewell to Collins

Much of Emmet Dalton's time was now taken up with matters to do with the obsequies for the fallen leader. Crowds gathered around Shanakiel Hospital where the body of Collins lay in state. Some members of the public were allowed into the room where Collins lay, to view the remains. Troops lined the avenue leading to the hospital. The Bishop of Cork, Dr Cohalan, was among those who attended. Before the coffin was closed, the Rev. Dr. Joseph Scannell, who was accompanied by other clergy, administered the Absolution. Dalton and a number of officers acted as pall-bearers as the coffin was removed – Colonel Commandant Kingston, General Liam Tobin, Colonel Commandant Byrne, Colonel Commandant Sean O'Connell and Lieutenant Commandant Dolan. The tricolour-draped coffin was carried out to the horse-drawn hearse, followed by a group of nurses carrying wreaths.

Collins's coffin was taken to the docks for transport to Dublin. Crowds turned out to line the streets and show their respect as the cortege passed. National Army officers marched on each side of the hearse, followed by a contingent of officers and troops, marching four abreast. Ordinary Cork citizens joined in the sombre procession as it proceeded by way of Sunday's Well, across Wellington Bridge and on by Western Road, Washington Street, Patrick Street to Penrose Quay, where the coffin was carried on to the waiting ship, *Classic*. Among the officers who stood on the quay by the gangway as the coffin was carried onto the ship were Tom Ennis and Frank O'Friel.

Dalton and other members of the contingent at Bealnablath were among those who went on board to accompany the remains on the voyage to Dublin. The armoured car that had escorted Collins on his tour was also loaded on board. The Rev. Dr. Scannell travelled with the coffin, which was placed on the after-deck, with a guard of honour. As the vessel sailed slowly past Cobh, a Royal Navy flotilla was drawn up in full dress parade formation. On the light cruiser HMS *Castor* sailors and marines stood to attention on the deck, and a bugle sounded the Last Post, the haunting sound coming across the water. Dalton was deeply moved by the salute, and would always remember it. Silent crowds assembled on the pier as *Classic* sailed by. The Bishop of Cloyne Dr. Browne and members of the cathedral clergy knelt in prayer, while the slow tolling of a cathedral bell sent out its own message of mourning. Parties of the National Army assembled and stood to attention to give a salute. Dalton would later recall how many of the people in Cobh had put lights in their windows overlooking the water, as a tribute to the dead leader. This experience would stay engraved in his memory to the end of his days.

Remains of Collins Arrive in Dublin

In Dublin port, dignitaries and clergy waited on the North Wall to receive the remains as a silent crowd looked on. The Reverend Patrick Doyle, a friend of Michael Collins, recalled that the ship was about two hours late, and it was not until about 2 am before the lights of *Classic* were spotted as it glided slowly up the Liffey in the rain.[78] The *Freeman's Journal* reported that as the lines of the ship *Classic* were made fast, the buglers on the quayside played the Last Post, and the sound of weeping could be heard: 'Men who had known and loved Michael Collins broke down. They wept and were not ashamed of their tears.'

Dalton, looking out from Classic onto the Dublin quays, saw in the gloom and the teeming rain a crowd of thousands of people, including women and children, waiting in an eerie silence for the ship.[79] The head of government, William T. Cosgrave, and the Chief of Staff of the National Army, General Richard Mulcahy were among the senior figures on the quayside. Collins's friend, the surgeon Oliver St. John Gogarty was also there. The Dublin Guards provided a guard of honour, standing to attention on either side of the gangway. Collins's sister, Mrs Mary Collins Powell and her husband, were brought onto the ship. They were followed by members of the Cabinet, and the officers who would act as pall bearers.

Father Doyle retained a vivid memory of what happened next: 'As we advanced towards the coffin, covered by the national flag, Emmet Dalton, Collins's companion in the fatal ambush, emerged from the companion-way bearing the dead hero's military cap, stained with blood and brain-matter, the physical remains of that wonder-brain that had served Ireland so nobly.'[80] (There has been much debate about what happened to Michael Collins's cap – it is possible that the cap referred to here was Dalton's own cap which had been used to cradle Collins's head.)

The casket was borne along the deck, followed by members of the Government as well as by Major General Dalton and others who had served under Collins. The coffin was carried from the ship and placed on a gun carriage drawn by four horses. The cortege moved slowly off, to the beat of muffled drums, and pipers of the Dublin Guards[81] playing the dirges, *The Flowers of the Forest* and *Lord Lovat's Lament*.[82] The cortege proceeded through silent streets, with cobblestones glistening in the rain. It was almost four o'clock, almost dawn, by the time the procession reached St. Vincent's Hospital on St. Stephen's Green where hospital staff were waiting to receive the remains. It was here that the body was embalmed by Oliver St. John Gogarty. The coffin was then placed in the hospital chapel.

Dalton, along with General Mulcahy, Sean O'Connell, Liam Tobin and other senior officers, was among the pall-bearers as Collins's coffin was taken in procession on a gun carriage from the hospital to City Hall, through vast crowds. The remains lay in state at City Hall, guarded by members of the National Army, including some of those who had been close to Collins in the Squad and in the intelligence apparatus. The coffin was taken on Sunday evening to the Pro-Cathedral, for the Solemn Requiem High Mass next day, 28 August. Listed among those in the women's section in the church was Katherine Dalton, mother of Emmet and Charlie. Charlie Dalton was chosen as one of the pall bearers at the funeral, along with Sean O'Connell and Joe Dolan who had both been with the Big Fellow at Bealnablath.

Emerging from the Pro-Cathedral after the Solemn Requiem High Mass, Charles Dalton joined with other officers of the National Army as they lined up to march behind the gun carriage. An unnamed writer in the *Irish Times* described how some of the pall bearers had 'wayward tears coursing down their sun-burned cheeks' as the oak coffin was carried from the church. A contingent of senior, uniformed army officers assembled to march in the cortege. A solemn, grim-faced Emmet Dalton had pride of place in this group, marching in the front row, with General Mulcahy and General Gearóid O'Sullivan. Noting the presence of Dalton, the *Irish Times* report referred to him as 'the flaxen-haired lad in whose arms he [Collins] had died'.[83] All the officers wore black armbands. Vast crowds, estimated to number up to a half million, lined the streets for the funeral procession from the Pro-Cathedral to Glasnevin Cemetery. It was reported that the funeral procession took one and half hours to pass a given point. Major Gubbins, the British officer who had supplied the field guns used by Emmet Dalton to bombard the Four Courts, also provided, with reluctance, the gun carriage and horses used to convey Collins's tricolour-draped coffin to the cemetery.[84]

Major General Dalton was one of the senior National Army officers who lined up at the graveside giving a final salute as the grave diggers lowered Collins's coffin into its last resting place. A choir chanted Latin hymns, a firing party fired three volleys and the Last Post was sounded. General Mulcahy then gave an oration, speaking in Irish and English, paying an eloquent tribute to his fallen comrade. In his address, Mulcahy made a special reference to Dalton, who was standing just a few feet away. He said that after Collins received his death wound, he had only a few minutes to live, and the only word he spoke in these few moments was, 'Emmet'. 'He called to the comrade alongside him, the comrade of many fights and many plans, and I am sure that he felt, in calling that one name, that he was calling around him the whole men of Ireland, that he might speak the last word of comradeship and love.'[85]

Republican Reaction

Among republicans there was regret over the death of Collins, who had played such an important role in the fight against the British during the Anglo-Irish War. Prominent anti-Treaty fighter Tom Barry said he saw about 1,000 republican prisoners on their knees in Kilmainham Prison saying the rosary for Collins when news came that the Big Fellow was dead. However, in the immediate aftermath of the ambush, the feeling of regret was not universal. General Richard Mulcahy talked of internees in the Curragh 'cheering and jeering when they heard of Collins's death'.[86] The writer Francis Stuart, a republican prisoner at Portlaoise, recalled 'a big cheer going up', although he did not cheer himself.[87]

Despite later speculation that Collins was killed by a member of his own convoy, IRA Chief of Staff, Liam Lynch, seemed to have no doubt but that it was his forces who killed Collins. In a memo to Ernie O'Malley just eight days after the ambush, he took the attitude that it was 'regrettable' that the 'National Position' made the shooting of such leaders with a splendid previous record, 'necessary'. He praised the performance of the nine republicans who took part in the engagement. He said it was a 'splendid achievement from a military point of view', as they were opposed by machine guns and greater numbers. 'Were it not that mines had been raised, armoured car would have been destroyed, as well as lorries.'[88]

It is not known with absolute certainty who shot Collins. A 'favourite' suspect has emerged – Denis 'Sonny' O'Neill who, according to the O'Donoghue report, was a member of the ambush party, although his relatives denied he killed Collins. Through a succession of events, O'Neill's name first emerged into the public domain in the 1980s. His name has featured in connection with the Collins killing in books, media reports and at least one TV documentary. In defence of O'Neill, his relatives released the transcript of a priest's 1989 interview with Tom Foley who was present in Bealnablath as a 17-year-old. Foley claimed that O'Neill left the ambush position an hour before the attack. Foley, incidentally, claims that Sonny's brother, Jackie O'Neill, was at Bealnablath, 'minding the landmine after it had been laid'.[89] (In military pension files released in 2014, Sonny O'Neill said he 'took part' in the 'engagement' at Bealnablath. He knew Collins and was 'attached' to his pre-Truce intelligence staff in Dublin, targeting 'enemy agents'. O'Neill, ex-RIC, ex-British Army and a 'first-class shot', became a Fianna Fáil councillor in Nenagh, County Tipperary. He died in June 1950, aged 62, after a pilgrimage to Knock.)

Conspiracy Theories

There was no inquest into Collins's death. The Provisional Government had ceased, from 30 June, to hold inquests into the deaths of members of the National Army killed in action. Technically, Collins fell into this category. It would have been useful had the government made an exception in the case of Collins. A public inquiry of some kind might have clarified matters about which there are still conflicting opinions and theories. Books have been written dealing in great detail with the death of Collins and still questions remain to be answered. Was he standing up or lying prone when hit? Was he hit directly by a bullet or indirectly by a ricochet? In addition to the large wound at the back of his right ear, did he also have a small entry wound in the forehead, at the hairline? Dalton always said he saw no such 'entry wound'. From his experience in the Great War, he believed that Collins had been hit either by a dum dum bullet or a ricochet.[90]

The lack of an inquest or public inquiry probably helped fuel the conspiracy theories. Some began pointing the finger of suspicion at Dalton. There was wild speculation that he had shot Collins either accidentally or as a British 'sleeper', that he was an assassin in the pay of British intelligence. It is unclear when such rumours started. The writer Ulick O'Connor recalled they were in circulation in the 1950s when he interviewed Dalton for his biography of Oliver St. John Gogarty. But he also recalled that people of any discernment dismissed the rumours as 'outrageous'. The rumours had no real acceptance. 'It was just pub talk.' He said he never discussed the rumours with Dalton himself, as it would probably have been 'bad manners' to even refer to them.[91]

Dalton was not the only target of the conspiracy theorists. For a period, the finger of suspicion was pointed at Éamon de Valera – had he engineered the death of his great rival? Despite his presence in Bealnablath, there is no evidence that Dev had anything to do with the killing of Collins. Others blamed John McPeak, the Scots-born gunner in *Slievenamon*, who would later defect to the republicans bringing the armoured car with him. Once again there was no hard evidence to stand up a theory that he shot Collins, either deliberately or accidentally.

Emmet Dalton was a strong-willed man and he may not have lost much sleep worrying about accusations made behind his back. He was more concerned with the thought – could I have done more to protect Collins? In the circumstances, it is difficult to see what else Dalton could have done. Yet, many years later, in an interview with Pádraig Ó Raghallaigh for RTÉ radio, Dalton admitted that in the wake of Collins's death, he had a 'feeling of guilt'. He could not excuse himself of responsibility. He was sorry that Collins had been killed, and also sorry that it had happened in his own command area. In addition, he felt the 'sad loss' of a friend.[92]

After arriving in Cork on 20 August, and after consultation with Dalton, Collins requested air reconnaissance on areas in West Cork where the 'Irregulars' were active. Dalton may have decided that a good way to get aerial surveillance was to have Collins order that it be carried out. Collins's message reached headquarters on the day of the Bealnablath ambush. Collins instructed that Colonel Charles Russell be told that Fermoy aerodrome was suitable for landing: 'Ask him if he can fly over West Cork area as follows, Macroom to Ballyvourney, to Inchigeelah, Bandon to Dunmanway. Am most anxious to have these places reconnoitred…'[93] The message, sent in cypher, was received at the wireless station in Portobello at 8.35 pm on 22 August and was translated at 10.20 pm. Collins was already dead at this stage and clearly this is one of the last messages he ever sent. Had Collins sent the message earlier in his tour of the south, and expanded the purpose of the air surveillance operation to include reconnaissance along the routes he was to travel, perhaps the IRA ambush party at Bealnablath might have been spotted and a warning given. It is one of the 'what if?' questions that occur about the last day in the life of Michael Collins.

Looking back on the events of that fateful day, 22 August 1922, timing played a crucial role. Had the Collins convoy arrived fifteen minutes later than it did, all the ambush party would probably have departed, the barricade and the mine would have been lifted and the Big Fellow could have proceeded safely to Cork. But it could also be said that Dalton and other members of the convoy were fortunate that they had not arrived fifteen minutes earlier, when the mine would still have been in place and probably many of the IRA riflemen as well. Convoy members were fortunate that the gregarious Big Fellow had delayed so long in the different towns he visited, conferring with military officers, mixing with the people, and chatting with his own relatives and friends. A full-scale attack on the convoy could have not only killed Collins but caused serious casualties among the other members of the convoy as well. Dalton himself would reflect in later life that the convoy members were lucky in that they only had to deal with a few gunmen, the main ambush party having departed. Had they been attacked by a numerically superior party, they would have been in a bad way, as they were in a very vulnerable situation, 'down in a road with no protection'.[94]

Once again Dalton had survived – his close friend Lady Luck, who brought him safely through the carnage of the Somme, was also watching over him on that chilly summer evening in the valley of Bealnablath when the Big Fellow's life came to an end.

CHAPTER ELEVEN

The War Continues

Emmet Dalton's trip to Dublin for the funeral of Michael Collins gave him an opportunity for face-to-face talks with General Richard Mulcahy, who succeeded Collins as Commander-in-Chief. After arriving in Dublin with Collins's remains in the early hours of the morning of 24 August, Dalton and other officers who accompanied him from Cork went to army headquarters at Portobello to meet with Mulcahy and other senior officers.[1] Clearly, Mulcahy and his colleagues wanted to discuss with Dalton the crisis that had arisen. They needed information on the circumstances surrounding Collins's death, the progress of the campaign in the south, and the challenges facing Dalton in the Cork region. When this initial meeting was over, Dalton grabbed the opportunity of some badly-needed sleep at Portobello. By now, he was probably physically and emotionally drained.

As a commander in charge of a most turbulent region, Dalton had many issues on his mind. Despite his success in driving the enemy from Cork city and the major towns and forcing them into remote areas, he now feared that his campaign was losing momentum. He felt that he did not have enough troops to keep the republicans under pressure, and that the enemy fighters were re-grouping to threaten his forces.

He had a number of urgent requirements as he sought to mount an effective counter-insurgency campaign. These included assistance with civil administration; the arrangement of proper accommodation for his troops, and the supply of additional armoured cars and motorized transport to enhance his forces' transport capabilities and mobility. Dalton believed in what today would be called 'rapid reaction', as he confronted enemy guerrillas in the countryside. Dalton maintained garrisons in the towns, but supplemented them with mobile 'columns'. These were intended to bring the war to the enemy, to round up anti-Treaty fighters, to seize arms and also to keep open lines of communication and supply. For these forces to operate effectively they needed good transport facilities.

He also sought dozens of Lewis machine guns, and extra rifles to arm new recruits. He wanted assistance to restore the railway system that had been sabotaged by republicans. He wanted greater cooperation and coordination from the forces of Limerick-based General Eoin O'Duffy and he requested maritime support from the *Helga*, as well as air support. Michael Collins had already given instructions for Dalton to get support in terms of aerial reconnaissance, with missions to be flown from the aerodrome at Fermoy over areas of West Cork where the anti-Treaty forces were active. Headquarters immediately contacted the air service to have the order implemented, and arrangements were made for Dalton to outline his requirements while in Dublin.[2]

After attending the Collins funeral on 28 August, Dalton returned to Cork to press ahead with his campaign. He was entering a difficult period when his forces would come under considerable pressure. Despite the takeover of Cork city by the National Army, control of the streets had not been firmly established. A Church of Ireland businessman, Mr W.L. Cooke, who had served as a Justice of the Peace, was shot dead at his home by armed men. A young National Army driver called Isherwood was abducted from his home by an armed group and reportedly accused of driving Michael Collins at Bealnablath – he was shot as a 'spy' but survived.[3] Sniper attacks on National Army posts became more frequent.

Travel by road in the Munster region remained hazardous for the National Army due to the threat from republican forces. Aided by an intimate knowledge of the countryside, republicans carried out regular ambush operations. For example, just a couple of days after Bealnablath, one of Emmet Dalton's closest associates in the army, Pat McCrea, was wounded in an ambush in Watergrasshill, County Cork.[4]

One of Dalton's priorities was to get the railway system working again, by fixing bridges and repairing facilities damaged by the anti-Treaty forces. He asked headquarters to send air pilot Colonel Charles Russell to help with this task.[5] Russell would later go on to head a new Railway Protection Corps.

At the end of August there was a re-organization of the National Army structure, with eight territorial commands created. One was the Cork Command, with Major General Dalton as general office commanding (GOC). Dalton had been pressing for his command area to be clearly defined. He was responsible for a large area stretching from the borders of County Waterford in the east to the borders of County Kerry in the west. The region was rife with republican guerrilla activity. Headquarters seemed to have supported Dalton's request for closer cooperation from General Eoin O'Duffy's command, and transferred some of O'Duffy's forces over to Dalton's area.[6]

Meanwhile, a Cork Command memorandum dated 31 August, outlined some of the command's immediate plans and requirements.[7] Dalton asked for two planes for the military airbase at Fermoy. He also requested use of the *Helga* for transporting troops and heavy equipment such as lorries and armoured cars. The memo proposed that the Victoria Barracks in Cork be made accommodate 600 men. Dalton also requested 1,000 rifles; 1,000 uniforms; two armoured cars; twelve tenders; twelve Lancias and fifty Lewis guns. It was quite a tall order, indicating the challenges that Dalton felt he was facing. Artillery was not included on the list. Dalton had artillery in his command, and field guns would continue to be deployed on certain operations, but he probably reckoned he had sufficient capabilities in this area. He appeared to be thinking more in terms of mobility in his request for armoured cars, tenders and Lancias. Such vehicles would have been necessary not only for carrying out counter-insurgency operations but also to re-supply outlying garrisons. It is also noteworthy that Dalton was thinking in terms of what would today be described as 'combined arms' operations. He was not simply concerned with the infantry, which formed the main element of his forces. He also focused on air power and sea power. An amended list of requirements subsequently supplied by Dalton included 'two good intelligence organisers', underlining the importance that Dalton continued to attach to good intelligence.

The pull-out from Fermoy on 11 August by Liam Lynch and his anti-Treaty forces enabled the National Army to use the former British aerodrome for air operations in the southern region. One of the Military Air Service pilots to use the base was James C. Fitzmaurice. He had flown with the Royal Flying Corps, later the Royal Air Force, during the First World War. He had then joined the new National Army air service at Baldonnel in August 1922.[8] He appeared quite happy to be transferred to serve in Cork under Dalton.

On flying into the airfield, he found that only the girders of the hangars were left and had to quickly set about re-building the hangars. He described his duties as consisting of reconnaissance and the distribution of Amnesty Proclamation leaflets over the mountainous districts of Cork and Kerry. An air transport service for senior officers was also operated between Fermoy and Baldonnel.[9]

Fitzmaurice force-landed on a number of occasions in areas held by anti-Treaty forces but managed to get away each time. It is reported that Fitzmaurice was the pilot of a Martinsyde Scout which dropped bombs and opened fire with a machine gun on a republican column that ambushed a Free State convoy between Drimoleague and Dunmanway on 3 December 1922 – an early example of 'rapid reaction' by the air service after assistance was sought by a Free State unit under attack.[10] Fitzmaurice went on secure his own place in aviation history – he was one of the pilots on the Bremen for the first East to West transatlantic flight, taking off from Baldonnel in April 1928.

Dalton's Anger and Frustration Over Attacks on Troops

Dalton expressed increasing frustration at the casualties inflicted on his forces by republican guerrillas. Despite being pushed out of the positions they held in Cork city and county, republicans still mounted regular hit and run attacks. Sniping, roadside ambushes and sabotage of railways and roads were among the tactics used. In Cork city, there were regular, night-time sniping attacks on National Army posts - Dalton's own headquarters in the Imperial Hotel came under fire. Telephone and telegraph wires were regularly cut. The insurgents also used land mines, including booby trap mines designed to detonate when a soldier tried to defuse or remove the device. This latter tactic was particularly lethal and provoked particular anger among National Army personnel.

Republicans in Cork and Kerry developed a tactic whereby a large number of fighters would assemble to attack a vulnerable Free State garrison in a town. Such town attacks put Dalton's garrisons under particular pressure.[11] In response, Dalton was obliged to send troops he could barely spare, to travel long distances under difficult conditions to reinforce garrisons under attack, or positions under threat of attack. In so far as Dalton's limited resources allowed, he sought to carry out raids and sweeps to seize arms and round up enemy fighters. Many of Dalton's troops were drawn from Cork city and county and had good local knowledge of the area and of their republican enemies. The republicans also had good local knowledge, and used their own information system to carry out attacks, as one particular killing in Cork city illustrates. A young National Army soldier, Denis McCarthy, was targeted while visiting his wife and young child at their home on Barrack Street on 29 August. Just after he bade them farewell and departed, he was shot dead outside his doorway. According to the *Cork Examiner*, the off-duty soldier was unarmed. The newspaper reported that a crowd chased after the killers but they got away.[12]

Another example of how Cork republicans were able to keep the pressure on the Free Staters by surprise attacks came on 2 September. National soldiers were lining up outside a military post at Cork City Club on Grand Parade to collect their pay when, from across the river on Sullivan's Quay, republicans travelling by motor bike and sidecar, opened fire with a machine gun mounted on the sidecar – an innovative tactic, a kind of 'drive-by shooting'. Snipers also opened fire with rifles. Two young Dublin soldiers were killed and two of the wounded later died.[13]

Dalton had a strong sense of loyalty to his troops and was angered by such attacks on his men. To stop them, he contemplated ruthless action against the perpetrators. On 2 September he sent a number of communications to General Mulcahy, expressing his views. Dalton also contemplated the execution of republicans found in possession of arms. In a letter to General Mulcahy, dated 2 September, Dalton said he believed he had suffered twenty-six casualties in twenty-two hours.[14]

Dalton said it was necessary for him to introduce martial law, and to bring in a curfew at midnight. If he had about 700 additional men it would not be necessary for him to take these steps. It was possible for him to hold all the towns in the south with the men he had at his disposal but he could not hope to clean up areas or keep open lines of communication. The issue of communications with outlying posts was also foremost in his mind. He asked for small wireless sets for places such as Fermoy, Macroom and Bantry. Dalton also wanted command boundaries clarified – there appears to have been an issue in regard to which command had control over particular areas. In a chilling sentence, Dalton also indicated that one of his men had been executed for treachery, showing a ruthlessness on the part of the Cork command towards anyone colluding with the enemy. 'One of our reserves was caught handing over ammunition to the Irregulars,' Dalton explained. 'He was court martialled and shot and buried in the prison.' Little is known about this episode, and details are unavailable about the court martial or who presided over it – Dalton had been away in Dublin for some days following the death of Collins. There are indications that the executed soldier was Private John W. Winsley, also known as Bernard Winsley, a native of Cork city who had previously served in the British Army. It is likely he was one of the ex-servicemen who joined the National Army after Dalton's forces took over Cork. Winsley's name does not figure in the well-known list of seventy-seven anti-Treaty republicans executed by the Free State during the Civil War. Bernard Winsley is recorded by Padraic O'Farrell in his 'who's who' reference book on the revolutionary period as having been executed at Cork County Prison in September 1922.[15] His remains were later exhumed, presumably for return to his family.[16] On being informed of the execution, General Mulcahy wrote back to Dalton: 'I note your action with regard to the man caught handing over ammunition to Irregulars, and I approve.'[17]

In a wireless message to headquarters on Saturday, 2 September, Dalton talked also of the casualties that had been inflicted on his men, and his desire to retaliate: 'Since I arrived here I have had casualties to the extent of six killed and twelve wounded, most inflicted Cork city. I must bring martial law or remain impotent. I will shoot without trial men found in possession of arms. Can I publish a notice to this effect?'[18] Dalton followed up quickly with another message, which was decoded at Portobello about two hours later, at 3.50 pm. There was a real note of urgency in this communication – Dalton said that all his posts were being strongly attacked, 'Macroom especially'. Dalton was appealing for reinforcements from headquarters and also, apparently, support from the neighbouring command.[19] In another message on 2 September, Dalton said that Macroom had been heavily attacked, and the garrison commander Peadar Conlon had sent word that he urgently needed reinforcements.[20]

Mulcahy replied the same day, saying that he had wired General O'Duffy to get his forces to close in on Macroom from Millstreet. He hoped to despatch 200 men from Dublin the following day.[21] Referring to the enemy who had inflicted '17 casualties' on his forces the previous day, Dalton now seemed to move away from the idea of summarily executing republicans found with arms, but still seemed eager to inflict dire punishment. He makes the comment: 'It would be better to try them and execute rather than shoot them out of hand when I catch them…'[22] He said the enemy had been beaten off from Macroom the day before, but his forces suffered two dead and three wounded. (It was reported that one of the soldiers killed, Volunteer John O'Leary from the Macroom area, had a brother fighting with the IRA.[23]) Dalton indicated that he would 'get active' when he received reinforcements. He estimated there were about 1,000 of the enemy grouped west, west-northwest and west-southwest of Macroom. He proposed moving against them from various points, with a force slowly closing in from Kenmare and Killarney. He asked for some indication of the intentions of neighbouring commanders, Prout and O'Duffy, 'so that I can cooperate'.

In regard to martial law, Mulcahy advised Dalton in a communication on Tuesday, 5 September that this simply involved setting up military courts and the trying of persons on charges of murder or attempted murder when they were caught in ambushes, 'preferably in ambushes in which any of our men are killed or wounded...' He advised that there should be no declaration of martial law. That day headquarters sent an additional 200 men and some officers under Sean O'Connell to Dalton by ship. Mulcahy also promised to see at once about getting smaller wireless sets for outlying areas.[24]

The following day there was an upbeat note in Dalton's communication with headquarters, when he confirmed that Commandant O'Connell had arrived with both officers and men. Dalton remarked: 'I think that from now on we will make a little bit of history here.'[25] Dalton said he was sending General Liam Tobin back to Dublin in order that he could receive treatment for his 'unfortunate ailment', an attack of scabies. (Tobin would go on to serve as the army's Director of Intelligence from October to December 1922.[26]) In a rather bleak addendum, Dalton said that Tobin, who had a good grasp of the situation in Cork, would be able to explain to Mulcahy how he (Dalton) had lost 'one of the most promising officers in the army, Captain Caprani'. Dalton said he had no definite information about Caprani but very much feared he had been murdered. Dalton said the morale of the Irregulars seems to have improved a little, 'but on what account I do not know'.

Captain Joseph Caprani, who came from a notable Irish-Italian family in Dublin, had been kidnapped or taken prisoner by the republicans and apparently held captive on a farm in the East Cork/West Waterford area. The anti-Treaty IRA, who had few facilities for holding prisoners after taking to guerrilla tactics, often released Free State soldiers shortly after they were taken captive, but there were cases in which National Army personnel were executed after falling into the hands of the enemy.[27]

Joe Caprani, from the Fairview district of north Dublin, had joined the Royal Dublin Fusiliers during the Great War as a private, and was later commissioned as a 2nd Lieutenant in the Connaught Rangers. In 1919, he was one of 139 former Irish officers to petition King George for Ireland's case for Home Rule to be referred to the Peace Conference in Versailles. Caprani joined the National Army, and while stationed in County Cork clearly made an impression on Major General Dalton. After his capture, Caprani somehow managed to escape and resumed his duties.[28] Caprani's nephew, the writer Vincent Caprani told the author that he received a mysterious phone call in the late 1990s from an anonymous woman caller. She believed Captain Caprani had been held at a particular farm, and there was a building there called 'Caprani's barn'. She mentioned that Caprani's captors were intrigued by his foreign-sounding name, and they wondered if the Free State was recruiting foreign mercenaries!

Liam Deasy

One of Dalton's key opponents in County Cork was Liam Deasy, commander of the IRA's 1st Southern Division. Dalton regarded him as a formidable opponent, reportedly telling the chairman of Cork County Council that they wanted to get Deasy 'as he is the most resourceful officer in the republican ranks and if they had him, the end would be in sight – while he is at large, the war will go on'.[29] While Dalton was feeling under extreme pressure in early September 1922, Deasy was expressing optimism about the general situation, even though the republicans had lost control of towns and urban centres. According to Deasy's memo to IRA headquarters, 'the position here is very satisfactory, especially in the Cork and Kerry Brigades'.[30] He stated that the enemy occupied forty-eight towns; total troops would be approximately 5,330. Practically all the posts were supplied with an armoured car or armoured Lancia. 'Their total [field] guns are approximately 18'. He claimed that all the posts were encircled, and constant harassing tactics were carried out.

While Deasy struck an optimistic note in this communication, years later Deasy looked back on this period as a very bleak one from a republican point of view. In his book *Brother Against Brother*, he reflected on the Free State landings at Passage West and commented on the aftermath: 'Any possibility of our forces mounting a full scale defence of Munster was by now discounted. The Free State forces were well organized and fully equipped with arms, artillery, armoured cars and transport'.[31]

The republican encirclement of the West Cork coastal town of Bantry in early September put the National Army forces under considerable pressure. A young officer in the Free State garrison, Sean O'Sullivan was asked by another officer, Michael Connolly, if he could get to Cork to arrange further supplies – they were running low on ammunition. O'Sullivan, who was active in the IRA in the War of Independence, would tell later how he dressed as a woman and travelled on a coal boat to Cork, where he went to see Major General Dalton. Dalton came to realise that O'Sullivan, from Eyeries, in the Bantry region, and his comrades, were fighting against men who were also from the region and they probably all knew each other. Dalton showed consideration towards O'Sullivan by saying he would transfer him and his company to County Waterford, with headquarters in Lismore Castle, 'as it could become very emotional when old comrades were killed'. O'Sullivan said he and his comrades were glad of this decision – about six men had already been lost in Bantry.[32] Meanwhile, the republicans withdrew from around Bantry, having lost Cork No. 5 commander Gibbs Ross and other men.

Peace Overtures

In his memo to IRA HQ, Deasy referred to 'numerous peace moves we are daily hearing about'. He said the latter were principally the work of Free State officers, including Tom Ennis and Emmet Dalton, through intermediaries, 'who are dealing with anybody, Politician or Military man, who is willing to act'. Deasy appeared to have a negative attitude to the overtures, stating that as the Republican Party were in no way responsible for this war he considered it unfair 'to put the responsibility for its continuance or end on them'.[33] It is clear that Dalton, while contemplating dire retribution for those who were killing his soldiers, was also seeking to explore ways of ending the conflict, although the death of Michael Collins cannot have helped the atmosphere in which a peace settlement could be pursued.

Various individuals came forward with peacemaking proposals. One of them was Father Thomas Dowling, with whom Dalton had already discussed aid for the impoverished in Cork.[34] A key player in the peace moves was Professor Alfred O'Rahilly. In his biography of O'Rahilly, J. Anthony Gaughan states that following the death of Collins, O'Rahilly redoubled his peace efforts, preparing a memorandum which he asked Dalton to pass on to the Provisional Government. O'Rahilly made a number of points, and said that many of the republican TDs were known to hold the view 'that a sufficient protest has been made and that it is time to quit'. Referring to the proposal for a Truce and the peace agreement ideas he and his ad hoc committee had already outlined, he suggested that the government should authorize somebody such as General Dalton to meet, in Cork, with representatives of the IRA's Cork No. 1 Brigade. Gaughan states that O'Rahilly's memorandum and peace proposals were considered by Defence Minister Richard Mulcahy 'and most probably by the Cabinet'.[35]

There were meetings in Cork between some of Dalton's senior officers and Cork No 1 Brigade officers. Among those from the National Army side involved in these contacts were Dalton's second in command, Ben Byrne, and Tom Ennis.[36] Liam Lynch, IRA Chief of Staff, ordered the contacts by his officers with those from the other side to stop. He appeared to oppose 'unofficial' negotiations, and was certainly in no mood for surrender. He remarked in a memo, 'Is anyone foolish enough to believe that either of them (Ennis or Dalton) would negotiate without orders of government? Then why not direct negotiations?'[37]

Nevertheless, Dalton and Tom Ennis pressed ahead with efforts to end hostilities. Through intermediaries they contacted senior republican officers. According to Liam Deasy, the feelers had the authority of the Free State Government but he interpreted what was on offer as 'unconditional surrender'. For this reason he believed they had little chance of success.[38] Lynch's view that Dalton and Ennis were acting with government approval was verified in a letter on 29 September from Dalton's staff officer, Captain T.C. Courtney to S.P. Cahalane, one of the peace intermediaries. He reported that Dalton was acting 'under definite instructions of the Ministry of Defence' and that he would make any effort towards ending the present needless strife, 'on the basis of an unconditional surrender'.[39]

In a memo from Liam Lynch to Acting Assistant Chief of Staff Ernie O'Malley dated 1 October 1922, Lynch refers to correspondence from Professor Alfred O'Rahilly and goes on: 'When [Emmet] Dalton and [Tom] Ennis got in touch they got rather a set back.'[40] By this stage, Tom Ennis appeared to have been leading the effort. Dalton was about to get married and go on leave, so this may have been a factor in his stepping aside. Ennis and the air pilot Charles Russell, met the republican officers Liam Deasy and Tom Barry near Crookstown on 13 October.[41] Like Ennis, Russell was close to Dalton. Deasy, Barry and another republican, Tom Hyde, were given safe conduct passes to the house of Tadhg O'Donovan, medical officer of the 1st Cork Brigade, where the meeting took place. Deasy did not consider the offer from the other side merited serious consideration.[42]

Details of the meeting with Ennis and Russell were outlined at a meeting of the IRA Executive on 16 October, attended by Chief of Staff Liam Lynch and other senior figures, including Deasy, Barry, Ernie O'Malley and Sean Moylan. Charles

Russell apparently proposed the disbandment of both armies; the formation of a volunteer army under an agreed independent executive, and the officers of that executive to take a pledge to force the government to delete the British veto etc from the Constitution within a stated time.[43] Other proposals included a police force modelled on the Canadian system. Russell said they would go to Dublin in an attempt to 'enforce these proposals' on the Minister for Defence. Nothing came of the proposals. The war would drag on until the following year.

Wedding Plans

Despite the enormous demands of the job, Dalton had another, more private matter on his mind – he wanted to get married. On 6 September he wrote a letter to General Mulcahy saying he had the 'temerity' to apply for leave of absence from the 9–16 October. He explained that he had arranged to be 'very quietly' married in Cork on the 9th. He pointed out that he had arranged to be married about the time that hostilities opened in Dublin but had postponed 'the great event'. It would be 'extremely difficult and disappointing' if he had to postpone again, so he was asking General Mulcahy to give his application 'your kind indulgence'. Dalton remarked that he had sent the application directly to Mulcahy, to 'keep the affair as quiet as possible'. In fact, the wedding would be a major event, with coverage and photographs in the newspapers. Dalton added that he expected to conduct a big round-up in West Cork the same week.[44] Eventually, Mulcahy gave permission for the wedding leave.[45]

The 'round-up' referred to by Dalton duly got under way, with his troops sweeping areas of County Cork, including Blarney, Coachford and Donoughmore and surrounding districts. With the arrival of Sean O'Connell and reinforcements from Dublin, Dalton may have felt he was now in a position to go on the offensive. General O'Duffy's forces carried out a sweep in coordination with Dalton's forces, with columns working south from Rathmore and Banteer to the Derrynasaggart Mountains; from Millstreet towards Macroom and from Killarney southeastwards.[46] It was reported that during the drive large quantities of war materiel were discovered by Dalton's troops, including ten machine gun 'drums' fully-loaded, and a large number of hand grenades, rifle grenades, and land mines.

The National troops returned to Cork on the evening of Saturday, 9 September.[47] There was a disturbing incident during the sweep when National Army troops shot dead anti-Treaty officer, Timothy Kenefick, at Nadrid, Coachford. Free State personnel were accused of torturing and summarily executing Kenefick after capturing him. Kenefick was signaling officer of the IRA's Cork No. 1 Brigade, and it was reported that he was taken prisoner on his way to his mother's funeral. An inquest was held at Mr Gilligan's house, Coachford. One of the witnesses claimed that the Free State convoy that captured Kenefick was commanded by Dalton but this was not corroborated and has to be treated with caution. The Coroner was pro-Treaty solicitor J.J. Horgan, formerly a prominent Redmondite. A verdict of 'wilful murder' was returned against the National troops.

The Provisional Government hit back at the verdict claiming that the inquest was held under the auspices of 'armed Irregulars'. Dalton placed a public notice in the Cork press stating that 'owing to acts of terrorism to the civil population, and more particularly to jurors', no inquests are to be held in future in the county unless written authority for the holding of same shall have been first given by him.[48] This move by Dalton to regulate the holding of inquests was condemned by the IRA publication *War News* which claimed that murder 'may go unchecked'.[49]

Labour Deputy Tomás de Nógla raised Kenefick's death in the Dáil. He said that a verdict of 'wilful murder' had been recorded against National troops, and asked if any attempts had been made to bring the guilty ones to justice. Defence Minister Mulcahy replied:

> I have ascertained that the inquest was held under the auspices of Irregulars armed to the teeth, and before a jury that was apparently selected by Irregulars. The Coroner, in directing the jury, pointed out that they had heard only one side of the case. This was inevitable under the conditions. An adjournment was suggested, but not agreed to. Under the circumstances no action has been taken to bring the so-called guilty troops to justice…[50]

Dalton's Security Concerns Discussed by Government

In early September, Major General Dalton's concerns about the security situation in West Cork were raised at government level. The Cabinet discussed his reports about the threat posed by anti-Treaty forces in certain mountainous areas of West Cork, and the lack of coordination between National Army commands in the region. Dalton had discussed his concerns with his airman friend Colonel Commandant Charles Russell, who had flown down to County Cork. Russell was by now the second in command of the National Army's Military Air Service. On 6 September Russell sent notes of his conversation with Dalton to army chief General Mulcahy who, conveyed Dalton's concerns to the Government, which discussed the matter on 8 September.[51]

On that date there was some positive news for Dalton in regard to air support. Four planes would now operate from Fermoy, and two more in Limerick. General Mulcahy also addressed the question of using the aircraft for rudimentary bombing missions. He said that he had arranged with the Quartermaster General 'to turn out a particular type of hand grenade for throwing from planes'.[52]

On Charles Russell's return to Baldonnel on 12 September, the airman detailed Dalton's concerns in a message to the secretary to General Mulcahy. Russell quoted Dalton as saying that the Irregulars were occupying the mountainous area immediately south of the towns of Mallow, Banteer, Millstreet and Killarney. They were occupying this ground unhindered 'because of lack of cooperation between the forces on either side of them'. Dalton believed that this lack of cooperation was the result of 'the dual command of this area'.[53]

Republican resistance in County Kerry was particularly strong and this posed a problem for Dalton, as he was required to send troops he could ill afford to reinforce National Army forces there. On 11 September, word came through of republican forces making headway in attacks in County Kerry, causing much anxiety among the army command in Dublin. A large IRA force had captured the town of Kenmare, seizing a considerable quantity of arms. At the start of the attack, local pro-Treaty OC Tom 'Scarteen' O'Connor and his brother were shot dead at their home. Army headquarters feared that Cahirciveen and Waterville with its vital cable station were now under threat. Dalton was instructed by General Mulcahy to send 100 men immediately to Waterville by sea; he was told that 100 men were being sent by sea from Dublin to replace them. Mulcahy also ordered reinforcements to be sent by sea from Limerick to the area under threat.[54]

Dalton continued to argue that a major cause of the difficulties in his campaign was the failure of General O'Duffy, based in Limerick, to cooperate with him. He claimed O'Duffy failed to move decisively against the republicans in the remote, barren areas where they were located. In a communication on 11 September to General Mulcahy, Dalton claimed that if O'Duffy's men 'had pushed in and cooperated with me, the fight would now be over'. O'Duffy, for his part, suggested that the problem was down to ineffectiveness of Dalton's command.[55]

Dalton explained to Mulcahy that after his forces landed at Passage West, the republicans whom he estimated to number about five thousand, had crowded into the barren area of the Boggeragh Mountains, without a base for supplies. These forces had retreated from Cork, Limerick, Waterford, Clonmel and Cahir. He considered that with their communications broken, the enemy's position was next to hopeless at this period. He wanted to harass the enemy and keep them moving, but did not have enough troops to do this. He asked for assistance from men in posts in O'Duffy's neighbouring command, but 'this did not take place'. The result was that the Irregulars had time to reorganize. They had now put their best men into what he described as the 'X' class – columns of ten to thirty men, given arms and good officers, and allocated specific areas in which to operate. The next class of men, the 'Y' class, were mostly disarmed and sent back to their own areas to do intelligence work, destroy roads and railways and cooperate with the flying columns as required. The third class, the 'Z' type, were disarmed and told to return home and be ready to mobilize again at any given time.[56] Dalton said that following systematic raids and searches, 100 prisoners had been taken, but mostly of the 'Z' class. Dalton said the anti-Treaty forces had now adopted a type of warfare 'of which they had years of experience'. He went on: 'They now operate over territory which they know. They are now better armed and better trained than they were against the British. In short, they have placed me and my Troops in the same position as the British were a little over a year ago.'[57]

On a more positive note, he said his forces enjoyed the good will of the people. The enemy had poor morale, owing to the indefinite nature of their objective and lack of confidence in their leaders. O'Duffy, for his part, claimed in a message to the Chief of General Staff in September that, as far as he could see, other commands were not engaging the Irregulars as they might, and the Irregulars 'had perfect freedom to move around as they wish'. O'Duffy insisted that in his own command, his forces engaged the Irregulars everywhere, 'and although we have suffered heavily, we have taught them a salutary lesson'.[58]

During September, the *Helga* proved useful to Dalton in circumventing the disruption by the republicans of travel by road and rail in West Cork. On 7 September the ship sailed from Cork and, in an operation overseen by Tom Ennis, delivered troops and Lancia vehicles, under fire, at Courtmacsherry.[59] In another operation along the West Cork coast in September, the *Helga* landed troops and armoured cars at Bantry.[60]

Land Mine at Carrigaphooca

On 11 September the National Army received a stern reminder of the lethal threat posed by the enemy. Free State troops suffered a heavy blow when a massive land mine explosion killed seven soldiers at Carrigaphooca, near Macroom, in the area under the command of Peadar Conlon. The dead included an officer who Dalton and his brother Charlie knew well – Colonel Commandant Tom Keogh who had been a member of Michael Collins's Squad and a close friend of Collins himself. Keogh had taken part with Emmet Dalton in the attempted rescue of Sean MacEoin from Mountjoy Prison, shooting a sentry in the process. Among the former Squad members who survived the blast were Jimmy Conroy, who had been with Collins at Bealnablath, and James Slattery.

The explosion was caused by a trap mine – when the mine was moved it set off a second device beneath it. This was designed to prevent any attempt to disarm the mine which had been placed on Carrigaphooca bridge, about three miles from Macroom on the road to Ballyvourney. National Army soldier John P. Haran much later described how he gave Keogh a drink of water from a water bottle, and said an Act of Contrition into the ears of men hit by the explosion. The exception was Ralph Conway – he was 'blown to pieces lifting the mine, which was a trap one'.[61] It was said that human flesh hung from thorn trees in the vicinity and that body parts were being found up to two weeks after the massive explosion. Michael Collins's sister, Mary Collins Powell was with Keogh as he died in hospital. She took a lock of his hair and sent it with an eloquent letter of condolence to Keogh's mother, Mrs Julia Keogh.[62] The remains of Keogh and four of the other men killed were taken to Dublin aboard the *Helga*.

On the day of the explosion, some of the outraged Dublin soldiers in Macroom decided to take revenge. A republican prisoner James Buckley was shot dead and his body thrown into the hole made by the explosion. National Army soldier Tom Daly blamed the 'Dublin Brigade' for taking the prisoner into custody from other troops and then carrying out this summary execution.[63] Buckley had apparently been captured earlier in the day when there was an engagement between a Free State contingent and an IRA group at Gortnalicka. Daly later told how troops protested over the Buckley killing and 'grounded arms' (i.e. went on strike) and General Tom Ennis had to come out from Cork to deal with the matter.[64]

Peadar Conlon, commander of the Macroom garrison, wrote to Dalton to complain about the killing of the prisoner. He said the shooting 'had caused considerable contempt among the Garrison here'. He went on: 'They have paraded before me and gave me to understand they would not go out on the hills anymore.

Therefore you will want to tell these officers from Dublin that they will want to stop that kind of work or they will corrupt the Army.' He remarked in his communication to Dalton: 'If I was taken a prisoner I would want to be treated as one.'[65]

Dalton brought the matter to the attention of headquarters in Dublin, and forwarded the communication from Conlon. Perhaps mindful of his own men who had been killed by the enemy, and angry over the loss of comrades such as Tom Keogh, Dalton failed to condemn the killing of the prisoner, even though there is no evidence that he sanctioned it. In a communication with General Mulcahy, Dalton said he approved of the action, but at the same time took steps to avoid a recurrence. He reported:

> The shooting was the work of the Squad. Now I personally approve of the action but the men I have in my Command are of such a temperament that they can look at scores of their companions being blown to atoms by a murderous trick without feeling annoyed – but when an enemy is found with a rifle and ammunition they will mutiny if he is shot. On this account, I think it would be better if you kept the 'Squad' out of my area. I would be glad to have the services of Sean O'Connell but I don't want the others.[66]

It is noticeable that Dalton wished to retain O'Connell, his comrade from Bealnablath.[67] Despite a move to send 'Squad' members back to Dublin, Dalton still needed extra troops to cover a region that was both turbulent and extensive. On Tuesday, 19 September he received a message from General Headquarters in Dublin to indicate he was getting an extra 300 men – they would be departing from Dublin the following Thursday.[68] Republican fighters would continue to keep up the pressure on Dalton's forces, though the Cork region would not be Dalton's responsibility for much longer.

CHAPTER TWELVE

Leaving the Army

In addition to waging a campaign against the anti-Treaty forces, Major General Dalton had to deal with issues within the National Army. An issue arose in September 1922 about the number of ex-British soldiers recruited locally into the National Army after Dalton's arrival in Cork. Dalton was asked by General Mulcahy to give him a report on the matter, and to report also if there was any feeling of grievance among the civilian Sinn Féin population in Cork about ex-soldiers being taken on. Mulcahy indicated that he sought the report in light of a letter sent to General O'Duffy 'on behalf of Galvin'. (This was Mallow-based Commandant General Denis Galvin, a prominent IRA leader in the War of Independence, who now commanded troops in north Cork, part of General O'Duffy's South-Western Command.) Mulcahy said he wanted to deal with the matter quickly 'to stop any of this type of complaints that there might be…'[1]

One could speculate that O'Duffy had passed on to Mulcahy various criticisms that Galvin was making of Dalton's neighbouring command to the south, and that this was part of the ongoing quarrel between O'Duffy and Dalton. Dalton sent a long, detailed and courteously assertive letter to Mulcahy, meeting criticisms and comments head-on.[2] In regard to the number of ex-servicemen he had taken on, Dalton said he only recruited 200 selected men: 'These men were uniformed and armed and placed in properly organized companies. They have since performed all duties imposed on them and they have been an unqualified success.' Dalton said he had interviewed prominent people in Cork and they repudiated any suggestion of grievance over the recruitment he had carried out. In an extraordinary account, Dalton said that the late General Collins, in conjunction with some of his secret agents in Cork, had made arrangements to have 700 ex-servicemen sworn in and ready to take up service with him 'upon my arrival in Cork city'. Collins had also arranged similarly for 500 ex-servicemen at Youghal. 'I was unaware of this until my arrival in Cork where I was consulted by his agents,' Dalton wrote.

When he arrived in Cork, 5,000 ex-service men offered their services, Dalton said. 'Upon reviewing the situation I foresaw the political effect of recruiting ex-service men. I was also of the opinion that in arming them, I would be assisting later potential enemies. In view of this and contrary to my instructions, I only recruited 200 picked men.' He said that all his officers agreed that the officers and men of this contingent were 'the most disciplined and effective troops' under his control.

Dalton said that with the assistance of several prominent Cork Volunteer officers, he endeavoured to recruit 'friendly IRA men'. He succeeded in recruiting sixty men, together with fifty prisoners whom he released upon his entry into the city. These men he placed under the control of Captain Dennehy. 'Without prejudice, I say that these men have given me much more trouble than any other unit.' Dalton added that it was 'absurd' to state that 'Sandow' Donovan and the leading Irregulars in Cork were walking about the streets 'flinging bombs at our troops'. He said that since he had been in Cork there were two cases of bomb throwing, and in both cases Fianna boys were responsible.

Dalton seemed to think that there was a desire on the part of Galvin to take over control of Dalton's command and told Mulcahy in no uncertain terms that the 'time has now arrived when it is necessary to definitely clear up Galvin's position with regard to me'. Dalton went on: 'If it is your desire and his [Galvin's] wish that he controls this Command, I will assist him in any capacity to successfully conclude operations in this area.' Mulcahy's reply is not available, but clearly the C-in-C had no wish to sideline Dalton, or have him superceded, in the crucial Cork command area. Galvin was fatally injured the following February when a bomb he was demonstrating exploded.

Efforts to Restore Railway Services

Dalton was anxious to restore to full activity the railway system in the County Cork region that had been sabotaged by the republicans. The repair of railway bridges that had been damaged or destroyed, and the protection of those carrying out the repair work, was a particular priority. On 19 September Dalton sent a wireless message to General Mulcahy: 'Protection for Rathpeacon and other bridges arranged, work about to go ahead.'[3] The following day, Mulcahy sent a message to Dalton to say that there were about 1,200 railway men out of work and without pay of any kind in the Cork area. It was proposed to enroll a number of these men in the army especially for work on the railways, both from the point of view of repairing and guarding the railway. Mulcahy added that he would arrange with the Quartermaster General to send a number of rifles 'for the immediate arming of some of these men'.[4] It had been decided to set up a special force of railwaymen which would be known as the Railway Preservation, Maintenance and Repair Corps, also referred to as the Railway Protection Corps. Dalton's friend, the airman Charlie Russell was appointed head of the new body. He proved an excellent selection, as he made swift progress organizing the new corps.

At one stage in September Dalton was told to provide war news to the National Army's field censor in Limerick – possibly another example of inter-command rivalries. He clearly felt that this instruction was inappropriate, and appealed to General Mulcahy. In a communication to headquarters in Dublin, he asked if this instruction was in order?[5] Mulcahy replied on 15 September: 'It is not in order that Limerick field censor should issue you instructions.'[6] No doubt, it was the answer that Dalton wanted to receive.[7]

Collins Barracks

As the National Army consolidated its presence in Cork city, the former Victoria Barracks became an important military base and was to be the location of the headquarters of Cork Command. The base was re-named Michael Barracks in honour of Michael Collins – this particular name was chosen to differentiate it from Collins Barracks (formerly Royal Barracks) in Dublin. Michael Barracks never really caught on as a name, and in 1925 it would be changed to Collins Barracks. It was estimated that about 600 troops were in temporary accommodation here by the end of the Civil War while hundreds more were accommodated in hotels, halls and schools in other parts of the city.[8] On 25 September Bishop Cohalan formally appointed a Catholic chaplain to the forces in Cork, Father Joseph Scannell DD, who, as indicated earlier, had been acting as *de facto* chaplain. As a devout Catholic, Dalton valued his services. Scannell had been a chaplain in the Great War, winning the Military Cross and the Croix de Guerre.

Major Sweep in West Cork

In September General O'Duffy's adjutant in the Southwest Command, Commandant General W.R.E. Murphy, drew up elaborate proposals for major operations against the republican forces, involving cooperation with Major General Dalton in the clearance of the Ballyvourney area of West Cork. This was the kind of cooperation which Dalton had been seeking, in order to prevent republicans from re-organising in the remote mountainous areas to which they had retreated after the Passage West invasion. Murphy had much military experience from his service in the Great War. In his suggested operational plan, which awaited the approval of the Commander-in-Chief, Murphy said that their information was that the Irregulars had established their headquarters at Ballyvourney, with outposts at various locations. His plan involved contingents of troops closing in on Ballyvourney from different directions, with air support and armoured car support.[9] The historian Michael Hopkinson writes that the prospects for the success of Murphy's plan were ruined by the capture of the instructions. As a result, Liam Lynch ordered all columns to leave the area.[10]

Nevertheless, at the end of September, Dalton launched a major sweep in West Cork, overseen by General Tom Ennis, to root out the remaining republican fighters in the region. Three Free State flying columns from Clonakilty, Bandon and Dunmanway were mobilized, setting off from Dunmanway to close in on anti-Treaty forces in the area of Inchigeelah, with troops from the County Kerry side helping to hem in the republican forces. In a novel development, it appears that some troops were mounted on horses – according to a news report, 'a detachment of cavalry operated in the mountains and captured an Irregular outpost.[11] It was reported that some of the republicans were also on horseback, having commandeered hunters in the Muskerry foxhunting district.[12] Meanwhile, a fourth Free State column from Macroom, under the redoubtable Commandant Peadar Conlon, also advanced on Inchigeelah. He encountered some resistance at Carrignacurra Castle, which was captured. Having taken possession of Inchigeelah, with reportedly a considerable number of prisoners captured, the National Army forces advanced to Ballingeary where resistance was encountered. It was reported that the army used artillery against Irregulars concealed in caves on the mountain sides.[13] The troops then pushed on to Ballyvourney, encountering further resistance along the way. It would appear that there were times when Dalton's artillery could still prove useful, despite the republicans resorting to guerrilla warfare. Some of the republicans retreated into County Kerry, and despite the advances made by Dalton's forces, resistance would continue in the mountainous areas of West Cork.

The Red Cow Killings

In Dublin, on the morning of 7 October, a grim discovery was made in the Red Cow area of Clondalkin – three youths, all from the Drumcondra area, were found shot dead. The victims were Edwin Hughes (17) of 107 Clonliffe Road; Brendan Holohan (17), of 49 St Patrick's Road, and Joseph Rogers (16), of 2 St Brigid's Road. They had been arrested the previous night while putting up republican posters at Clonliffe Road by three National Army officers. These were named at an inquest as Charlie Dalton, younger brother of Emmet; Sean O'Connell who had been with Michael Collins at Bealnablath, and Nicholas Tobin, younger brother of Liam Tobin – Nicholas had been at Carrigaphooca when Tom Keogh was killed. The inquest heard evidence indicating that at least one gun was recovered from the youths. Only Tobin gave evidence at the inquest – he denied that he and his colleagues had any role in the killings. Tobin told of the men arrested at Clonliffe Road being taken by car to Wellington Barracks where they were later released – he claimed that the young men detained at Clonliffe Road were not the young men found dead at Clondalkin. (Two days after giving evidence, Captain Tobin was shot dead accidentally by a fellow officer, Sean 'Flash' Bolger, while taking part in a raid on an IRA bomb factory. Emmet and Charlie Dalton both attended the funeral.)

At one stage the inquest heard that Charlie Dalton had been arrested in connection with the killings.[14] At the inquest, Charlie's lawyer, the eminent barrister Tim Healy, later to be Governor General, protested his client's innocence and argued that he had been targeted because he was the brother of Major General Emmet Dalton, and because Charlie had a promising career ahead of him. Healy seemed to imply that there was a vendetta against Charlie Dalton waged by elements out to destroy him. Ultimately, an open verdict was recorded, finding that the deceased had met their deaths by gunshot wounds inflicted by a person or persons unknown. Charlie Dalton was cleared by a military court of inquiry.[15]

Nobody was ever convicted of the murders, which have been the focus of media attention in recent years. Such extra-judicial killings by State forces were a disturbing feature of the Civil War, even though it could be said they were the exception rather than the rule, in light of the fact that about 12,000 republican prisoners survived the war. Nevertheless the killings by shadowy state forces left an ugly stain on the reputation of the Free State. The young age of the victims at Clondalkin made these particular killings all the more shocking.[16]

Wedding of Emmet Dalton

Despite the turmoil of the Civil War, Major General Emmet Dalton was married in Cork on 9 October 1922 just a few weeks after the death of Michael Collins. For security reasons, the ceremony was held, not in a church, but in the closely-guarded Imperial Hotel in Cork city where the 24-year-old general had his headquarters and where he resided. Dalton's bride was Alice Shannon (21), who lived with her widowed mother in Phibsboro, Dublin. Her late father was Dick Shannon, an accountant. Alice had family connections in Newcastle West, County Limerick. The two had been friends from childhood. Alice travelled to her wedding in Cork by ship – the most practical way to travel given the disruption of the road and rail network.

Alice was said to have taken part as an actress in an early Irish film, foreshadowing Emmet's own future career as a pioneering Irish film producer. According to a newspaper report, Alice had appeared in the 1919 film *Willie Reilly and His Dear Colleen Bawn*.[17] It was produced by Irish film maker Jim Sullivan, and directed by John MacDonagh, a brother of executed 1916 leader Thomas MacDonagh. During the filming, John McDonagh also made a short film for Sinn Féin known as the Republican Loan film, which included footage showing Michael Collins sitting at a table, giving Dáil Bonds to a number of individuals prominent in the nationalist cause. (When I interviewed her in 2012, Dalton's daughter Audrey recalled her mother being 'teased' about appearing in a film but could not confirm the story that her mother had actually taken part.)

Reporting on the wedding of the youthful general, the *Freeman's Journal* described how a 'beautiful altar' had been erected for the ceremony on the concert stage in the Imperial Hotel's Clarence Hall. Irish tricolour flags stood on each side of the altar.[18] The ceremony was performed by military chaplain, Father Scannell. Dalton's parents Mr. and Mrs James F. Dalton, and Mrs Shannon, the mother of the bride, managed to attend despite the unsettled state of the country. Other relatives were present as well as a number of Catholic clergymen and many army officers. Dalton's brother Charles was best man and the bridesmaid was Mary Mullen from Boston USA. Among Dalton's officer friends present were Tom Ennis, the airman Charles Russell and Pat McCrea. The groom was presented with a silver salver by his fellow officers. The inscription read: 'Presented to Major General J.E. Dalton by his brother officers IRA engaged with him on active service in Cork on the occasion of his marriage, October 1922.'

There was a guard of honour of twelve men under Commandant Scott. They presented arms during the Elevation following the Consecration, and two bugles sounded the general salute. The Bishop of Cork, Dr. Cohalan sent his blessing, and congratulations were also received from the Bishop of Cloyne and a number of local clergy. It was stated that a large body of troops assembled on the quays to give a hearty send-off to Major General Dalton and his bride on the honeymoon trip. Dalton would take up residence with his wife at his mother-in-law's home.

The sense of celebration at the Imperial was marred by a shocking incident at the hotel that evening. A young soldier, Andrew Rooney, had been drinking and a row developed between himself and another soldier Charles Kearns. A Sergeant Lowry separated the two, but did not disarm Rooney. Later, in the guard room, Rooney shot and killed Kearns and was immediately arrested. At a court martial on 27 October presided over by Dalton's deputy Ben Byrne, Rooney was found guilty and sentenced to death. General Mulcahy commuted the sentence to five years. Mulcahy, who was often the recipient of complaints from Dalton about lack of facilities and logistical support, now wrote a rather assertive letter to Dalton about the incident, asking for a special report as to whether 'indiscipline and irresponsibility' is in any way general among the garrison in Cork, and suggesting disciplinary action against Lowry. Dalton's reply is unavailable.[19]

By late 1922 the Quartermaster and his personnel at Portobello were becoming better organized, and on 9 October, a considerable quantity of ammunition and stores was dispatched to Dalton's forces in Cork on board the ship *Walnut*.[20] After Dalton's return from honeymoon there was a musical event on the evening of 31 October organized by the Cork Garrison Concert Committee, of which Dalton was President.[21] A priest, Father Sexton, various civilians, male and female, as well as Volunteers O'Brien and Keating and Lieutenant O'Shea, sang songs, accompanied by Mrs Lyons on the piano. The holding of the concert, which concluded with *The Soldier's Song*, underlines the fact that even in the midst of a Civil War, garrison social life continued.

Death List

There was one person who would not have been in the mood to send best wishes to Dalton on getting married – his former schoolmate Ernie O'Malley. Dalton was excoriated in posters put up in his native Dublin by two youths from his own home neighbourhood of Drumcondra/Glasnevin, brothers of O'Malley, now prominent on the anti-Treaty side. In his memoir, *The Singing Flame*, O'Malley described how his younger brothers Paddy and Kevin were nearly captured bill-posting in Dublin. He gave the text of the poster: 'Mulcahy call off the murder gang. Dalton, Lawlor, you have murdered prisoners. Up the Republic.'[22] 'Dalton' is identified in the index to the book as Emmet Dalton. It was not explained why Dalton was being accused of murder – the allegation may have been inspired by the verdict of murder against National forces in the Timothy Kenefick inquest. 'Lawlor' probably refers to Tony Lawlor who, during a riot at Athlone jail, was reported to have shot a prisoner, who later died.[23]

Allegations about the treatment of prisoners were to lead to Emmet Dalton and other senior National Army officers being placed on a death list by Ernie O'Malley. On 30 October, O'Malley, as Acting Assistant Chief of Staff, sent a memorandum to Michael Carolan, Director of Intelligence for Northern and Eastern Command of the republican forces, instructing him to compile a list of all those Free State Officers, NCOs and men who had ill-treated prisoners, or who had acted on the 'murder gangs'. The list was to be compiled from all Officers Commanding of areas in the Command. The names would be circulated to all units in the Command, and personnel would be instructed that these men are to be 'shot at sight'. The memo went on: 'Included in the list will be McKeown [Seán MacEoin], Lalor [possibly a reference to Tony Lawlor] and Emmet Dalton.'[24]

Despite O'Malley's accusation against Dalton over the treatment of prisoners, there is some evidence around this period of an attempt, in Dalton's command area, to stop the extra-judicial killing of prisoners and to hold culprits to account. In the latter part of October a military tribunal was set up in Cork to inquire into the shooting dead of a republican, Sean O'Donoghue, and the wounding of another man, Seamus Collins, after they had been taken prisoner at Dublin Hill, near Cork city, on 28 September.[25] The tribunal recommended that two members of the National Army should be court-martialled.

Lady Lavery Correspondence

During a raid on Ernie O'Malley's Dublin hideout at 36 Ailesbury Road on 4 November by National Army intelligence officers and troops from Wellington Barracks, documents were seized.[26] These documents were later examined by Charlie Dalton as part of his work in army intelligence. Among the papers was a letter from Michael Collins's London-based society friend Lady Hazel Lavery to his brother Emmet. It had been written in August 1922 in the week that Collins was shot, and apparently was a letter of sympathy to Emmet. This letter had been intercepted by republicans. Emmet wrote to Lady Lavery to explain about her letter being intercepted. He did not see what use it could be to the enemy but they had retained it and marked it as a 'valuable document'.[27]

On 22 November, Lady Lavery wrote a long letter in reply to Dalton.[28] She indicated that she took the precaution of sending it, not through the usual postal system, but through the Colonial Office. Her personal friendship with the powerful British Colonial Secretary, Winston Churchill may have facilitated her use of the internal mail system of his department. She indicated she had also been sending letters to Collins via this route and they had arrived safely. Presumably, there was nothing in the letters that would have been of interest to the British from an intelligence point of view. It appears that in a previous letter Dalton had asked her for a pencil sketch by her husband, Sir John Lavery, of Collins. This, apparently, was not feasible but she promised Dalton that her husband would send him a signed, coloured print of the well-known Lavery painting of Collins lying in state. (The print in question was sent by Sir John and was among the items, along with the Lady Lavery letter cited here, that were acquired by the National Library from Dalton's son Richard in 2008.[29])

In her letter, Lady Lavery addressed Dalton as 'My Dear General Dalton' and thanked him profusely for getting in touch.[30] She came across as being upset and worried. She wrote of being 'constantly threatened and blackmailed' in recent months through anonymous telephone calls and letters. She referred to two letters that had been sent to Collins the previous spring that contained political information useful to Collins, and that had been intercepted and used against him by the Irregulars. She said the letters fell into the hands of Harry Boland. Boland had been a close friend of Collins and was also friendly with Emmet Dalton, but he had taken the anti-Treaty side. He was shot and fatally injured in a National Army raid in July 1922 on the hotel in Skerries, County Dublin, where he was staying.

Lady Lavery described how the writers of anonymous letters threatened her with 'exposure'. She insisted she did not care what happened to her but she could not bear that the memory of Michael Collins could be touched by 'scandal'. She also added that her husband would be unhappy if he knew, 'and he is wonderfully good and kind to me'. Lady Lavery appears to be hinting at a romantic relationship with Collins which had left her, and Collins, open to blackmail and which, if exposed, could have seriously damaged Collins. Dalton had obviously informed Lady Lavery of his marriage to Alice. In her letter, Lady Lavery said that she was so glad 'that you have found happiness' and she prayed that the marriage 'may be ever blessed'. She mentioned that she still kept in touch with Mr Kevin O'Higgins (by then a Minister in the Provisional Government).

It is interesting that in this letter, Lady Lavery points to Harry Boland as the republican suspected of intercepting her letters. (It is not known if Boland was, in fact, involved in this activity – Lady Lavery's husband had received a threatening anonymous letter which claimed that republicans had her letters which 'the late Harry Boland had secured'.[31]) According to some reports prior to the Lavery letter emerging into the public domain in 2008, it was another republican, Noel Lemass, brother of Sean Lemass, whom she was supposed to have named in correspondence with Emmet Dalton as the suspect for stealing her letters.[32] These reports seemed to fuel a conspiracy theory, which surfaced in the public domain in recent years, that Dalton was somehow responsible for the murder of his former schoolmate Noel Lemass. Noel, who was on the anti-Treaty side in the Civil War, was abducted after that conflict in July 1923, and his decomposed body was found dumped in the Dublin Mountains the following October. Dalton was Clerk of the Senate during this period and it seems highly unlikely that he would have taken time off from his official duties to arrange a murder. The fact that Harry Boland, not Noel Lemass, has emerged in a Lady Lavery letter as the alleged 'suspect' for intercepting the Lavery-Collins correspondence, further undermines the unlikely conspiracy theory that Emmet Dalton engineered the death of Noel Lemass.

Horse Racing, and Blessing the Colours

Even while he was a serving officer in the National Army during the Civil War Emmet Dalton still managed to find the time to go racing. A report in the *Irish Independent* on the race meeting at Leopardstown on 3 November 1922 noted that 'Gen. Dalton of the Free State Army' was among those who attended. He was developing what would become a life-long passion for horse racing, and would become a semi-professional punter. Dalton's attendance at the races is a reminder that in many areas of Irish life normality often prevailed during the Civil War – it was, after all, a limited, low-intensity conflict and many citizens emerged relatively unscathed.

Despite the demands of the Civil War, there were also some social events to attend. One of the last official events Dalton attended as Commander of the Southern Area was the Blessing of the Colours at Fermoy. Father Scannell, Army Chaplain, said Mass in St. Patrick's Church for the repose of the souls of the officers and men of the Fermoy garrison. Later, Dalton presided at a lunch given by the officers of the garrison. There was an ecumenical flavour to the lunch. On Dalton's right was seated the Catholic parish priest, Canon J. Murphy, and on his left was the Church of Ireland rector, the Venerable Archdeacon Abbott. (A series of murders of Protestants in West Cork in late April, while condemned by both pro- and anti-Treaty sides, may have encouraged anxious local Protestants to look all the more for protection to the National Army and the new police force, the Civic Guard. The atrocity occurred in a region dominated by anti-Treaty republicans, and nobody was brought to book for the murders.)

Proposing the toast of 'Ireland a Nation', the Archdeacon said the people of the country had recently spoken and given a very definite decision as to what they wished for and wanted. They prayed that the day of peace would soon dawn in Ireland. The toast of 'The Army' was replied to by Dalton himself, who said the army was the army of the people; they were not the dictators of the people; the people were their masters. The army was there to protect and to help the people in maintaining their rights and their property, and to carry out their wishes. According to the *Freeman's Journal* report, Dalton received loud applause.[33]

The Officers Who Served With Dalton

Details that have emerged about the Southern Area Command Headquarters staff at this period indicate that Dalton had gathered around him a couple of trusted Collins loyalists. Lieutenant Commandant Pat McCrea had a Transport role and Colonel Commandant Ben Byrne had the important role of Command Quartermaster.[34] Both had been members of Michael Collins's Squad. The two officers now faced their own challenges – Dalton was constantly unhappy with the level of support from GHQ in Dublin in terms of transport and equipment, the areas covered respectively by McCrea and Byrne. Details of the two men appear on the same page as Dalton's entry in the Military Census carried out on 12/13 November 1922.[35]

Dalton seems to have had an instinct for choosing young men of ability who would later distinguish themselves in various fields. The Assistant Command Adjutant was 20-year-old Captain Eamon Butler (Éamon de Buitléar) from Dublin.[36] He went on to become a distinguished Irish Army intelligence officer during the Second World War, playing a key role in breaking a sophisticated code used by German agent Dr. Herman Goertz.[37] Dalton chose another talented young man as his aide de camp, Cork-born Staff Captain T.C. 'Ted' Courtney, an engineer by profession. He would go on to play an important role in organizing the Corps of Engineers, and in later life served as Chairman of the national public transport body, CIE.[38]

In late 1922 the Southern Area Command was organized on the basis of four districts. Command City District, with its headquarters in Cork city, had a strength of 1,200, and was under the command of Brigadier General Ashton; South West District, with headquarters at Bandon, had a strength of 1,020 and was in charge of Dalton's friend Commandant General Tom Ennis; Eastern District, with headquarters at Fermoy, had a strength of 500 and was under the control of Commandant McGrath; Western District, with headquarters at Macroom, also had a strength of 500 and was under Colonel Commandant Peadar Conlon. Dalton thus had overall command of forces with a strength of 3,220.[39]

Dalton Decides to Resign

Some time in late 1922, Dalton took a momentous step – he decided to leave the army. It was a decision that caused much surprise when it eventually became known. The historian Michael Hopkinson, in his book on the Civil War, says that Dalton 'left the command in mysterious circumstances'.[40] Dalton, with his experience, bravery, leadership abilities and his capacity for tactical and strategic thinking, was a huge loss to the National Army. In light of his record and achievements, had he stayed in the army he might have risen even higher, possibly even attaining the position of Chief of Staff. In the years following his resignation, Dalton declined to state publicly why he abandoned a highly promising military career.

In an interview in July 1970, Dalton still did not wish to discuss publicly the reasons why he left the army.[41] However, by the late 1970s, he was more willing to discuss the decision. He explained his reasons in an RTÉ series of radio interviews with Pádraig Ó Raghallaigh broadcast in 1977, and in his RTÉ TV interview with Cathal O'Shannon broadcast the following year. Dalton told how he was concerned over the passing of legislation authorizing military courts to execute republican prisoners for certain offences. Though Dalton had earlier lobbied for the death penalty for 'Irregulars' caught in the possession of arms, when the government brought in formal arrangements for such death sentences he appeared reluctant to go along with the policy. He may well have discussed the matter with his friend Tom Ennis, one of his senior fellow-officers in the command and they may have come to the same conclusion. Ennis was said to have refused to have any republicans executed in his area.[42]

The appointment to Dalton's command staff of a young Legal Officer, Lieutenant Commandant Charles Wyse-Power to help with the arrangements for military trials may have helped to concentrate his mind. Wyse-Power, a former actor with the Abbey Theatre and a Trinity College-educated barrister, was the son of Jennie Wyse Power, businesswoman, suffragist and founder member of the republican women's organization Cumann na mBan.

Dalton said that he went to see the army commander, General Mulcahy. He pointed out that he had a prison in Cork with 1,800 prisoners, caught in the possession of arms and so forth. Was he expected to try these people and execute them? Mulcahy said that was not expected of him, but the government had got to the stage where it decided that strong action would have to be taken.[43] Still concerned over what might be required of him under the new legislation, Dalton believed the only honourable course open to him would be to resign. Dalton described the interview with Mulcahy as friendly, and said the Chief of Staff was understanding. Mulcahy suggested that if Dalton had the same type of responsibility that he himself as Chief of Staff had, he might not be so broadminded. It was a gentle reproof. Dalton may have decided to delay talking about his reasons for resigning because he did not wish to let down the Free State side, or cause embarrassment to senior figures such as Mulcahy or Cosgrave.

Mulcahy clearly believed that the State could still make use of Dalton's talents, and he sent him to see William T. Cosgrave, the Acting Chairman of the Provisional Government. Because of the threat of assassination, Cosgrave and most of his ministers resided at their offices in the heavily-guarded Government Buildings on Merrion Street. It was at the latter location that Dalton was interviewed by Cosgrave, who was apparently surprised at Dalton's decision to leave the army. Cosgrave wanted to assist a man who had done the Free State some service, and offered Dalton the post of Clerk of the new Senate. Dalton accepted. Cosgrave arranged for Dalton to get advice on the performance of his Senate duties from the Ceann Comhairle of the Dáil, Michael Hayes, and the Clerk of the Dáil, Colm Ó Murchadha.

According to Military Pension records, Dalton resigned from the army on 11 November.[44] However, he continued for some weeks in his post, and was on the army payroll until 9 December. Even as he prepared to leave, he remained anxious over the lack of resources for his forces. On 18 November he wrote an outspoken letter to General Mulcahy complaining about the lack of transport and equipment generally, and warning of possible dire consequences if deficiencies were not addressed.[45] Dalton copied the letter to the other members of General Headquarters - the Adjutant General; the Director of Organization, and the Director of Intelligence. Dalton seemed to be in very low spirits when he penned the letter. In his long, anguished and rather emotional communication, Dalton said that transport continued to be 'hopelessly impoverished down here'. Unless the matter was immediately attended to, the garrisons must continue as they are – 'comparatively ineffective'. They could rest assured that their weakness was well known to the Irregulars, 'and the fullest advantage will be taken of it'. He also complained about the cost of food being bought by the army and said that where possible the army should have issued stores, bought wholesale from wholesale houses, and thus avoid enormous retail profit charges. He complained about the lack of visible presence on the ground of Free State troops, saying that one may travel seventy or eighty miles in parts of County Cork without meeting even one Free State soldier. He admitted: 'I am beginning to lose hope.'

Dalton complained of a lack of zeal and discipline. He returned again to the issue of transport – 'a horrible lack of transport, competent drivers, lack of machine guns and equipment generally – spares for motors…' He referred to several Cork priests who told him that the public 'are absolutely disgusted and disheartened'. Dalton wrote that he hoped he did not look as if he were 'scolding ye'. 'I quite appreciate the difficulties but, old friend, we must speed up or the poor country will run into bankruptcy and ruin.' He concluded on a bleak note: 'In Cork we are going to be beaten unless we wake up and at once. The state of things is very bad – it is my plain duty to say so.'

Dalton's Account of Bealnablath Ambush

In the third week of November, Dalton found time to write up an account of the ambush that resulted in the death of Michael Collins three months previously. The headline on the typewritten account was in capital letters, 'THE DEATH OF MICHEAL O'COILEAIN'. A carbon copy of the typescript still survives in the possession of the Dalton family. The document is signed 'J. Emmet Dalton' and the date is 23 November 1922.[46] Emmet Dalton's youngest brother Dermot Patrick was only about three years old at this stage. Dalton dedicated his written account to his young brother with a handwritten note on the typescript: 'I dedicate this, my first little work to my youngest brother Pat, hoping that when he witnesses the improvement in Ireland's welfare, he will occasionally allow his mind to dwell upon the memory of my dearest friend [Michael Collins].'

Later in November, Dalton was outraged by yet another booby trap bomb explosion, this time at Ballyvolane, near Cork city, which killed one of his men and injured two other soldiers. It was reported that body parts of Sergeant Major McCann were found in a field some distance away. Dalton issued a proclamation in the *Cork Examiner* on 25 November stating that his soldiers had been the victims of a 'diabolical death trap'. He announced every time a road mine was found, he would use prisoners to clear it from the road. Dalton declared that the men killed or wounded were doing their duty to the people, 'a duty of extreme peril'. He went on: 'The "trap" mine is an improvement on the German "Booby Trap" which was decried by the civilized world – its victims have scarcely a chance – and casualties are mangled beyond recognition. Methods such as this would not be countenanced by any man claiming for himself the title of soldier.'

The treatment and sanitary conditions of prisoners held in Cork came into focus in late 1922. Some weeks before, in September, there had been trouble at Cork County Gaol. Thirty-nine prisoners escaped by means of a tunnel; there was also a hunger strike, as well as a disturbances during which a prisoner was shot dead. On 22 November Dalton sent an urgent message to General Mulcahy stating that a commission was appointed by Cork Corporation to investigate the prison conditions. Dalton needed guidance as to how to deal with this development: 'Wire me instructions. Urgent.'[47]

At the end of November, Dalton seemed to become a little more optimistic. On the night of 29 November, he sent a message to Mulcahy, 'Military position here very satisfactory, improving daily, expect further good stunts.'[48] Some days previously, the IRA's Cork No. 3 Brigade commander Tom Hales was taken prisoner by Tom

Ennis's troops. This breakthrough may have boosted Dalton's flagging morale. On 20 November National Army troops in Cork city had made another important arrest when they captured Mick Kenny, who apparently commanded the city's Active Service Unit.[49] Also arrested in November was the County Cork anti-Treaty figure, Martin Corry.

Gunner McPeak Defects to the Republicans with Slievenamon

In early December startling news brought back bitter memories of the Bealnablath ambush. John 'Jock' McPeak, the gunner in the armoured car when Michael Collins was killed, had abandoned his post at Bandon and defected to the enemy, taking the vehicle with him. Losing a precious and much-valued Rolls Royce Whippet was a serious blow to the National Army's Cork command. Only about ten days before his defection, McPeak was travelling with General Tom Ennis from Bantry in *Slievenamon* when the vehicle was ambushed near Drimoleague. After Ennis and other occupants of the car emerged to clear a barrier, fire was opened on them by an IRA ambush party. After a lengthy firefight the armoured car managed to push through the remains of the barrier and continue on its way. Like at Bealnablath, McPeak's Vickers machine gun in the armoured car experienced a stoppage.

After McPeak's defection, the stoppages that had occurred with the Vickers at Bealnablath and Drimoleague acquired sinister significance in the minds of some. This helped form the basis of a conspiracy theory that McPeak had been in league with the IRA all along and was responsible for the death of Collins. This was highly unlikely. McPeak, born in Scotland of Irish parents, had served as a machine gunner with the British Army at the Somme and in Palestine during the Great War. A native of Peterhead, he had been involved in Irish republican activity, and was jailed in Glasgow for possessing arms apparently destined for the IRA. After release from prison in early 1922, McPeak went to Dublin and joined the National Army, stating later that he did not know the difference at this stage between the pro- and anti-Treaty versions of the IRA.

After its capture, *Slievenamon* was soon in action against the National Army but was recovered by the Free Staters. After the Civil War, McPeak was arrested in Glasgow and in July 1923 extradited to Ireland where he was jailed for six years for the theft of the armoured car. The Special Branch of New Scotland Yard reported that McPeak was suspected of being in touch with Communists on behalf of 'Irish extremists'.[50] In later life, having changed his name by deed poll to John Logan, he was married with a family and living in Essex, and working as a crane driver. In 1971, the year before his death, McPeak gave an interview to the *Irish Independent* in which he refuted any suggestion he had shot Collins, pointing out that he had the Vickers machine canted upwards during the ambush, firing at the attackers on the high ground overlooking the road.[51] Dalton may well have read the interview with McPeak, but did not make any comment in the public domain.

McPeak claimed that one of the reasons he defected was disgust at the shooting of two prisoners at Dublin Hill in late September 1922. This is the incident referred to above, in which Sean O'Donoghue was fatally injured and Seamus Collins wounded. He said he heard shooting after the prisoners were put into a Crossley tender and found one man dead and the other injured.

Dalton's departure from the army meant that the Free State had lost an outstanding soldier. The army had some trouble finding a successor to the very capable Cork commander. Colonel Commandant Stephen Murphy was informed on 14 December that he was to act as General Officer Commanding (GOC) for the present. Then the Cork Command was informed on 21 December that Commandant Seamus Hogan was to be appointed GOC.[52] Seán Ó Murthuile took over the post for a while in January 1923, and was then succeeded by General David Reynolds.[53] Meanwhile, the army's temporary occupation of the Imperial Hotel came to an end in January. The owners of the hotel would later sue the state claiming they were still owed money for accommodating the army.

Just a few weeks after Dalton stepped down, the Cork command carried out its only official execution of an anti-Treaty fighter. William Healy had been captured after an attempt by republicans to burn down the home of Michael Collins's sister Mary Collins Powell. He was executed by firing squad at Cork County Gaol on 13 March 1923. Dalton was by now working in a less contentious role as Clerk of the Senate. Looking back in later years on his time as army commander in Cork, Dalton said that he tried 'to keep the copybook clean'. He reflected that 'other commands had their problems'. This was probably a reference to neighbouring County Kerry where the Civil War was particularly vicious, and where notorious incidents such as the Ballyseedy atrocity had taken place, involving republican prisoners being tied to a mine and blown up. Dalton told RTÉ interviewer Pádraig Ó Raghallaigh, 'We like to think we fought a clean fight.'[54]

CHAPTER THIRTEEN

Senate Clerk

As he settled into his prestigious new post of Clerk of the Senate in late 1922, Emmet Dalton may not have felt particularly welcome in his new surroundings. Dalton found himself at the centre of a dispute. He had been given the job by William T. Cosgrave, President of the Executive Council, in advance of the Senate convening for the first time. Members of the Senate, while they had nothing against Dalton personally, believed that Cosgrave did not have the authority to make this appointment. They insisted it was the prerogative of the Senate itself, not of the head of government, to appoint the Clerk and other senior officials.

Lord Glenavy, Cathaoirleach (Chairman) of the Senate, took particular exception to Cosgrave's action. Cosgrave, for his part, argued that he had the right to make the appointment. James Henry Mussen Campbell, 1st Baron Glenavy, came from Terenure, Dublin and qualified as a barrister. He served as a Unionist MP for a Dublin constituency and had been elevated to the post of Lord Chief Justice of Ireland, in which he served until 1921. He had a reputation for arrogance, and was one of the members of the Anglo-Irish ascendancy class who had been appointed to the Senate by Cosgrave.

In the interests of inclusiveness, Cosgrave gave particular representation in the Senate to the Protestant minority, many of them former southern Unionists. Members of this community were feeling vulnerable as a result of the Troubles. In appointing Dalton as Clerk of the Senate, Cosgrave may have considered that Dalton's background as a British Army officer would help him establish a rapport with this element in the Senate.

Among the Senators were seven peers, a dowager countess, five baronets and several knights. In addition, of course, there were figures from other elements of Irish society, including the literary world – examples being the poet William Butler Yeats and Oliver St. John Gogarty, poet, writer and surgeon. It was said that one of the achievements of the Senate was to show that those from the Nationalist and Unionist traditions could work together for the common good. However, the country was still unsettled and the Civil War was still in progress. Ironically, by entering the Free State Senate, the former landed gentry, and others, were to be targeted all the more by anti-Treaty republicans. Many would suffer intimidation and have to endure the trauma of having their houses and valuable possessions burned.

The weeks preceding the opening of the Senate in December 1922 was a particularly grim period in the Civil War. There had been increasing frustration at the level of casualties being inflicted on the National Army and in October, as indicated earlier, the government pushed through emergency powers legislation with draconian measures that permitted military courts to impose penalties, including the death penalty, for a variety of offences, including the illegal possession of arms or ammunition. Soon, the executions began. Four young men caught in possession of arms were executed on 17 November. The prominent republican Erskine Childers was executed on 24 November for being found in possession of a small revolver said to have been given to him by Michael Collins.

Shocked by the executions, the anti-Treaty IRA chief Liam Lynch sent out an order that all TDs who had voted for the 'Murder Bill' should be shot at sight. In line with this policy, on 7 December, in an attack in Dublin, republicans shot and killed a Dáil deputy, Sean Hales, and wounded another deputy, Pádraic Ó Máille. Hales had, in fact, been absent from the debate on the Bill and had not voted. Dalton had conferred with Hales less than an hour before the Bealnablath ambush in which Michael Collins died.

Members of the government were appalled at the assassination of Sean Hales and feared that if such killings were to continue the very survival of the state could be put in jeopardy. The Cabinet made a ruthless decision to execute four anti-Treaty prisoners in reprisal even though they had nothing to do with the Hales killing. The four, who had all been captured after the siege of the Four Courts, were shot by firing squad at Mountjoy Prison on 8 December – Rory O'Connor, Liam Mellows, Dick Barrett and Joe McKelvey. In London, *The Times* commented: 'The British Government never adopted such drastic measures, even in the darkest days of the fighting before the Truce...' The Labour Party, official opposition in the Dáil, vigorously condemned the executions, Labour Deputy Cathal O'Shannon describing them as the worst crime in Ireland in the previous ten years.

In response to the executions, the IRA chief, Liam Lynch, broadened the targets for reprisals to include Senators and newspaper editors. In fact, no more assassinations of members of the Oireachtas (the parliament comprising Dáil and Senate) would take place, although family members of some politicians would be killed, and the homes and possessions of members of the Oireachtas including Senators, would be destroyed. Favourite targets for destruction included the big houses and mansions of the Anglo-Irish Senators. Members of the Senate were facing into a very turbulent time.

On 10 December, the day before the opening of the Senate, there was a reminder of the threat to members of the Oireachtas when anti-Treaty republicans raided the Dublin home of pro-Treaty TD Sean McGarry. As they sprinkled petrol around to burn the dwelling, the raiders ignored the frantic pleas of women in the house that there were children upstairs. The house went up in flames and McGarry's disabled daughter was rescued but his seven-year-old son Emmet was badly burned and died. The government pressed ahead with its ruthless policy of capital punishment, ultimately officially executing up to eighty-one republican prisoners.

It was against a very tense background that the first meeting of the Senate took place at the museum adjacent to Leinster House on Monday, 11 December 1922, with Dalton as Clerk. A Free State government representative, Eamon Duggan, Minister without Portfolio, entered the chamber and announced that he had been authorized by the Governor-General to administer the Oath to the members. This was, of course, the Oath that had been rejected by the anti-Treaty element and which was a crucial factor in the Civil War. With the Oath duly administered, the Senate began its work, electing a Committee on Standing Orders, and a temporary Chairman, and then adjourning until the next day, when the formal opening of the new Free State Parliament or Oireachtas would took place. It was a bright, sunny day as the Governor-General, Tim Healy, was driven by limousine from his official residence, the former Vice-Regal Lodge in the Phoenix Park, to Leinster House for the opening ceremony. There were no crowds of onlookers on the street, just a few spectators at the main gates. Healy was accompanied by two aides, Liam Tobin and Tom Cullen, who had been key members of the IRA intelligence staff under Michael Collins. Today they were assigned a ceremonial role. However, the two would have been more than capable of protecting Healy if anyone tried to harm the Governor-General.

After a private session, Lord Glenavy was elected Chairman of the Senate and James Douglas was elected Vice-Chairman. These men were effectively Dalton's superiors and he would work closely with them. Douglas, a businessman and Quaker, had been a Home Ruler and was noted for his charitable work and his liberal, tolerant views. After the Dáil approved the Treaty, at the request of Michael Collins, he served on the committee charged with drawing up a constitution for the new Free State. Dalton got on well with him and liked and respected him.

Now that they were members of the upper house of the parliament, some of the Senators were eager to assert their independence. When Lord Glenavy and a delegation of Senators met the President of the Executive Council, Mr Cosgrave, they insisted that the Senate had a constitutional right to appoint the Clerk. Cosgrave pointed out that he was in a difficult situation in regard to Dalton, apparently suggesting that Dalton had taken the position after being 'induced' to resign a very high position in the Free State Army. Glenavy indicated that they would interview Dalton, and, if satisfied with his credentials, would favourably consider him for the post.[1]

After the Christmas recess, the Senate met on 10 January 1923. The Committee of the Senate reported on a number of matters, including the appointment of senior staff. The Committee was satisfied to recommend the appointment of General Dalton – in effect, to rubber-stamp Cosgrave's decision. (Two Committee members, Senator Farren and Colonel Moore, dissented.) However, it was clear that Glenavy and the Committee were asserting the right of the Senate to make such senior appointments. The Senate formally voted to appoint Dalton as Clerk, at a salary of £1,000 a year, with Donal O'Sullivan appointed as Assistant Clerk and Diarmid Coffey as Second Assistant Clerk. Later, in 1924, a compromise arrangement would be worked out whereby the Clerk and Clerk Assistant to the Senate would be appointed by the President of the Executive Council on the recommendation of the Chairman of the Senate and the Minister for Finance.[2]

Dalton's two colleagues were men with lively minds and interesting backgrounds. Donal O'Sullivan was born in Liverpool of County Kerry parents and joined the British civil service in London, later being transferred to Dublin. He learned Irish during visits to the Kerry Gaeltacht. He served as an officer in the Royal Navy in the Great War and qualified as a barrister. He would later become a noted expert in Irish constitutional matters and Irish folk music. In 1940 he published a learned study, *The Irish Free State and its Senate* – oddly, Emmet Dalton does not get a single mention in the book. Diarmid Coffey was a barrister from a Dublin literary family. He had been a crew member of the *Kelpie*, which transported rifles that were landed for the Irish Volunteers at Kilcoole, County Wicklow in August 1914. He was an unusual figure in nationalist circles in Dublin in that he was an atheist. During the Civil War he served as a lieutenant in the National Army, and captained a patrol boat on the River Shannon.

Having had his appointment as Clerk approved by the Senate, Dalton now faced criticism in the Dáil of his appointment. In a debate in the Dáil on 19 January 1923, Labour leader Thomas Johnson said they should not be asked to concur in the appointment of Dalton and other officials as they knew nothing about these persons or their qualifications.[3] Another Labour member of the Dáil, Cathal O'Shannon, also questioned the appointment of Dalton to the important Senate post. He said he was told, and he did not know if it was true or not, that the gentleman appointed as Clerk did not have a working knowledge of Irish. He also questioned why a man who had been a senior officer in the army should come into a post like this: 'It seemed to me personally a rather extraordinary thing that a Major-General in the Army – and I understand that he has been a very dashing soldier, indeed – should come out of the Army or be brought out of the Army and come into a post like this.'

Despite the misgivings of the Labour members, the Dáil voted to approve the appointment of Dalton and the other Senate officials. It cannot have been a pleasant experience for Dalton to have his qualifications queried in such a public manner. As mentioned by Deputy O'Shannon, an issue arose in regard to Dalton's fluency, or lack of it, in the Irish language and the impact this might have on the performance of his official duties. Dalton had learned Irish at O'Connell's and Roscrea but was not fluent in the language. The Senate heard that two Assistant Clerks had been appointed who had good Irish, because of the need to ensure that there were personnel employed who could ensure that all the proceedings and official documents could be dealt with not only in English but in Irish, as the Constitution demanded. The question of Dalton's inadequacy in Irish gave Glenavy an opportunity to score a point vis-a-vis Cosgrave.

In his new role of Senate Clerk, Dalton was still interested in finding ways of ending the Civil War. He took particular notice of Liam Deasy's capture in County Tipperary on 18 January 1923. Deasy had apparently been having serious doubts about continuing with the struggle, and as a prisoner agreed to publicly advocate an end to the war. He avoided the firing squad but his statement caused outrage among republican leaders such as Liam Lynch, Tom Barry and Ernie O'Malley. On 13 February Dalton sent a memorandum to Senator Douglas, who was eager to bring about a peace settlement, recommending that a truce be called.[4] Dalton expressed the belief that 80 per cent of the Irregulars were only looking for a chance 'to get out and save their faces before their comrades...' He saw no point in talking to anti-Treaty leader Éamon de Valera 'and his alleged government'. Dalton maintained that their tactics should be to invite the acknowledged Irregular military leaders to a meeting where they could discuss the terms upon which a truce could be called. 'We should view the truce as a truce of surrender – but then call it a truce of peace or a compromise.' He suggested that in public comments it could be stated that the government has offered a very generous amnesty and that it was the action of 'Mr Decies' [Deasy] that was responsible for this amnesty. However, hostilities were destined to continue.

In March 1923 Dalton travelled to London to visit the House of Lords. He was accompanied by James Douglas, vice-chairman of the Senate. It would appear that they wanted to see how the House of Lords went about its business, and to learn any lessons that might be relevant to the Senate back in Dublin. According to a news report some question arose as to where they were to sit. It was finally decided by the officials of the House to accommodate them in the Foreign Visitors' Gallery.[5] While Dalton seemed to have a good working relationship with Douglas, he found that Glenavy could be unpredictable and difficult.

Attacks on Homes of Senators

Meanwhile, members of the Senate and their families were coming under enormous pressure from anti-Treaty republicans. The burning of houses was a particular tactic. In December 1922, armed men ordered a family out of their home, a fine detached residence, Clonard, at Terenure, Dublin and then set it on fire. It was the home of Lord Glenavy's son Gordon Campbell, a senior civil servant with the Irish Free State. Also in December, men threw bombs through the windows of the Dublin business premises of one of the few female Senators, Mrs Wyse Power. Worse was to follow in early 1923. In January and February that year, it was estimated that thirty-seven houses of Senators were burned by the anti-Treaty forces.[6] Among the Senators whose mansions were destroyed was Senator John Bagwell, whose home near Clonmel, County Tipperary was burned with its valuable works of art and one of the finest private libraries in the country. Senator Oliver St. John Gogarty, a good friend of Dalton's, was kidnapped from his Dublin home but managed to escape by swimming the Liffey. However his home in Connemara, Renvyle, was destroyed with its collection of paintings and its extensive library. Shots were also fired into the house of poet W.B. Yeats, with a bullet striking close to Yeats's wife and toddler.[7]

Senator Douglas would later recall this period as one of great tension for Dáil Deputies and Senators alike. Threats were made that they might be shot if they did not resign, and Senators were told their homes would be burned. Douglas declined a government offer of armed guards on his house, though he received many threatening letters. He tried to keep them from his wife but she saw some of them and could not sleep.[8]

Many senior republicans now viewed the war as a lost cause. However, Liam Lynch was determined to press on with the fight. On 10 April 1923 Lynch was shot and fatally wounded in the Knockmealdown Mountains. He was succeeded as Chief of Staff by Frank Aiken, who issued a ceasefire and 'dump arms' order on 24 May. This effectively ended the Civil War. Donal O'Sullivan, the Senate Assistant Clerk who would later succeed Dalton as Clerk, was impressed by the bravery of the Senators during the Civil War. In his book about the Free State Senate, he paid tribute to the Senators who persisted in their work despite the danger, 'when no man knew on whom the blow might next fall...'[9]

As August 1923 came around, memories of the ambush at Bealnablath in which Michael Collins died were very much on Dalton's mind. His account of the ambush, which he wrote in November 1922, a few months after the death of Collins, was published in the *Freeman's Journal* on the first anniversary of the death of the Commander-in-Chief.[10] On the day of that first anniversary, Dalton joined in the commemoration ceremonies at Bealnablath. Among the army officers present was Commandant Sean O'Connell, who had also been with Collins at Bealnablath, and who was now serving as aide-de-camp to the Governor-General, Tim Healy. Among others present was Mrs Mary Collins Powell, Collins's sister.[11]

O'Connell realized that Dalton's account of the final moments of Michael Collins would be of great interest to Lady Lavery. O'Connell had himself met Lady Lavery and knew of her devotion to the Big Fellow. A few weeks after Dalton's article appeared, O'Connell sent a copy to Lady Lavery in London, and in a covering letter endorsed Dalton's account, saying it was 'fairly accurate'. O'Connell also gave details of how he had carried out Lady Lavery's instructions in regard to securing rosary beads which she had placed on Collins's grave.[12]

Emmet Dalton and wife Alice had their first child in December 1923. The esteem in which Dalton was held by senior figures in the government was illustrated by the fact that William T. Cosgrave acted as godfather for the infant boy when he was baptised. The child was christened Emmet Michael Dalton, the middle name commemorating Michael Collins.[13] Dalton was unwell around this period. The *Freeman's Journal* reported in early January 1924 that he had been seriously ill, was now recovered, but 'still confined to his bed'.[14] No details were given as to the nature of the illness.

Winston Churchill, Lady Lavery and Kevin O'Higgins

While serving as Clerk of the Senate, one of the places where Dalton socialized was the fashionable bar at the Theatre Royal, one of Dublin's premier theatres. He became friendly with the manager, J.H. Hamilton, and sometimes Dalton and others would adjourn to Hamilton's office for a drink and conversation. One evening Dalton was approached at the Royal by Alfie Byrne, who had served as an MP with the Irish Parliamentary Party, and was now an Independent TD, and would go on to become one of the best-known Lord Mayors of Dublin. Dalton and Byrne adjourned to Hamilton's office, and there they met a well-known bookmaker, Richard Duggan. Byrne and Duggan had a problem. They were organizing a sweepstake, with some of the funds going to a local hospital, and an office had been set up in Switzerland to get around legal difficulties. However, post destined for the lottery office in Switzerland was being blocked in Britain, where sweepstakes were illegal. Duggan had gone guarantor for the prize money and he faced a huge financial loss if the sweepstake collapsed.

Dalton later described in his RTÉ radio interview with Pádraig Ó Raghallaigh how Alfie Byrne asked him if he would approach Winston Churchill.[15] Churchill at this stage was Chancellor of the Exchequer. Dalton got permission from the Senate Chairman, Lord Glenavy for three days leave and he travelled to London on the evening mail boat with Byrne and Duggan. In London, Dalton phoned his friend Lady Lavery describing how he needed to meet Churchill. The following day she invited him to tea at her residence, 5 Cromwell Place. When he arrived, a footman announced him as 'General Dalton'. Winston Churchill was present, as were some others, including Commander Joseph Kenworthy, a former naval officer who had become a Liberal MP, and a Government Minister, William Bridgeman. Eventually, various guests withdrew, leaving Dalton in the presence of Lady Lavery, Churchill, Kenworthy and Bridgeman. Lady Lavery explained to Churchill why Dalton was there, and the nature of the problem he was trying to solve. Churchill remarked that the hospital to benefit from the sweepstake seemed like a good cause and asked Bridgeman if something could be done about it. It was indicated to Dalton that at least some of the mail would go through.

In his RTÉ interview with Ó Raghallaigh, Dalton told how he reported back to his friends who were pleased at his progress and very grateful to Lady Lavery. Eventually, Spencer Freeman, who was based at the office in Switzerland, reported that they were inundated with mail, and that all was well – the sweepstake was a success. This is one of the sweepstakes that was the prelude to the highly lucrative Irish Hospital Sweepstake that would involve both Duggan and Freeman, and would be headed for many years by Joe McGrath, who had been part of Michael Collins's inner circle.[16]

Dalton returned to Dublin and what happened next was to come as a big surprise. He received a summons from the Home Affairs Minister, Kevin O'Higgins. O'Higgins asked him if he had been to London recently and Dalton confirmed that he had indeed been there. O'Higgins asked him if he had left his post without permission. Dalton denied this was the case, pointing out that he had permission from Lord Glenavy to be absent. O'Higgins asked him if he had seen Lady Lavery and Winston Churchill. Dalton confirmed that he had – Lady Lavery was a friend, and he had been asked to speak to Churchill for a very deserving reason. O'Higgins accused Dalton of misrepresenting the Irish Government, a charge which Dalton vehemently denied. Then O'Higgins revealed that the British had been holding up the mail at his request, and that Dalton had put him in an impossible position. Dalton said he was very sorry, but he had no way of knowing of the Minister's involvement in this matter.[17] O'Higgins had emerged as a strong opponent of legalizing sweepstakes even in aid of worthy causes, voicing his suspicion that the promoters of such sweepstakes were not true philanthropists.

O'Higgins may well have learned of Dalton's visit to London through Lady Lavery. It would only emerge in later decades that the married father of two had developed a romantic friendship with Lady Lavery. She was greatly upset in 1927 when O'Higgins was assassinated by IRA gunmen, just five years on from her grief over Michael Collins's death. Following Dalton's confrontation with O'Higgins, the two men had no further contact. Dalton's assessment of O'Higgins was that he could be a 'very good friend', but a 'very bitter enemy'.[18]

Charlie Dalton and the Army Mutiny

In 1924, long-simmering discontent in the Free State Army burst to the surface in the affair that became known as the Army Mutiny. Emmet Dalton did not make any public comment on the mutiny controversy – he was a public servant at this period. But he may well have had a certain sympathy with the dissidents if only on the basis of his personal links to the leaders. One of them was Liam Tobin who had campaigned with Dalton in the Civil War and was now serving as aide-de-camp to the Governor-General. The other was Dalton's own brother Charlie. Emmet was also close to some of the other officers involved, and who, like himself, had been part of the Michael Collins coterie.

The army dissidents had formed their own group, the IRA Organisation (IRAO). The first formal meeting of discontented officers to discuss the situation in the army was held on 29 January 1923.[19] Those attending could be described as Collins loyalists, and they included both Emmet and his brother Charlie, even though Emmet was no longer in the army. Some of Emmet's close associates were there, including Tom Ennis, Pat McCrea and Sean O'Connell. Emmet was present the following April at a general meeting of the group that had been formed. However, there is no indication that he attended subsequent meetings. Possibly, having regard to his position as a public servant, he may have decided it was inappropriate for him to be further involved. However, his brother Charlie took a prominent role in the dissident officers' group.

Members of the Army Council of the National Army had revived the secret Irish Republican Brotherhood (IRB) and officers like Tobin and Charlie Dalton felt excluded. The Tobin group response was to form the IRAO, comprised of pre-Truce IRA veterans. They had a sympathizer in the Cabinet, Joe McGrath, who mediated between the disaffected officers and the government. The head of government, William T. Cosgrave, President of the Executive Council, tried to humour the dissidents in private meetings.

The catalyst for the outbreak of open protest was resentment over massive army demobilization. At the end of the Civil War, the cash-strapped Free State was saddled with a huge army and it was found necessary to drastically reduce the strength, while some retained officers were reduced in rank. Men were being let go from the military at a time of widespread unemployment and there seemed little future for them. There was a perception that officers who had served in the British Army and who had never been in the IRA were getting preference over men who had fought the British as IRA Volunteers. The influence of trusted members of the Michael Collins inner-circle such as Liam Tobin and Charlie Dalton had begun to diminish. They no longer had a patron like the Big Fellow to fight their corner for them. Risteárd Mulcahy, son of General Mulcahy, has suggested that Tobin, Charlie Dalton and other leaders of the mutiny were 'never reconciled' to the death of Collins, and resented having to serve under another leader.[20]

On the night of Thursday, 6 March 1924, acting on behalf of the IRAO, Major General Tobin and Colonel Dalton sent an ultimatum to Mr Cosgrave. They demanded an end to the reforms taking place within the army, including demobilization; they demanded the removal of the most senior general staff officers, including General Richard Mulcahy, who held the joint posts of Minister of Defence and Commander in Chief; and stated that they and the IRAO members had accepted the Anglo-Irish Treaty of 1921 as a 'means to secure and maintain a Republican form of government' and that the Cosgrave government no longer had this aim in view. They insisted on a conference with the government to discuss how a republic could be achieved. Meanwhile, there were reports of officers resigning, and also of incidents in various parts of the country, involving officers absconding with arms or with stores. Tensions within the Cabinet on the issue led to the resignation of Joe McGrath as Minister for Industry and Commerce, in sympathy with the IRAO.

Cosgrave raised the Tobin-Dalton demands in the Dáil on Monday, 11 March, saying the communication from the army officers 'is a challenge to the democratic foundations of the State, to the very basis of parliamentary representation and of responsible government'. The Tobin-Dalton group backed down. The following day Cosgrave read out to the Dáil a contrite second letter from the group, accepting that both police and army had to be subject to civil authority and claiming that the original ultimatum had been inspired by 'a serious menace to the proper administration of the Army'.

However, the dissent rumbled on, and there were still concerns in the upper echelons of the army about the intentions of the IRAO. Amid fears that the IRAO was plotting a coup, army intelligence, under Colonel Michael J. Costello, maintained close surveillance on the activities of IRAO activists, through phone tapping and other methods. On 18 March the dissidents assembled at Devlin's pub on Parnell Street, Dublin, an old haunt of Michael Collins. Two lorry loads of troops were sent to the pub. Liam Tobin and Charlie Dalton avoided arrest but some others were detained. They included Pat McCrea, a close friend of Emmet Dalton's; Christopher O'Malley, with whom Emmet had shared a hideout during the War of Independence, and Joe Dolan, who had been with Emmet at Bealnablath. Among the others were such Collins loyalists as Jim Slattery, Frank Thornton and Charles Byrne. They were released after a few days.

The Executive Council met the day after the raid. Mr Cosgrave, President of the Council, was absent due to illness. There was concern over the army's action in raiding the pub. There had long been rivalry in the Cabinet between Kevin O'Higgins and Richard Mulcahy, and O'Higgins was highly critical of the army raid. Mulcahy defended the action, insisting it was legal. However, the Council decided to request the resignations of the Chief of Staff, Adjutant General and Quartermaster General – two resigned and one was sacked after refusing to resign. It also asked head of government William Cosgrave to remove Mulcahy as Minister of Defence. Mulcahy stepped down from his positions and General O'Duffy was put in charge of the army. In the latter part of March, Liam Tobin and Charlie Dalton, as well as many other officers associated with the IRAO resigned from the army. One of those who left was the head of the Military Air Service, Jack McSweeney, who had taken part in Dalton's air rescue scheme for Michael Collins. Another who resigned was Sean O'Connell, who had been at Bealnablath.[21] Jimmy Conroy, who had also been at Bealnablath, was another officer who left the army at this period. (It emerged in recent years that Conroy, who emigrated to America, was a suspect for the anti-semitic murder of Emmanuel Kahn, one of two Jewish men shot dead in Dublin in late 1923.[22])

Emmet Dalton, still working at his important job in the Senate, stayed out of the mutiny controversy. But in reports of the mutiny saga in newspapers at home and abroad, references to Charles Dalton sometimes included the information that he was the brother of Emmet Dalton. The saga had claimed a number of notable casualties – Joe McGrath; Richard Mulcahy and three members of the Army Council who lost their jobs, and members of the IRAO who left the army. Richard Mulcahy would in later years make a comeback, becoming leader of Fine Gael, successor party to Cumann na nGaedheal, and serving as a Government Minister.

On 22 August 1924, the second anniversary of the death of Michael Collins, Charlie Dalton, as secretary of the IRAO, organized a Solemn Requiem Mass at St. Peter's Church, Phibsboro, Dublin, for the repose of the soul of the Big Fellow. There was a big attendance of former army officers who had been involved in the IRAO. Among others listed in newspaper reports as being present were members of the Dalton family. Emmet's wife Alice was present, as was James F. Dalton, father of Charlie and Emmet, but Emmet himself appears to have been absent – probably a wise move in light of his public service job. A few days later, on 26 August, the IRAO organized a big gathering of friends and associates of Collins in Vaughan's Hotel. It was reported that all the officers who were with Collins when he was shot were present, with the exception of Major General Dalton.[23]

The army mutiny affair, the spat between the IRB and the IRAO factions within the army, led to the formation of a short-lived breakaway group from Cumann na nGaedheal. This was the National Group, formed by Joe McGrath and eight other TDs who resigned from the Cumann na nGaedheal party. In late October 1924 they vacated their Dail seats and only one, Sean Milroy, contested one of the seats in the March 1925 by-elections. Among those who supported him was James F. Dalton. He became a member of Cumann na nGaedheal after it was formed in April 1923, was actively involved in fund-raising for the new party, and also became a Peace Commissioner. Milroy failed to gain a seat, and James F. Dalton's active involvement in Irish politics appeared to come to an end.

During all this turmoil, Emmet Dalton retained his interest in a wide range of sports. Apart from playing soccer and golf and following horse racing, he also played cricket. In the summer of 1925, while still Clerk of the Senate, he took part as a sidecar passenger in a challenging 24-hour motor cycle trial, and met with a serious accident. The driver of the motorcycle was Frank Wallen, an Irish motorcycle racing pioneer.[24] It appears that Wallen took a bend too quickly at Grange, County Sligo, and the machine did a complete somersault. The motor cycle was badly damaged, and while Mr Wallen suffered no serious injury, Dalton sustained a broken collar bone and slight concussion.

Dalton's Resignation as Senate Clerk

During his term as Senate Clerk, Dalton became concerned about some family difficulties with the banks. In his RTÉ interview with Cathal O'Shannon, he said that he had the misfortune 'to have backed bills for relatives with the bank, and the bank was calling these in, and the wherewithal was not there to meet them…'[25] Dalton said that he explained the situation to Lord Glenavy and to Mr. Cosgrave, and that they made overtures to the banks about 'sparing' Dalton. However, the bankers were not for turning on the issue. It is likely that Dalton was particularly concerned about a pending court case in which a bank was bringing an action arising out of his father's finances. Dalton felt he had no option but to resign from his job. In November 1925 Dalton tendered his resignation as Senate Clerk – the stated cause was ill health.[26] He would never again work as a public servant. According to one account, Dalton's tenure in the Senate was characterized by absences, and his absences and resignation can in part be explained by ill health, 'but the financial strain of his father's debts, of which he was guarantor, proved to be equally debilitating and far more embarrassing'.[27] The name of Emmet's father James would ultimately be dragged into court in connection with a civil case. The Provincial Bank sued Mrs Josephine Culhane, aunt of Emmet's wife Alice, over a complex loan deal of which James was the beneficiary. Mrs Culhane won the case but it brought unwelcome publicity to the family finances.[28]

In his memoirs published posthumously in 1998, Senator James Douglas recalled working with Dalton as Clerk, and the difficulties the former army officer had with the Chairman, Lord Glenavy. Douglas would have had particularly close dealings with Dalton as, during the first year of the Senate, as Vice-Chairman he handled much of the work of the Senate office as Glenavy was often away in London. Douglas did not consider Dalton to have been a success in the post of Clerk. He considered that this was partly due to the fact that Dalton did not want the job, and partly because Glenavy intensely disliked his appointment. Douglas said he personally liked Dalton, and believed he had ability, but as Clerk he was a 'fish out of water'. According to Douglas, Glenavy only accepted Dalton as Clerk on condition that a 'trained civil servant' was appointed as Assistant Clerk. Applicants for this post were considered by a Senate committee, and Donal O'Sullivan was given the post. He was already a civil servant, and accepted the job on condition that his rights and remuneration as a civil servant should not suffer in any way. According to Douglas, after O'Sullivan was appointed he was virtually acting Clerk, as Glenavy 'always ignored Dalton' and it was clear that Dalton 'would not last as Clerk for very long'.[29]

Having experienced the excitement and the challenges of life as a soldier, Dalton, may well have become a little bored with the conservative lifestyle of a senior public servant. In an interview in later life, he reflected that most members of the Senate were kind to him – however, he also made the point that the Senate did not meet very often, and reminded him more of a club than a functioning legislative body. As already indicated, the initial venue for Senate sessions was the museum adjacent to Leinster House. With his trademark dry humour, Dalton told the interviewer: 'It was a pretty dull place – a museum usually is.'[30]

Making a Living

After leaving his Senate post, Dalton was facing an uncertain future. Apart from a wife to support, he also had two children – a daughter, Sybil Marie, had been born in 1925. As he struggled to make a living after resigning as a public servant, he was assisted by a Free State pension from his period of military service – in 1927 this amounted to £117 per annum. It was only a fraction of his generous Senate salary but nevertheless would have been a useful addition to his finances.

He followed in his father's footsteps, becoming an entrepreneur, marketing a variety of products, including Scotch whiskey, Avery weighing scales and encyclopedias.[31] He also worked at selling insurance. The journalist and author Tim Pat Coogan, biographer of Michael Collins, recalls that his father, Eamon Coogan, bought a set of encyclopedias from Dalton at this period and the set remained 'a treasured family possession'.[32] According to another account, Dalton 'caused a stir' when he called to the Duty Officer at the Curragh Camp to sell a set of encyclopaedias. Dalton achieved a sale and the books formed part of the library in the Officers' Mess.[33]

During the 1920s, Dalton was drinking heavily. There has been speculation as to the reasons he turned to drink. Writer Ulick O'Connor believes it is quite obvious why Dalton became a heavy drinker: 'He had gone through the First World War, got the Military Cross, came back and had gone through another war. And then Michael Collins dies in his arms. It was a natural progression...'

Dalton would eventually give up the drink completely and become a teetotaller, but in the meantime, there were some memorable binge incidents. It was surprising that he did not get into trouble over some of his Wild West-style exploits, but then he was well-known and liked in the various places where he socialized around Dublin. He would later tell his son Richard about some of his drinking escapades. Said Richard: 'He told some marvellous stories about what happened when he was drunk. We always felt my poor mother, Lord rest her, had a rough time. He used to go on the razzle. As he said, "I was able to clear every bar in town", because he carried his revolver with him.'

One story told to Richard had to do with Dalton disrupting a dance at the Metropole ballroom on O'Connell Street, when he insisted on the band playing his favourite tune, *Indian Love Lyrics*, which none of the couples present could dance to. Another story was about Dalton striking a policeman on Grafton Street after he held up his hand to stop a car in which Dalton was travelling with a driver. Dalton apparently told the policeman: 'I'll have you transferred to Ballydehob.'

Richard told of another extraordinary episode as described by his father. One day, while drinking at the Wicklow Hotel, he decided to order a taxi to go and visit Tim Healy, the Governor General at his official residence (now Áras an Uachtaráin) in the Phoenix Park. Dalton and Healy began drinking together and 'the two of them got pissed'. Then Dalton told Healy he had a problem – he had to get home to Alice and needed 'some kind of excuse'. Healy wrote a note for Alice, asking for Emmet to be excused as he had been with the Governor-General. Then Healy sent him back with an escort to his Phibsboro home.

Emmet Dalton told Ulick O'Connor about another episode. Dalton had a hangover when he met his friend, Senator Oliver St. John Gogarty who insisted that Dalton needed a 'flip'. Soon Gogarty was flying Dalton in his Puss Moth aircraft over the Hill of Howth, with Dalton being ill and shouting to be let down. Gogarty managed to land safely and they went off for a drinking session to the Lamb Doyle's pub in the Dublin Mountains.[34]

Dalton continued to meet up with old comrades from the army and with former political colleagues. He was among the attendance in May 1927 when the President William T. Cosgrave and his Ministers, assembled for a Solemn Requiem Mass and a military parade at Arbour Hill Barracks, to honour the executed leaders of the 1916 Rising, whose remains are buried there. Among the Cabinet members present was Justice Minister Kevin O'Higgins. Just a few weeks later, O'Higgins was assassinated near his home at Booterstown, County Dublin, while on his way to Sunday Mass. This was a reminder of the potential threat against some of those who were prominent on the Free State side during the Civil War. Dalton sent a message of sympathy to Mrs O'Higgins following the murder of her husband.

From time to time, in the years after he left public life, Dalton's name figured in the media, often in a positive sense, but there was the occasional negative connotation as well. He was mentioned in a Fianna Fáil political advertisement prior to the September 1927 general election. The advertisement quoted from the memoirs of British General Sir Nevil Macready, explaining his loaning of artillery to Emmet Dalton to shell the Four Courts at the outset of the Civil War.[35]

Charlie Dalton's Book

Charlie Dalton's last post in the army before his resignation was adjutant in the army's air service, serving under Jack McSweeney. In his final period in the army Charlie and other officers had been reduced in rank as part of the cutbacks and downsizing – he was demoted from colonel to commandant. On leaving the army he worked for a period for his father before setting up in business as a manufacturer's agent with an office at 18 Duke Street in Dublin city centre. He also sold insurance. In October

1928 he married Dubliner Theresa Morgan, and they went on to have three sons and a daughter.[36] In the latter part of the 1920s, he concentrated on writing a book detailing his experiences as a Volunteer in the pre-Truce IRA and as a member of Michael Collins's intelligence apparatus. The book, *With the Dublin Brigade, 1917–1921*, was published in 1929 by the London firm Peter Davies. Dalton described his role in gathering intelligence on British officers who were assassinated on Bloody Sunday in November 1921 and other exploits with Michael Collins's Squad. It would have been interesting to read of his experiences of the Civil War, but that period is not covered in the memoir. Emmet receives some mentions in the book.

One of Michael Collins's female admirers, Moya Llewelyn-Davies may have had a role in the publication of the memoir. She was an aunt by marriage of the publisher Peter Davies, who is said to have helped inspire the character Peter Pan in the writings of playwright J.M. Barrie. The publication of the book was heavily condemned in the House of Lords in May 1931.[37] Lord Banbury assailed the author's admitted role in the Bloody Sunday operation, branded him a 'criminal' and indicated a wish that if Dalton ever came to England he could be arrested. Lord Passfield, Secretary for the Colonies, chided Lord Banbury for giving a large, gratuitous advertisement to the book, and indicated that Dalton could not be arrested, pointing out that the King had granted a general amnesty in respect of offences committed in Ireland from political motives prior to the Truce of July 1921.

James F. Dalton Returns to America

In 1931 Emmet Dalton's father, James F., moved back to the United States with younger members of the family, taking up residence in Taunton, Massachusetts. It appears the move was made essentially for economic reasons, and that James F. figured there was a better chance of making a decent living in the US, even though the country had moved into depression following the Wall Street Crash of 1929. For James F. the journey back to his Irish roots at the turn of the century had been a most remarkable adventure, but it was now time to return to his native America. James took up employment again, working as a salesman with the venerable wholesale grocery and liquor company, S.S. Pierce. One of his daughters, Nuala, became a nun, entering a convent in Fall River. Emmet remained in Ireland, as did his brother Charles and half-brother Martin Joseph.

Emmet kept in touch with former comrades in the pre-Truce IRA and the National Army through involvement in the Association of the Old Dublin Brigade (AODB). This group was founded in 1925 and attracted men who had been close to Michael Collins or who had been members of the IRAO during the period of the Army Mutiny. At a meeting in Dublin in May 1931 Dalton was elected one of the Vice-Presidents of the group – the President was Piaras Béaslaí and the Treasurer was Vinny Byrne.

Charlie Dalton found attractive new employment opportunities with the launch of the Irish Hospitals Sweepstake in 1930. It was set up following legislation passed by the Dáil, and was a lottery based on horse races and designed to raise funds for cash-strapped Irish hospitals. Joseph McGrath, the former Civil War intelligence chief under Michael Collins, who had resigned from the Free State Government in March 1924 in sympathy with the army mutineers, became the managing director of the Sweepstake. The directors would become extremely wealthy and the Sweepstake became the subject of considerable controversy.

Among the individuals McGrath employed were men who had also been close to Michael Collins. Apart from Charlie Dalton, they included Liam Tobin and Frank Saurin, members of Collins's Squad.[38] Another former Squad member, Sean O'Connell, also served as a Sweepstakes agent to supplement his civil service salary.[39] Jobs also went to men who had been on the anti-Treaty side in the Civil War. In America, where the sweepstake was highly popular with the public despite being illegal, one of the key Sweep agents was Cork-born republican Connie Neenan, head of the IRA in the US. Another agent in the US was the prominent republican Joseph McGarrity who also had close links to the IRA. When Charlie Dalton, circulation manager of the Sweep, was on his first visit to America with wife and two children in July 1936 to visit his parents in Taunton, Massachusetts, he heard the unwelcome news that federal officials and New York police had seized a million dollars' worth of sweepstake tickets.[40]

Turning Over A New Leaf

Emmet Dalton's drinking binges, which continued into the early 1930s, caused problems in his marriage. According to Military Pension files that came into the public domain, at one stage apparently his wife Alice contemplated getting a legal separation.[41] Dalton had arranged for his military pension to be paid directly to Alice but later revoked that arrangement, causing further tension. The pension files detail an incident in which it was alleged that Dalton and two companions, named Poynton and Teeling, confronted postal workers at the sorting office in Sandwith Street – Dalton was seeking a letter being sent to him by the Department of Defence – obviously his pension payment. There was also an indication in the files that he considered emigrating to America and making a new start, with the idea of bringing Alice and the children over when he had established himself. Finally, Dalton came to his senses and, through sheer willpower, stopped drinking, halted the downward spiral, and restored harmony and happiness in his marriage.

The factor that prompted Dalton to sort himself out was Alice's pregnancy with her third child in the latter part of 1933. According to son Richard, there was a difficulty with the pregnancy and Emmet was worried. At a pub in Dublin he pledged that he would not drink again if Alice came safely through this pregnancy. In Richard's words, he 'gave it up, stone dead'. Audrey was duly born in January 1934, and mother and child were well. The Daltons went on to have two more children, Richard, born in August 1935 and Nuala, born in January 1937.

Meanwhile, in 1935, Dalton had a poignant reminder of times past. Lady Lavery died at her home in London after a long illness. Dalton was moved to receive a letter from Sir John Lavery, saying that when his wife was dying she wished to be remembered to him, recalling the time she had intervened on his behalf (with

Winston Churchill) on the issue of the sweepstake. Dalton was clearly emotional when he recalled the letter in his interview with Pádraig Ó Raghallaigh. Asked if he still had the letter, Dalton replied, 'I have.'[42]

By now, Dalton's old adversary, Éamon de Valera had become head of government, having led his Fianna Fail party into the Dáil in 1927. He formed a government with Labour after the 1932 general election. The Free Staters of Cumann na nGaedheal obeyed the dictates of the ballot box and handed over power to their former Civil War adversaries. Dalton himself cannot have been pleased at de Valera coming to power, and would continue to blame him for the Civil War. The Long Fellow may have been the loser in that war but it could be said that in the longer term he won the political battle. The party that he founded was destined to play a dominant role in Irish politics for decades. In America, Dalton's father, James F., seemed to take a more pragmatic attitude to de Valera's political success. In June 1935 Dalton senior gave a talk to the weekly meeting of the Rotary Club in Newport, Rhode Island, in which he predicted 'a good future for Ireland under its present leaders'. A local newspaper reported that Dalton produced at the meeting a silk Irish Free State flag which was on the casket of Arthur Griffith – clearly a treasured memento of Dalton's eventful thirty-one-year sojourn in Ireland.[43]

By the latter part of the 1930s Emmet Dalton had moved with wife and family from his mother-in-law's home at St. Benedict's Gardens, Phibsboro to a much bigger family house at 90, Iona Road, Glasnevin directly opposite St. Columba's Church. The semi-detached residence is located on a corner site and was a very fine family home. It is very close to the house where Dalton himself had grown up. Some of his children attended St. Columba's National School, directly opposite the family home, before moving on to other schools. It was run by the Holy Faith nuns from Glasnevin, where Emmet had his first experience of school. Eithne McKeon (née Sheerin) who was a pupil at St. Columba's remembers that the Daltons stood out – they were well-dressed and had an air of prosperity. Mrs Dalton was a very attractive lady, and Audrey, with her dark hair and ringlets, was always 'beautifully groomed'.

Private Detective

By now, Dalton had found another interesting occupation from which to make a living – he had become a private detective. It was the era of fictional 'private eyes' such as Sam Spade and Philip Marlowe. Dalton is unlikely to have experienced the adventures of these fictional investigators. Unlike his detective novel counterparts, it would appear that Dalton did not have to venture out too much on those 'mean streets'. Said Dalton's son Richard: 'My father knew everybody and he solved [virtually] everything without moving out of the office.' Richard said that until recently he had his father's list of garda stations around Ireland, with the names of members of the force from garda to superintendent rank. All he had to do was to phone a garda contact, ask them about a particular matter and they would tell him. 'That was it, it was solved.' He added: 'The one thing he did not handle was divorce.'

Dalton's firm was called General Enquiries (Ireland) Ltd., and it was based in a rented two-room office at a five-storey Georgian building, 79 Dame Street, in central Dublin. The office was just a few doors from the Olympia Theatre, and across the street from City Hall. It was also close to Dublin Castle, where elements of the Garda Síochána were located – the Special Branch had its offices there. For a time his old army friend from the Civil War days, Tom Ennis, worked with him in the 'private inquiry' business.[44] Like Dalton, Ennis had some very useful contacts, especially in law enforcement, which would have been a major help to them in working on cases.

Ennis and Dalton had, of course, been in the pre-Truce IRA, had been part of the Michael Collins coterie, and had soldiered together in the Civil War. Clearly, there was a bond between the two men that persisted over the years. Details are unavailable of the cases undertaken by Dalton and Ennis. It is unclear if either man had to give evidence in court as part of the private detective business. It is also unclear if they used newspaper advertising, or if they simply attracted clients through word of mouth, or through contacts in the legal profession. There were just a few other private detectives working in Dublin at this period. A small ad that appeared in the *Irish Independent* on 23 February 1939 could have applied to Dalton: 'Private Inquiry Agency, conducted by ex-Government Official; strictest confidence. Box 17697.'

In the latter part of 1939, Dalton became involved in a committee to raise funds for a memorial to Sean Treacy, the prominent IRA man who was killed in a gun fight with British agents in Talbot Street, Dublin on 14 October 1920. Treacy and his close friend Dan Breen had operated with members of Michael Collins's Squad after moving to Dublin from their native Tipperary. Membership of the All-Party Dublin sub-committee of the Sean Treacy Memorial Fund meant that Dalton was now a member of the same group as some old adversaries from the Civil War, such as Liam Deasy.[45] At a later stage Dalton became a member of the 1916–21 Club, which sought to heal the divisions of the Civil War – another indication on his part of the easing of old animosities. Deasy was also a member. A prominent figure in the club was Commandant D.V. Horgan, who had served under Dalton in Cork, and who became President of the club. Horgan, who became a hotelier in Dublin, had much respect for Dalton.[46] During this period Dalton also retained his interest in soccer. In 1924, he had been elected President of the Bohemian Football Club.[47]

For Dalton, golf continued to be a major part of his life. One advantage of his job as Senate Clerk and his subsequent career was that it gave him the opportunity to pursue the sport. In early 1923 while the Civil War was still in progress, he was listed as participating in a Hermitage club competition.[48] In a very short space of time he became one of the Hermitage club's most accomplished players. It was a long way from El Arish in the Sinai desert (where he had first played) to the well-tended greens of the majestic Hermitage parklands. In summer 1924 Dalton was a member of the Hermitage team that won the Junior Cup. Dalton reached the last eight of the Irish Close Championship that same year, and also played for the National Army's Golfing Association. In 1935 he was a member of the Hermitage team that won the Junior Cup at Galway. In 1938 he won the Club Singles.

Meanwhile, he had the opportunity to play outside of Ireland – in 1936 he played in the Open Foursomes at Addington in Surrey. This experience inspired him to propose at a Hermitage committee meeting in April 1939 that the Hermitage Foursomes be set up.[49] During the period the competition lasted, from 1939 to 1950, the professional-amateur matchplay foursomes proved extremely popular, attracting big crowds of spectators. Dalton and his partner, the Hermitage club professional Paddy Gunning, were beaten 2 and 1 in 1940-41 by the formidable duo, amateur Joe Carr and professional Harry Bradshaw, who would dominate the competition for years.

In early 1938 Dalton was interviewed by one of the leading golfing journalists of the day, Major Lionel Hewson, for a column in the *Irish Independent*.[50] Hailing the Hermitage member as 'one of the new Selectors', Hewson said he did not think a wiser choice could have been made, 'for he reeks with cold, incisive criticism of golf, however played'. According to Hewson, it was Dalton's 'wonderful accuracy' that had brought him to scratch, great accuracy with a rifle standing him in good stead. 'No other Irish amateur can produce his accuracy when near the green – it is deadly.' Hewson, while noting Dalton's 'stone wall' demeanour, also said that with this imperturbability 'goes a very pleasing disposition that wins him all the friends he wants'. In the interview itself, Dalton expressed the view that his home course, Hermitage, was the best inland course in the country. His favourite links course was Newcastle, County Down. His favourite shot was one of about sixty yards to the green with a mashie-niblick. His best tip for gaining proficiency was 'to take lessons from a professional when one has reached single figures'.

Dalton met some interesting people while playing golf, and an encounter at Hermitage would have a life-changing effect.

CHAPTER FOURTEEN

Moving to England

For Emmet Dalton, a meeting on the golf course opened up an exciting new career and a new life in England. David Rose, the head of the British branch of Paramount, the major Hollywood film studio, visited Dublin from time to time on business. He was in charge of Paramount film distribution in the United Kingdom and Ireland. On his trips to Ireland, Rose liked to play golf, especially with Dalton at Hermitage. In 1939, Dalton had become Honorary Secretary of the club. Rose was clearly impressed by the soft-spoken former military man with such an intriguing past. Recalled Dalton's son Richard: 'Rose got on with my father, most people got on with him. My father was talking about what he was doing, and Rose said, "Why don't you come and join me?"'

Dalton was eventually persuaded to accept a sales job in England with Paramount. The war had disrupted his whiskey brokerage business. Dalton's daughter Audrey believes his move to England at this period was prompted essentially by economic reasons. The new job also enabled Dalton to pursue his passion for horse racing at race meetings in the UK. According to his son Richard: 'What you have to understand too, is doing that sort of thing [film distribution], which was not paying very much money, he was a speculator on the horses. Where he was making little on the real job, he was making money on the horses as a gambler. I suppose in a way he was very professional about it.' In addition to gambling, Dalton went on to become an owner, or part-owner of racehorses, although with no great success. The move to Britain also allowed him to play golf in interesting new surroundings.

No doubt American-born David Rose, considered that Dalton had the necessary skills to sell Paramount films to the cinemas. But Dalton probably impressed him for another reason as well. After the start of the Second World War, Rose was anxious to ensure that his wife Elizabeth and their young son returned safely to the United States. In the summer of 1940, the US Government sent a liner, *SS President Roosevelt*, to Galway to enable US citizens located in war-time Europe to return to

America. Dalton, with his problem-solving skills, ensured that Mrs Rose and her boy got tickets for the voyage. They were among the 725 passengers crammed on board when the ship finally departed Galway Bay for New York on the evening of 3 June. David Rose was clearly grateful to Dalton for his assistance.[1]

David E. Rose was immersed in the film culture of Hollywood. The American had been a travelling salesman when he became acquainted with the silent screen film star, Douglas Fairbanks Senior. For some decades he was Fairbanks's manager and financial adviser. When the swashbuckling actor formed United Artists Studios with Charlie Chaplin, Mary Pickford and D.W. Griffith, Rose became the studio vice president. Rose later worked as a financial adviser for movie mogul Samuel Goldwyn before taking a job in 1938 as head of Paramount Film Services in the UK, with a London office at Wardour Street, Soho. Rose oversaw a network of sales personnel selling Paramount films to the cinemas, covering England, Scotland, Wales, Ireland and Northern Ireland. He seems to have had a good instinct for public relations. In 1943 Paramount filmed the Requiem Mass at Westminster Cathedral for Cardinal Hinsley. Rose arranged for the newsreel to be presented to the formidable Archbishop of Dublin, Dr. John Charles McQuaid, who was not noted for his fondness for Hollywood.[2]

During the period 1941 to 1942 Dalton was based in Liverpool where he was a trainee salesman, dealing with cinema managers. He made swift progress, and was promoted to sales supervisor for the North of England, spending much time in Leeds. In 1943 Dalton set up his base in London, renting premises at 1 Bank Chambers, 25 Jermyn Street, in the exclusive St. James's area of the City of Westminster, which he used as an apartment and an office. However, it was a dangerous time to be in London – the aircraft of Germany's Luftwaffe were still carrying out bombing raids over the city. Dalton's contribution to the British war effort was to become an air raid warden. Dalton's wife and family stayed in their much safer home area of Dublin in neutral Ireland, but they would eventually join him in England.

During this period, Dalton was very concerned about his brother Charlie, who had been experiencing severe mental health problems from about 1938. Charlie was admitted to St. Patrick's psychiatric hospital in Dublin in 1939 and over the following years would spend extended periods of time in psychiatric institutions. He suffered from hallucinations and fears that those around him were conspiring to kill him. For a period he was a ward of court, judged to be of unsound mind. Doctors and former comrades attributed Charlie's psychiatric torment to his military service during the War of Independence, when he had taken part in operations such as Bloody Sunday, and the Civil War. One doctor, Harry Lee Parker, expressed the view that Charlie's experiences had preyed on his mind and conscience so that in the following years 'he has gradually lost his reason'.[3] In 1940, Charlie's wife Theresa wrote to the Minister for Defence, Oscar Traynor, seeking a disability allowance for her husband, pointing out that she had four small children, that Charlie's military pension was insufficient for his upkeep at St. Patrick's and that she was 'completely without income'.[4]

Emmet visited Charlie in hospital. It must have been a traumatic experience for him to see the brother who was once so full of dynamism now trapped in a dark world of paranoia. Emmet secured a letter from Seán Ó Murthuile, a former senior army officer and a prominent figure from the revolutionary period, supporting the contention that Charlie's psychiatric problems were due to his military service. Ó Murthuile showed magnanimity in the gesture as he was on the opposite side to Charlie in the Army Mutiny affair and was one of the Army Council members who had to resign during that controversy. Ó Murthuile was not surprised that Charlie was now affected by the strain of his service: 'He was young and impressionable when he first took up his National activities and had serious responsibilities thrust upon him early,' he said in his letter to Emmet. Various former comrades of Charlie's wrote letters supporting the pension application, including Liam Tobin, Frank Thornton and Frank Saurin. The latter said that because of Charlie's duties he was under 'continual strain', and for most of his service he knew that his life was in danger. During the War of Independence the British were constantly raiding for him and on one occasion he fell into the hands of a plainclothes RIC posse known as 'Igoe's Gang'. (Dalton bluffed his captors into releasing him.) Dalton was equally unpopular with the 'Irregulars' during the Civil War, said Saurin. He recalled Dalton's duties with GHQ Intelligence during the latter conflict – these were mainly concerned with raids and arrests 'and a little shooting, as the exigencies of the situation demanded from time to time'.[5]

Theresa Dalton contacted Sean Lemass, who was then Minister of Supplies, to ask him to give testimony in support of the claim. Lemass generously provided the required statement to assist a former Civil War opponent. On 12 May 1941 Lemass sent a handwritten five-page letter to Mrs Dalton recalling his own association with Charlie in the latter part of 1920. (Understandably, Lemass did not mention his own role in the Bloody Sunday operation.) Lemass said that at that time, he himself, Charlie 'and some others' were lodging together at a billet in Dublin. Lemass understood that Charlie was engaged in 'intelligence work': 'He was of highly strung disposition and on more than one occasion I came to the conclusion that his work was telling on his nerves.'[6] Lemass said he first became seriously concerned about Dalton on the evening of 21 November 1920 'since called Bloody Sunday'. When Dalton returned to the billet Lemass realised that he had become 'unnerved by his experience of the morning'. Lemass went on: 'So obvious was his condition that I and one of the others took him out for a walk although it was an undesirable and risky thing to do.' In October 1941 it was decided to award Charlie Dalton, then a patient at Grangegorman Mental Hospital, a pension of £200 per annum 'in respect of delusional insanity'. Charlie later recovered sufficiently to resume some consultancy work with the Hospital Sweepstake[7], though his mental health problems would continue.

Peter Wentworth-Fitzwilliam

One of Emmet Dalton's friends in England in the 1940s was the dashing and very wealthy Peter Wentworth-Fitzwilliam, whom Dalton had got to know through racing. Peter Fitzwilliam, as he was known among his friends, was a fun-loving English aristocrat with Anglo-Irish family connections. He maintained an opulent lifestyle, owned racehorses and, like Dalton, was a very keen gambler. He became the Earl Fitzwilliam on his father's death in 1943. His family seat was the magnificent Wentworth-Woodhouse near Rotherham, Britain's biggest stately home, and his family's very fine Irish residence was Coollattin House, set in a sprawling estate near Shillelagh in south County Wicklow. Fitzwilliam's wife Olive was the daughter of a wealthy Church of Ireland cleric, Bishop Benjamin Plunket, who was related to the Guinness brewing dynasty. Fitzwilliam had high-level connections in the British establishment. One evening at the Ritz in London, Fitzwilliam introduced Dalton to the enigmatic Brendan Bracken, a Conservative MP who had become a member of Winston Churchill's war-time government. It was not a happy encounter.

A native of Templemore, County Tipperary, Bracken was the son of an ardent Irish republican who co-founded the strongly nationalist Gaelic Athletic Association. As a boy Bracken was brought to Dublin by his widowed mother who enrolled him at O'Connell School. One of his teachers, Brother William Allen, later recalled him as a boy 'with brains to burn' who was up to pranks of every description, and who was also 'the most scruffy and untidy boy' in the school.[8] Bracken was later sent to Mungret College in County Limerick. Moving to England after a period in Australia, Bracken went on to re-invent himself as an English public schoolboy, spending a year at Sedbergh school. Rejecting his Irish roots, he claimed to be English-born of Anglo-Irish stock, with parents who had died in an Australian bush fire. He became a media magnate, and close associate of Winston Churchill. He rose to the position of Minister for Information in Churchill's government in July 1941.

On being introduced by Fitzwilliam, Dalton remarked that Brendan and he knew each other of old: 'We were schoolmates in Dublin.' The atmosphere cooled, and it must have been an extremely embarrassing moment for Bracken, who feigned puzzlement at any such connection, clearly not wishing to re-live his early days in Ireland. Dalton was in no mood to tolerate such subterfuge and remarked that if Bracken did not remember his former schoolmate, he certainly remembered Bracken, and the 'stink of those corduroy trousers which you wore day in and day out...'[9]

As his friendship with Dalton developed, Fitzwilliam was clearly impressed by Dalton's military record and his decoration for bravery. He tried to persuade him to return to soldiering, believing him a natural fit for a commando or special forces unit.[10] At that time Lord Louis Mountbatten was creating special commando units, designed for operating behind enemy lines.[11] However, Dalton declined the offer, preferring to stick with civilian life.

Martin S. Quigley, an undercover agent of the US Office of Stra-tegic Services (OSS), who spent time in Ireland during the Second World War, recorded that he heard 'rumours' that Dalton had been approached early in the war to head the British Commandos, 'a post made famous by Lord Louis Mountbatten'. According to the story told to Quigley, Dalton, being aged over forty, could not meet the medical and physical requirements for commando-style operations.[12] Even if this is accurate, Dalton may not have wanted to fight another war. He appeared happy with his new job in the film world with Paramount, which also allowed him to operate as a semi-professional punter frequenting race meetings throughout the UK.

Fitzwilliam joined the commandos, and served with the shadowy Special Operations Executive (SOE). A captain in the Grenadier Guards, he was awarded the Distinguished Service Cross, 'for distinguished services in a special operation'. Although still married, he began having a relationship around 1946 with an attractive young American widow, Kathleen 'Kick' Kennedy, sister of the future US President John F. Kennedy. In 1944, she had married another aristocrat, William Cavendish, the Marquis of Huntingdon, who was killed in Belgium four months later. Cavendish was heir to the Dukedom of Devonshire, whose Irish seat was Lismore Castle which had been captured intact by Emmet Dalton's troops during the Civil War. Kathleen liked to visit Lismore Castle and during one of her house parties there, in August 1947, the guests included her brother John, who, during the trip, went off to find his ancestral home at Dunganstown in neighbouring County Wexford. In May 1948 Kathleen Kennedy and her boyfriend Peter Fitzwilliam were travelling to Cannes aboard a private plane when the aircraft crashed. Both were killed. No doubt the tragedy came as a shock to Emmet Dalton as it did to other members of Fitzwilliam's wide circle of friends.

The Treaty Ports

The American agent Martin Quigley became closely acquainted with Emmet Dalton in mid-1943. They got on well, sharing a number of traits. They both had a strongly Catholic, Irish-American family background and they were both involved in the film world. Quigley had been working for his father's film trade publishing company, and while in Ireland posed as a representative of the American film industry. In reality, he had been sent to Europe as a secret agent to gather intelligence by another Irish-American, Bill Donovan, head of the OSS. During his time in Ireland, Quigley's cover was never blown, and with his clean-cut appearance and his charm he managed to gain access to many influential people, as well as individuals involved in the Irish film world. He was introduced to Dalton by Norman Barfield, the young branch manager of Paramount Pictures. Quigley would meet Dalton in the private back room of the Paramount film exchange in Dublin.[13] (Paramount had opened commodious new offices at 35 Lower Abbey Street in 1942.) After winning Dalton's confidence, Quigley decided to sound him out on an extraordinary proposition. Quigley wanted to explore the possibility of the Treaty ports, which the British had handed back to the Irish just before the outbreak of the Second World War, being made available to American forces for the remainder of the conflict. In outlining his ports proposal to Dalton, Quigley, who, of course, did not reveal that he was working for OSS, envisaged a quid-pro-quo for the Irish – in return for opening up the coastal bases to the US, President Roosevelt would support an end to Partition and back the re-unification of Ireland. Quigley considered that such an objective would be highly desirable from the point of view of the de Valera government and of nationalists such as Emmet Dalton.[14]

In reality, there would have been no prospect of the Irish government giving approval for US forces to occupy Irish bases – it would have undermined Irish neutrality, and led to Irish facilities being targeted by the German war machine. Already Ireland was covertly pro-Allied, with assistance being given discreetly to the Allied war effort despite the country's official neutrality. Nevertheless, Quigley wanted to sound out the British on the ports proposal and decided that the only man with the proper qualifications to present the idea to the British was Emmet Dalton. Quigley remarks in his memoir: 'I never knew whether he [Dalton] had or did not have intelligence duties in addition to his film distribution activities. So far as I was concerned, it made no difference one way or another.'[15] It is unclear why Quigley decided to adopt this oblique approach. Presumably the Americans could simply have asked the British directly what their thinking would be on the issue. Perhaps Quigley wanted to use his own contacts to gain whatever insights were available.

In his memoir, Quigley says he knew that Dalton 'had maintained excellent contacts in the British government'. Quigley did not identify these contacts, but clearly Dalton had come face to face with members of the British establishment over the years, during the Treaty talks, as Chief Liaison Officer and during his time as Clerk of the Senate. He had come to know Winston Churchill, now Prime Minister. Dalton agreed to get the reaction of the appropriate British authorities to Quigley's ports idea on his next trip to London. (Dalton may have checked with Churchill himself – Dalton's daughter Audrey said that she always understood from her father that 'Churchill was involved in the request'.[16])

When Dalton returned to Dublin, his news gave Quigley no reason to rejoice. The British Imperial General Staff were happy with the current situation regarding the Treaty ports and preferred to leave things as they were. It appeared that the Allies had all the bases they needed. If the US were given access to the ports, they would need to be refurbished; Germany would regard Ireland as a belligerent, and resources such as anti-aircraft artillery would have to be supplied so that the Irish could defend their territory. Quigley wondered if the British rejection might have been also motivated by the idea of heading off US pressure for a British withdrawal from Northern Ireland.[17]

In his capacity as a US film industry representative, Quigley was brought along by Dalton to meet his former military superior, General Richard Mulcahy, now a member of the Senate, who would become leader of the opposition party Fine Gael, whose origins lay in Cumann na nGaedheal. Representing Paramount, Dalton was concerned about the strict censorship of films by Éamon de Valera's Fianna Fáil government – two American films had been suppressed, apparently on grounds that they might undermine Irish neutrality. Mulcahy appeared rather cynical about this type of censorship. He expressed the view that the political purposes of de Valera's party required that the country be kept in constant fear of some danger to neutrality – he pointed out that there was a by-election to take place shortly and there was also the possibility of a general election.[18]

Brothers in Arms

America's entry into the Second World War impacted on Dalton's younger brothers now living in the United States – both Dermot and Brendan joined the US Army. Dermot, a graduate of Holy Cross College and Boston University's law school, was commissioned as an officer in 1942. Brendan enlisted at Boston the following year. Dermot had an eventful career in the US Army, showing some of Emmet's youthful physical courage and sense of adventure. He served in three wars – the Second World War, Korea and Vietnam. During World War Two, he commanded a field artillery battery in Europe and was assistant secretary to the General Staff Headquarters of the 7th Army, commanded for a period by the legendary General George S. Patton.

While in Europe, Dermot contacted Emmet in London. Emmet's daughter Audrey explained: 'They had not seen each other in many years. My father sitting waiting in the hotel lobby saw the American in uniform, figured who it was, walked up to him with outstretched hand and said, "Hello, I'm your brother."'[19] Audrey recalled that Dermot later visited Emmet's wife Alice in Dublin. In uniform, he walked with her in town one day. Emmet duly received an anonymous letter telling him his wife 'was fooling around with an American soldier in Dublin'! In October 1945 Dermot, still in uniform, was back in Dublin and had a day out at the Leopardstown races with his two brothers, Emmet and Charlie. The latter had made some recovery but would remain deeply troubled. A photograph of the three brothers at the races still survives as a treasured item in Audrey's collection.

After service as a combat officer in the Korean War, Major Dermot P. Dalton LL.B taught Military Science and Tactics at Boston College.[20] He saw additional service in the Vietnam War, as a staff officer in the 1960s and early 1970s. He died of a heart ailment, at sixty years of age, at the George Washington Memorial Hospital in May 1980. The *Washington Post* recorded that his decorations included the Legion of Merit with one oak leaf cluster, and the Bronze Star with two oak leaf clusters.[21] He was buried with full military honours at Arlington National Cemetery.

Meanwhile, the years were taking their toll on some of Emmet Dalton's former comrades. Tom Ennis passed away in March 1945. Dalton was in England but he ensured that he was represented by his son Emmet junior.[22] Some of the bitterness of the Civil War had by now healed, and it was noteworthy that senior figures from both sides were at the funeral Mass. (Ennis suffered a great tragedy in 1942 when his daughter Una, aged 19, was shot dead by her fiancé who then killed himself. Emmet and wife Alice were at Una's funeral.)

Dalton may have noticed a rather sad item in the newspapers in January 1946 about the death of an Irishman who had served with him in the 2nd Leinsters in the Great War. Martin Moffatt, a private who won the Victoria Cross, and who, it will be remembered, was one of the decorated soldiers pictured with Dalton at Dhunn, Germany in early 1919, was drowned in his native County Sligo. It was reported that he had worked for many years as a harbour constable with Sligo Harbour Commissioners but was laid off. A few days later, the body of the 63-year-old father of three was recovered from the sea at Rosses Point.

In late 1946 Dalton was asked to write an article for the *Irish Independent* to mark the twenty-fifth anniversary of the signing of the Anglo-Irish Treaty. As an intrepid young reporter, the newspaper's Editor Frank Geary had witnessed the triumphal entry of Dalton's troops into Cork city after the Passage West landings. The article mixed opinion with some warm, personal memories of Collins and first-hand accounts of historic events and various incidents that occurred during the Treaty saga. Dalton had a clear, vivid, writing style, indicating that he might have been a successful journalist had he chosen that route. The article, 'Collins, Happy Warrior, Born Leader' was one of a number of articles to do with the Treaty published in the *Irish Independent* on 6 December 1946.

Working for Sam Goldwyn

In 1947 there was a parting of the ways between Dalton and Paramount. Many years later Dalton said he had a 'falling out' with Paramount over a 'matter of principle' but he did not elaborate.[23] A couple of years later, Dalton's former boss David Rose would move from film distributor to film producer – a path that Dalton himself would eventually follow. David E. Rose Productions made such films as *Sea Devils, Island of Desire, The Safecracker, Port Afrique* and the 1955 version of *The End of the Affair*.

Meanwhile, another bright vista opened up for Dalton – an opportunity to work for David Rose's former boss, the legendary Hollywood movie-maker Samuel Goldwyn. In June 1947 Dalton sailed to New York and travelled on to California to meet Goldwyn. Born in Poland of a Hasidic Jewish family, Sam Goldwyn had come to the United States as an impoverished immigrant and realised the American dream. He emerged as perhaps the most successful independent film producer in the USA. He hired the most accomplished writers, such as Ben Hecht, Dorothy Parker and Lillian Hellman, and provided Hollywood platforms for such notable actors as Gary Cooper, David Niven, Lawrence Olivier and Barbara Stanwyck. Among his movies were *Wuthering Heights, Guys and Dolls*, and *The Secret Life of Walter Mitty*.

In the year that Dalton met him, Goldwyn was in his mid-sixties but was still a major player, having experienced huge success with *The Best Years of Our Lives*, a film about the problems faced by veterans returning home from the Second World War. The powerful movie-maker was regarded by some as tyrannical, but Dalton got on well with him.

Goldwyn was very familiar with the story of Michael Collins. In fact Goldwyn was so intrigued by the Collins saga that, in 1936, he produced a film loosely based on the Big Fellow's life, *Beloved Enemy*. English-born actor Brian Aherne played the role of the clean-cut hero, Dennis Riordan, clearly based on Collins, while Merle Oberon played an English aristocrat, Lady Helen Drummond, who falls in love with him – a role obviously inspired by Lady Lavery. David Niven played a

British Army officer. In the closing scenes, Riordan is shot by one of his own men – an echo, perhaps, of the rumours and speculation that arose after Collins's death at Bealnablath.

In regard to the way the film ends, Goldwyn hedged his bets, with two alternative closing scenes being filmed. As he once said himself, he never liked to end a film with corpses and it may have been against his better judgement that a version of the film was released in which the hero dies at the end. There was a negative reaction at the box office so Goldwyn and his director H.C. Potter released a version with a happy ending in which the wounded hero turns to his Lady Lavery-inspired sweetheart and declares, 'It's all right, darlin', I'm not going to die.' In performing the Lazarus-style feat of bringing the hero back to life, Goldwyn did not have to worry about the niceties of Irish history – in fact there is a screen note at the start of the film making clear the story is 'legend inspired by fact'. In light of his interest in Collins, Goldwyn must have been intrigued to meet the man who was with Collins when he died. The movie mogul appointed Dalton as his representative in the British Isles, in charge of film distribution.

Family Moves to London

Dalton took advantage of his four-week trip to America to spend time with his parents and other members of his family in Taunton, Massachusetts. He had not seen his parents in around sixteen years. Returning to Europe, it was clear that Dalton's long-term future lay in London and he decided to move wife Alice and family over as well. In the meantime, there was an important family event – eldest daughter Sybil became the first of his five children to wed. In November 1949 Sybil (24) married a young army officer, Lieutenant Justin Collins. The following month, Emmet and Alice, with their remaining children, left their very attractive home on Iona Road for a new life in England.

Around this time, some important mementoes from Dalton's past came to light. A newspaper reported that the items had been found in a chest in an attic.[24] One could speculate that this occurred when the Daltons were leaving Iona Road to emigrate to England. Among the items were rare photographs; Arthur Griffith's handwritten note on the signing of the Treaty, as mentioned in Chapter Four; the keys supplied by Michael Collins which Dalton carried with him into Mountjoy Prison in the attempt to 'spring' Sean MacEoin; the flag that draped Griffith's coffin, and a memorandum from Michael Collins to Dalton about retrieving the National Loan lists from Dublin Castle. These items were put on show at the National Museum in Dublin around that period, and are still on loan to the museum.[25]

Dalton met Goldwyn when the movie mogul made trips to Europe. In London, Goldwyn would stay in opulent style at Claridge's, and Dalton would send his secretary Norma Garment around to type letters for him. Dalton liked Paris, and on one occasion met up in the 'city of light' with Goldwyn. While at dinner at the plush George V Hotel, finger bowls were supplied by the attentive staff. Dalton was astonished when Goldwyn removed his dentures and washed them in the finger bowl. Nobody dared say a word.[26] Dalton became friendly with senior figures in the

Goldwyn organization such as Al Crown and James Mosley – the latter was a co-owner of the Brooklyn Dodgers baseball team. Dalton greatly respected Goldwyn's pioneering role in cinema, and later said that while Goldwyn was difficult, he was also wonderful to work for. If you did what Goldwyn asked you to do, and were able to do it, it was 'rewarding'.[27]

Dalton continued to operate from his office in Jermyn Street, in the Piccadilly area of central London, a street noted for its exclusive gentlemen's outfitters, including the venerable shirtmakers Turnbull & Asser. Dalton's son Richard recalled some of the battles his father fought on behalf of Goldwyn. Dalton had a difficult relationship with John Davis, of the Rank organization, which had a powerful position in film distribution in the UK. The Dalton family settled in an attractive area of Kensington. With Sybil married off, the couple's remaining four children – two sons and two daughters, ranged in age from teens to twenties. Their daughter Audrey, who had been a student back in Dublin at the Sacred Heart convent on Leeson Street, was interested in acting and she went to study at the Royal Academy of Dramatic Art (RADA). Nuala transferred from Mount Anville school in Dublin to a school in Notting Hill. Richard was a boarder at the Jesuit-run Clongowes Wood College in County Kildare until 1953, and he also lived at the family home in Kensington. Emmet junior, like his father, was educated at O'Connell's and then Roscrea, before going on to study medicine at UCD. After qualifying, he practised at St. Mary's Hospital, New York, before moving to London, where he lived with his parents while working as a general practitioner. Like his father, Emmet junior was a gifted golfer, with a handicap of 2 or 3, and the two became members of Sunningdale golf club, in Berkshire.

The Daltons lived at Plane Tree House, on Duchess of Bedford's Walk. It was a big house divided into four flats – the Daltons had a spacious, comfortable duplex apartment on the ground floor. The house was in a tranquil, most desirable area beside Holland Park, just a few minutes' walk from bustling Kensington High Street. Richard recalls the period at Plane Tree House as 'the best years of our lives'. The residents in the other three sections of Plane Tree House were all interesting people. One was Carl Foreman, a renowned Hollywood scriptwriter who was a friend of Emmet's. The two later worked together in the film business. Another resident, J.E. Ferguson was a wealthy Old Etonian who shared Emmet's passion for horse racing. Ferguson owned the racehorse Airborne, that won the Derby in 1946 at 50-1. Finally, there was Harold Chadwick, the wealthy boss of a fur trading concern Anning Chadwick & Kiver, and his wife Madeleine. Dalton got to know the couple after they moved into Plane Tree House in the 1950s.[28]

Richard remembers Plane Tree House as 'a marvellous place'. He believed his father paid £25 a month for the two-storey flat, 'which is a little bit different from what you would pay now'. When they first moved there in 1949, Holland Park was a wild area. 'There was certainly no activity there, except the birds and the bees.' But then it was opened up and developed and became a 'lovely spot'. Life at Plane Tree House was enlivened by the visits of young people, friends of the Dalton children. Dubliner Brian Chambers has fond memories of visiting Plane Tree House in the

1950s – his sister was a friend of Audrey's. On the piano, he played for Emmet one of the popular tunes of the day, and remembers a big portrait of Michael Collins in the room.[29]

Dalton Pursues his Interest in Horse Racing

Dalton continued to pursue his interest in horse racing, and was a regular at the major race meetings. He was sufficiently prosperous to have owned, or part-owned, a couple of horses that were trained by Noel Murless, one of the finest trainers of thoroughbred horses in England at the time. He was Queen Elizabeth's trainer, and had the legendary jockey Gordon Richards on a retainer. According to Emmet's daughter Audrey, her father's horses never amounted to much. Audrey recalled being taken with her parents on Sunday visits to the Murless yard to see the horses. She recalled Noel's wife Gwen being very excited, having just received a visit from Queen Elizabeth (destined to become the Queen Mother). Audrey said her own mother enjoyed selecting the racing colours for the horses. Dalton's son Richard recalled that his father and Murless got on very well. 'They became very great friends.' Richard said his father would sometimes hire a chauffeur-driven car to go to the races: 'He was very involved with a lot of bookmakers. They all knew him and they would do things for him that they would not do for anybody else.' Dalton did achieve a little success with a promising racehorse that ran in his colours, Amour d'Or. In the Ashtead Stakes at Epsom, during the major June 1947 meeting that culminated in the Epsom Derby, the racehorse came third in a £522 six furlong race for three-year-olds.

Friendship with Howard Taubman

A member of Emmet's circle of friends in the early 1950s was the music critic of the *New York Times*, Howard Taubman, later to become the newspaper's drama critic. He was a critic at large of the prestigious newspaper, with the freedom to roam the world and write about whatever cultural happening that he thought worthwhile. In the spring of 1951 he thought he should have a look at the British racing scene, for the sake of writing an article but also because he was interested. He was friendly with two Goldwyn executives in the US, who both shared his interest in racing. They arranged for Taubman to meet their colleague Emmet Dalton as soon as he arrived in London. Taubman phoned Dalton at his office on Jermyn Street and Dalton told him to come right over. In his memoirs, Taubman relates how he found a 'slim, wiry, forceful man who exuded a sense of authority'.[30] Dalton brought him to a local restaurant for lunch. Taubman had a drink at Dalton's invitation. Dalton himself did not take a drink, indicating that he had learned how to abstain.

Taubman explained that he hoped to cover the Derby for the *New York Times*. Dalton told him severely that in order to understand British racing, he had to do a lot more than go to the Derby – he had to visit other courses, such as Newmarket, Ascot and less-renowned venues, and if he really cared about the sport, the place to find it in its purest form was Ireland, especially at the Curragh. Dalton, in his decisive way, said the first thing was to begin immediately. In his memoirs,

Taubman recalled Dalton's words: 'We shall go to Hurst Park on Saturday.'[31] This was a racecourse located in West Molesey, Surrey.

On the day of the races, Dalton collected Taubman from his hotel. Dalton was accompanied by a 'tall, pink, sandy-haired friend', a former RAF war-time 'daredevil' who Taubman referred to in his memoirs by the pseudonym 'Colonel Dickie'. According to Taubman, Colonel Dickie was co-owner with Dalton of the horses in training with Noel Murless, and was a man of few words – indeed he hardly said anything as Dalton drove them to Hurst Park.[32] Taubman noted with obvious fascination how Dalton and Colonel Dickie placed their large bets – they bet with bookies passing by at the foot of the stands. 'Hand gestures were all that were necessary,' he recalled in his memoirs. Clearly, the two were highly experienced punters.

The former British war-time leader Winston Churchill, was present at Hurst Park that day. On this cold, overcast day, the youthful Princess Elizabeth, the future Queen, was also present, and she had lunch with Churchill, before the Winston Churchill Stakes, run at a distance of just over one mile. Churchill had a runner in the race he was sponsoring, a grey colt, Colonist II, which went on to win.[33] Taubman recalled how Dalton pointed with pride as Churchill stomped to the winner's circle. He had the racing man's respect for a winning owner. There was another flurry of excitement within Dalton's small group when Colonel Dickie won a large sum. He invited his companions to join him at the bar for champagne. As they raised their glasses, the taciturn Colonel Dickie turned to Taubman and declared: 'Now, you are one of us.'[34] According to Taubman, they were virtually the only words he spoke during the entire day.

Dalton also brought the American to the races at Newmarket, the home of British racing, which has the largest concentration of training yards in the UK, and is the home base of the all-powerful Jockey Club. Taubman noted that Dalton 'despite his intense Irish patriotism, had great respect for English civility and adherence to tradition'. Dalton insisted on leaving Taubman in the car in the car park until he found a member of the Jockey Club who could countersign Dalton's invitation to him to enter the members' enclosure. It was a rule, and Dalton made it clear forcefully to his friend that it had to be strictly observed.[35]

Having completed his apprenticeship in the art of English racing, Dalton introduced Taubman to the heady excitement of the Epsom Derby, the prestigious Classic flat race. Taubman travelled in Dalton's car to the meeting at Epsom Downs on 30 May with two of Dalton's Irish friends. One was a relative of Joe McGrath, the extremely wealthy Irish Sweepstake boss and owner of one of the runners, Arctic Prince. (Dalton had remained a close friend of Joe McGrath's over the years, and the two often had lunch together.[36]) Charlie Dalton was also at Epsom for the race, and was part of Emmet's group on the day.

There was, as usual, a carnival atmosphere for the Derby, with a huge crowd present in festive mood. Arctic Prince was a 28-1 outsider, but after just a half furlong into the straight the colt went out in front and in a highly impressive performance trounced the opposition, scoring a runaway victory in what was the richest Derby to date. It was said that onlookers were stunned at the unexpected victory of an outsider. But the Irish among the crowd cheered lustily and there was predictable jubilation in the McGrath camp.

As a journalist covering a story, Taubman was lucky on the day. He was in the company of men connected to the winning owner, and in this pre-internet era had access to all the background information that he needed. He got a quote from Charlie Dalton to include in the story he filed to the *New York Times* – Dalton said there would be 'bonfires and lavish drinking of toasts in Dublin and in other parts of Ireland tonight'. It had been many years since an Irish-owned horse had won the legendary Derby, adding to the Irish sense of victory.[37] During the summer of 1951, on his travels around Europe, Taubman would call to see Emmet at his home whenever he was in London.

Audrey Dalton's Break in Hollywood

There was an exciting development within the Dalton family in 1952 when Audrey now aged 18, still a drama student at RADA, auditioned for a Hollywood film. A Paramount executive had seen her in a student play in London and asked her to audition for a movie being planned, *The Girls of Pleasure Island*. She was just one of hundreds of young women who auditioned in England for roles in the romantic comedy. The auditions were overseen by F. Hugh Herbert, the Vienna-born writer and film-maker who wrote the script and would direct the movie.

Audrey and two English drama students, Joan Elan (22) and Dorothy Bromiley (21) were finally selected and given contracts by Paramount. The film tells the story of three young English women who live with their planter father, played by veteran actor Leo Genn, on a South Sea island. In the film, their first encounter with men comes with the arrival on the island of a couple of thousand US Marines and Navy Seabees to build an airstrip. The romantic lead was played by Don Taylor as a US Marine.

Audrey's breakthrough gave rise to excited coverage in the Irish newspapers. Audrey and the two other young women travelled to California in March 1952 to begin work, with Alice Dalton accompanying her daughter initially.[38] The studio mounted a vigorous publicity campaign to promote the film, and Audrey and her companions received much media attention. They figured on the cover of the 28 July 1952 edition of *Life* magazine – the front-page photo of the three bore the headline: 'British Starlets in Hollywood'.

Emmet Dalton, through his film industry work, had a range of useful movie connections. He wrote to the film star Alan Ladd and his wife Sue to ask them to 'keep an eye' on his daughter. At the time Alan Ladd was one of the most popular Hollywood film stars, best known for his leading roles in the films *Shane* and *This Gun for Hire*. According to one account, Dalton asked, 'If she [Audrey] gets lonely out there, where she knows no one, maybe you can find a nice, unattached young man with steady head who might take her out an evening or two.'[39] Emmet Dalton and Alan Ladd had an interest in common – horse racing. The two men had become friendly after Ladd sought Dalton's advice on horses and trainers – Ladd owned a number of racehorses. Audrey said, 'Alan and his wife Sue did indeed watch over me and were very good to me.'

The Ladds had a young man in mind for Audrey. Their daughter Alana Ladd (also an actress) introduced Audrey to James Brown on a 'blind date'. The couple announced their engagement in January 1953 and were married shortly afterwards in San Francisco. They went on to have four children. Audrey told a journalist that she had originally planned to return to London immediately after completing her six-month contract with Paramount but her plans changed because of that 'blind date'.[40]

Paramount arranged for Audrey, Joan Elan and Don Taylor to travel to Seoul, South Korea, in March 1953 for the local premiere of *Girls of Pleasure Island*. There were many thousands of American soldiers in Korea – the Korean War was still on. Emmet and Alice were worried about their daughter going into a war zone. Audrey said her parents were 'very relieved' when she reassured them that the film director's wife would be acting as chaperone. The stars toured various military camps and Audrey herself and Don Taylor travelled in a general's helicopter to the front line area. A crowd of soldiers gathered around the muddy landing field and cheered as the helicopter set down. Audrey recalled: 'In newly learned movie star style I waved back enthusiastically as I descended the steps and promptly fell flat on my rear into the mud as the first foot on the ground slipped out from under me. That took me down a peg or two, I can tell you!'[41]

Back in Hollywood, Audrey had a swift rise to further success. After her debut in *Girls of Pleasure Island*, she appeared with Richard Burton and Olivia de Haviland in *My Cousin Rachel*. She had a role in a major production *Titanic* with Clifton Webb, Barbara Stanwyck and Robert Wagner. She appeared with comedian Bob Hope in *Casanova's Big Night*. She played opposite her father's friend Alan Ladd in *Drum Beat*. She had a role in *The Prodigal* which starred Lana Turner and Edmund Purdom. All this work came in a very short space of time. She went on to enjoy a busy and successful career in films and TV. Clearly her success was a source of great pride to Emmet and Alice.

Emmet Dalton Junior Weds

While working as a general practitioner in London, Emmet Dalton's son Emmet Michael met a charismatic Australian-born socialite, Robin Eakin, and there was instant mutual attraction. Emmet junior had recently received disturbing news when he went for a medical examination as part of call-up for National Service. He learned he had a potentially fatal rare heart deformity – a subaortic stenosis, and probably did not have much longer to live.[42] Some months later Robin met Emmet again and it was the beginning of a romance that would lead to marriage. She was hoping that heart surgery would improve enough to save him.

Robin Eakin had grown up in a big house in the bohemian King's Cross area of Sydney, survived a divorce in her twenties, before moving in the late 1940s to London. She became immersed in the post-war world of English high society, rubbing shoulders with royalty, members of the aristocracy and the celebrities of the day. Her social circle included John F. Kennedy, Lord Mountbatten, and the actor Laurence Olivier.

Emmet junior and Robin decided to marry, but could not do so in the Catholic Church, as she was a divorced Presbyterian. The Daltons being devout Catholics, a marriage outside the church posed a serious religious dilemma. (Emmet junior was said to have once considered studying for the priesthood.) The couple married at Caxton Hall registry office in London in May 1953. A photo of the newly-weds was published in the society column of the *Australian Women's Weekly*. Also in the photo were the witnesses, the society photographer Baron (a friend of the Duke of Edinburgh and the man who took the first photographs of the infant Prince Charles), and the film actress, Kay Walsh, the then-wife of noted film director David Lean.

Robin records in her memoir that Emmet senior and his wife did not attend the wedding.[43] Her father-in-law disapproved of the match for religious reasons. Robin told me how, with the encouragement of Audrey, she went to see her in-laws and was warmly welcomed and embraced. There was never a problem after that. 'It was the beginning of our friendship,' she said. She remembers her late father-in-law with great affection.

> We became very, very close friends, and I loved him very much …
> He was full of integrity. He had a great sense of humour, but it was
> very dry and very quiet, and he was very stubborn. But not nastily
> stubborn. I think that's a good description of him anyway.

CHAPTER FIFTEEN

Making Films

As he worked in film distribution in the UK, Emmet Dalton became increasingly tempted by the prospect of making films himself. He was always interested in the cinema and the theatre, and as his income from Sam Goldwyn's organization began to decline, the idea of moving into film production became more appealing. He relished a challenge; he had gained valuable contacts in the film business, and he seemed to have inherited his father's entrepreneurial spirit. He finally ceased to work for Goldwyn in 1955, and as he moved into the challenging world of independent film and TV production, he still operated from his London offices at Bank Chambers, 25 Jermyn Street. He was clearly excited by the idea of becoming a film producer but would initially work in association with others in their movie production ventures.

Among his early contacts in the film business were two men who had been combat cameramen with the British Army during the Second World War, Monty Berman and Robert S. 'Bob' Baker. Both had worked in films before the war, and they met during the desert campaign in North Africa. After being demobilized they decided to operate together, producing many low-budget films for the cinema as well as TV series such as *The Saint*. Their prolific output included horror movies and melodramas. They specialized in second features – it was an era when many cinema-goers expected value for money in the form of a double bill. With few resources to build sets or pay hotel bills many of the Berman-Baker films were shot on location near London. Their main production company was Tempean, but they also worked through a company called CIPA Productions. Under the aegis of CIPA, they teamed up with Dalton and others to produce a number of second features, *Barbados Quest* (1955); *Breakaway* (1956) and *High Terrace* (1957).[1] A burly, cigar-smoking American, Joe Vegoda, sales director of RKO films in the UK, was also involved in CIPA.[2] Berman and Baker would later work with Dalton on film projects in Ireland. Berman, a skilled cameraman, specialized in cinematography and film finance, while Baker concentrated on directing and script development.

Dalton had another important film business partner – Hannah Weinstein, a dynamic American in her forties who worked as a journalist and publicist before entering film and TV production. Weinstein had been active in various radical causes, and moved to Europe to escape the 'red scare' in the US, as the House Committee on Un-American Activities (HUAC) pursued those in the film world suspected of having Communist sympathies. Weinstein was not herself blacklisted though she was a 'person of interest' to HUAC. She initially resettled with her children in Paris – it was said that she was an 'Un-American in Paris' – before moving on to London.[3]

Although of the left, Hannah Weinstein was also a hard-nosed businesswoman. She approached Dalton with some business proposals and he became involved with her in the production of a TV crime-mystery series *Colonel March of Scotland Yard*, starring Boris Karloff. The *Colonel March* series was made during the mid-1950s at Nettlefold Studios in Walton-on-Thames, Surrey. Dalton invested in the studio, and became one of the owners.[4] The series was shown in the UK on ITV and sold to US interests for showing in America. Dalton became a director of a company involved in Weinstein's production of another TV series *The Adventures of Robin Hood*, starring Richard Green.[5] The makers of *Robin Hood* bought a mansion set on 34 acres, Foxwarren Park, near Cobham, Surrey, to film the series. A replica of Nottingham Castle was built in the deer park to be used in various scenes. Other filming work was carried out at Nettlefold studios. Weinstein employed a range of writers on the Hollywood blacklist to write scripts for the series under pseudonyms – they included Ring Lardner Jnr., Waldo Salt and Ian McLellan Hunter,[6] as well as a writer who Dalton would get to know well, Hyman 'Hy' Kraft. In his memoirs, Kraft praised Weinstein, saying that 'no single person did more for the personal and professional sustenance of condemned American writers and directors during these grave years...'[7]

It appears that Dalton's involvement in the *Robin Hood* project did not entitle him to a share of the huge finances generated by the US sales, his interest being confined to a percentage of British sales. Dalton's son Richard said his father had 'no direct role as such' in the making of the series – he was a director of a company with Weinstein whom he called 'a tough cookie'. He did not believe his father made much money from the *Robin Hood* project. It appears that Ms Weinstein drove a hard bargain when Emmet's interest was bought out after the project had become a success. Emmet was beginning to learn some tough lessons about the business. In an interview in later life, Dalton said that the Robin Hood project became very big and Weinstein was not prepared to share with anybody at this stage. He was told that he could not be forced out, but if he wanted to remain in, he had to invest more capital, and he was not prepared to do so.[8]

Apart from Hannah Weinstein, Dalton also came to know some of the other figures from the US film world who had moved to London because of difficulties with the HUAC. Joseph Losey was a prominent director and Carl Foreman was an established scriptwriter – he wrote the screenplay for the acclaimed film *High Noon* (1952) starring Gary Cooper and Grace Kelly. Both had joined the Communist Party in America and were targeted as a result. In London, Losey became a close friend of Hannah Weinstein. According to a memoir penned by Dalton's daughter-in-law, Robin Dalton, Emmet provided work to Joe Losey and Carl Foreman after they came to Europe, writing and editing films 'under pseudonyms'.[9] Robin said that even though they worked under assumed names, 'everybody in England in the film industry knew it'.[10] The use of pseudonyms was a way of getting around the Hollywood blacklist. Dalton was not normally a man to engage in subterfuge, but it seems he made an exception in regard to Hollywood exiles. With wry humour, Robin recalled Emmet as someone quite unusual in the film production world, as 'he could not tell a lie'.

Dalton could not be described as a Marxist or Communist sympathiser. He probably took the pragmatic view that the Hollywood exiles were people of talent and that it was worthwhile to work with them. There may also have been an element of sympathy for the underdog. Dalton became a director of Carl Foreman's film production company, Open Road Films. The concern was based at Dalton's London business address at Jermyn Street. Robin said that Emmet remained a director of Foreman's company until he died. Among the film projects undertaken by Foreman through Open Road Films was the highly successful war film *The Guns of Navarone* (1961), which he scripted and produced. It remains one of Foreman's most popular films. Foreman had by now sorted out his difficulties with HUAC, with the aid of his very resourceful lawyer Sidney Cohn, who also did legal work for Dalton in America. It was through Foreman that Dalton became friendly with Joe Losey, and Dalton's son Richard would go on to work for Losey as an assistant director on major films.

An Irish Film Industry

Buoyed up, perhaps, by the popular success of the *Robin Hood* venture, Emmet Dalton began working on a project close to his heart – the idea of making films in Ireland or with an Irish theme, using Irish actors. He envisaged that, as in the case of the *Robin Hood* series, there could be a lucrative market in America for such films. He may also have been encouraged by the success of John Ford's film, *The Quiet Man* (1952), which had been shot on location around Cong, County Mayo, and was based on a book by Irish writer Maurice Walsh. In the mid-1950s Dalton's company Medal Films optioned another of Walsh's novels, *Blackcock's Feather*, set in the Elizabethan period. Dalton engaged the screenwriter Cecil Maiden, based in La Mesa, California, to write a treatment and a film script. However, it seems that the film world was moving away from historical, swashbuckling movies at this period, and despite Dalton's enthusiasm for the project, nothing came of it.[11]

One of Dalton's Irish collaborators in the Irish film venture was Ria Mooney, who had become the first female producer of Dublin's renowned Abbey Theatre.

Dalton had much respect for the Abbey tradition and for Mooney personally. Born in 1904, she had been personally chosen by Sean O'Casey to play the prostitute Rosie Redmond in the first production of his play *The Plough and the Stars*, which famously sparked a riot at the Abbey in February 1926. Dalton and Mooney became good friends and collaborators as Dalton struggled to get an Irish film industry off the ground. Dalton was originally interested in making a series of TV films based on Irish folklore tales to be sold in America, and he sought advice from Mooney who was interested in archaeology and antiquities.

She was glad to assist with 'something different', and hinted that she was a little frustrated with some of her work at the Abbey: 'Years of routine work on Irish kitchen comedies is somewhat stifling…'[12] She came up with some ideas and Dalton also took advice from the aforementioned Cecil Maiden, who had worked for Walt Disney. Maiden did not think much of Mooney's proposals for the folklore series, telling Dalton in 1954 that Ria's concept was 'art', rather than money-making 'entertainment'.[13] Ultimately, the series was not made, but Ria Mooney would work closely with Dalton on film projects linked to the Abbey, advising in a range of areas, including scripts, casting and costumes.

As he developed ideas for Irish film production, Dalton had conceived the idea of using actors from the Abbey Theatre. He saw in the Abbey players a ready-made pool of talent that could be deployed for his ambitious project. Actors who had honed their skills at the Abbey had gone on to successful careers in Hollywood, such as Barry Fitzgerald and his brother Arthur Shields. Another Abbey product, Maureen O'Hara, was at that time one of the biggest stars in Hollywood. All three had prominent roles in *The Quiet Man*.

Dalton enlisted the help of businessman Louis Elliman, who had extensive interests in the Irish cinema and theatre world, and had campaigned for the setting up of an Irish film industry. Dalton had preliminary talks with Elliman in the summer of 1956. Later that year, the two men met the managing director of the Abbey Theatre, Ernest Blythe, with a view to making films using Abbey players. Dalton and Blythe were both prominent on the pro-Treaty side during the Civil War, Blythe serving as a government minister.

The proposal was to form a holding company to act as an intermediary between the Abbey and Dalton's London-based company, Emmet Dalton Productions Ltd. This would facilitate collaboration on the filming of a number of scripts with Abbey players taking the various roles. Blythe, who had a reputation for being difficult, was initially reluctant to let the Abbey become involved. The Abbey had had an unhappy relationship with the film world. Apart from the fact that some talented Abbey players had been lured away from the theatre by the bright lights of Hollywood, there had been several proposals over the years for Abbey plays to be filmed, and these proposals had failed to come to fruition. Blythe was never noted for hasty decisions – it was inevitable that he would be cautious, and probably the most difficult member of the Abbey board to be won over.

Dalton became frustrated as he waited for a decision from Blythe. He confided in a letter to Ria Mooney, 'I cannot understand the attitude of Earnan [Ernest

Blythe] but after all, who does understand his various changes of mind? For my part, my project is very much alive and I have Louis Elliman constantly harassing Blythe, seeking agreement.'[14]

Blythe asked Dalton and Elliman to submit a detailed memorandum of how the scheme might work.[15] In their memo, the two proposed that a new company would be set up, Dublin Film Productions, which would make motion pictures and TV films for worldwide distribution and which would have access to the Abbey name and its players. The Abbey would receive a payment for each film made, regardless of whether or not the film was based on a play from the Abbey repertoire.[16] After much initial reluctance, Blythe, in consultation with the Abbey board, eventually went along with the project. Among the advantages for the Abbey would be that the players would get extra exposure and the scheme would help promote the Abbey. In addition to the above-mentioned company, a management company was also set up, with Louis Elliman as Chairman and Managing Director, and with Dalton and Blythe as First Directors.[17] Dalton was worried about the delay in concluding a deal, and the short time available to produce a pilot film to show to potential American backers. He commented to Ria Mooney, 'From the all-important aspect of American TV participation, we are in a serious spot due to the time element.'[18]

In late 1956 Dalton had exploratory talks with a senior American TV executive about his idea for Irish-made films to be shown in the US. The executive, a Mr Harris who was Vice-President of the Columbia Broadcasting Company, felt that only a limited number of intelligent people appreciated the art of theatrical companies such as the Abbey or the Old Vic. Harris suggested the Abbey players spend about a month in New York, and he would organize a celebrity spot on a national TV network, for which they would be paid $150,000 – this would publicize them to millions of American viewers. At the same time, the Abbey could do a season of repertory plays in a suitable theatre in New York. Harris suggested that one or two pilot films should be ready for viewing at the end of April or the beginning of May. Dalton reported on these developments in a letter to Louis Elliman, asking him to report in turn to Blythe. Dalton felt sure that Blythe would agree that the 'entire project is sound' and can have no other result than 'great benefit to the Abbey Theatre.'[19]

In November 1956, after Dalton consulted with Ria Mooney, it was decided that the pilot film to begin production would be based on the play *Professor Tim* by George Shiels. For this project, Dalton called in two trusted collaborators to act as producers – Monty Berman and Bob Baker. The director was Henry Cass, an experienced English director who had worked on other Berman-Baker films. Ria Mooney worked on script adaptation and was Dialogue Director. It appears that Baker wanted to bring in guest actors to play some older characters and Dalton was against this, considering that younger Abbey actors, with suitable make-up, could play these roles. In a letter to Mooney, Dalton said, 'It is my idea to do these plays with the Abbey Players and I do not want to create a situation where they would be overshadowed by guest actors, no matter where they come from. You must not give way to Baker on any issue that you feel confident you can justify your views.' Dalton added that he liked Baker immensely but in this matter 'is a little different from us Irish'.[20] Considerable friction would develop between Mooney and Baker – the two came from very different backgrounds. Mooney was a distinguished actress and director whose experience was entirely in the theatre, while Baker had mainly worked in popular, low-budget films.

Introductory scenes for *Professor Tim* were filmed at Dunboyne, County Meath in January 1957, and the *Irish Independent* reported that the company directors hoped it would be followed with an order for twenty to thirty more such TV films for showing in America.[21] The low-budget black-and-white film starred Ray McAnally and Maire O'Donnell, with Seamus Kavanagh playing Professor Tim. Abbey actors played a range of other parts. While location scenes were filmed in Ireland, Abbey players had to travel to England for interior scenes shot at Nettlefold Studios. The film had its premiere at the Regal Rooms in Dublin in April 1957 and there was a generally positive reaction. All was going well at this stage and, despite the challenges and hard work involved, Dalton was greatly enjoying the experience of film producing.

With a well-received *Professor Tim* as a pilot to show to potential US backers, Dalton went to America to secure financial support for a series of films. It was an exciting time for Dalton. Ultimately Dalton, with the advice of lawyer Sidney Cohn, concluded a deal in New York, not with Columbia, but with a concern headed by Thomas F. O'Neil. He was a wealthy Irish-American businessman who had begun his career with General Tire and Rubber, founded by his father William O'Neil. For a massive purchase price of $25 million, Tom O'Neil had bought a major film company, RKO Pictures from the reclusive tycoon Howard Hughes, which gave him access to the company's impressive library of 600 films. O'Neil needed a ready supply of films for showing on the TV stations that he controlled on the east coast. In his early forties, he was described as an affable, strapping, six foot four inch-tall war veteran, with an unassuming manner.[22] He apparently liked Dalton's film *Professor Tim*. He had a particular regard for the Abbey Theatre and liked the idea of films based on Abbey plays. Under the deal, as he would describe it later, Dalton was to supply sixteen half-hour films, with O'Neil's concern supplying 50 per cent of the finance, provided O'Neil's people approved the script, chose the director and had approval of the leading artist, who was expected to have American and worldwide appeal. O'Neil would have the American rights while Dalton and his people would have the rights for Europe and the rest of the world. For Dalton it was a very attractive deal, and he was very pleased at this breakthrough. In line with this arrangement, Dalton set about making films based on Abbey plays and using Abbey players. However, to Dalton's great dismay, the deal was later changed, with the number of films requested being reduced to six, and the running time expanded from a half-hour to one hour. It was a frustrating development for Dalton. As he would later recall, he had to arrange the re-writing of scripts and various arrangements had to be re-negotiated.[23]

It was unsatisfactory for Abbey players to have to travel to England for interior filming so the idea of setting up a dedicated film studio in Ireland came to the fore.

Dalton purchased, for a modest £5,000, a Georgian mansion, Ardmore House, set on extensive grounds of more than thirty acres at Bray, County Wicklow. He may have been partly inspired by the purchase of a mansion and estate, Foxwarren Park, for the making of the *Robin Hood* TV series. With generous financial assistance from the Irish state, the work began of building a fully-equipped studio at Ardmore. It was a time when Sean Lemass, as a very innovative Minister for Industry and Commerce, was diligently promoting Irish industry and exports. Lemass had long been interested in setting up an Irish film industry.[24] The Ardmore studio venture received a grant of £45,000 from the Industrial Development Authority and a debenture loan of £217,750 from the state development bank, the Industrial Credit Company.[25] Dalton and Elliman were the joint managing directors of the enterprise, other directors being Abie Elliman and bookmaker Con McGrath, a friend of Dalton's.

Ardmore was a good location for film-makers and provided much variety in terms of location shooting. It was close to the sea and to the scenic woods and valleys of the Wicklow Mountains. Exterior shots could be filmed in the grounds or in the nearby countryside. In addition, Ardmore was close to Dublin, which facilitated the transport of film to London for processing. It was envisaged that Ardmore would eventually have its own processing facilities.

At the end of July 1957, Dalton updated Blythe on the studio plans. 'So far, the Minister [Sean Lemass] has proved to be enthusiastic and cooperative.' Although he did not say it in so many words, Dalton indicated that he had an essentially patriotic motive in trying to found a film studio. 'In all of my discussions with my associates and with our American collaborators I have been insistent that my primary object is the welfare of the State. No one of us is greedy for money but we are very conscious that commercial success is essential if we are to achieve our object and create an industry in Dublin.'[26]

Dalton's daughter Audrey says that her father was a 'believer in Ireland, a patriot to the core' and that the Ardmore venture came from his belief that Ireland was in need of a film industry, that this was an area where he could make a contribution. He knew that Ireland had so much to offer film-makers – 'the scenery, the people, the actors, and this pool of skilled workers'.[27]

'The Kid Stays In The Picture'

As he embarked on this ambitious project, Dalton decided to enrol the services of the experienced American scriptwriter Hyman Kraft, as writer and editor of the series. Kraft had been born around the turn of the century on New York's Lower East Side, and had made his name as a scriptwriter, playwright and theatrical producer. He was noted for his lively wit and his celebrity contacts, and was friendly with Dalton's business colleague Carl Foreman and, as indicated above, with Hannah Weinstein. Kraft had also run into difficulties with the HUAC, and moved to London. To avoid any possible banning of the film in the US owing to the writer being blacklisted, Kraft used the pseudonym Howard Kent in his work for Dalton.

Kraft told in his memoir *On My Way to the Theatre* how a draft of the first screenplay was mailed to New York with Harold Kent listed as the writer. He believed the alias 'must have caused a few flurries'. A man from RKO arrived in London. There was a tense meeting at Dalton's office on Jermyn Street between Dalton, the RKO representative and Hy Kraft. The RKO man told Dalton that Kraft had to be sacked. Dalton was furious and was not about to give in. His legendary stubbornness came into play. Dalton's attitude could be summarized in the words of the old Hollywood cliché: 'The kid stays in the picture.' Kraft commented in his memoir: 'Apparently they had not done a very thorough research job on Emmet Dalton or they would have known that he was American-born, that at twenty-seven he was a general in the Irish Republican Army [sic], that Michael Collins, the leader and hero of the rebellion, had died in Emmet's arms. You don't fool around with a guy of such lofty courage and integrity.'[28]

Kraft says in his memoir that everything Dalton had was tied up in this deal. 'If it collapsed, Emmet Dalton would collapse with it.' In order to get Dalton off the hook, Kraft offered to pull out. Dalton seemed to be more enraged by this offer of capitulation than by the RKO demand. Then Dalton made a dramatic gesture. He opened his desk drawer, pulled out the RKO contract and said he was ready to tear it up. The ultimatum had the required effect. In Kraft's words: 'The RKO man backed down. Harold Kent stayed on.'[29] Players at the Abbey theatre may not have realized how close Dalton came to losing US financial support. Meanwhile, the second television film selected to be made was another comedy, based on the play *Boyd's Shop* by St. John Ervine. As the Ardmore studios would not be ready for use for some time, the Abbey players again travelled to England for studio filming. Among the players with roles in the film were Eileen Crowe, Geoffrey Golden and Aideen O'Kelly. Under the auspices of Emmet Dalton Productions, the producers, once again, were Monty Berman and Bob Baker, with Henry Cass directing.

A friendship developed between Dalton and his American attorney Sidney Cohn. Apart from Carl Foreman, the lawyer's clients included Hy Kraft and Joe Losey. Cohn specialized in movie world legal affairs and used to come to London on business to see his American clients. Cohn was diligent in assisting his friends and his clients. On one occasion, Audrey Dalton stopped in New York on her way to a film set in London. Cohn met her with a limousine at the airport, and ensured she was safely escorted to the airport the next day.[30]

Cohn worked for liberal causes, and had a long record of representing workers trying to organize trade unions. He also counselled Hollywood personalities called before Congressional committees investigating Communist influence. Cohn acted for Foreman and Kraft when they came under investigation. He sat beside Kraft to advise him as he was quizzed by the HUAC at a public hearing in Washington. Kraft always remembered the advice given to him by Cohn before the hearing: 'Remember, never say, "I refuse to answer." Say, "I *decline* to answer."' Apparently, this was not just a matter of semantics. Kraft was given to understand that the use of the proper word could decide if you continued to live in a comfortable five-room flat, or 'in solitary confinement at government expense'.[31]

Cohn was so fascinated by Dalton's charismatic personality and extraordinary past that he presented him with a special gift. It was a portrait of Dalton based on his image in the renowned painting executed in 1922 by Leo Whelan of the members of the pre-Truce IRA General Headquarters staff. Dalton's son Richard recalled: 'Cohn presented the painting to my father who hated it. It was a huge painting so he gave it to his eldest daughter to put in her house in Clontarf [Dublin], and it just dominated the bloody place. Subsequently we had it cut down to size, and I have it now in my dining room, which is fine.'[32] The presentation of a painting as a gesture to a friend would have made sense to Cohn as he was an art connoisseur with a multi-million dollar collection.

As he moved into film production, Dalton considered the idea of making a film about his friend Michael Collins, many aspects of whose life seemed ideal for transfer to the silver screen. For this project, Dalton made a rare foray into scriptwriting. He worked on various rough drafts of an outline script for a film, drawing on his own experiences with Collins and the plan to rescue Sean MacEoin from prison.[33] In one version of the script, the main focus is on the Dalton-inspired character – a young American-born man of Irish descent called Riley (Dalton's mother's maiden name) who has served in the British Army in the Great War and who now wants to join the Volunteers. He meets Collins at Volunteer Headquarters and a clearly cautious Big Fellow asks why a former officer in the British Army 'wants to render us service'. Riley explains that down through the ages his folks 'have never lost the love of Ireland'. He says he was one of the many thousands of Irishmen who felt that this service in the British Army was 'in the best interests of their native land'. He believed Ireland could now best be served 'by armed resistance with your Volunteer Army'. Collins thanks Riley for his application, and tells him they will tell him of their decision later. Collins also expresses appreciation for 'the motive that activated your gesture'. The script describes other meetings with Collins as plans for the rescue of MacEoin take shape.

In another draft, the 'love' interest is provided by the Dalton character's girlfriend Katie, who supports his involvement with the Volunteers. At one stage, as an ex-British officer, he says to Katie, 'You must remember we were promised that the question of Home Rule would be reopened and made law at the end of the War. Since that has not been done we feel no further obligation to the Crown.' Dalton's idea for a film on Michael Collins would not become a reality. In a later era, Neil Jordan would write and direct *Michael Collins* (1996) starring Liam Neeson as the Big Fellow. In that film, Dalton is merged into the character of the Big Fellow's ever-faithful aide, Joe O'Reilly. (Richard Dalton remarked that he felt his father had been 'airbrushed' out of the film.[34])

Even though Dalton, in his Collins movie script, included details of the attempt to rescue Sean MacEoin from Mountjoy, he was becoming a little tired of the emphasis being put on this aspect of his career. He indicated his thoughts in a letter in reply to Ria Mooney who appears to have mentioned a plaque unveiled at the Curragh in December 1955, during the annual Cavalry Corps dinner, to commemorate the event. MacEoin and a number of those who had taken part in the rescue attempt were present for the black tie occasion – Joe Leonard, Pat McCrea,

Frank Bolster, Bill Stapleton, Sean Caffrey and Peter Gough. Dalton sent a telegram regretting he was unable to attend because of illness, but conveying his best wishes. In his letter to Mooney he remarked, 'I feel complimented by the Cavalry Corps' action, but they are inclined to over-emphasize the incident. Almost annually this thing is in the news and I am thoroughly fed up with it. I could tell of a half dozen other incidents that I participated in, which are never referred to, but which were to me more daring and certainly more important.'[35]

A Time of Bereavement

While developing Ardmore studios, Dalton continued to reside in London and would travel to Dublin as required, staying in one of the leading hotels, the Gresham, where he was formerly based in 1921–2 and which had been re-built after the Civil War. He was a friend of the celebrated Gresham manager, the urbane Toddy O'Sullivan. At one stage, Dalton planned to reside with wife Alice at an apartment at Ardmore House. It would have been a pleasant place to retire but tragedy intervened.

On 1 September 1957, Alice and Emmet had an American friend to lunch at their home in Kensington – this was Al Crown, who was head of international sales for Sam Goldwyn. Their son Richard was also present. Crown had been president of Moulin Productions when it produced *Moby Dick* (1956), starring Gregory Peck and directed by John Huston. Some of the *Moby Dick* scenes were filmed in Youghal, and Crown told how he had to visit Ireland to restrain Huston, who was spending money 'as if it was going out of fashion'. Dalton also had unfortunate personal experience of films exceeding budget.

The next day, Richard found his mother dead at the family home. Alice had been unwell but nevertheless her sudden death came as a huge shock to the family. It was decided that after funeral Mass she would be laid to rest at Glasnevin Cemetery. Emmet and members of the family, including Richard and Emmet junior, took a night-time flight into Dublin Airport while the coffin was flown in on another flight. Emmet senior's hotelier friend, Toddy O'Sullivan was waiting loyally at the airport with a big car to bring them all to the Gresham.

It was said that Emmet found it extremely difficult to cope with this devastating loss. The couple had been married for thirty-five years, and their friendship went back to their childhood. Audrey was working in America and unable to attend the funeral. She recalled how close Emmet had been to Alice. 'My father just adored her and I have the letter he wrote to me after her funeral saying they had been childhood sweethearts. It was the most moving letter. He never really recovered his will, the battle was too much.'[36] Robin Dalton believed that after Alice died, 'the heart went out of him, he did not want to go on, it really gave him a terrible, terrible knock.'[37]

The year 1957 proved to be an *annus horribilis* for Emmet Dalton. His widowed mother Katherine died in the US, and just a few weeks after Alice passed away, there was a further heavy blow when his son Emmet junior died on 3 December, at thirty-three years of age, after heart surgery. His wife Robin, who had been working as a press attaché for the Royal Thai Embassy in London, was left as a single mother with two small children, Seamus and Lisa. For Emmet senior it was particularly difficult to cope with such a loss, so soon after losing Alice.

Robin went on to become one of London's leading literary agents, her clients including Iris Murdoch, John Osborne and the Irish writer Edna O'Brien. By the mid-1980s she had followed in the footsteps of her father-in-law by moving into film production. Her movie production projects included *Madame Sousatzka* (1988) starring Shirley Maclaine, and a movie adaptation of Peter Carey's *Oscar and Lucinda* (1997), starring Ralph Fiennes and Cate Blanchett. She wrote books – her childhood memoir, *Aunts Up The Cross*, was a bestseller in Australia, and she followed up with a volume about her later life and times, *An Incidental Memoir* (1998).

While traumatised by the loss of loved ones, Emmet Dalton had embarked on a major business enterprise and he could not now turn back. Perhaps the resilience he had shown in his younger days as a soldier came back into play. There was a range of projects to be pursued, and he got on with the job. In the period 1957 to 1958 Dalton corresponded with noted Irish playwright Sean O'Casey with regard to the proposed adaptation by Hy Kraft of *The Shadow of a Gunman* for a television film. Kraft himself also wrote directly to O'Casey about this project. Dalton was also in touch with O'Casey about the rights for film production of *The Plough and the Stars*, in which Abbey Players would be used. Dalton's business partner Louis Elliman also wrote to O'Casey – one idea put forward was for live television broadcasts of *The Plough and the Stars* and *Juno and the Paycock*.[38] The irascible O'Casey rejected all these requests – he had refused other approaches at this period to televise his early plays, as he disliked the way that plays were cut and edited for television. For O'Casey, it meant losing out on the sizeable sum of £3,000 offered by Dalton for *The Shadow of a Gunman*.[39]

In the latter part of 1957 Dalton may have given some consideration to writing a memoir about his role in Ireland's revolutionary period. There survives in his papers a memorandum from an unidentified person providing a suggested outline of chapters, and indicating sources that could be used, including documents in Dalton's possession and newspaper files.[40] It is unclear if the initiative for the project came from Dalton or the writer of the memo. Ultimately, Dalton did not proceed with the memoir project.

Hurdles to Cross

As he pressed ahead with his film projects, there were constant hurdles that Dalton had to surmount. Before having an Abbey play turned into a film script, he had to get approval from his RKO backers in the US. In October 1957 he received a letter from Nathan Keats of RKO Television in Manhattan, emphasizing that it was most important 'that we have the opportunity to exercise the approvals outlined in our contract by reading every play before you go to the expense of a screenplay'.[41] Keats also sounded an ominous note when he warned that it might be necessary at some stage to include the work of authors better known to Americans than

Irish playwrights such as John McCann, Lennox Robinson or St. John Ervine. The following month Dalton wrote to Ria Mooney saying that he just had a letter 'from the crazy RKO people asking me to do plays by Ibsen and Chekov with the Abbey Players, and I have said "No"'. Dalton also mentioned that he had bought the Joseph Tomelty play *The End House*, adding, 'I hope you can agree that this can be made into a good strong drama.'[42]

Production was completed on *Boyd's Shop* in early 1958, (although it would not appear until 1960), and work was well advanced on the building of Ardmore studios. The first film shot at Ardmore was *Home is the Hero*, based on a book by Walter Macken, who was also an accomplished actor. After a couple of comedies, Dalton's US backers wanted a more serious drama, and Macken's work appeared to fit the bill. The film deals with the survival of an Irish family after the father is sent to prison.

In early 1958 Dalton and Elliman were in touch with Macken to acquire the film rights to his book and also to line up Macken to play the lead part. The popular American character actor Arthur Kennedy played his son. The respected American director Fielder Cook was hired to direct the film, while under the umbrella of Emmet Dalton Productions, Bob Baker and Monty Berman handled the production side. Cook, an urbane southerner and acclaimed television director (he won three Emmy awards) was impressed by Ardmore Studios, partly because everything was brand new. He described Emmet Dalton as 'a man of absolute steel and a great gentleman.'[43]

Meanwhile, Abbey players and members of the press were given a tour of Ardmore on 13 March. Dalton may have been eager to reassure the Abbey that progress was being made on the construction of the studio. It appears that Blythe was getting impatient. The visitors were told that within the next few weeks the first of four modern sound stages, eighty feet long by 100 feet wide, would be completed on the thirty-five-acre site. Captain Justin Collins, a member of the studio management team, who was married to Dalton's daughter Sybil, gave a briefing to the visitors. He said that over the following two years, three more large sound stages would be built, with a smaller one for making advertising films and short films. The plans also included a large workshop, while Ardmore House itself was housing administration offices and would accommodate cutting and editing rooms, a projection theatre as well as a canteen and executive restaurant. Among the advanced film equipment shown to the visitors was a £7,500 Mitchell BNC studio camera which had arrived from Los Angeles.[44] Dalton was always proud of the high quality of the technical equipment and the facilities generally at Ardmore.

Official Opening of Ardmore

Work was still in progress on the filming of *Home is the Hero* when Ardmore Studios were formally opened on 13 May 1958. The opening was performed by Dalton's old Civil War adversary and former O'Connell School contemporary, Sean Lemass in the latter's capacity as Minister for Industry and Commerce. It was thirty-six years since they had fought on opposing sides at the siege of the Four Courts but this was not the occasion for looking back on old conflicts. Lemass was never seen as a man to hold a grudge from the old Civil War days, and clearly he had no problem doing business with Dalton. The Minister complimented those behind the new venture for their initiative and enterprise. He observed that Irish people were being trained in the highly-complicated business of film-making and that the new studio was aimed at the export market, and that it marked an important development in the economic history of the country. Dalton made a short speech, thanking the Minister for opening the studio. Lemass and other guests were shown around the studios and watched a scene from *Home is the Hero* being filmed. (The film was completed in 1959 and released in America in January 1961.)

Writing next day in the *Irish Times*, the columnist Quidnunc welcomed the brevity of all the speeches. He remarked that in view of the ballyhoo generally associated with show business, it was an agreeable surprise that the official opening of the studios was marked by 'a complete absence of the usual stunting claptrappery'. He commented that Elliman and Dalton 'said their pieces with the minimum of words' and that Mr Lemass 'kept to the same terseness'.[45] The setting up of the studio was probably the single most important event in the history of Irish cinema, and there were high hopes for the future of Ardmore. Now that Ardmore was in operation, Dalton and Elliman were eager to attract international films to the studio, and earn some badly-needed income for the venture. Revenue generated by the Abbey films would not be enough to sustain the studio. Dalton's friend and business colleague Carl Foreman made his first trip to Ireland in July 1958 to visit Ardmore. During his visit to Dublin, Foreman met the noted Irish writer Liam O'Flaherty. Foreman hoped to make a film based on O'Flaherty's story *Insurrection* which deals with the 1916 Rising, and envisaged filming being carried out at Ardmore and on location in Dublin.

Ardmore began receiving international publicity. Hugh D. Smith, in an article in the *New York Times* in September 1958, noted approvingly that Dalton and Elliman were putting thousands of pounds into 'what promises to be one of the finest movie and TV film studios in Europe'. Smith noted that a recent visitor to Ardmore was the actor Cary Grant, who said of Dublin and its environs, 'Where have I been all my life, that I haven't come here before?'[46]

Meanwhile, Dalton pressed ahead with his collaboration with the Abbey. It was decided to make a film based on the play *The New Gossoon* by George Shiels. The film version would be known as *Sally's Irish Rogue* (1958), with the title further changed for the US market to *The Poacher's Daughter*. The American director Allen Reisner was initially hired, but he and Dalton disagreed over the script. Reisner withdrew and was replaced by George Pollock, who later directed the popular Agatha Christie mystery, *Ten Little Indians*.[47] *Sally's Irish Rogue* starred Julie Harris and Tim Seely, with Harry Brogan and a range of other Abbey players also taking part. The producers, under the aegis of Emmet Dalton Productions, were Dalton's collaborators, Bob Baker and Monty Berman.

There was ongoing tension between Ria Mooney and some of the outside production people who were brought in to work on films. She had differences with Bob Baker in particular on *The New Gossoon* project, in which she advised on casting. In a letter to Dalton she talked bitterly of being 'snubbed' or 'politely tolerated like an unwanted hanger-on'.[48] She talked of the extra strain she had to endure in 'churning out productions' at the Abbey while key players were absent from rehearsals because they were away making films. It also emerged that Dalton had differences with Fielder Cook and Bob Baker over an attempt by Dalton to make a film based on the T.C. Murray play, *Autumn Fire*. In letters to Mooney, Dalton complained that Cook and Baker 'completely sabotaged my efforts to produce *Autumn Fire*'. He also complained that he had to pay $5,000 to Cook 'for letting me down' on the project.[49] Dalton felt that between Cook and the 'crazy Reisner', he had 'a very bad deal'.

The next play to be turned into a film was Hugh Leonard's popular 1956 comedy *The Big Birthday*. The film version was re-titled *Broth of a Boy*. Once again, George Pollock was called in to direct. The film-makers succeeded in enticing Oscar-winning actor Barry Fitzgerald over from America to play the lead role of a 110-year-old poacher. The film tells the story of how an English TV producer (Tony Wright) discovers the oldest man in the world and tries to get him onto television. Among the other actors taking part were Harry Brogan, Marie Kean and Dermot Kelly. The film was completed in the latter part of 1958 and released the following year.

While Dalton undoubtedly enjoyed producing films there were signs that the frustrations of film-making and setting up Ardmore were taking their toll. In a letter to Ria Mooney he questioned the commitment of Ernest Blythe to the Abbey film project.[50] Dalton indicated he was also unhappy about Abbey players working for outside film-makers – he thought that after the Abbey, his own productions had first call on their services. 'One of these days I will sit down and work out why I have got myself so involved when life could have been so much easier without this project.'[51] He confided that he was not going to confine himself to the Abbey players for the future. 'So I will consult with you later about extending the field of talent.'

Shake Hands With The Devil

The efforts to bring international film projects to Ardmore bore fruit in 1958, when it was decided to make a Hollywood film, *Shake Hands With The Devil* at the County Wicklow studio. The film told the story of an American medical student, played by Don Murray, who, while studying in Dublin, is caught up in the struggle between the IRA and the Black and Tans. A major star, James Cagney was lined up for the film, along with Dana Wynter, Glynis Johns and Dame Sybil Thorndike. A youthful Richard Harris was among the many Irish actors who also played roles. The director was Michael Anderson, who had made *The Dam Busters* (1955).

Apart from the filming at Ardmore, location shooting took place at various places, including County Wicklow and the Dublin docks. The author recalls as a schoolboy watching the filming of a scene as a 59-year-old Jimmy Cagney nimbly ran along the North Wall quay. The film had personal resonance with Emmet Dalton. His son Richard was hired as the Third Assistant Director, and would go on to have a successful career in films and TV. The armoured car that the author saw being used on the North Wall that day as part of a scene, and which had been loaned by the Irish Army, would have had particular significance for Emmet. It was none other than *Slievenamon*, part of the convoy on the fateful day of the Bealnablath ambush in which Michael Collins died.

Shake Hands With The Devil received its Irish premiere at the Savoy Cinema on O'Connell Street, Dublin on 21 May 1959. Dalton and Elliman were, of course, present, as were the American producers of the film, George Glass and Walter Seltzer of Troy Productions. A glittering array of acting talent from home and abroad attended, along with President Sean T. O'Kelly, Government Ministers, academics, senior army officers, members of the diplomatic corps – even Monsignor Gerada, secretary to the Papal Nuncio. One can detect a real sense of pride in Ireland over the release of *Shake Hands With The Devil*. It was the biggest production so far from Ardmore, and showed that Ireland's new film industry could handle a major feature film. A range of other movie-makers would make their way to Ireland to make films at Ardmore and the studio would have quite a prolific output. The premiere of the film must have been a proud moment for Dalton, even though he had come under great pressure in running Ardmore and in his film production activities generally. In a letter to Ria Mooney, he talked of having to bear 'almost unendurable anguish and disillusionment', but also tried to cheer her up, adding, 'Ria, don't be too depressed, life is full of problems, but we must just learn to take them in our stride.'[52]

This Other Eden

The English film director Muriel Box was lined up for the next film to be made at Ardmore in collaboration with the Abbey. The film, *This Other Eden*, was based on a play by Louis D'Alton. Muriel Box was the most prolific of English female directors and had her own ideas as to whom she wanted to act in the film. Some at the Abbey were deeply unhappy with her approach, feeling the theatre's experienced players had not been given sufficient prominence. Box was not for turning on the issue. Abbey boss Ernest Blythe complained to the theatre board that Mrs Box would not take Bill Foley to play a leading character, and brought over Niall MacGinnis from England instead.[53] The employment of Hilton Edwards from the other major theatre in Dublin, the Gate, was noticeable – he was cast as a parish priest, Canon Moyle.

Box became the first woman to direct an Irish feature film. Although the producer was Alec C. Snowden, Dalton undoubtedly played a key role in selecting the play to form the basis for the film, which was produced under the aegis of Emmet Dalton Productions. At one stage the Abbey Players' Council held a meeting with Snowden on the issue of casting. He told them that although Dalton was eager to use as many Abbey players as possible, often the actual decisions were made by the director, and that certain decisions could not be overruled.[54]

Ria Mooney was particularly upset over the way the production was being handled. She clearly felt that she was being sidelined in regard to casting, and wrote to Dalton to tell him that she was withdrawing from the project. She was also turning down the role she had been offered in the film, that of Mother Superior, even though she would have liked to take the part: 'I cannot pay lip service to you and the Abbey Theatre, in return for a cheque, no matter how large.'[55] It was obvious that she retained a personal loyalty to Dalton, going on to say, 'You may call on me at any time and I'll be only too happy to help you, while at the same time serving our Theatre.'

This letter must have come as a particular blow to Dalton. Dalton's response is not available but, doubtless with his support, the producer Alec Snowden pleaded with Mooney to reconsider her decision. No doubt much to the relief of Dalton, Mooney signed a contract to act in the film, and went on to play the Mother Superior. Both Dalton and Snowden expressed delight with her performance in the role.

This Other Eden, which has been described as a 'caustic comedy' is set in the Ireland of 1945, but the story it tells goes back to the Troubles of an earlier era. Some of the locals in a small town have decided to erect a statue to an IRA hero, Jack Carbery (Gerald Sullivan), who was shot dead in an ambush by the Black and Tans during the War of Independence. Carbery was on his way to a meeting with a British Army officer to engage in peace talks when he was killed. His friend Mick Devereaux (played as a young man by Peadar Lamb and as an older man by Niall MacGinnis) cradles Carbery's head as he dies. There is an element of greed and hypocrisy among the elderly men behind the monument project, because they believe it will bring business to the town. The monument is blown up by the patriot's illegitimate son Conor (Norman Rodway). Some saw in the film echoes of the story of Dalton and Collins at Bealnablath, and the subsequent wild speculation that Dalton was somehow responsible for Collins's death.

Fidelma Farley, in her academic study of *This Other Eden*, sees the character of the cynical and weary Mick Devereaux as having echoes of Emmet Dalton, while Devereaux's friend Jack Carbery she sees as 'loosely based on Michael Collins'. Farley goes on: 'Carbery, like Collins, was intent upon entering negotiations to end the war. Devereaux, like Dalton, is suspected of complicity in Carbery's death and has become worn down by his own disillusionment and by the largely unspoken accusations which have dogged him.'[56] Farley believes that the character of Devereaux can be viewed 'as the means through which Emmet Dalton revisited a traumatic past...'[57] At one stage in the film an Anglophobic character, Clannery (Harry Brogan), says to Devereaux, 'You were there when he died,' and Devereaux replies, 'I was. I have heard it hinted at more than once that it was myself that had him killed.'

The film may have been Dalton's way of sending a defiant message to his anonymous detractors who had spread wild rumours about his supposed role in Michael Collins's death. The film, of course, deals with a far broader range of issues. Farley describes the film as a 'remarkable early treatment of the concerns which would exercise Irish film-makers from the 1970s onwards'. She comments that through its exploration of the legacy of the past, *This Other Eden* addresses a wide range of issues, 'including emigration, the power and wealth of the Church, the reverence of nationalist martyrs, illegitimacy and anti-English hostility'.[58]

Box lined up English actor Leslie Phillips to play a wealthy Englishman with a romantic vision of Ireland. Emmet's daughter Audrey, who had already made her name in Hollywood, had the lead female role. Phillips, in his autobiography, referred to Emmet Dalton as 'a powerful individual with a formidable reputation', who was trying to bring international film-making to Ireland. He described Audrey, whom he played opposite, as 'a very striking and likeable woman' who, it seemed to him, 'had the eyes and colouring of the Armada sailors who had run adrift on the Irish west coast in the late 17th century [sic] and subsequently infused the Celtic population with strong Hispanic genes'.[59]

Location filming was carried out in Chapelizod village near Dublin's Phoenix Park, and a hotel in Wicklow town, while Ardmore House was pressed into service as the 'big house' in the film, Kilgarrig House. The script was written by veteran screenwriter Patrick Kirwan and Blanaid Irvine. There were last-minute script revisions as filming was in progress. Box re-worked the script herself, according to Farley.[60]

There was a social side to work on the film. Phillips recalled being invited by Dalton to a 'big dinner in the Shelbourne in Dublin with all his family'.[61] Nevertheless Muriel Box, in her diary, told of a conversation she had with Dalton during filming, when he recalled the deaths a couple of years previously of his wife, mother and eldest son. Box remarked that he seems 'a very lonely man'.[62] The film had its Irish premiere at the Cork Film Festival in September 1959. Dalton, noted for his cool nerve as a soldier in times of war, admitted at a press conference that he was 'on tenterhooks' waiting for the reaction to the film. Leslie Philips had high praise for Dalton in comments to the media. 'I have worked with many producers but never one like Emmet Dalton. He is the straightest, sincerest and least calculating man in films'.[63]

Dalton was extremely proud of this film. In a letter to Ria Mooney, he said he believed it was 'easily our best film to date'. He said he knew she was not too happy about this particular picture but he also felt she was big enough to admit she was wrong if this proved to be the case. He complimented Mooney on her own performance as the Reverend Mother, describing it as a 'perfect gem'.[64] Relations between Dalton and the Abbey appeared to become more distant following the making of *This Other Eden*. Barry Monahan notes that at the film's premiere in Cork, Dalton told Maxwell Sweeney of *Kinematograph Weekly* that he had plans for a non-Irish story, with locations in Cornwall and London.[65] Monahan comments that Emmet Dalton Productions 'never again engaged the Abbey players wholesale'.[66] Some Abbey players were employed on subsequent Dalton-produced films but in smaller numbers.

Other Dalton Productions

In the early 1960s the English director Don Chaffey made two films at Ardmore for Emmet Dalton Productions. The first, in 1960, was *Lies My Father Told Me*, starring American actress Betsy Blair and Abbey actors Harry Brogan and Eddie Golden. Like other American movie figures linked to Dalton, Blair had moved to Europe as a result of the Hollywood blacklist. (She is best remembered for playing the love interest of Ernest Borgnine in the critically acclaimed *Marty*.)

The next Don Chaffey film at Ardmore was made the following year, 1961. For this production, *The Middle of Nowhere* (later re-named *The Webster Boy*) the film-makers cast the young American actor, John Cassavetes. He later emerged as a major film star and an acclaimed director. In *The Webster Boy* Cassavetes plays an American who meets the woman from whom he was divorced many years before. She is now re-married, with a growing son, but they fall in love again, leading to complications. *The Webster Boy* also starred Elizabeth Sellars and David Farrar, with smaller roles going to Harry Brogan and his colleague in the Abbey players, Aideen O'Kelly.

Don Chaffey was a prolific director who worked in film and TV. Dalton would have been familiar with his work directing episodes of *The Adventures of Robin Hood*. Chaffey was not an 'art house' director or part of the *avant garde* but he was seen as an efficient, no-nonsense director who could bring in films and TV episodes on time and on budget. John Trumper, a film editor who worked with Chaffey on a number of projects, wrote a letter to the British newspaper *The Independent* in January 1991 after Chaffey died, drawing attention to his two Ardmore films, saying these were remarkable films which never got the distribution they deserved.

The last film made with Dalton as producer at Ardmore was *The Devil's Agent* (1962). It is a spy story about a wine salesman caught up in an espionage drama involving Russian and US intelligence in Austria, Germany and Hungary. Directed by John Paddy Carstairs, the film starred Peter van Eyck, Marianne Koch, Macdonald Carey and Christopher Lee, who was famed for playing Dracula, among other roles. Like Dalton, Lee was passionate about golf, and Dalton ensured that the actor enjoyed some good golfing during his period in Ireland. In an interview in 1990, Lee recalled how Dalton arranged many games for him, including rounds with a couple of the great names – with Harry Bradshaw at Portmarnock and Christy O'Connor at Royal Dublin.[67]

Dalton had continued to play golf at Hermitage during trips back to Dublin and Liam Murray recalls, as a schoolboy, acting as caddy for him in the 1950s. He told how fellow golfers treated Dalton with enormous respect and addressed him as 'General'. Among the boy caddies, Dalton was seen as a 'good bag' – he gave a good tip.[68]

Emmet Dalton Productions made just one foray into the documentary world. In 1960 the company made *Meet the Quare Fella*, consisting of a lengthy interview by Eamon Andrews with the writer Brendan Behan. It was produced by Louis Elliman and directed by Fred O'Donovan. Because of Behan's reputation for hell-raising and unpredictability, it was decided to book him into the Royal Hotel, Bray, close to Ardmore where the interview was filmed. Andrews and O'Donovan, accompanied by impresario Lorcan Bourke, collected Behan from his Dublin home and brought him to the hotel. They stayed there too, to keep an eye on Brendan.[69] In the interview, the gravel-voiced Behan talked about his views on fame, religion, writing and his time in Borstal. He said he believed that the world was divided into two classes – invalids and nurses. 'I'm a nurse,' he announced helpfully. 'In my books and plays I try to find out why everybody is unhappy.'

Film Distribution

Dalton ran into difficulties getting distribution for his films in Britain. He was very familiar with the distribution aspect of the film business, and knew only too well how major players largely controlled which movies were shown in cinemas. In August 1958 he confided in a letter to Ria Mooney, 'The past year has been one of trial and trouble for me, mainly caused by the worst possible distribution of my pictures...' He went on, 'It does not matter how good your pictures are, if the people do not get the opportunity to see them.' He said that from the economic standpoint, it had been 'ruinous' for him, as he would personally lose money on each picture that had been released. He expressed hope in regard to the distribution of *This Other Eden*, as it was being handled by a different distributor – Regal Films International, run by Joe Vegoda – 'who will take much greater pains to ensure that the film can be seen and earn money'.[70]

Sean Lemass, now Taoiseach, was concerned about the film distribution problem, as the government had invested heavily in Ardmore. According to Barry Monahan, one of the Ardmore directors Con McGrath contacted Lemass pointing out that two major distributors in the UK, who controlled 50 per cent of the market, were refusing films made at Ardmore. Lemass, in turn, wrote to Jack Lynch, Minister for Industry and Commerce, asking him to have one of his officials talk to Emmet Dalton with a view to helping Ardmore with its problem.[71] Dalton was able to get distribution but not the major distribution he had hoped for.

Attracting overseas film-makers to Ardmore was also important for the future of the studio. Apart from the films associated with Dalton, other films were made at Ardmore following *Shake Hands With The Devil*. American film legend Robert Mitchum came to Ardmore to film *A Terrible Beauty* (1960), a story about the IRA in a Northern Ireland border town in the 1940s. Produced by Raymond Stross and directed by Tay Garnett, the cast list also featured Anne Heywood, Dan O'Herlihy and Richard Harris. In this early period other films made at Ardmore included *The Siege of Sidney Street* (1960), shot partly on location in north inner city Dublin. The film, another Berman-Baker production, was based on the story of a police siege of a house occupied by anarchists in Edwardian London. Another film made in this era was *Johnny Nobody* (1961), starring Aldo Ray, Nigel Patrick and Cyril Cusack. A controversial film, Guy Green's *The Mark* (1961) was nominated for the Palme d'Or award at Cannes, while its star Stuart Whitman was nominated for an Oscar. The veteran Belfast-born director, Brian Desmond Hurst, made *The Playboy of the Western World*, adapted from the Synge play, at Ardmore in 1962 – his last film. Gary Redmond played the lead role.

In the early 1960s, Ardmore hosted an eager young American, Francis Ford Coppola. He had been working as a sound man for prolific, low budget producer Roger Corman. Coppola persuaded Corman to let him make what he promised would be the cheapest film Corman had ever produced. The result was a horror film made in three weeks, written and directed by Coppola. *Dementia 13* (1963) remains a cult favourite with gothic horror fans. The black and white movie starred William Campbell, Luana Anders and the Irish actor Patrick Magee, and features an axe-wielding lunatic who stalks an Irish family at a reunion in Castle Haloran. The historic Howth Castle near Dublin was used to depict the fictional castle. Coppola became one of America's most acclaimed film directors, making such classics as *The Godfather* and *Apocalypse Now*. Emmet Dalton's son Richard worked as assistant director on Coppola's Ardmore film. Richard remembers Coppola as 'very enthusiastic, a nice guy, and off the wall at times'. Coppola had a very expensive Alfa Romeo sports car but during his time in Ireland he preferred Richard's bigger MG Magneto. 'We swapped cars for the few weeks he was here, which was fine with me.'

Problems at Ardmore

As part of a drive to entice foreign film makers to Ardmore and to assist the Irish film industry generally, the Industrial Credit Company set up a subsidiary, the Irish Film Finance Corporation (IFFC) in February 1960. It has been said that Emmet Dalton played a key role in persuading the Industrial Credit Company to set up the IFFC.[72] The IFFC assisted film producers in Ireland by providing financial loans. The first film made with the assistance of the IFFC was *The Siege of Sydney Street*. Other early film projects to receive loans included *Lies My Father Told Me, Middle of Nowhere* and *The Devil's Agent*, all three the work of Emmet Dalton Productions, and *Johnny Nobody*. By December 1961, the IFFC had helped to finance thirteen films, all but one of which was made at Ardmore.

However, problems persisted for the studio. Dalton had a fight on his hands to ensure that films made at Ardmore continued to qualify for British state funding known as Eady finance. Dalton complained that elements in the British film industry had tried to get the British government to exclude Ardmore from the fund. This would have made it much more difficult to attract British film-makers to the County Wicklow studio. Apparently, some in the British film world objected to a UK 'subsidy' for an Irish competitor. Dalton explained in a letter to Ria Mooney that 'by way of retaliation' he had joined the Federation of British Film Makers whose members included Carl Foreman, Sidney Gilliat, the Boulting Brothers and Sir Michael Balcon.[73] The federation had written a very strong letter to the President of the Board of Trade, and as a result Dalton seemed certain there would be no change in the status quo.

Unfortunately, Eady finance posed its own problems. To avail of the funding, Ardmore had to be regarded as a UK studio. This meant employing British technicians on British productions at Ardmore. As a result, there were fewer opportunities for the development of native Irish technical expertise in film-making, although the productions were a benefit to the local economy and helped sustain the studio. There was labour unrest arising out of conflicts between the Irish Electrical Trades Union and its British counterpart on the employment of electricians at Ardmore on British-produced films.

Dalton later recalled that when pickets were placed on the gates of Ardmore, he had to close the studio for a lengthy period. It was a particularly frustrating time for him. There were large overheads, the borrowing from the Industrial Credit Company was considerable, and the amount owed in interest was increasing all the time.[74] With the studio closed, the venture was falling into greater difficulty. Eventually, in 1963, Ardmore went into receivership, with the Industrial Credit Company appointing the receiver. Dalton's own company went into liquidation. He told an interviewer, 'I lost my entire investment.'[75] Dalton was sixty-five years old at the time. Although he remained a director of Carl Foreman's Open Road Films, Dalton's direct involvement in Irish film production was at an end. Dalton greatly regretted that his great adventure, his attempt to start an Irish film industry, had ended in this way.

Ardmore ultimately survived under other managements. Despite all the early difficulties, Dalton's vision was vindicated in the longer term. Overseas producers came to make films at Ardmore with local crews, while indigenous producers also used the facilities. It is more than fifty years since Ardmore was opened and many major films and TV series have been made at the facility that was Dalton's brainchild, helping to maintain Ireland's reputation around the world as a highly respected centre for film-making.

CHAPTER SIXTEEN

Life After Films

In the latter stages of his film production work, Emmet Dalton continued to live alone at Plane Tree House in Kensington. In 1960 his old friend Harold Taubman was planning a return trip to London – this time with his family – and Dalton offered him the use of his flat at Plane Tree House. It was only after arrival that Taubman realised that Dalton was also in residence – but the apartment was big enough for Dalton and the Taubmans. Neither did Dalton look for rent – Taubman had to force him later to accept some payment.[1] The Taubmans also stayed in Dalton's home on another trip in 1962. At this period, in the midst of his loneliness as a widower, Dalton found some companionship in a platonic friendship with next-door neighbor Madeleine Chadwick[2] – he would sometimes have dinner with her in her apartment. Madeleine's husband Harold had died in 1958.

Taubman's sons William and Philip retain very happy memories of their visits to Plane Tree House. William, an academic who won the Pulitzer Prize for his biography of Nikita Kruschev, was nineteen years old at the time of his first visit to the Dalton home: 'I recall that Emmet seemed rather formal and somewhat stern (and ramrod straight), but that he was also warm and hospitable, and a very nice person.'[3] Philip, who had a distinguished career as a journalist with the *New York Times*, recalled his two month-long sojourns at the apartment in 1960 and 1962: 'We stayed in a cozy ground floor flat, went to the theatre every evening and I explored London during the days on my own or spent many beguiling afternoons in Holland Park … Emmet and Howard would get together occasionally to talk, usually upstairs in the main residence or in the garden.' Philip recalled that the garden was 'beautifully maintained' – he thinks by Emmet's neighbour Madeleine.

Philip recalled his father and Emmet talking, among other things, about the Wimbledon tennis championship, which was under way during both their visits, and horse racing: 'Emmet set us up with a small black & white television and I greatly enjoyed the extensive coverage of Wimbledon matches in our flat. Like [my brother] Bill, I remember Emmet as rather formal and a bit detached, but always polite and welcoming.' Philip added that he attributed his abiding affection for London 'to our two summers at Plane Tree House'.[4]

With Ardmore studios going into receivership, the early 1960s was not a happy time for Dalton. One consolation would have been that his daughter Audrey and son Richard were both enjoying ongoing career success in films and TV. Audrey was in constant demand in America as an actress, her work including roles in major TV serials. Richard, during the 1960s, worked as assistant director on the popular TV series *The Avengers*. Amid other work, he also began a long-term collaboration with Joseph Losey, working as Assistant Director on a range of films made by the acclaimed movie-maker. These included *Accident* (1967) with Dirk Bogarde and Stanley Baker; *Secret Ceremony* (1968), with Elizabeth Taylor and Mia Farrow, and *The Go-Between* (1970), with Julie Christie and Alan Bates, which won the Palme d'Or at the Cannes Film Festival.

Emmet Dalton suffered a major setback when he gave a large file of personal papers to a friend to sort out. Unfortunately, the file was lost, and the person concerned has passed on.[5] Other documents survived, and as earlier indicated, a file of the more significant papers is now with the National Library of Ireland. While living at Kensington, Dalton would attend Mass at the Jesuit church on Farm Street. He got to know some of the priests and they would visit him at Plane Tree House where a housekeeper would provide dinner, and they would debate the issues of the day. One visitor was Father Joseph Christie, a missioner renowned for his preaching.[6]

Pat McCrea, one of Dalton's old comrades, died in February 1964 and his passing elicited an eloquent tribute from Dalton. In a newspaper interview, he talked of McCrea as 'one of my dearest friends'.[7] Dalton paid particular tribute to McCrea's great skill in driving the hi-jacked armoured car during the attempt to 'spring' Sean MacEoin from prison. 'He was a power of strength and steady as the rock of Gibraltar in all our operations...' The interview was read with interest by the Sisters of Charity at the Stella Maris convent in Howth. Their annals recorded how Dalton, Joe Leonard and a third man had taken refuge at the convent after the prison rescue attempt. Sister Francis Colombiere wrote to Dalton wondering if the third man in the group that day was McCrea.[8] In fact it was the wounded Tom Walsh. She invited Dalton to visit Stella Maris the next time he was in Dublin.

In the mid-1960s, the good life at Plane Tree House came to an end. The property was sold for re-development, and the residents moved out. Madeleine Chadwick got a good price for her apartment and bought a large detached house at Watford Road, Radlett, near the Hertfordshire countryside, about a half hour by train from London. Dalton became one of the residents at the house, and lived there in an apartment for some time.[9] His son Richard, who was working at nearby Elstree film studio, would sometimes call around for lunch.

Dalton retained his low opinion of Éamon de Valera, whom he blamed for the Civil War. He cannot have been pleased when de Valera was re-elected as President for another term in 1966, occupying the official residence, Áras an Uachtaráin in the Phoenix Park. In a letter to a friend in Dublin in August 1966, Dalton considered that the curse of the Civil War could be attributed to one man, 'the sanctimonious, hypocritical megalomaniac' in the Phoenix Park.[10]

Remembering Tom Kettle

With the approach of the fiftieth anniversary of the death of his friend Tom Kettle, Dalton sent a letter to the *Irish Times* and it appeared on the anniversary itself, 9 September 1966. He observed that 1966 was the fiftieth anniversary of the 1916 Rising – it was a year when Ireland paid tribute to the memory of her sons 'whose lives were forfeit but whose sacrifice was not in vain'. Dalton reflected that 1966 was also the fiftieth anniversary of the Battle of the Somme, 'where thousands of young Irishmen fought with great gallantry before losing their lives', and were 'motivated by a just cause'. He recalled that Tom Kettle 'had left his testimony in a little poem dedicated to his daughter, and written four days before his death'. In his letter, Dalton quoted in full, the poem *To My Daughter Betty, The Gift of God*.

After years in England, Dalton's children persuaded him to return to live in Dublin. His married daughters were eager to look after him in his declining years. He divided his time between Sybil who lived at Vernon Avenue, Clontarf and Nuala who resided at Sydney Parade Avenue, Ballsbridge. To avoid the cold, damp Irish winter, he also spent time with daughter Audrey and her family in the California sunshine. Audrey recalled that he stayed with her for six or seven winters up to the mid-1970s: 'My children grew up knowing him at a very crucial age in their lives. He featured in their lives and they remember him with great affection.' She recalled how he would bring her sons Jim and Richard to a local driving range, even though he had long given up golf, 'or as he liked to say about many things – "it had given him up".' While in America, Dalton called to see his sister Nuala, the nun, who later told Audrey about the visits. He would take her out to dinner and she would bring him back into the convent to meet the other nuns, who would be in their dressing gowns, watching television. Dalton was used to the more austere religious life of pre-Vatican Two. 'It was not his idea of a convent,' said Audrey with wry amusement. Dalton became ill with respiratory problems during a visit to California and received treatment. He decided to forego further visits in case he became an imposition on Audrey and her family.

Dalton never realized his wish to make a film about Michael Collins, but in 1968 he was one of the advisers to Irish producer/director Kevin McClory who planned to make a movie about Collins with Richard Harris in the title role. McClory, who was associated with James Bond films, proposed to make the film at Ardmore, but the project never came to fruition.

Return to Bealnablath

Emmet Dalton was a private man, not prone to courting personal publicity. However, in his later years, he agreed to do some interviews with writers and journalists. In the 1960s, while living at Radlett, he gave a number of interviews to the late Calton Younger for his book *Ireland's Civil War*. In 1970, after returning to Dublin, he talked to Cormac MacCarthaigh and the interview was published in the *Sunday*

Independent.[11] The interviewer asked who chose the escort for Collins on his final trip to the south. Dalton said he did not know. As far as he was concerned, it was the escort party that had come down from Dublin and he would not have chosen any such unit. 'They had no notion of what conditions in the country were like.'[12] In 1974 Dalton was interviewed by historian Meda Ryan. (In January that year, he suffered another bereavement when his brother Charlie died at age 70 at St Patrick's Hospital, Dublin.)

Dalton went on to give an important series of interviews to Pádraig Ó Raghallaigh, which were broadcast on RTÉ radio in early 1977. Dalton also agreed to cooperate with an RTÉ TV documentary about his life and times, *Emmet Dalton Remembers.* The interviewer was the late Cathal O'Shannon, one of the most accomplished journalists of that era. Ironically, his father Cathal O'Shannon senior had raised a query in the Dáil in 1922 about Dalton's suitability for the post of Senate Clerk. In addition to studio interviews at RTÉ, Dalton returned to places of significance in his varied career. O'Shannon interviewed him at Kilworth Camp, where he first heard of the 1916 Rising. On 9 September 1976, the sixtieth anniversary of the taking of Ginchy during the Battle of the Somme, Dalton re-visited the battle site and showed O'Shannon the approximate location where Tom Kettle died. Dalton was interviewed at Guillemont Road Cemetery, beside the grave of his superior officer, Captain W.J. Murphy, killed on the same day as Kettle. In London, Dalton was filmed outside the house in Cadogan Gardens where he stayed with Michael Collins during the Treaty talks.

O'Shannon and his producer, the late Niall McCarthy, knew how important it was to film an interview with Dalton at the site of the ambush in Bealnablath. O'Shannon told how it took all the powers of persuasion of himself and McCarthy to guide Dalton's footsteps back to a location 'that must have been a place of horror for him'.[13] Dalton, who was almost eighty years old, ultimately agreed to return to the valley where he had witnessed the death of Michael Collins. The documentary makers applied to the Department of Defence for the *Slievenamon* armoured car to be brought back to Bealnablath for a reconstruction of the ambush but permission was refused.[14]

An intermediary (who was not identified) asked O'Shannon if two surviving members of the IRA ambush party could meet Dalton at Bealnablath. To film such an encounter would have been a golden opportunity for O'Shannon. However, Dalton was having none of it. The response of the feisty old soldier was typically terse and to the point: 'If their only claim to fame is that they shot at me from behind a wall, I don't want to meet the bastards.'[15]

Cameraman Godfrey Graham was in the car with Dalton and O'Shannon as they drove into the valley of Bealnablath. 'Emmet was emotional, no doubt about it,' Graham told me. The crew felt enormously privileged to be in the presence of history.'[16] Graham recalled Dalton as having a good memory and being 'very lucid'. The film shows Dalton as he emerged from a car near the Michael Collins memorial. He was, as usual, smartly dressed, wearing blazer, grey trousers, hat, shirt and tie and carrying a walking stick. Despite his age, he still had an erect, military bearing.

Talking to O'Shannon, Dalton calmly re-lived the events of 22 August 1922 in that secluded valley - the ambush, the firefight, the death of Collins, and the nightmare journey back to Cork with the body of the Commander-in-Chief. Dalton told how shots came not just from a low hill to their left as they moved northwards through the valley but also from a hill ahead and to the right of the convoy. He talked also of his deep regard for Collins whom he felt he had got to know very well in a very short space of time. 'My love for Collins – I use no other word – has not altered one iota in the passage of time,' Dalton said in a remarkable tribute.

O'Shannon admitted that it was with some trepidation that he later raised the question as to who shot Collins. Off-camera, Dalton said he knew what some people were saying, they were claiming he shot the Chief. Nobody had the guts to say it to his face, he said. He loved Collins, and anyone who knew Collins and who knew him (Dalton) knew what a lot of nonsense it was.[17] O'Shannon would have liked to get such comments on camera but Dalton did not want to dignify the rumours by discussing them on the record. O'Shannon respected Dalton's decision.

Death of Emmet Dalton

With military-style precision, Emmet Dalton died on his eightieth birthday, 4 March 1978, the 200th anniversary of the birth of the patriot after whom he was named, Robert Emmet. He passed away at the residence of his daughter Nuala. That night, the documentary, *Emmet Dalton Remembers* was broadcast by RTÉ, to much acclaim. The chief mourners at his funeral were son Richard, and daughters Nuala Cuddy, Audrey Browne and Sybil Collins. Dalton's elderly surviving siblings in America were unable to travel, except for Nuala, the nun. Emmet and Nuala had always been close. Recalled Richard: 'There was a whiparound, Nuala got an air ticket and she was straight over on the plane. She was marvellous.'

There was controversy over the failure of the Fianna Fáil government to send a Minister to represent it at the funeral. An editorial in the *Irish Times* excoriated the government's omission, referred to the Civil War and asked: 'How can we expect the Taoiseach and his Ministers to make an open, generous approach to the one million [Protestants] in the North of Ireland when they find it impossible even to try to get over old antagonism down here?'[18] Various senior figures from Fine Gael, including former Taoiseach, Liam Cosgrave TD, were present at the funeral in the Church of Our Lady Queen of Peace, Merrion Road. Among other dignitaries were Colonel P.J. Dempsey, representing the Defence Forces, Chief Justice Mr T.F. O'Higgins, and Michael Collins's nephew, Major General Sean Collins Powell.

Full military honours were rendered. The band of the Curragh Command played the Dead March. The tricolour-draped coffin was drawn on a gun carriage to Glasnevin Cemetery, followed by an army vehicle carrying wreaths and floral tributes. At the graveside, army buglers sounded the Last Post, and a military party fired volleys. A guard of honour was formed by members of the Old IRA, under Dalton's former comrade, Commandant Vinny Byrne, who gave a last salute. Dalton was not buried with his beloved wife Alice. Alice's mother was also in that grave in Glasnevin and according to Dalton's son Richard, he did not want to spend eternity in the same plot as his mother-in-law. His own man to the end, Dalton opted to be interred alone in the republican plot, close to Michael Collins and other figures from Ireland's revolutionary past. Reporting on Dalton's death, journalist Michael McInerney commented that Collins's death affected Dalton deeply, and 'he seemed to have lost interest in Irish politics afterwards...'[19]

Following the absence of Government Ministers from the funeral, the poet Paul Durcan wrote a poem *Lament for Major General Emmet Dalton* in which he denounces the 'mob' who disowned Dalton. Jim Haughey comments on the poem in his book on Irish war poetry, and reflects that Dalton in death joined the other forgotten dead – those whose ideals and actions 'are no longer serviceable to the republican myth of a unified nationalist front against British rule'. He says that Dalton 'is a discomforting reminder of another branch of Irish nationalism, one that saw the value of political compromise rather than unyielding and unrealistic devotion to a nationalist ideal'.[20]

Controversy Over Who Shot Collins

Within a few years of Dalton's passing, there was a public debate over who shot Michael Collins. The debate was sparked by the 1981 publication of Captain John M. Feehan's book, *The Shooting of Michael Collins, Murder or Accident?* Captain Feehan hotly denied suggestions he had accused Dalton of shooting Collins. He said nobody knew who fired the shot. 'All I have tried to do in my book is to show that he [Collins] could have been murdered. I do not say that he was.'[21] Others would go on to air conspiracy theories about the death of the Big Fellow. Some old friends, acquaintances and former comrades of Dalton came out strongly in his defence, as well as two men who were on the republican side in the Civil War, Aodogan O'Rahilly and Sean Dowling.

Cathal O'Shannon labelled as 'contemptible' the insinuations against Dalton and also defended his competence as a military man.[22] O'Shannon said he had no doubt, having spent many months with Dalton, that he was innocent of the calumnies 'which lesser men have uttered about that day'. O'Shannon added: 'Dalton was an honourable man, and few in his lifetime dared to say publicly what they have hinted at now that he is safely dead.'[23] Dalton's former schoolmate, statistician R.C. Geary declared: 'I would stake my life on the absolute integrity of Emmet Dalton.'[24] Sports commentator Brendan O'Reilly quoted former IRB man Martin Walton: 'There was not an ounce of deception in Dalton's nature. No more honourable man ever walked this earth.'[25]

General M.J. Costello, former army intelligence chief, said he never knew of any responsible person who doubted that Collins was killed 'by a single shot fired by one of an ambush party which went into action for the specific purpose of attacking him'.[26] Ulick O'Connor also defended Dalton, saying that he often discussed the ambush with Joe Dolan who was on the Collins convoy. 'If there had been any question of anyone in the convoy deliberately shooting Collins, Joe would have blown the head off him before they reached Cork.'[27]

Dalton's daughter-in-law Robin Dalton said that claims that Emmet was somehow responsible for Collins's death 'upset the family terribly, nothing could be further from the truth'. In America, Dalton's daughter Audrey wrote a memo for her own family. She castigated the pundits who, knowing they were beyond the libel laws, 'dug up and embellished every rumour, no matter how far-fetched' about the death of Collins.[28]

Sean Dowling, a senior figure in the anti-Treaty IRA in the Civil War, made an important contribution. He refuted the rumour that Dalton may have been responsible for Collins's death, 'accidentally or otherwise'. He revealed that during the Civil War some members of the IRA HQ staff interviewed one of the Bealnablath ambush party 'who believed he had fired the fatal shot that killed Collins'. Dowling commented: 'Emmet Dalton was not only the most fearless of soldiers (was he not the "boy hero of Guinchy"?), he was also among the noblest of men – and he idolized Collins'.[29]

Postscript

Emmet Dalton packed much into his eighty years. His soldiering took him on a hazardous journey, from the Somme to Bealnablath, from Palestine and Salonika to the Battle of the Four Courts. He had an amazing record – a founding father of the Irish Defence Forces; first Senate Clerk; pioneering Irish film-maker and founder of Ireland's first film studio. It is noteworthy that a former Civil War enemy described him as 'a fearless soldier' and 'among the noblest of men'. Not a bad epitaph for Major General James Emmet Dalton.

Notes

CHAPTER ONE

1. *Boston Daily Globe*, 27 September 1893.
2. See Family Search website, https://familysearch.org/pal:/MM9.3.1/TH-267-11782-2386-96?cc=1469062. See also: https://familysearch.org/pal:/MM9.3.1/TH-267-11782-3721-15?cc=1469062 (accessed 20 May 2014).
3. Dalton family history website: Daltons in History, Volume 3, No. 5, *Major General James Emmet Dalton, An American in Ireland*, http://www.daltongensoc.com/diharchive/3_5_May_2000/text.html#3 (accessed 20 May 2014).
4. Dalton family history website.
5. Letter from Ernie O'Malley, Kilmainham Prison, to Mrs Erskine Childers, November 1923, reproduced in Cormac K.H. O'Malley, & Anne Dolan, *No Surrender Here, The Civil War Papers of Ernie O'Malley, 1922–24*, (Dublin: Lilliput Press, 2007), p.422.
6. Ibid., O'Malley to Mrs Childers.
7. 'Pearse', letter to the *Irish Times*, 28 September 1972.
8. Letter from Ernie O'Malley to Molly Childers, *No Surrender Here*, p.426.
9. *Sunday Independent*, 23 March 1952.
10. James Meenan (ed.), *Centenary History of the Literary and Historical Society, 1855–1955*, The Kerryman, Tralee, p.131.
11. 'The Great Home Rule Meeting', *Freeman's Journal*, 1 April 1912.
12. 'Coming Prospectus', *Irish Times*, 24 October 1913.
13. 'Action for Wrongful Dismissal Settled', *The Citizen*, 26 April 1916.
14. Information to author from private source.
15. Emmet Dalton, interview with Pádraig Ó Raghallaigh, RTÉ radio, February–March 1977.
16. Ibid.
17. 'James Emmet Dalton', *Dictionary of Irish Biography*, Cambridge University Press/Royal Irish Academy.
18. 'Meeting of Dublin Magistrates', *Irish Times*, 1 August 1914.
19. 'Irish National Volunteers: Meeting of Mr. Redmond's Supporters; New Organisation Formed', *Irish Times*, 1 October 1914.
20. Patrick Moylett, BMH, WS 767.
21. Emmet Dalton interview with Cathal O'Shannon, *Emmet Dalton Remembers*, RTÉ TV, 4 March 1978.
22. Patrick Moylett, BMH, WS 767.
23. Roscrea: 'Distinguished Past Pupil's Death', *Nenagh Guardian*, 11 March 1978.
24. Emmet Dalton interview with Pádraigh Ó Raghallaigh, RTÉ; see also Myles Dungan, *They Shall Not Grow Old* (Dublin: Four Courts Press, 1997), p.25.
25. Emmet Dalton interview with O'Shannon, RTÉ.
26. Ibid.
27. Letter, Colonel W. Elliot, for Military Secretary, War Office, London S.W., to J. E. Dalton Esq., 8 Upper St Columba's Road, Dublin, 29 December 1915; letter courtesy of Audrey Dalton Simenz.
28. Dalton interview with O'Shannon, RTÉ.
29. Ernie O'Malley, *The Singing Flame* (Cork: Mercier, 2012), p.198.
30. Charles Dalton, *With the Dublin Brigade, 1917–1921*, Peter Davies, London, 1929, pp.37–43.
31. Dalton, p.40.

32. Ibid.
33. Dalton, p.43. See also Padraig Yeates, A *City in Wartime* (Dublin: Gill & Macmillan, 2011), p.118.
34. Dalton, p.41.
35. Lieutenant-Colonel Frederick Ernest Whitton, *The Prince of Wales's Leinster Regiment*, Volume 2, Andrews UK Ltd, 2012, pp.263, 264, 268.
36. Francis Carty, BMH, WS 1,040.
37. 'The Real Danger, Apathetic Voters The Enemy, A Candidate's Warning', *Irish Independent*, 12 September 1927.
38. Robert Brennan, BMH, WS 779, Section 1.
39. Emmet Dalton interview with Padraigh Ó Raghallaigh, RTE Archives, quoted in Dungan, *They Shall Not Grow Old*, p.33.
40. Dalton RTÉ interview with Ó Raghallaigh.
41. Ibid., p.37.

CHAPTER TWO

1. Emmet Dalton papers, NLI, MS 46,687/1.
2. Myles Dungan, *They Shall Grow Not Old* (Dublin: Four Courts Press, 1997), p.124, quoting from Emmet Dalton interview with Pádraigh Ó Raghallaigh, RTÉ archives.
3. Michael MacDonagh, *The Irish on the Somme* (London: Hodder and Stoughton, 1917), pp.161–2.
4. Dalton interview with Cathal O'Shannon, *Emmet Dalton Remembers*, RTÉ, March 1978.
5. Robin Prior & Trevor Wilson, *The Somme*, (New Haven: Yale University Press, 2005), pp.170–1.
6. MacDonagh, pp.162–3.
7. Ibid.
8. Ibid.
9. Second Lieutenant William Hatchell Boyd (29) was the son of a Methodist clergyman from Lucan, County Dublin. He had worked for an accountancy firm in Derry and his name is inscribed on the Diamond War Memorial.
10. McDonagh, pp.162–3.
11. See Tom Burke, 'In Memory of Lieutenant Tom Kettle, 'B' Company, 9th Royal Dublin Fusiliers', *Dublin Historical Record*, Vol. 57, No. 2, Autumn 2004.
12. Myles Dungan, *Irish Voices from the Great War* (Dublin: Irish Academic Press, 1995), p.138, quoting RTÉ radio interview with Dalton by Pádraig Ó Raghallaigh.
13. Figures from Official History, quoted in Tom Johnstone, *Orange Green & Khaki* (Dublin: Gill and Macmillan, Dublin), p.253.
14. See entry dated 19 Jan 1918, Diary, Emmet Dalton Papers, NLI MS 46,687/3.
15. 'Court Circular', *The Times*, 3 May 1917.
16. Howard Taubman, *The Pleasure Of Their Company, A Reminiscence* (Portland, Oregon: Amadeus Press, Portland, 1994), p.84.
17. L.M. 'Golfers I Have Met', No. 32, Mr. E. Dalton (Hermitage), *Irish Independent*, February 1938, cutting courtesy of Audrey Dalton Simenz.
18. F.E. Whitton, *The History of the Prince of Wales's Leinster Regiment*, Volume 2, Andrews UK, 2012, pp.339–40.
19. Ibid., p.330.
20. Ibid., p.334.
21. 'Dalton's War Record Gallant', *Boston Daily Globe*, 27 August 1922.
22. Tom Johnstone, *Orange Green & Khaki* (Dublin: Gill & Macmillan, 1992), p.329.
23. Whitton, p.510.
24. Lt. J. Emmet Dalton, Diary, Dalton Papers, NLI MS 46,687/3.
25. Ibid.
26. Ibid.
27. Entry dated 2 February 1918, Dalton diary, NLI.
28. See entries dated 10 & 11 February, Dalton diary, NLI.
29. Entry dated 23 January 1918, Dalton diary, NLI.

30. Entry dated 3 February 1918, Dalton diary, NLI.
31. Entry dated 4 February 1918, Dalton diary, NLI.
32. Entry dated 20 January 1918, Dalton diary, NLI.
33. Entry dated 28 January 1918, Dalton diary, NLI.
34. Entry dated 2 February 1918, Dalton diary, NLI.
35. Entry dated 16 January 1918, Dalton diary, NLI.
36. Entry dated 13 February 1918, Dalton diary, NLI.
37. Entry dated 15 February 1918, Dalton diary, NLI.
38. Entry dated 16 February 1918, Dalton diary, NLI.
39. Entry dated 25 February 1918, Dalton diary, NLI.
40. Entry dated 26 February 1918, Dalton diary, NLI.
41. Entry dated 27 February 1918, Dalton diary, NLI.
42. Ibid.
43. Memorandum, Emmet Dalton papers, NLI, MS 46,687/1.
44. Text of *The Sniper* supplied courtesy of Audrey Dalton Simenz.
45. Whitton, p.515.
46. Ibid.
47. Officer's Record of Services, Emmet Dalton papers, NLI, MS 46,687/3.
48. 'Dalton's War Record Gallant', *Boston Daily Globe*, 27 August 1922.
49. Emmet Dalton papers, NLI, MS 46,687/1.
50. Ibid.
51. Captain F.C. Hitchcock, *Stand To: A Diary of the Trenches, 1915–1918* (Norfolk: Gliddon Books, 1988), p.301.
52. First published in March 1937 by Hurst & Blackett, London, Hitchcock's *Stand To* was reissued by Gliddon Books, Norfolk in 1988.
53. Hitchcock, p.301.
54. Emmet Dalton papers, NLI, MS 46,687/3.
55. Hitchcock, p.312.
56. Emmet Dalton papers, NLI, MS 46,687/3.
57. Hitchcock, pp.262–263.
58. Emmet Dalton papers, NLI, MS 46,687/3.
59. Record of Officer's Services, Emmet Dalton papers, NLI, MS 46,687/1.
60. Hitchcock, pp.329, 330.
61. 'Operation Orders', 14 February 1919, Emmet Dalton Papers, NLI, MS 46,687/3.
62. Emmet Dalton papers, NLI, MS 46,687/1.
63. B.B. Cubitt, War Office, London, S.W.I, to Lieut. J. E. Dalton, 15 Wicklow St., Dublin, 4 June 1919; copy of letter courtesy of Audrey Dalton Simenz.

CHAPTER THREE
1. Charles Dalton, *With The Dublin Brigade, 1917–1921* (London: Peter Davies, 1929), p.56.
2. Dan Breen, BMH, WS 1739.
3. Dublin Castle file on Emmet Dalton, TNA, WO 35/206/52.
4. Charles Dalton, BMH, WS 434.
5. Dalton, p.80.
6. Mattie McDonald, Ernie O'Malley Notebooks, UCDA p17b/105(79); quoted in Anne Dolan, 'Killing and Bloody Sunday, November 1920', *The Historical Journal*, Vol. 49, No. 3 (September 2006), Cambridge University Press.
7. Dalton, p.124.
8. Emmet Dalton interview with Pádraig Ó Raghallaigh, RTÉ radio, February–March 1977.
9. Colonel Joseph V. Lawless, BMH, WS 1,043.
10. TNA, WO 35/206/52.
11. Emmet Dalton interview with Pádraig Ó Raghallaigh, RTÉ radio, February–March 1977.
12. 'Ex-Army Captain and J.P. Arrested', *Irish Independent*, 11 December 1920.

13. Dalton, p.126.
14. James T. Sullivan, 'Gen Dalton of Free State Fall River Boy', *Boston Daily Globe*, 5 August 1922.
15. Oscar Traynor, BMH, WS 340.
16. *An t-Óglach*, 11 November 1922.
17. Commandant Gerald Davis, BMH, WS 1,361.
18. Ibid.
19. Ibid.
20. Author's interview with source, 5 May 2013.
21. St. John Ervine, *Craigavon, Ulsterman* (London: George Allen & Unwin, 1949), pp.409–10.
22. Calton Younger, *Ireland's Civil War* (London: Fontana Press, 1986), p.144.
23. Sean Harling, BMH, WS 935.
24. St. John Ervine, p.411.
25. M.J. MacManus, *Eamon de Valera* (Chicago: Ziff-Davis Publishing Company), p.91.
26. Tim Pat Coogan, *Michael Collins* (Arrow Books, 1991), p.211, quoting Emmet Dalton in RTÉ interview, 6 June 1978.
27. Emmet Dalton, interview with Pádraig Ó Raghallaigh, RTÉ radio, February–March 1977.
28. 'An Irishman's Diary', by Kevin Myers, *Irish Times*, 6 November 1981.
29. Oscar Traynor, BMH, WS 340.
30. Emmet Dalton, interview with Cathal O'Shannon, *Emmet Dalton Remembers*, RTÉ TV, March 1978.
31. Emmet Dalton, 'Collins, Happy Warrior, Born Leader', *Irish Independent*, 6 December 1946.
32. Charles Dalton, BMH, WS 434.
33. See Chapter 17, *IRA Jailbreaks, 1918-1921* (Cork: Mercier Press, 2010), pp.158–67.
34. Article by Joe Leonard in *The Kerryman*, 23 October 1954.
35. Emmet Dalton, BMH, WS 641.
36. Leon Ó Broin, *Revolutionary Underground: The Story of the Irish Republican Brotherhood, 1858–1924* (Dublin: Gill & Macmillan, 1976), p.149.
37. Emmet Dalton, 'Collins, Happy Warrior, Born Leader', *Irish Independent*, 6 December 1946.
38. Michael Lynch, BMH, WS 511; see also statement by Michael Lynch, 2 November 1935, J.J. O'Connell Papers, NLI, MS 22,117 (i).
39. Accounts by some of the participants of the rescue attempt have varied in different ways. I have relied mainly on Dalton's own version of events about his own role, as he outlined in interviews with Cathal O'Shannon (RTÉ TV) and Pádraig Ó Raghallaigh (RTÉ radio); in a statement in his papers at the National Library of Ireland (MS 46,687/5); in an article in the *Irish Independent* on 6 December 1946, cited above, and in a statement to the BMH (WS 641). See also other Witness Statements to the BMH: Sean MacEoin, WS 1716; Patrick Lawson, WS 667; Joseph Byrne, WS 461; Vincent Byrne, WS 423; William James Stapleton, WS 822; Peter Gough, WS 401; Patrick McCrea, WS 413; Joe Leonard, WS 547; John Anthony Caffrey, WS 569; Oscar Traynor, WS 340; Charles Dalton, WS 434, and Joe Hyland, WS 644.
40. Sean MacEoin, BMH, WS 1716.
41. The keys carried by Emmet Dalton are now with the National Museum, Object number HE:EW.401 (Loan).
42. Joe Leonard, BMH WS 547.
43. Patrick McCrea, BMH WS 413.
44. William Sheehan, *Fighting for Dublin: The British Battle for Dublin 1919--1921* (Cork: Collins Press, 2007), p.49.
45. 'Daring Prison Rescue Plot', *The Times*, 16 May 1921.
46. Michael Lynch, BMH WS 511.
47. Statement by Michael Lynch, 2 November 1935, J.J. O'Connell Papers, NLI, MS 22,117 (i).
48. Michael Lynch, BMH WS 511.
49. Niall C. Harrington, *Kerry Landing, August 1922* (Dublin: Anvil Books, 1992), p.184.
50. 'Armoured Car In Jail Break', *Irish Independent*, 5 February 1964.
51. Dalton, p.159.
52. 'Emmet Dalton, 'Collins, Happy Warrior, Born Leader', *Irish Independent*, 6 December 1946.

53. Memo by Emmet Dalton re MacEoin rescue attempt, titled 'Period – Early 1921', Dalton papers, NLI, MS 46,687/5.
54. 'Daring Prison Rescue Plot', *The Times*, 16 May 1921.
55. See website, http://www.cairogang.com/soldiers-killed/saggers/saggers.html (accessed 20 May 2014).
56. Report by the GOC-in-Chief of the Situation in Ireland for Week Ending 14th May, 1921, TNA, CAB/24/123.
57. Sheehan, p.134.
58. 'Armoured Car In Jail Break', *Irish Independent*, 5 February 1964.
59. See *Guide to the Military Service (1916–23) Pensions Collection*, published online by the Defence Forces, 2012, pp.127–8.
60. Dublin Castle file on Emmet Dalton, TNA, WO 35/206/52.
61. 'Castle and Dead Caretaker', *Irish Independent*, 28 May 1921.
62. Dalton interview, Ó Raghallaigh, RTÉ.
63. James Brendan Connolly, BMH WS 849.
64. 'Burning of the Dublin Custom House, May 25 1921', Emmet Dalton papers, NLI, MS 46,687/5.
65. Emmet Dalton interview with Cathal O'Shannon, 'Emmet Dalton Remembers', RTÉ TV, March 1978.
66. See Peter Hart, *The IRA at War 1916–1923* (Oxford: Oxford University Press, 2003).
67. P.J. Paul, BMH WS 877.
68. Catherine Rooney, BMH, WS 648.
69. Charles Dalton, BMH, WS 434.
70. Emmet Dalton, 'Collins, Happy Warrior, Born Leader', *Irish Independent*, 6 December 1946.
71. Emmet Dalton, interview with Pádraig Ó Raghallaigh, RTÉ radio, February–March 1977.
72. 'James Emmet Dalton', *Dictionary of Irish Biography*, Cambridge/Royal Irish Academy.
73. IE/MA/MSPC/24SP1347.
74. C.S. Andrews, *Dublin Made Me* (Dublin: Lilliput, 2001), pp.209–10.
75. Seamus Finn, BMH, WS 1,060.
76. *Southern Star*, 21 February 2009, quoting extract from Uinseann MacEoin, *Survivors*, 1987.
77. Letter from W. Corri to Colonel J.J. O'Connell, Griffith Barracks, 2 February 1936, filed in 'War Service Officers, Accession of 1919-21, Ex-Members of British Army Who Joined IRA', IE/MA, LE/24.
78. Emmet Dalton, interview with Pádraig Ó Raghallaigh, RTÉ radio, February–March 1977.
79. O'Malley, pp.34–5.
80. David Fitzpatrick, *Harry Boland's Irish Revolution* (Cork: Cork University Press, 2003), p.226.
81. Cormac MacCarthaigh, 'The Shooting of Michael Collins, Shock Disclosures', *Sunday Independent*, 23 August 1970.
82. Fitzpatrick, p.255.
83. See Fitzpatrick, pp 251–52, quoting letter from Emmet Dalton (London) to Harry Boland, 14 October 1921, in Boland Papers, in possession of Harry Boland, jnr.
84. Author's conversation with Barry McGovern, 19 April 2013; see also Chrissy Osborne, *Michael Collins - Himself* (Cork: Mercier Press, 2003), p.71.
85. Ulick O'Connor, *Michael Collins and the Troubles* (Edinburgh: Mainstream, 2007), p.145.
86. The biography by Ulick O'Connor, *Oliver St John Gogarty*, was originally published by Jonathan Cape, London in 1964 and has appeared in other editions since.
87. Author's interview with Ulick O'Connor, Dublin, 4 September 2012.
88. L. H. 'Golfers I Have Met, No. 32 – Mr. E. Dalton (Hermitage)', *Irish Independent*, February 1938, clipping supplied courtesy of Audrey Dalton Simenz.

CHAPTER FOUR

1. 'Dalton's War Record Gallant', *Boston Daily Globe*, 27 August 1922.
2. Emmet Dalton, BMH, WS 641.

3. Emmet Dalton, 'Collins, Happy Warrior, Born Leader', *Irish Independent*, 6 December 1946. See also interview with Cathal O'Shannon, *Emmet Dalton Remembers*, RTÉ, 1978.
4. Emmet Dalton, BMH, WS 641.
5. 'Promenade Concert', *Irish Independent*, 5 October 1935.
6. Emmet Dalton, BMH, WS 641.
7. Ibid.
8. Eamon Broy, BMH, WS 1,280.
9. Ibid.
10. Emmet Dalton, BMH, WS 641.
11. David Fitzpatrick, *Harry Boland's Irish Revolution* (Cork: Cork University Press, 2003), p.395.
12. Leon Ó Broin, *Revolutionary Underground: The Story of the Irish Republican Brotherhood, 1858–1924* (Dublin: Gill & Macmillan, 1976), p.149.
13. Emmet Dalton, 'Collins, Happy Warrior, Born Leader', *Irish Independent*, 6 December 1946.
14. Ibid.
15. Robert Barton, BMH, WS 979.
16. Emmet Dalton, 'Collins, Happy Warrior, Born Leader', *Irish Independent*, 6 December 1946.
17. Tim Pat Coogan, *Michael Collins, A Biography* (London: Arrow Books, 1991), pp.234–5.
18. Peter Hart, *Mick, The Real Michael Collins* (London: MacMillan, 2005), p.298.
19. Piaras Béaslaí, *Michael Collins and the Making of a New Ireland* (Dublin: Phoenix Publishing, 1926), Volume II, p.448.
20. Ibid.
21. Emmet Dalton, 'Collins, Happy Warrior, Born Leader', *Irish Independent*, 6 December 1944.
22. See Fitzpatrick, pp.251–2, quoting letter from Emmet Dalton (London) to Harry Boland, 14 October 1921, in Boland Papers, in possession of Harry Boland, jnr.
23. Meda Ryan, *Tom Barry, IRA Freedom Fighter* (Cork: Mercier Press, 2012), p.204.
24. Dalton, Ó Raghallaigh RTÉ interview.
25. Ibid.
26. León Ó Broin (ed.), *In Great Haste, The Letters of Michael Collins and Kitty Kiernan* (Dublin: Gill & Macmillan, 1996), p.42.
27. Eamon Broy, BMH, WS 1,280.
28. Meda Ryan, *Michael Collins and the Women who Spied for Ireland* (Cork: Mercier Press, 2006), pp.117, 131.
29. Ibid., pp.134–5.
30. Draft article in Dalton Papers, NLI, MS 46,687/4.
31. Emmet Dalton, *Irish Independent*, 6 December 1944.
32. T. Ryle Dwyer, *'I Signed My Death Warrant': Michael Collins and the Treaty* (Cork: Mercier Press), pp.91–2.
33. Shane O'Brien, MA Thesis, 'Piaras Béaslaí and An tÓglach', pp.31–32, quoting letters Béaslaí to D/T [Emmet Dalton], 19 November and 2 December 1921, Béaslaí Papers, NLI, MS 33,914/3.
34. Charles Townshend, *The Republic: The Fight for Irish Independence, 1918–1923* (London: Alan Lane, 2013), pp.1051–6.
35. TNA, WO 35/206/52.
36. Emmet Dalton interview with Pádraigh Ó Raghallaigh, RTÉ radio, February–March 1977.
37. Undated press clipping from unidentified newspaper, possibly late 1940s, with headline 'Family Chest Gives Up Secret', courtesy of Audrey Dalton Simenz.
38. Information to author from National Museum re Griffith note (Object number HE:EW.402 - loan), 5 February 2014.
39. 'Mr Griffith Speaks; Believes Treaty Will Lead To Peace and Friendship; Stands By What He Has Signed', *Irish Independent*, 9 December 1921.
40. Emmet Dalton, 'Collins, Happy Warrior, Born Leader', *Irish Independent*, 6 December 1946.
41. Dalton, Ó Raghallaigh RTÉ interview.

CHAPTER FIVE

1. Report by the GOC-in-Chief on the Situation in Ireland for week ending 3 December 1921, TNA CAB/24/131.
2. Ibid.
3. 'Breach of Parole, Prisoner Returns', *Irish Times*, 2 December 1921.
4. Emmet Dalton, interview with Pádraig Ó Raghallaigh, RTÉ radio, February–March 1977.
5. Patrick Moylett, BMH, WS 767.
6. Dalton interview, Ó Raghallaigh, RTÉ.
7. Ibid.
8. C.S. Andrews, *Dublin Made Me* (Dublin: Lilliput Press, 2001), p.224.
9. Emmet Dalton memorandum, IE/MA/LE/4.
10. Dalton interview with Ó Raghallaigh, RTÉ; Ernie O'Malley, *The Men Will Talk To Me, Galway Interviews* (Dublin: Mercier Press), p.190.
11. Nevil Macready, *Annals of an Active Life*, Volume Two, Hutchinson, London, 1924; quoted in 'The Rathkeale Workhouse Incident, November 1922', *Old Limerick Journal*, Winter Edition, 1992.
12. Michael Hopkinson (ed.), *The Last Days of Dublin Castle – The Diaries of Mark Sturgis* (Dublin: Irish Academic Press, 1999), pp.223–4.
13. See A. Kinsella, 'The Rathkeale Workhouse Incident, November 1921', *The Old Limerick Journal*, Winter Edition, 1992. See also 'Rathkeale Raid', IE/MA/LE/B/3/7.
14. W. Doolin, Dublin Castle, to CLO, 21 February 1922, IE/MA; Correspondence between Dalton and Colonel Brind, British Headquarters, and correspondence between Dalton and Superintendent, Grangegorman, March-April 1922; Captain T. Hughes, for Deputy Adjutant General, GHQ., Dublin to CLO, Government Buildings, 10 April 1922; Lieutenant Colonel Pickering, GHQ, Dublin to CLO, 4 March 1922, IE/MA/LE/11/3.
15. Dalton to O.C., Dublin Brigade, 20 December 1921, IE/MA, LE/11/3.
16. Commandant Emmet Dalton to O.C. Dublin Brigade, 11 January 1922, IE/MA, LE/11/3.
17. Liaison Office to Captain Whistler, Dublin District, 14 January 1922, IE/MA, LE/11/3.
18. Letters from W. Doolin, Dublin Castle to CLO, 27 January 1922, IE/MA, LE/11/2.
19. Siobhan Lankford, *The Hope and the Sadness* (Cork: Tower Books, 1980), p.225.
20. Kenneth Griffith and Timothy E. O'Grady, *Curious Journey, An Oral History of Ireland's Unfinished Revolution* (London: Hutchinson, 1982), pp.245–6; see also David Neligan, *The Spy in the Castle* (London: Prendeville Publishing Ltd., 1999), pp.150–1, and David Neligan, BMH, WS 380.
21. Macready, p.635.
22. Neligan, p.155.
23. Travers Wolfe to Captain Thomas Healy, Liaison Officer, Bandon, 28 November 1921, IE/MA, LE/11/1.
24. Gerry White & Brendan O'Shea, *The Burning of Cork* (Cork: Mercier, 2006), pp.99, 237.
25. Commandant E. Quinlan, Liaison Officer, Nenagh, County Tipperary, Weekly Report Sheet, 27 January 1922, IE/MA, LE 11/2.
26. National Police Officers, Roll of Honour, http://www.rollofhonour.org/ (accessed 20 May 2014).
27. Travers Wolfe to Captain Healy, Liaison Officer, Bandon, 26 November 1921, IE/MA, LE/11/1.
28. 'Cork Farmers Murdered', *Irish Times*, 21 February 1921.
29. Patrick O'Sullivan, BMH, WS 1481.
30. Acting Chief Liaison Officer to Captain Healy, Bandon, 9 December 1921, IE/MA, LE/11/1.
31. Affidavit of E.B., 10 December 1921 re alleged sexual assault; Captain Liam Murphy, IRA Liaison Officer for Kildare, to Dalton, CLO, 14 December 1921; Dalton to Captain Murphy, Court House, Naas, 15 December 1921; A. W. Cope, Chief Secretary's Office, Dublin Castle to Dalton, 10 January 1922; Dalton to Minister for Home Affairs, 11 January 1922; Department of Home Affairs to Dalton, 13 January 1922; IE/MA, LE 11/2.
32. John Donnelly, WS 626, BMH.
33. Hopkinson, *The Last Days of Dublin Castle*, p.235.
34. 'Collins To Make Announcement', *New York Times*, 11 December 1921.
35. John Sharkey, BMH, WS 1,100.

36. 'Collins To Make Announcement', *New York Times*, 11 December 1921.
37. TNA, CAB/24/131.
38. Ibid.
39. Michael MacEvilly, *A Splendid Resistance, The Life of IRA Chief of Staff, Dr. Andy Cooney* (Dublin: Edmund Burke Publishers, 2011), p.58.
40. 'The True Voice of Ireland, Cork Majority for Peace, "The Past is Past"', *The Times*, 28 December 1921.
41. John Borgonovo, *The Battle For Cork, July–August 1922* (Cork: Mercier, 2011), p.36.
42. Lankford, pp.228–9.
43. 'Kidnapped, Adventures of Our Correspondent', *The Times*, 7 January 1922.
44. Ibid. J. Anthony Gaughan, Alfred O'Rahilly, Volume II (Dublin: Kingdom Books, 1989), p.146. See also, Borgonovo, Chapter 1, 'The Treaty Debate in Cork'.

CHAPTER SIX

1. Winston Churchill, House of Commons, Hansard, 9 February 1922.
2. Ibid.
3. Object no. HE.EW.402 (loan), Dalton collection, National Museum of Ireland.
4. Gerard O'Brien, 'The Missing Personnel Records of the R.I.C.', *Irish Historical Studies*, November 1999.
5. Ibid. See also Neligan, p.155, and *Irish Independent*, 17 Jan 1922.
6. Neligan, p.155.
7. 'Hunger Strike Ends, Expected Release of Derry Prisoners', *Irish Independent*, 19 January 1922. See also, 'Liaison Officer Acts, Political Prisoners' Hunger Strike Called Off in Derry', *Freeman's Journal*, 19 January 1922.
8. Comdt Dalton to Comdt Shields, Derry, 18 January 1922, IE/MA, LE/21.
9. Memorandum for Cabinet, 2 February 1922, by the Chief Secretary for Ireland, 'Weekly Survey of the State of Ireland', for week ending 30 January 1922, TNA, CAB/24/132.
10. Emmet Dalton, Dublin Castle file, TNA, WO 35/206/52.
11. Tim Carey, *Hanged For Ireland, The Forgotten Ten* (Dublin: Blackwater Press, 2001), pp.183–4.
12. 'Armed Soldiers, An Eloquent Symbol', *Irish Independent*, 2 February 1922.
13. Comdt Dalton to M.D., 10 February 1922, IE/MA, LE/11/3.
14. 'To Prevent Robbery; Pay Clerks' Armed Escorts', *Irish Times*, 6 February, 1922.
15. Comdt Dalton to Minister for Foreign Affairs, 18 February 1922, IE/MA, LE/21.
16. Undated memorandum, J.J. O'Connell Papers, NLI, MS 22,126.
17. Emmet Dalton, BMH, WS 641.
18. Report by GOC-in Chief on the situation in Ireland for week ending 18 March 1922, TNA, CAB/24/134.
19. Dalton interview with Cathal O'Shannon, RTÉ TV.
20. Report by General Officer Commanding-in-Chief on the situation in Ireland for week ending 25th February 1922, TNA, CAB/24/133.
21. David Fitzpatrick, *Harry Boland's Irish Revolution* (Cork: Cork University Press, 2003), p.278.
22. 'Developing Dublin Port', *Freeman's Journal*, 17 March 1922.
23. C.S. Andrews, *Dublin Made Me* (Dublin: Lilliput, 2001), pp.224–7.
24. Michael McEvilly, *A Splendid Resistance, The Life of IRA Chief of Staff Dr. Andy Cooney* (Dublin: Edmund Burke Publisher, 2011), p.61.
25. W. J. Slattery, BMH, WS 882.
26. See 'Object of the IRA, Four Courts Statement', *Irish Independent*, 22 April 1922; also Dublin Castle file on Emmet Dalton, TNA, WO 35/206/52.
27. Macready, pp.625–7.
28. T. Ryle Dwyer, *Michael Collins and the Civil War* (Cork: Mercier Press, 2012), p.140.
29. Andrews, p.233.
30. Emmet Dalton interview with Pádraig Ó Raghallaigh, RTÉ radio, February–March 1977.
31. 'The Official Reports', *Irish Independent*, 21 April 1922.

32. Ibid.
33. Denis Fitzpatrick, Military Service Pension Collection, MSP34REF816.
34. Undated memorandum, J.J. O'Connell Papers, NLI, MS 22,126.
35. See 'Object of the IRA, Four Courts Statement', *Irish Independent*, 22 April 1922; also Dublin Castle file on Emmet Dalton, TNA, WO 35/206/52.
36. Emmet Dalton memorandum, IE/MA/LE/4.
37. Gregory Allen, *The Garda Síochána, Policing Independent Ireland 1922-82* (Dublin: Gill & Macmillan, Dublin, 1999), p.13.
38. Macready, pp.635–8.
39. See Sir L. Worthington-Evans, House of Commons, Hansard, cc. 1067–1068, 11 July 1922.
40. For more detail, see Borgonovo, pp.38–40.
41. Macready, pp.635–8.
42. See Daniel Corkery, BMH, WS 1719, and James Murphy, WS 1633.
43. See Timothy Buckley, BMH, WS 1674.
44. Colonel E. Evans, Staff of the Deputy Quartermaster General, GHQ Ireland, to CLO, Evacuation Office, Government Buildings, 9 May 1922.
45. Hopkinson, pp.85–6.
46. Memorandum, J.J. O'Connell Papers, NLI, MS 22,126.
47. Mulcahy, Dáil Éireann Debate, Vol. 1 No. 3, 12 Sept 1922.
48. John Linge, 'British Forces and Irish Freedom: Anglo-Irish Defence Relations 1922-31', Thesis, Department of History, University of Stirling, December 1994; See also Dalton to Minister of Defence, 10 May 1922, UCDA, MP, P7/B/102.
49. 'How Portobello Passed Into Irish Hands', *Freeman's Journal*, 18 May 1922.
50. Ibid.
51. Dublin Castle file on Emmet Dalton, TNA, WO 35/206/52.
52. How Portobello Passed Into Irish Hands', *Freeman's Journal*, 18 May 1922.
53. *Kilkenny People*, 13 May 1922; see also Younger, p.280.
54. *An t-Óglach*, 3 June 1922.
55. Report to the Cabinet by General Officer Commanding-in-Chief of the situation in Ireland for week ending 10th June 1922, TNA, CAB/24/137.
56. Dalton to A. W. Cope, 3 June 1922, IE/MA, LE/11/3.
57. Comdt Dalton to Captain Hughes, Castle Street, Castlebar, 30 December 1921, IE/MA, LE/11/1.
58. N. Loughnane, Dublin Castle, to Evacuation Office, 'Particulars of further cases of old RIC Pensioners who have been ordered to leave their homes', 14 June 1922, IE/MA, LE/11/3.
59. Reports Furnished to Army Finance Department', 2nd Bureau, Occupation of Barracks by Irregulars etc 1922, IE/MA, LE/15/1.
60. Richard English, *Armed Struggle, The History of the IRA* (London: Pan Books, 2004), p.34.
61. Liam Deasy, *Brother Against Brother* (Dublin: Mercier Press, 1982), p.43.

CHAPTER SEVEN

1. Major General Dalton to DQMG, British General HQ, Parkgate, 26 June 1922, IE/MA, LE/11/3.
2. Michael Hopkinson, *Green Against Green, The Irish Civil War* (Dublin: Gill & Macmillan, 2004), p.116.
3. *Manchester Guardian* report quoted in Dorothy Macardle, *The Irish Republic* (Dublin: Irish Press, 1951), p.739.
4. Hopkinson, *Green Against Green*, p.116.
5. Meda Ryan, *The Day Michael Collins Was Shot* (Dublin: Poolbeg, 1995), p.20.
6. Emmet Dalton interview with Cathal O'Shannon for RTÉ documentary, *Emmet Dalton Remembers*, 1978; reproduced also in RTÉ documentary, *The Shadow of Béal na Bláth*, 1988.
7. Younger, p.321.
8. Macready, *Annals of an Active Life*, p.655.
9. Calton Younger, *Ireland's Civil War* (London: Fontana Press, 1986), p.322.

10. Younger, pp.321, 322.
11. Report by the General Officer Commanding-in-Chief on the situation in Ireland for the week ending 20th May 1922, CAB24/136.
12. 'Opening Shots of the Civil War', William Mullen, letter to the *Irish Times*, 1 November 2012.
13. Aaron R.B. Linderman, *Lessons Learned by SOE from the Irish War of Independence*, p.5.
14. Macready, p.656.
15. Wilkinson and Astley, p.26.
16.' Conclusions of a Conference of Ministers held in the Prime Minister's Room, House of Commons, on Wednesday, June 28, 1922, at 9.50 p.m.' TNA, CAB/23/39.
17. *Document*, BBC Radio 4, 29 October 2012.
18. Report from CS, General O'Duffy, 28 June 1922, UCDA, MP, P7/B/106.
19. Liz Gillis, *The Fall of Dublin* (Cork: Mercier Press, 2011), p.51.
20. Ernie O'Malley, *The Singing Flame* (Cork: Mercier Press, 2012), p.127.
21. Report from CS, General O'Duffy, 28 June 1922, UCDA, MP, P7/B/106.
22. Dalton interview with Ó Raghallaigh, RTÉ.
23. Emmet Dalton interview with Cathal O'Shannon for RTÉ documentary, *Emmet Dalton Remembers*, 1978; reproduced also in RTÉ documentary, *The Shadow of Béal na Bláth*, 1988; see also Dalton interview with Ó Raghallaigh, RTÉ.
24. Conor Cruise O'Brien, *Memoir, My Life and Themes* (London: Profile Books, 1999), p.25.
25. Report from Chief of Staff, General O'Duffy, 28 June 1922, UCDA, MP, P7/B/106.
26. Macready, p.655.
27. Memo signed ROM [Risteárd Ó Maolcatha], UCDA, MP, P7/B/107.
28. Younger, pp.336–7.
29. Ibid., pp.337-8.
30. Liam Deasy, *Brother Against Brother* (Cork: Mercier Press, 1982), pp.50–1.
31. Macready, p.655.
32. Ibid., p.656.
33. Ibid.
34. 'The Brave And Fair, Cumann na Saoirse Stand Nobly By Irish Army', *Freeman's Journal*, 7 July 1922.
35. Younger, p.326. Emmet Dalton interview with Cathal O'Shannon, *Emmet Dalton Remembers*, RTÉ TV, March 1978.
36. John P. Duggan, *A History of the Irish Army* (Dublin: Gill & Macmillan, 1991), pp.83, 332.
37. http://www.militaryarchives.ie/collections/document-of-the-month/july (accessed 20 May 2014).
38. Younger, p.324.
39. Ibid.
40. Dalton to Ria Mooney, 29 November 1957, NLI, MS 49,603/9.
41. Younger, p.327.
42. Ibid., p.328.
43. 'The Fight for the Four Courts', *Galway Observer*, 1 July 1922.
44. Younger, p.328.
45. Ibid.
46. Ms Catriona Crowe of the Irish National Archives has written that the anti-Treaty forces, after occupying the Four Courts and placing their munitions in the Record Office, were reminded on three occasions, in person and in writing, that 'that the history of the country was in their safekeeping', but they did not seek another location for their munitions. When the shelling of the Four Courts began it was 'inevitable that calamity would follow'. See 'Ruin of Public Record Office Marked Loss of Great Archive', *Irish Times*, 30 June 2012.
47. O'Malley, p.136.
48. UCDA, MP, P7/B/107.
49. Diarmuid O'Connor & Frank Connolly, *Sleep Soldier Sleep: The Life and Times of Padraig O'Connor* (Miseab Publications, 2011), pp.98–100.
50. Ibid.

51. Younger, p.332.
52. Liz Gillis, *The Fall of Dublin* (Cork: Mercier, 2011), p.79.
53. Eoin Neeson, *The Civil War, 1922–23* (Dublin: Poolbeg, 1989), p.122.
54. http://www.militaryarchives.ie/collections/document-of-the-month/july (accessed 20 May 2014).
55. Gillis, p.125.
56. 'Impressions of a Sightseer – Watching the Fighting at Close Quarters', *Irish Times*, 8 July 1922.
57. TNA, WO 35/206/52.
58. Letter from Frank Saurin, Charles Dalton file, IE/MA/MSPC/24SP1153.
59. 'General O'Duffy's Tour', *Irish Times*, 4 July 1922.
60. Macready to War Office, Report on Situation in Ireland for week ending 1 July, 1922, TNA, CAB/24/137.
61. Michael Joseph Lawless, BMH, WS 727.
62. Ibid.
63. 'Death of General Emmet Dalton', *Irish Times*, 6 March 1978.
64. See 'Artillery - Men Who Worked The Guns', *Irish Times*, 3 July 1922.

CHAPTER EIGHT

1. Younger, pp.383–4; Macardle, pp.761–2.
2. Patrick J. Casey, BMH, WS 1,148.
3. Jack McElhaw, BMH, WS 634.
4. Younger, p.383.
5. Macardle, p.762.
6. Ibid.
7. Hopkinson, p.170.
8. Adjutant General Gearóid O'Sullivan to C-in-C, 19 July 1922, UCDA, MP, P7/B/27.
9. Michael Rynne, Staff Captain, to Major General Dalton, Eastern District Command, Portobello, 3 August 1922, UCDA, MP, P/7/B/16.
10. Younger, p.348.
11. Comdt. P. Cronin, Narrative of Operations, 4 to 8 July 1922, UCDA MP P7/B/109.
12. Report by Macready on situation in Ireland for week ending 8 July 1922, TNA, CAB/24/138.
13. Major General Dalton, to Minister for Defence, 10 July 1922, UCDA, MP, P7/B/59.
14. Letter from Frank Saurin re Charles Dalton pension claim, IE/MA/MSPC/24SP1153.
15. Captain C. Daltúin, acting Intelligence Officer, Eastern Command HQ, Portobello to Minister of Defence, 10 July 1922, UCDA, MP, P7/B/106.
16. See Army Census, November 1922 and *An t-Óglach*, October 1923, Irish Military Archives.
17. Ernie O'Malley, *The Singing Flame* (Cork: Mercier, 2012), pp.176–7.
18. Younger, p.348.
19. See Younger, p.348–53; Hopkinson, p.144.
20. 'The Man Who Praised Civil War Opponent', *Irish Press*, 8 March 1978.
21. Minister for Defence to Major General Dalton, 14 July 1922, UCDA, MP, P7/B/109.
22. Younger, p.354.
23. Paul Gorry, *Baltinglass Chronicles* (Dublin: Nonsuch, 2006), p.190, cited in 'the Irish Civil War', Turtle Bunbury website, www.turtlebunbury.com (accessed 20 May 2014).
24. O'Malley, pp.183–4.
25. Major General Dalton to Adjutant General, Portobello, 19 July 1922, UCDA, MP, PB/7/109.
26. Ibid.
27. Commandant General W.J. McSweeney, Baldonnel Aerodrome, to Adjutant General, 17 July 1922, UCDA, MP, PB/7/109.
28. 'Aeroplane Damaged at Naas', *Kildare Observer*, 22 July 1922.
29. 'Irregulars Lose Baltinglass', *Carlow Nationalist*, 22 July 1922, cited in Turtle Bunbury website, www.turtlebunbury.com (accessed 20 May 2014).
30. Pilot Captain Russell, Reconnaissance Report, 9.15 am, 17 July 1922 to General Headquarters, UCDA, MP, PB/7/109.

31. Younger, p.354.
32. 'Irregulars Lose Baltinglass', *Carlow Nationalist*, 22 July 1922, cited in Turtle Bunbury website, www.turtlebunbury.com (accessed 20 May 2014).
33. Younger, p.354.
34. Major General J.E. Dalton to Adjutant General, 17 July 1922, UCDA, MP, PB/7/109.
35. Ibid.
36. 'Fall of Baltinglass', *Kildare Observer*, 22 July 1922.
37. Robert Brennan, WS 779, BMH.
38. 'She was Aide to Austin Stack', *Kerryman*, 21 May 1982.
39. C.S. Andrews, *Dublin Made Me* (Dublin: Lilliput, 2001), p.263.
40. Major General J.E. Dalton to Adjutant General, 17 July 1922, UCDA, MP, PB/7/109.
41. Minister of Defence to Dalton, Eastern Command, 19 July 1922, UCDA, MP, P7/B/59.
42. C-in-C to Chief of General Staff, 28 July 1922, UCDA, MP, P/7/B/1.
43. Office of C-in-C to Dalton, Eastern Command, 3 August 1922, UCDA, MP, P/7/B/16.
44. Colonel Commandant Aodh MacNeill, Wellington Barracks, to Dalton, GOC, Eastern Command, 2 August 1922, UCDA, MP, P/7/B/16.
45 'Irregulars' Plan to Isolate Dublin Frustrated by Army', *Weekly Irish Times*, 12 August 1922.
46. John Borgnovo, *The Battle for Cork* (Cork: Mercier, 2011), p.62.
47. Dalton, Eastern District Command HQ, Portobello to C-in-C, 4 August 1922, UCDA, MP, P/7/B/9.
48. M.R. Walker, 3 Molesworth Street to Major General Dalton, Portobello Barracks, 5 August 1922, UCDA, MP, P/7/B/9.
49. TNA, WO 35/206/52.
50. See Emmet Dalton interview with Cathal O'Shannon, *Emmet Dalton Remembers*, RTÉ, March 1978.
51. Patrick McCarthy, *The Twilight Years – the Irish Regiments 1919–1922*; essay in *Irishmen in War, Volume II* (Dublin: The Military History Society of Ireland and Irish Academic Press, 2006), p.146.

CHAPTER NINE

1. Michael Hopkinson, *Green Against Green,* p.163.
2. Dalton interview with Cathal O'Shannon, RTÉ TV documentary, *Emmet Dalton Remembers*, 1978.
3. Niall C. Harrington, *Kerry Landing, August 1922* (Dublin: Anvil Books, 1992), p.174.
4. Timothy Collins, 'The "Helga/Muirchú": Her Contribution to Galway Maritime History', *Journal of the Galway Archaeological and Historical Society*, Volume 54 (2002).
5. Hopkinson, p.155.
6. Emmet Dalton interview with Pádraig Ó Raghallaigh, RTÉ radio, February–March 1977.
7. Meda Ryan, *Michael Collins And The Women Who Spied For Ireland* (Cork: Mercier Press, 2006), pp.179–80.
8. O'Hegarty to Minister for Defence, 5 July 1922, UCDA, MP, P7/B/106.
9. Dalton to C-in-C, GHQ, Dublin, 11 September 1922, Appendix I, Harvey & White, p.258.
10. MOC [Mícheál Ó Coileáin], 'Air Services', 4 August 1922, UCDA, MP, P7/B/10.
11. Borgonovo, p.81.
12. See photograph captioned 'An Open Air Ballroom', *Sunday Independent*, 13 August 1922.
13. Dalton interview, Ó Raghallaigh, RTÉ.
14. John Linge, *The Royal Navy and the Irish Civil War*, Irish Historical Studies, May 1998.
15. Younger, p.410.
16. Eoin Neeson, *The Civil War, 1922-23*, Poolbeg, Dublin, 1989, p. 224.
17. Borgonovo, *The Battle for Cork*, p.71.
18. Neeson, pp.224–5.
19. 'The Relief of Cork, How the City was Entered', *Irish Times*, 15 August 1922.
20. O'Shannon RTÉ TV interview.

21. 'The Relief of Cork, How the City was Entered', *Irish Times*, 15 August 1922.
22. 'Landing at Youghal, Troops Celebrate the Arrival of the Helga', *Freeman's Journal*, 10 August 1923.
23. *Freeman's Journal*, 10 August 1922.
24. Patrick J. Twohig, *The Dark Secret of Béalnabláth* (Ballincollig: Tower Books, 1991), p.195.
25. Dan Harvey & Gerry White, *The Barracks: A History of Victoria/Collins Barracks, Cork* (Cork: Mercier Press, 1997), pp.105–6.
26. Younger, p.412.
27. http://www.militaryarchives.ie/collections/document-of-the-month/july (accessed 20 May 2014).
28. Borgonovo, p.92.
29. Neeson, p.227.
30. 'The Fight at Cork', *Cork Examiner* report reproduced in the *Southern Star*, 19 August 1922.
31. Borgnovo, p.100. See also Paul McMahon, *British Spies and Irish Rebels: British Intelligence and Ireland 1916–1945* (Surrey: The Boydell Press, 2008), pp.85–6.
32. Hopkinson, p.163.
33. HOGW 169, NLI.
34. See Borgonovo, pp.105–6.
35. Twohig, p.17.
36. Younger, pp.412–20.
37. 'The Relief of Cork', *Irish Times*, 15 August 1922.
38. 'The Fight at Cork', *Cork Examiner* report reproduced in the *Southern Star*, 19 August 1922.
39. See Borgonovo, p.109.
40. Aerial Reconnaissance Report, Baldonnel, 10 August 1922, UCDA, MP, P/7/B/10.
41. Younger, p.421.
42. Ibid.
43. Liam to C-in-C, 8 pm, Douglas; Liam to C-in-C, 9 pm, Douglas, 10 August 1922, UCDA, MP, P/7/B/16.
44. *Sunday Independent*, 13 August 1922.
45. Captain P. Dalton to Adjutant General, Portobello, 12 August 1922, UCDA, MP, P7/B/70.
46. IE/MA/DOD/A/1178.
47. 'Cork's New Freedom', *Irish Times*, 14 August 1922.
48. Frank Geary, 'The Taking of Cork', *Irish Independent*, 12 August 1922, reproduced in John Horgan (Editor), *Great Irish Reportage*, Penguin Ireland, 2013.
49. General Macready, Report on Situation in Ireland for Week Ending 12 August 1922, TNA, CAB/24/138.
50. 'Irish Nationalists' Coup', *The Times*, 12 August 1922.
51. Neeson, p.230.
52. Hopkinson, p.164, quoting Dalton to C-in-C, 12 August 1922, MP, P7/B/20.
53. Dan Harvey & Gerry White, p.110.
54. Harvey & White, p.111.
55. Dalton interview, Ó Raghallaigh, RTÉ.
56. Transport Order, 10 August 1922, UCDA, MP, P7/B/70.
57. Chief of General Staff to Quartermaster General, 11 August 1922, UCDA, MP, P7/B/70.
58. Liam Deasy, *Brother against Brother* (Cork: Mercier, 1982), pp.72–3.
59. Siobhan Lankford, *The Hope and the Sadness* (Cork: Tower Books, 1980), p.241.
60. Deasy, p.73.
61. J. Anthony Gaughan, *Alfred O'Rahilly*, pp.179–82.
62. John A. Murphy, 'Alfred O'Rahilly', *Dictionary of Irish Biography*, Cambridge/Royal Irish Academy.
63. For an image of the proclamation, see J. Anthony Gaughan, *Alfred O'Rahilly*.
64. CGS to Dalton, Cork, UCDA, MP, P7/B/70.
65. 'Arrival of National Troops at Cove, Enthusiastic Reception', *Cork Examiner*, 14 August 1922.
66. Robert Briscoe, with Aidan Hatch, *For the Life of Me* (London: Longmans, 1958), p.5.

67. *Cork Examiner*, 14 August 1922.
68. Dalton to C-in-C, 12 August 1922, UCDA, MP, P/7/B/20.
69. Jim Herlihy, *Issues Affecting Irish Policing, 1922–1932*, Garda Síochána Historical Society, PoliceHistory.com.
70. Dáil Éireann Debates, Vol. 1, No. 5, 14 Sept 1922.
71. Dalton to C-in-C, 12 August 1922, UCDA, MP, P/7/B/20.
72. Dalton to Mulcahy, 13 Sept 1922, IE/MA/CW/OPS/04/01.
73. Dalton interview, Ó Raghallaigh, RTÉ.
74. Dalton to C-in-C, 12 Aug 1922, UCDA, MP, P/7/B/20.
75. CGS to Major General Dalton, Cork, 14 August 1922, UCDA, MP, P7/B/70.
76. Leon Ó Broin, *Joseph Brennan, Civil Servant Extraordinary*, Studies, Vol. 66, No. 261, Spring, 1977, pp.25–37.
77. Acting Military Secretary to C-in-C, to Major General Dalton, O/C Cork expedition, 17 August 1922, UCDA, MP, P/7/B/20.
78. Twohig, pp.207–9.
79. UCDA, Mulcahy Papers, P7/B/70/80
80. CGS to Major General Dalton, Cork, cypher telegram, 19 August 1922, UCDA, MP, P7/B/70.
81. Dalton, Cork, to C-in-C, 'Cork Report', 11 Sept 1922; see Harvey & White, Appendix 1.
82. 'Midleton College; Distribution of Prizes; Bishop of Cork's Tribute', *Irish Times*, 16 December 1933.
83. IE/MA/DOD/A/6869.
84. Hopkinson, pp.164–5.
85. Report of the Situation in Ireland for the Week Ending 19th August 1922; Memorandum to the Cabinet by the Secretary of State for War, TNA, CAB/24/138.
86. J. Anthony Gaughan, pp.182–4.
87. Ibid.
88. C-in-C, Portobello to CGS, 15 July 1922, UCDA, MP, P7/B/1.
89. Lt. A. Barry, Publicity, Command Headquarters, Cork, Report, Week Ending 13 Jan [1923], IE MA CW/OPS/04/13.
90. Major General J. E. Dalton, Cork Command HQ, to C-in-C, 12 August 1922, UCDA, MP, P/7/B/20.

CHAPTER TEN

1. James Conroy senior, MSPC, MSP34REF743; James Patrick Conroy, MSPC, 24SP80.
2. William James Stapleton, BMH, WS 822.
3. Charles Dalton, 'Memories Of A Tragic Time In Irish History', *Sunday Independent*, 25 August 1944.
4. Patrick Moylett, BMH, WS 767.
5. Finola Kennedy, *Frank Duff, A Life Story* (London: Burns & Oates, 2011), p.74.
6. CGS to C-in-C, Limerick, 20 August 1922, UCDA, MP, P7/B/70.
7. Interview with Cathal O'Shannon, *Emmet Dalton Remembers*, RTÉ TV, 1978.
8. 'Cork Towns Occupied. General Collins's Tour', *Irish Times*, 23 August 1922.
9. Comdt. D.V. Horgan, 'Shooting of Michael Collins', *Irish Press*, 10 July 1981.
10. Interview with Cathal O'Shannon, *Emmet Dalton Remembers*, RTÉ TV, 1978.
11. Emmet Dalton, 'Grim Tragedy of a Year Ago', *Freeman's Journal*, 22 August 1923.
12. Younger, p.431.
13. C-in-C, Cork, to Intelligence Dept., Portobello, 21 Aug 1922, UCDA, MP, P7/B/70.
14. Meda Ryan, *The Day Michael Collins Was Shot* (Dublin: Poolbeg Press, 1995), pp.55–6.
15. Dalton interview with Pádraigh Ó Raghallaigh, RTÉ radio, February-March 1977.
16. Meda Ryan, p.185.
17. Borgonovo, p.131.
18. A.J.S. Brady, *The Briar of Life* (2010), Chapter 18.
19. Diary is preserved at the Military Museum, Collins Barracks, Cork.

20. Edward O'Mahony, *Michael Collins, His Life and Times*, 1996, Chapter 11, Collins 22 Society website.
21. Florence O'Donoghue Papers, NLI MS 31,305; see also Edward O'Mahony, *Michael Collins*, Appendix 1.
22. Liam Deasy, *Brother Against Brother* (Cork: Mercier Press, 1982), pp.77–8.
23. Twomey Papers, UCDA; report reproduced in Brian Hanley, *The IRA, A Documentary History 1916-2005* (Dublin: Gill & Macmillan, 2010), pp.48–9.
24. Emmet Dalton, 'Grim Tragedy of a Year Ago', *Freeman's Journal*, 22 August 1923.
25. Raymond Smith and Jim Nicoll, 'The Mistake That Cost Collins His Life', *Irish Independent*, 19 May 1971.
26. Cormac MacCarthaigh, 'The Shooting of Michael Collins: Shock Disclosures', *Sunday Independent*, 23 August 1970.
27. MacCarthaigh interview with Dalton, *Sunday Independent*.
28. Dalton interview, Ó Raghallaigh, RTÉ.
29. Emmet Dalton account, *Freeman's Journal*, 1923.
30. Raymond Smith and Jim Nicoll, 'The Mistake That Cost Collins His Life', *Irish Independent*, 19 May 1971.
31. Deasy, p.78.
32. Transcript of interview with Tom Foley, 2 September 1989, Sean O'Mahony Papers, NLI MS 44,104/4.
33. Hanley, pp.48–9.
34. Ibid.
35. 'A Survivor's Narrative', *Irish Times*, 2 September 1922.
36. Ibid.
37. TV archive interview with John O'Connell, featured in 2007 BBC TV documentary, *The Assassination of Michael Collins*.
38. Hanley, pp.48–9.
39. Emmet Dalton, in *Freeman's Journal* article, 1923.
40. Ibid.
41. Margery Forester, *Michael Collins, The Lost Leader* (Dublin: Gill & Macmillan, 1989), p.337.
42. Raymond Smith and Jim Nicoll, 'The Mistake That Cost Collins His Life', *Irish Independent*, 19 May 1971.
43. Rex Taylor, *Michael Collins* (London: Four Square, 1961), p.270.
44. Ibid.
45. Emmet Dalton, *Freeman's Journal* article, 1923.
46. Younger, p.438.
47. Dalton, *Freeman's Journal* article, 1923.
48. Taylor, p.270.
49. See interview with Lieutenant Smith, *Cork Examiner*, 26 August 1922.
50. Taylor, p.270.
51. Deasy, pp.78–9.
52. Martin Brennan, interview with former garda John Hickey, *Evening Herald*, 12 September 1970, quoted by J. Anthony Gaughan in letter 'Shooting of Collins', *Sunday Independent*, 7 January 1990.
53. Cormac MacCarthaigh, 'The Shooting of Michael Collins: Shock Disclosures', *Sunday Independent*, 23 August 1970.
54. Ibid.
55. Meda Ryan, *The Day Michael Collins Was Shot* (Dublin: Poolbeg, 1995), pp.110–1.
56. Taylor, p.205.
57. See detail given in Catalogue, 14 March 2009, for items for auction by Whyte's Irish Art Auctioneers and Valuers.
58. Ibid.
59. Meda Ryan, p.113.
60. 'General Dalton Unhurt', *Freeman's Journal*, 24 August 1922.

61. See 'Mr Collins's Tragic Death', Morning Bulletin, Rockhampton, Queensland, 25 August 1922.
62. Harvey & White, p.112.
63. 'Kinsale Taken', Irish Times, 25 August 1922.
64. Oliver St John Gogarty, BMH, WS 700.
65. Ibid.
66. 'The Shooting of Michael Collins: Shock Disclosures', interview with Emmet Dalton by Cormac MacCarthaigh, Sunday Independent, 23 August 1970.
67. John M. Feehan, The Shooting of Michael Collins, Murder or Accident? (Cork: Royal Carbery Books, 1991), pp.95–6.
68. Piaras Béaslaí, 'Memories', Irish Independent, 22 August 1962.
69. Pádraig Ó Siadhail, An Béaslaíoch, Beatha agus Saothar Phiarais Béaslaí (1881–1965) (Dublin: Coiscéim, 2007), pp.594–8.
70. Charles Dalton, Sunday Independent, 1944.
71. Ibid.
72. See interview with Cathal O'Shannon, Emmet Dalton Remembers, RTÉ.
73. J.J., 'Emmet Dalton', Southern Star, 15 April 1978.
74. Dalton to General Staff, Dublin, received 9 am, 23 August 1922, UCDA, MP, P7/B/70.
75. Younger, p.443.
76. Adam's, Dublin, auction catalogue, 2008.
77. Dalton interview, Ó Raghallaigh, RTÉ.
78. Very Rev. Patrick J. Doyle, P.P., BMH, WS 807.
79. Dalton interview, Ó Raghallaigh, RTÉ.
80. Doyle, BMH, WS 807.
81. Freeman's Journal, 24 August 1922.
82. Risteárd Mulcahy, My Father, The General; Richard Mulcahy and the Military History of the Revolution (Dublin: Liberties Press, 2009), pp.99–100.
83. 'General Collins's Funeral', Irish Times, 29 August 1922.
84. Wilkinson & Astley, p.27.
85. 'General Collins's Funeral', Weekly Irish Times, 2 September 1922.
86. Mulcahy, p.150.
87. Eileen Battersby, 'Nothing But Doubts', Irish Times, 14 November 1996.
88. No. 108 UCDA P17A/61; P80/763 (21) (1-4); Memo from Liam Lynch, IRA Chief of Staff, to Ernie O'Malley, Assistant Chief of Staff, Field General Headquarters, 30 August 1922. (Dept C/S; Ref. No. C/S/29). Quoted in No Surrender Here, p.135.
89. Transcript of interview with Tom Foley, 2 September 1989, Sean O'Mahony Papers, NLI MS 44,104/4.
90. Dalton interview, O'Shannon RTÉ TV.
91. Interview with author, 4 Sept 2012.
92. Dalton interview, Ó Raghallaigh, RTÉ.
93. Message from Collins, Cork to Intelligence Department, Dublin, 22 August 1922, UCDA, MP, P7/B/70.
94. Dalton interview, Ó Raghallaigh, RTÉ.

CHAPTER ELEVEN

1. Emmet Dalton, interview with Pádraig Ó Raghallaigh, RTÉ radio, February–March 1977.
2. Portobello to O/C Baldonnel aerodrome, 10.30 pm, 22 August 1922, UCDA, MP, P7/B/67.
3. 'Cable Cut By Rebels', The Times, 30 August 1922. See also Census 1922, Military Archives.
4. 'Troops Ambushed, Officer and Soldier Wounded', Southern Star, 26 August 1922.
5. IE/MA/DOD/A/6943.
6. CGS, Portobello to General O'Duffy, Limerick, 31 August 1922, UCDA MP, P7/B/70.
7. Memorandum, Cork Command, 31 August 1922, UCDA MP, P7/B/70.
8. Colonel J.C. Fitzmaurice, 'Back to the Old Love', Irish Times, 17 December 1951.
9. Colonel J.C. Fitzmaurice, 'The Civil War', Irish Times, 19 December 1951.

10. Lt. Colonel M. O'Malley, 'Modest Beginnings in Times of Strife, The Air Service Years', *The Irish Air Corps, 1922-1997*, Air Corps 75 Committee, 1997; see also 'Aeroplane Surprise, Ambush Party Attacked and Scattered', *Irish Times*, 5 December 1922.

11. Poblacht na hEireann, *War News* no. 58, 15 September 1922; extract reproduced in Colonel, J. Brind report to War Office, 'Report On Situation in Ireland for the Week Ending 16 September 1922', TNA, CAB/24/139.

12. 'Terrible Cork Tragedy, Unarmed Soldier Shot Dead, Crowd Chase Assailant', *Cork Examiner*, 30 August 1922.

13. Interview with Joseph Duhig, *The Madness From Within*, RTÉ documentary on the Irish Civil War, broadcast 21 January 1998.

14. Dalton, Command HQ, Cork to CS, 2 September 1922, UCDA, MP, P7/B/70.

15. Padraic O'Farrell, *Who's Who in the Irish War of Independence and Civil War 1916–1923* (Dublin: Lilliput Press, 1997), p.400.

16. 'Exhumation of late Pte John W. Winsley – executed by sentence of court martial', IE/MA/DOD/A/13056.

17. CGS to Major General Dalton, Cork, 5 September 1922, UCDA, MP, P7/B/70.

18. Dalton to headquarters, wireless message, 2 September 1922, UCDA, MP, P7/B/71.

19. Ibid.

20. Dalton, Command HQ, Cork to CS, 2 September 1922, UCDA, MP, P7/B/70.

21. CGS to Major General Dalton, Cork, 2 September 1922, UCDA, MP, P7/B/70.

22. Major General Dalton to C-in-C, 3 September 1922, UCDA, MP, P7/B/70.

23. 'Trench Mortar Used At Macroom', *Irish Times*, 9 September 1922.

24. CGS to Major General Dalton, Cork, 5 September 1922, UCDA, MP, P7/B/70.

25. Dalton to CGS, 6 September 1922, UCDA, MP, P7/B/70.

26. Liam Tobin, MSPC, 24SP2764.

27. Two officers, Lts Cruise and Kennedy, were shot by the IRA in County Tipperary – the IRA alleged they were spies; also in that county, Sergeant Thomas McGrath, who was home on leave, was shot by the IRA after being accused of spying. (See Daniel Breen, BMH WS 1,763.) In County Wexford, four National Army prisoners were shot as a reprisal for the execution of republican prisoners. (See Hopkinson, p.246.)

28. 'Captures Near Fermoy, Nineteen Irregulars Taken In Castlelyons Area', *Freeman's Journal*, 23 September 1922; 'Fight on a Mountain, 19 Prisoners Taken', *Irish Times*, 23 September 1922.

29. Michael Harrington, *The Munster Republic* (Cork: Mercier Press, 2009), p.117.

30. No. 130 UCDA P17A/62, quoted in *No Surrender Here*, p.159.

31. Deasy, *Brother Against Brother*, p.72.

32. 'Eyeries Man Active During Civil War', *Southern Star*, 31 January 1981.

33. No. 130 UCDA P17A/62, quoted in 'No Surrender Here', p.159.

34. Dalton to CGS, 5 Sept 1922, UCDA, MP P7/B/70.

35. J. Anthony Gaughan, *Alfred O'Rahilly, Volume II, Public Figure*, pp.184–5.

36. Gaughan, pp.186–7.

37. Florence O'Donoghue, *No Other Law* (Dublin: Irish Press, 1954), p.282.

38. Deasy, *Brother Against Brother*, p.83.

39. O'Donoghue, p.282.

40. No. 205 UCDA P17A/64, quoted in *No Surrender Here*, p.246.

41. Meda Ryan, *Tom Barry, IRA Freedom Fighter* (Cork: Mercier, 2012), pp.246–7.

42. Deasy, p.84.

43. NLI MS 10,973(7); UCDA P17A/12; P69/179(3-9), quoted in *No Surrender Here*, pp.494–5.

44. J.E. Dalton to General Mulcahy, 6 September 1922, UCDA MP, P7/B/66.

45. Mulcahy to Major General Dalton, 30 September 1922, UCDA, MP, P7/B/66.

46. Headquarters to Dalton, Cork, re: O'Duffy's intentions, 7 September 1922, UCDA, MP, P/7/B/66.

47. 'Activities in Cork, Big Area Combed Out', *Irish Independent*, 11 September 1922.

48. 'The Cork Prison Tragedy', *Irish Independent*, 28 September 1922.

49. See *War News*, No. 71.

50. General Mulcahy, Written Replies, 'Coachford (County Cork) Inquest', Dáil Éireann, 1 November 1922.
51. Rúnaí don Rialtas [Government Secretary] to C-in-C, 9 September 1922, UCDA, MP, P/7/B/66.
52. C-in-C to Major General Dalton, Cork, 8 September 1922, UCDA, MP, P7/B/70.
53. Colonel/Commandant Charles Russell to Secretary, C-in-C, 12 September 1922, UCDA, MP, P/7B/66.
54. C-in-C to Major General Dalton, Cork, 11 September 1922; C-in-C to Commandant Murphy, Limerick, 11 September 1922, UCDA, MP, P7/B/66.
55. Hopkinson, p.201.
56. Harvey & White, p.259.
57. Hopkinson, p.174.
58. O'Duffy to CGS, 6 September 1922, UCDA, MP, P7/B/71; see also Fearghal McGarry, *Eoin O'Duffy, A Self-Made Hero* (Oxford: Oxford University Press, 2005), p.110.
59. Tom McGinty, *The Irish Navy* (The Kerryman Ltd., 1995), p.99.
60. *Connacht Tribune*, 16 September 1922.
61. John P. Haran, St. Camillus Hospital, Limerick, 'Emmet Dalton', letter to *Irish Independent*, 29 March 1978.
62. Mary Collins Powell, letter to Mrs Keogh, 28 September 1922, Vinny Byrne collection, www.wartalk.com.
63. See Patrick J. Twohig, *The Dark Secret of Bealnablath*, p.210. See also Timothy Buckley, BMH, WS 1674.
64. Twohig, pp 230–1.
65. Colonel Commandant Peadar Ó Conlain, O/C No. 2 Column, Southern Area, Macroom to Major General Dalton, Cork, 18 September 1922, UCDA, MP, P7/B/82.
66. Dalton, Southern Area Command HQ, Cork, to C-in-C, 19 September 1922, UCDA, MP, P7/B/82.
67. C-in-C to Major General Dalton, 21 September 1922, UCDA, MP, P7/B/82.
68. GHQ to Major General Dalton, 19 September 1922, UCDA, MP, P/7/B/66.

CHAPTER TWELVE

1. C-in-C to Major General Dalton, 11 September 1922, IE/MA, CW/OPS/01/03/02.
2. Dalton to Mulcahy, 13 September 1922, IE/MA/CW/OPS/04/01.
3. Dalton to C-in-C., 19 September 1922, IE/MA, CW/OPS/01/02/06.
4. C-in-C to Major General Dalton, Cork, 20 September 1922, UCDA, MP, P/7B/66.
5. Dalton to C-in-C, Dublin, UCDA, MP, P/7/B/66.
6. C-in-C to Major General Dalton, Cork, 15 September 1922, UCDA, MP, P/7/B/66.
7. Lt. Comdt. Liam Archer to C-in-C, 27 September 1922, UCDA, MP, P/7/B/48.
8. Harvey & White, p.121.
9. Commandant General W.R.E. Murphy, Adjutant Southwest Command, proposed operational plan, UCDA, MP, P7B/113.
10. Hopkinson, p.204.
11. 'Successes in Co. Cork; Inchigeela Taken; Pursuit Towards Kerry; Irregular Cavalry', *Irish Times*, 2 October 1922.
12. Ibid.
13. 'Co. Cork Operations, Advance on Ballyvourney', *Irish Times*, 5 October 1922.
14. See, for instance, *Irish Times*, 21 Oct 1922.
15. IE/MA/DOD/A/09177.
16. Anti-Treaty forces also carried out executions. For instance, during the same month of October, in Emmet Dalton's own command area in County Cork, republicans shot dead a number of civilians. The body of William Aherne was found at Bishopstown with a label inscribed, 'Shot as spy – IRA'. (During the Civil War the IRA continued to kill people accused of spying, although not in the same numbers as during the Anglo-Irish War.) In Carrignavar, Patrick Byrne and Daniel Hanlon were taken from their homes by armed men and were later found riddled with bullets in

a field. A military court of inquiry found they had been murdered because of assistance they had given to Free State forces – see IE/MA/CW/OPS/08/10. According to one estimate, anti-Treaty forces carried out 53 executions during the Civil War – see John P. Duggan, *A History of the Irish Army* (Dublin: Gill & Macmillan, 1991), p.113.

17. London Letter, *Irish Independent*, 14 March 1952.
18. 'Major General J. E. Dalton's Marriage in Cork', *Freeman's Journal*, 11 October 1922.
19. IE/MA/DOD/A/07556.
20. IE/MA, CW/OPS/01/01/22.
21. Copy of concert programme supplied courtesy of Audrey Dalton Simenz.
22. Ernie O'Malley, *The Singing Flame* (Cork: Mercier, 2012), p.205.
23. Hopkinson, p.216.
24. No. 276 UCDA P17A/58, quoted in Cormac K.H. O'Malley & Anne Dolan, *No Surrender Here, The Civil War Papers of Ernie O'Malley, 1922–24* (Dubin: Lilliput Press, 2007), p.309.
25. See 'Cork Irregular's Death, Prisoner's Accusations', *Irish Independent*, 23 October 1922; 'Sequel to Arrest, Wounded Prisoner's Account of Brutal Treatment', *Irish Times*, 23 October, 1922.
26. Eastern District Command, Reports of raids carried out, 1/11/1022 – 29/12/1922, IE/MA, CW/OPS/07/25.
27. Sinead McCoole, *Hazel, A Life of Lady Lavery, 1880–1935* (Dublin: Lilliput Press, 2012), Location 2,717, Kindle edition.
28. Lady Lavery letter to Dalton, Emmet Dalton papers, NLI, MS 46,687/6.
29. 'Recent Library acquisition includes important Lady Lavery letter', National Library of Ireland News, Issue 34: Winter 2008.
30. Letter from Hazel, Lady Lavery, to Major General Emmet Dalton, 22 November 1922, Dalton papers, NLI, MS 46,687/6; summary given in National Library of Ireland News, Issue 34: Winter 2008.
31. McCoole, Location 2703, Kindle edition.
32. See Cathal O'Shannon, 'Beal na mBlath – No Easy Road Back', *An Cosantóir*, November 1990.
33. 'The Irish Flag, Blessing of the Colours in Fermoy', *Freeman's Journal*, 9 November 1922.
34. Irish Army Census Collection 1922, Irish Military Archives.
35. Ibid.
36. List of Cork Command HQ Staff and District Command staffs, UCDA, MP, P7/B/67; see also Irish Army Census Collection 1922.
37. Éamon de Buitléar, 'An Irishman's Diary', *Irish Times*, 11 November 2008.
38. List of Cork Command HQ Staff and District Command staffs, UCDA, MP, P7/B/67.
39. Southern Area, Command HQ, to C-in-C, Portobello, 14 November 1922, IE/MA, CW/OPS/04/13; List of Cork Command HQ Staff and District Command staffs, UCDA, MP, P7/B/67.
40. Hopkinson, p.203.
41. Interview with Cormac MacCarthaigh for *Agus* magazine, July 1970, reproduced in John M. Feehan, *The Shooting of Michael Collins, Murder or Accident?* (Cork: Royal Carbery Books, 1991), p.108.
42. Hopkinson, p.202.
43. Dalton interview with Cathal O'Shannon, RTÉ TV documentary, *Emmet Dalton Remembers*.
44. IE/MA/MSPC/24SP13470.
45. Major General Dalton to C-in-C, 18 November 1922, UCDA, MP, P7/B/67.
46. See 'Chris Dalton Personal Development Blog', http://chris-dalton.com/tag/bael-na-mblath/ (accessed 20 May 2014).
47. Major General Dalton to C-in-C, 22 November 1922, IE/MA, CW/OPS/01/02/06.
48. Dalton to C-in-C, 29 November 1922, UCDA, MP, P7/B/67.
49. 'Extensive Raids, Attacks on Troops; Arrests and Captures', *Irish Times*, 22 November 1922.
50. Special Branch, New Scotland Yard, 'Report on Revolutionary Organisations in the United Kingdom', 5 July 1923, TNA, CAB/24/160.
51. Ray Smith and Jim Nicoll, 'Who Killed Michael Collins? I did not shoot him – McPeak', *Irish Independent*, 18 May 1971.

52. C-in-C to Stephen Murphy, Acting GOC, Cork, 14 December 1922; C-in-C to Cork Command, 21 December 1922, UCDA, MP, P7/B/67.
53. Hopkinson, p.203.
54. Dalton interview, Ó Raghallaigh, RTÉ.

CHAPTER THIRTEEN
1. Seanad Éireann Debate, Volume 1, 'Powers of the Seanad', Wednesday 24 January 1923.
2. Report on the Committee on the Appointment of the Clerks, Seanad Éireann Debate, Volume 2, Number 21, Friday, 7 March 1924.
3. Dáil Éireann Debates, Volume 2, 19 January 1922.
4. 'Memo from Dalton', 13 February 1923, Senator James G. Douglas Papers, NLI, MS 49,581/57, Folder 3.
5. See *Freeman's Journal*, 9 March 1923.
6. Hopkinson, *Green Against Green*, p.195.
7. R.F. Foster, *W. B. Yeats, A Life* (Oxford: Oxford University Press, 2003), p.230.
8. J.Anthony Gaughan (ed.), *Memoirs of Senator James G. Douglas (1887–1954), Concerned Citizen* (Dublin: University College Dublin Press, 1998), p.95.
9. Donal O'Sullivan, *The Irish Free State and its Senate* (London: Faber & Faber, 1940), p.108.
10. Major General Emmet Dalton, 'Comrade's Moving Story of Michael Collins' Last Fight', *Freeman's Journal*, 22 August 1923.
11. 'Where Collins Fell, Tributes of Comrades', *Irish Independent*, 23 August 1923.
12. Copy of letter, Sean O'Connell to Lady Lavery, 11 October 1923, courtesy of Louis O'Connell.
13. 'President as Godfather. Incident Which Recalls the Death of Michael Collins', *Freeman's Journal*, 17 December 1923.
14. *Freeman's Journal*, 2 January 1924.
15. Dalton interview, Ó Raghallaigh, RTÉ.
16. For background, see also Chapters 2 and 3, Damian Corless, *The Greatest Bleeding Hearts Racket in the World*, (Dublin: Gill & Macmillan, 2010).
17. Dalton interview, Ó Raghallaigh, RTÉ.
18. Ibid.
19. Internal, unsigned memo by the dissident group, with the heading *History of Events*; Military Archives; copy also in possession of Louis O'Connell.
20. Risteárd Mulcahy, *My Father, The General* (Dublin: Liberties Press, 2009), p.169.
21. Sean O'Connell, MSPC, 24SP1606.
22. James Patrick Conroy, MSPC, 24SP80.
23. 'Collins' Comrades', *Anglo-Celt*, 30 August 1924.
24.' Accident in Motor Cycle Trial', *Irish Independent*, 29 June 1925.
25. Emmet Dalton TV interview with Cathal O'Shannon, *Emmet Dalton Remembers*, RTÉ, 4 March 1978.
26. 'Seanad Clerk Resigns', *Nenagh Guardian*, 14 November 1925.
27. 'James Emmet Dalton', *Dictionary of Irish Biography*, Cambridge/Royal Irish Academy.
28. See 'Suit Against Bank', *Irish Independent*, 12 & 13 November 1926; 'Bank's Appeal Dismissed', *Irish Times*, 7 April 1927.
29. J. Anthony Gaughan (ed.), p.92.
30. Dalton interview, Ó Raghallaigh, RTÉ.
31. Ibid.
32. Tim Pat Coogan, *Michael Collins* (London: Arrow Books, 1991), p.417.
33. Colm Connolly, *Michael Collins* (London: Weidenfeld & Nicholson, 1996), p.83.
34. Ulick O'Connor, *Oliver St. John Gogarty* (London: New English Library, 1967), pp.206–7.
35. 'The Borrowed Guns', *Irish Independent*, 7 September 1927.
36. James Emmet Dalton, *Dictionary of Irish Biography*, Cambridge/Royal Irish Academy, 2009.
37. House of Lords Debate, 6 May 1931, Vol 80 cc1036-44.
38. Marie Coleman, *The Irish Sweep, A History of the Irish Hospitals Sweepstake* (Dublin: University College Dublin Press, 2009), p.31.

39. Information to author from Louis O'Connell.
40. *Daily Boston Globe*, 5 July 1936.
41. IE/MA/MSPC/24SP13470.
42. Dalton interview, Ó Raghallaigh, RTÉ.
43. 'Captain Tambs and James Dalton Speak', *Newport Mercury and Weekly News*, 21 June 1935.
44. 'Major General Ennis's Will', *Irish Times*, 15 December 1945.
45. 'The Sean Treacy Memorial Fund', *Irish Press*, 17 December 1938.
46. Comdt. D. V. Horgan, letter, 'Robert Kee's Ireland', *Irish Times*, 9 March 1981.
47. See Brian Trench, 'A Bohemian of Many Parts', on website of Bohemian Football Club.
48. *Irish Independent*, 6 April 1923.
49. Eamonn T. Doyle & Seán Óg Ó Ceallacháin, *Hermitage Golf Club, Celebrating 100 Years 1905–2005*, Hermitage Golf Club, p.47; see also *Irish Times*, 3 December 1945.
50. L.M. 'Golfers I Have Met', No. 32, Mr. E. Dalton (Hermitage), *Irish Independent*, February 1938. Clipping courtesy of Audrey Dalton Simenz.

CHAPTER FOURTEEN
1. Emmet Dalton interview with Pádraig Ó Raghallaigh, RTÉ radio, February–March 1977; see also *Irish Independent*, 31 May 1940.
2. 'Cardinal Hinsley Mass Reel', *Irish Times*, 16 April 1943.
3. Charles F. Dalton file, IE/MA/MSPC/24SP1153.
4. Ibid.
5. Ibid.
6. Ibid.
7. See Charles Dalton, *Dictionary of Irish Biography*, Cambridge/Royal Irish Academy.
8. Charles Lysaght, *Brendan Bracken, A Biography* (London: Allen Lane, Penguin Books, 1979), p.30.
9. Lysaght, pp.236–7.
10. Information to author from Richard F. Dalton; Tim Pat Coogan, *Michael Collins* (London: Arrow Books, 1991), p.418.
11. Coogan, p.417.
12. Martin S. Quigley, *A U.S. Spy in Ireland* (Dublin: Marino Books, 1999), p.92.
13. Ibid., pp.90–2.
14. Ibid., pp.91–6.
15. Ibid., pp.90–1.
16. Audrey Dalton Simenz email to author, 2 November 2012.
17. Quigley, p.96.
18. Ibid., pp.179–80.
19. Information provided to author by Audrey Dalton Simenz.
20. Boston College Bulletin, University General Catalogue 1958-1959, Volume XXX, No. 13.
21. 'Retired Col. Dermot P. Dalton Served in Last Three Wars', *Washington Post*, 23 May 1980.
22. 'Major-General T. Ennis', *Irish Independent*, 13 March 1945.
23. Dalton interview, Ó Raghallaigh, RTÉ.
24. 'Family Chest Gives Up Secret', undated clipping from unidentified newspaper, supplied courtesy of Audrey Dalton Simenz.
25. Information to author from Lar Joye, National Museum of Ireland, 12 February 2014.
26. Information to author from Richard Dalton, 18 February 2014.
27. Dalton interview, Ó Raghallaigh, RTÉ.
28. Information to author from Richard Dalton.
29. Conversation with the author, December 2012.
30. Taubman, p.83.
31. Ibid., p.84.
32. Ibid., pp.84–6.
33. 'Holiday Sport, Princess Elizabeth at Hurst Park', *The Times*, 15 May 1951.
34. Taubman, p.85.

35. Ibid., p.86.
36. Information to author from Audrey Dalton Simenz.
37. Howard Taubman, 'Arctic Prince, 28-1 in Books, 50-1 in Mutuels, Wins Epsom Derby', *New York Times*, 31 May 1951.
38. 'London Letter', *Irish Independent*, 10 June 1952.
39. Harold Heffernan (NANA), 'Audrey Dalton's Role A Reel-Life Paradox', *Toledo Blade*, 13 February 1958.
40. Ibid.
41. Audrey Dalton Simenz, email to author, 5 February 2014.
42. Robin Dalton, *An Incidental Memoir* (Australia: Viking, 1998), pp.86–7.
43. Robin Dalton, p.91.

CHAPTER FIFTEEN

1. Ian MacKillop & Neil Sinyard (ed.), *British Cinema in the 1950s: An Art in Peacetime* (Manchester: Manchester University Press, 2003), p.179.
2. Brian McFarlane, *An Autobiography of British Cinema* (London: Methuen, 1997), p.46.
3. Rebecca Prime, *Hollywood Exiles in Europe, The Blacklist and the Cold War Film Culture* (New Jersey: Rutgers University Press, 2014), Kindle edition location, 1,338.
4. Emmet Dalton interview with Pádraig Ó Raghallaigh, RTÉ radio, February–March 1977.
5. Information from Richard Dalton. See also Barry Monahan, *Ireland's Theatre on Film* (Dublin: Irish Academic Press, 2009), p.194.
6. Tise Vahimagi, *Hannah Weinstein (1912–1984)*, Screenonline, British Film Institute.
7. Hy Kraft, *On My Way to the Theatre* (New York: Macmillan, 1971), p.192.
8. Dalton interview, Ó Raghallaigh, RTÉ.
9. Robin Dalton, *An Incidental Memoir* (Australia: Viking, 1998), p.171.
10. Phone interview with author, 30 August 2012.
11. Maurice Walsh correspondence with Medal Films, London, 1954–5, Maurice Walsh papers, University of Limerick.
12. Mooney to Dalton, 28 October 1954, Ria Mooney Papers, NLI, MS 49,603/9.
13. Cecil Maiden to Dalton, 6 November 1954, NLI MS 49,603/9.
14. Dalton to Mooney, 10 October 1956, NLI MS 49,603/9.
15. Monahan, p.195.
16. Ibid.
17. Monahan, p.198.
18. Dalton to Mooney, 25 October 1956, NLI MS 49,603/9.
19. Dalton to Elliman, 1 November 1956, NLI MS 49,603/9.
20. Dalton to Mooney, 15 December 1956, NLI, MS 49,603/9.
21. 'Shooting of TV Film at Dunboyne', *Irish Independent*, 16 January 1957.
22. James L. Kilgallen, 'Tire and Rubber Executive Becomes Biggest Figure In TV, Radio and Movies', *Cumberland Times*, 14 August 1955.
23. Emmet Dalton interview with Pádraig Ó Raghallaigh, RTÉ radio, February–March 1977; see also interview with Cathal O'Shannon, *Emmet Dalton Remembers*, RTÉ TV, March 1978.
24. Brian Girvin and Gary Murphy, *The Lemass Era, Politics and Society in the Ireland of Sean Lemass* (Dublin:: University College Dublin Press, 2005), p.177.
25. Kevin Rockett, Luke Gibbons, John Hill, *Cinema and Ireland* (Kent: Croom Helm, 1987), p.99.
26. Dalton to Blythe, 31 July 1957, NLI, MS 49,603/9.
27. Audrey Dalton Simenz, email to author, 1 March 2014.
28. Hy Kraft, *On My Way to the Theatre* (New York: Macmillan, 1971), pp.194–5.
29. Ibid.
30. Audrey Dalton Simenz, email to author, 9 February 2014.
31. Kraft, p.166.
32. Phone interview with author, 19 March 2013.
33. Emmet Dalton Papers, NLI, MS 46,687/6.

34. Comment to author, 18 February 2014.
35. Dalton to Mooney, 29 November 1957, NLI, MS 49,603/9.
36. Phone interview with author, 19 October 2012.
37. Phone interview with author, 30 August 2012.
38. Sean O'Casey Papers, NLI, MS 38,086.
39. Christopher Murray, *Sean O'Casey, Writer at Work* (Dublin: Gill & Macmillan, 2006), p.399.
40. 're Irish Story', 15.9.57, Emmet Dalton Papers, NLI, MS 46,687/5.
41. Nathan Keats, RKO Television to Dalton, 29 Oct 1957, NLI MS 49,603/9.
42. Dalton to Ria Mooney, 29 November 1957, NLI, NLI MS 49,603/9.
43. Anthony Slide, *The Cinema and Ireland* (1988), p.30.
44. 'Work Starting Soon in Bray Film Studio', *Irish Times*, 14 March 1958.
45. 'An Irishman's Diary', *Irish Times*, 14 May 1958.
46. Hugh D. Smith, 'New Studio Thrives in Eire's Country Air', *New York Times*, 7 September 1958.
47. Monahan, pp.204–5.
48. Mooney to Dalton, 14 September 1958, NLI, MS 49,603/9.
49. Dalton to Mooney, 26 August 1958, and 5 December 1958, NLI, MS 49,603/9.
50. Dalton to Mooney, 6 August 1957, NLI, MS 49,603/9.
51. Ibid.
52. Dalton to Mooney, 15 September 1958, NLI, MS 49,603/9.
53. Monahan, p.206.
54. Ibid.
55. Mooney to Dalton, 9 January 1959, NLI, MS 49,603/9.
56. Fidelma Farley, *This Other Eden* (Cork: Cork University Press, 2001), p.19.
57. Farley, p.21.
58. Ibid., p.3.
59. Leslie Phillips, *Hello, The Autobiography* (London: Orion Books, 2006), pp.208–10.
60. Farley, p.29.
61. Phillips, pp.208–10.
62. Farley, p.19.
63. *Irish Press*, 26 September 1959.
64. Dalton to Mooney, 11 June 1959, NLI, MS 49,603/9.
65. Monahan, p.207.
66. Ibid., pp.207–8.
67. Michael Dwyer, 'Christopher Lee – Lots of Life after Dracula', *Irish Times*, 27 July 1990.
68. Information to author by interview and email, December 2013.
69. Gus Smith, *Eamonn Andrews, His Life* (London: W.H. Allen, 1988), pp.96–7.
70. Dalton to Mooney, 26 August 1958, NLI, MS 49,603/9.
71. Monahan, pp.208–9.
72. Kevin Rockett, Luke Gibbon, John Hill, *Cinema and Ireland* (Kent: Croom Helm, 1987), p.100.
73. Dalton to Mooney, 11 June 1959, NLI, MS 49,603/9.
74. Dalton interview, Ó Raghallaigh, RTÉ.
75. Ibid.

CHAPTER SIXTEEN
1. Howard Taubman, *The Pleasure of their Company* (Portland, Oregon: Amadeus Press, 1994), pp.87–8.
2. Information to author from Richard Dalton, and Audrey Dalton Simenz.
3. Email to author, 10 January 2013.
4. Email to author, 22 January 2013.
5. Information to author from Richard Dalton and Robin Dalton.
6. Information to author from Richard Dalton.
7. 'Armoured Car in Jail Break', *Irish Independent*, 5 February 1964.
8. Sister Francis Colombiere (McCarthy), Sisters of Charity, Stella Maris, Baily, County Dublin to Emmet Dalton, 9 February 1964, NLI, MS 46,687/3.

9. Information to author from Richard Dalton.
10. Letter, Emmet Dalton to Mrs Albert Ryan, Dublin, 24 August 1966, details given in Adam's catalogue, Dublin; see http://www.adams.ie (accessed 20 May 2014).
11. Cormac MacCarthaigh, 'The Shooting of Michael Collins: Shock Disclosures', *Sunday Independent*, 23 August 1970.
12. Ibid.
13. Cathal O'Shannon, 'Beal na mBlath – No Easy Road Back', *An Cosantóir*, November 1990, reproduced in the magazine with permission of *The Cork Examiner* and Mr O'Shannon.
14. Ibid.
15. Ibid.
16. Phone interview with author, 18 January 2014.
17. Cathal O'Shannon, *An Cosantóir*.
18. 'Reconciliation', *Irish Times*, 9 March 1978.
19. Michael McInerney, 'Death of General Emmet Dalton', *Irish Times*, 6 March 1978.
20. Jim Haughey, *The First World War in Irish Poetry* (Pennsylvania: Bucknell University Press), p.268.
21. *Irish Press*, 15 July 1981.
22. Cathal O'Shannon, letter to the *Irish Times*, 1 September 1981.
23. Cathal O'Shannon, *An Cosantóir*.
24. R.C. Geary, letter to the *Irish Times*, 10 September 1981.
25. Brendan O'Reilly, letter to the *Irish Times*, 10 September 1981.
26. M.J. Costello, letter to the *Irish Times*, 3 September 1981.
27. Ulick O'Connor, 'Treating Pub Guff As History', *Sunday Independent*, 6 September 1981.
28. Memorandum supplied to author, courtesy of Audrey Dalton Simenz.
29. Sean Dowling, letter to the *Irish Times*, 22 October 1981.

Select Bibliography

PRIMARY SOURCES
Irish Military Archives
Bureau of Military History
Civil War Operations and Intelligence Reports Collection
Department of Defence 'A' files
Irish Army Census Records
Liaison and Evacuation Papers
Military Service Pensions Collection

The National Archives, Kew, United Kingdom
Cabinet Papers (CAB)
War Office (WO)

National Library of Ireland
Emmet Dalton Papers
Piaras Béaslaí Papers
Senator James G. Douglas Papers
Ria Mooney Papers
J.J. O'Connell Papers
Sean O'Mahony Papers

University College Dublin Archives
Richard Mulcahy Papers

MEDIA
Radio and TV Programmes
Interviews with Emmet Dalton by Pádraig Ó Raghallaigh, RTÉ radio, February-March 1977; *Emmet Dalton Remembers*, RTÉ TV documentary, March 1978; *Shadow of Béal na Bláth*, RTÉ TV documentary, 1988; *The Madness From Within*, RTÉ TV documentary, 1998; *The Assassination of Michael Collins*, BBC TV documentary, 2007.
Newspaper Archives
Boston Daily Globe; *Cork Examiner*; *Freeman's Journal*; *Irish Independent*; *Irish Press*; *Irish Times*; *Limerick Leader*; *Munster Express*; *Nenagh Guardian*; *New York Times*; *Southern Star*; *Sunday Independent*; *The Times* (London), *Washington Post*. Also, *An t-Óglach* magazine, Irish Military Archives.

OFFICIAL PUBLICATIONS
Dáil Éireann Parliamentary Debates
Seanad Éireann Parliamentary Debates
Hansard: House of Commons Debates
Hansard: House of Lords Debates
London Gazette

SECONDARY WORKS

Allen, G., *The Garda Síochána: Policing Independent Ireland, 1922–82* (Dublin: Gill & Macmillan, 1999).

Andrews, C.S., *Dublin Made Me* (Dublin: Lilliput, 2001).

Bacon, Captain Alban F.L., *The Wanderings of a Temporary Warrior* (London: H.F. & G. Witherby, 1922).

Béaslaí, P., *Michael Collins and the Making of a New Ireland*, Volumes I & II (Dublin: Phoenix Publishing, 1926).

Borgonovo, J., *The Battle For Cork, July–August 1922* (Cork: Mercier, 2011).

Coogan, T.P., *Michael Collins* (London: Arrow Books, 1991).

Costello, Con, *A Most Delightful Station: The British Army on the Curragh of Kildare, Ireland, 1855–1922* (Cork: The Collins Press, 1999).

Dalton, C., *With the Dublin Brigade, 1917–1921* (London: Peter Davies, 1929).

Dalton, R., *An Incidental Memoir* (Australia: Viking, 1998).

Deasy, L., *Brother Against Brother* (Cork: Mercier Press, 1982).

De Búrca, P., & J.F. Boyle, *Free State or Republic? Pen Pictures of the Historic Treaty Session of Dáil Éireann* (Dublin: Talbot Press, 1922).

Doyle, E.T. & S. Ó Ceallacháin, *Hermitage Golf Club, Celebrating 100 Years, 1905–2005* (Dublin: Hermitage Golf Club).

Duffy, C., *Through German Eyes: The British & The Somme, 1916* (London: Phoenix, 2007).

Duggan, J.P., *A History of the Irish Army* (Dublin: Gill & Macmillan, 1991).

Dungan, M., *Irish Voices from the Great War* (Dublin: Irish Academic Press, 1995).

Dungan, M., *They Shall Grow Not Old* (Dublin: Four Courts Press, 1997).

Dwyer, T.R., *The Squad and the Intelligence Operations of Michael Collins* (Cork: Mercier Press, 2005).

Dwyer, T.R., *'I Signed My Death Warrant': Michael Collins & the Treaty* (Cork: Mercier Press, 2007).

Dwyer, T.R., *Michael Collins and the Civil War* (Cork: Mercier Press, 2012).

English, R., *Armed Struggle, The History of the IRA* (London: Pan Books, 2004).

English, R., *Ernie O'Malley, IRA Intellectual* (Oxford: Oxford University Press, 1999).

Ervine, St. John, *Craigavon, Ulsterman* (London: George Allen & Unwin, 1949).

Evans, B., *Seán Lemass, Democratic Dictator* (Cork: The Collins Press, 2011).

Fanning, R., *Fatal Path: British Government and Irish Revolution 1910–1922* (London: Faber & Faber, 2013).

Farley, F., *This Other Eden* (Cork: Cork University Press, 2001).

Fitzpatrick, D., *Harry Boland's Irish Revolution* (Cork: Cork University Press, 2003).

Feehan, J.M., *The Shooting of Michael Collins, Murder or Accident?* (Cork: Royal Carbery Books, 1991).

Gaughan, J.A., *Alfred O'Rahilly, Volume II, Public Figure* (Dublin: Kingdom Books, 1989).

Gaughan, J.A. (ed.), *Memoirs of Senator James G. Douglas (1887–1954), Concerned Citizen* (Dublin: University College Dublin Press, 1998).

Gibbs, P., *The Battles of the Somme* (Toronto: McClelland, Goodchild & Stewart, 1917).

Gilbert, M., *Somme, The Heroism and Horror of War* (London: John Murray, 2007).

Gillis, L., *The Fall of Dublin* (Cork: Mercier, 2011).

Griffith, K. & T.E. O'Grady, *Curious Journey, An Oral History of Ireland's Unfinished Revolution* (London: Hutchinson, 1982).

Harrington, M., *The Civil War in North Cork* (Cork: Mercier, 2009).

Harrington, N.C., *Kerry Landing, August 1922* (Dublin: Anvil Books, 1992).

Hart, P., *Mick, The Real Michael Collins* (London: Macmillan, 2005).

Harvey, D. & G. White, *The Barracks, A History of Victoria/Collins Barracks, Cork* (Cork: Mercier Press, 1997).

Hitchcock, Captain F. C., *Stand To: A Diary of the Trenches 1915–1918* (Norfolk: Gliddon Books, 1988).

Hopkinson, M., *Green Against Green, The Irish Civil War* (Dublin: Gill & Macmillan, 2004).

Hopkinson, M. (ed.), *The Last Days of Dublin Castle - The Diaries of Mark Sturgis* (Dublin: Irish Academic Press, 1999).

Horgan, J., *Seán Lemass, The Enigmatic Patriot* (Dublin: Gill & Macmillan, 1997).

Johnstone, T., *Orange, Green and Khaki, The Story of the Irish Regiments in the Great War, 1914–18* (Dublin: Gill and Macmillan, 1992).

Kautt, W.H., *Ambushes and Armour, The Irish Rebellion, 1919-1921* (Dublin: Irish Academic Press, 2010).

Kennedy, F., *Frank Duff, A Life Story* (London: Burns & Oates, 2011).

McCoole, S., *Hazel: A Life of Lady Lavery, 1880-1935* (Dublin: Lilliput Press, 2012).

McGarry, F., *Eoin O'Duffy, A Self-Made Hero* (Oxford: Oxford University Press, 2005).

MacDonagh, M., *The Irish on the Somme* (London: Hodder and Stoughton, 1917).

Macardle, D., *The Irish Republic* (Dublin: Irish Press, 1951).

Macready, N., *Annals of an Active Life*, Volume Two (London: Hutchinson, 1924).

Massey, W.T., *How Jerusalem Was Won* (New York: Scribner, 1920).

Mulcahy, R., *My Father, The General; Richard Mulcahy and the Military History of the Revolution* (Dublin: Liberties Press, 2009).

Neeson, E., *The Civil War, 1922–23* (Dublin: Poolbeg, 1989).

Neligan, D., *The Spy in the Castle* (London: Prendeville Publishing Ltd., 1999).

Ó Broin, L., *In Great Haste, The Letters of Michael Collins and Kitty Kiernan* (Dublin: Gill & Macmillan).

O'Connor, U., *Oliver St John Gogarty* (London: New English Library, 1967).

O'Connor, U., *Michael Collins and the Troubles* (Edinburgh: Mainstream, 2007).

Ó Dochartaigh, T., *Cathal Brugha, A Shaol is a Thréithe* (Baile Átha Cliath: Foilseacháin Náisiúnta Teoranta, 1969).

O'Donoghue, F. (Foreword), *IRA Jailbreaks 1918-1921* (Cork: Mercier Press, 2010).

O'Flaherty, L., *Drumcondra and its Environs* (Dublin: Drumcondra Publications, 2009).

O'Mahony, E., *Michael Collins: His Life And Times*, Collins 22 Society website.

O'Malley, C.K.H. & A. Dolan, *No Surrender Here, The Civil War Papers of Ernie O'Malley, 1922-24* (Dublin: Lilliput Press, 2007).

O'Malley, E., *On Another Man's Wound* (Cork: Anvil Books, 2012).

O'Malley, E., *The Singing Flame* (Cork: Mercier, 2012).

Osborne, C., *Michael Collins – Himself* (Cork: Mercier Press, 2003).

Ó Siadhail, P., *An Béaslaíoch, Beatha agus Saothar Phiarais Béaslaí (1881-1965)* (Dublin: Coiscéim, 2007).

O'Sullivan, D., *The Irish Free State and its Senate* (London: Faber & Faber, 1940).

Quigley, M.S., *A U.S. Spy in Ireland* (Dublin: Marino Books, 1999).

Rockett, K., L. Gibbon & J. Hill, *Cinema and Ireland* (Kent: Croom Helm, 1987).

Ryan, M., *The Day Michael Collins Was Shot* (Dublin: Poolbeg, 1995).

Ryan, M., *Liam Lynch, The Real Chief* (Cork: Mercier, 2012).

Ryan, M., *Tom Barry: IRA Freedom Fighter* (Cork: Mercier, 2012).

Sheehan, W., *Fighting for Dublin: The British Battle for Dublin, 1919-1921* (Cork: Collins Press, 2007).

Taubman, H., *The Pleasure Of Their Company, A Reminiscence* (Oregon: Amadeus Press, 1994).

Taylor, J.W., *The 2nd Royal Irish Rifles in the Great War* (Dublin: Four Courts Press, 2005).

Taylor, R., *Michael Collins* (London: Four Square Books, 1961).

Townshend, C., *The Republic: The Fight for Irish Independence, 1918–1923* (London: Alan Lane, 2013).

Twohig, P.J., *The Dark Secret of Bealnablath* (Ballincollig: Tower Books, 1991).

Younger, C., *Ireland's Civil War* (London: Fontana Press, 1986).

Walsh, M., *G2, In Defence of Ireland – Irish Military Intelligence 1918-45* (Cork: The Collins Press, 2010).

Whitton, Lieutenant-Colonel F.E., *The Prince of Wales's Leinster Regiment*, Volume 2 (Andrews UK Ltd., 2012).

Williams, D. (ed.), *The Irish Struggle 1916-1926* (London: Routledge & Kegan Paul, 1966).

Valiulis, M.G., *Portrait of a Revolutionary, General Richard Mulcahy and the Founding of the Irish Free State* (Dublin: Irish Academic Press, 1992).

Index

Bloody Sunday killings, 34–5, 87, 214, 221
Blythe, Ernest, 87, 237–8, 240, 245, 247–8
Bohemian Football Club, 6, 34, 217
Boland, Harry, 49, 53, 55, 86, 114, 116, 194
Bolger, Sean 'Flash', 190
Bolster, Frank, 45, 102
bombing of train at Thurles, 74
Boundary Commission, the, 84
Bourke, Lorcan, 251
Box, Muriel, 248, 250
Boyd's Shop (play), 241, 245
Boyle, John Kemmy, 32
Brabazon, Capt. Alan, 27
Bracken, Brendan, 222
Brady, A.J.S., 155
Breen, Dan, 33, 217
Breslin, Peadar, 42, 44
Bridgeman, William, 207
Brind, Col. J.E., 66, 99, 106
Briscoe, Robert, 145
Bristol F2B fighter plane, 115, 120, 138
British military base camp at Kantara, 26
British obstruction of the National Loan, 81
British refusal to vacate Naas barracks, 88
Brooks, Pte. J.R., 92
Brother Against Brother (book), 96, 105, 157, 163, 180
Browne, Dr., Bishop, 169
Brugha, Cathal, 63, 111
Buckley, James, 185
burning of houses of Anglo-Irish Senators, 202, 205
Byrne, Ben, 88, 130, 181, 192, 195
Byrne, Charlie, 91, 209
Byrne, Vinny, 83, 214, 259

Cagney, James, 1, 247
'Cairo Gang', the, 34
calls by Dalton for reinforcements and logistical support, 139, 142, 178, 197
camel convoys, organisation of, 22
Caprani, Joseph, 179
Caprani, Vincent, 179
capture of Cork, 129, 133–40, 141–3
capture of Jerusalem, 22–3
Capuchins, the, 140
casualties at assault on Ginchy, 19
Catholic Church, the, 57
Cavendish, William, 223 (*see also* Devonshire, Duke of)
CCP (Cork Civic Police), the, 146
Chadwick, Harold, 228
Chadwick, Madeleine, 255–6
Chambers, Brian, 228
change in attitude of the Irish people after Easter Rising executions, 14–5
Childers, Erskine, 10, 49, 59, 202
Christian Brothers, the, 25

Christie, Rev. Joseph, 256
Churchill, Winston, 59–60, 80, 89–90, 92, 99, 131, 131, 206–7, 216, 222, 224, 230
CID (Criminal Investigation Department), 65, 67, 72, 84, 116, 152
Cistercian College, Roscrea, 9
Civil War, the, 1, 3, 28, 53, 90, 96, 111, 113, 117, 123, 125, 127, 199–200, 202–3, 205–6, 256; capture of Baltinglass, Tullow and Newtownbarry, 122; capture of Cork by the National Army, 133–6, 138, 140–2, 145–6; counter-insurgency campaign against republicans, 174, 182–4, 189–90, 198–9; seaborne landings in Cork, 127–8 (*see also* ambush at Bealnabalath by republicans; anti-Treaty republican forces)
Clancy, Peadar, 35, 62
Classic (ship), 168–9
clearance of Ballyvourney area by National Army, 189–90
Clifford, Madge, 76, 122–3
coded letter from Dublin Castle, 71
Coffey, Diarmid, 204
Cohalan, Dr., Bishop, 145, 168, 189, 191
Cohn, Sidney, 236, 239, 241–2
Collins, Justin, 227, 245
Collins, Maurice, 158
Collins, Michael, 14, 36, 52, 62, 69, 76–8, 87, 92–3, 96, 99, 147, 191, 173–4, 227; ambush and death at Bealnablath, 159–60, 171–2, 198–9, 206, 210, 258; as Commander-in-Chief of the National Army, 124–5, 150, 189; conspiracy theories about his death, 171, 199, 260–7; establishment of Provisional Government and British withdrawal, 81–3, 88, 99**; frustration at de Valera's opposition, 153-4, 167; funeral of, 168–70; inspection tours, 144, 151; oversees intelligence, 33, 34, 35; and the recapture of Cork, 180, 182–3, 184; relationship with Dalton, 1, 41–2, 46–7, 49–50, 55, 58–9, 66, 241; at the Treaty negotiations, 57–8, 62
Collins-Powell, Mary, 129, 169, 185, 200
Collins Powell, Sean, 259
'Colonel Dickie', 230
Columbia Broadcasting Company, 238
commandeering of ferry boats, 130
commemorative Cavalry Corps dinner, 242
communication channels, 71, 139, 164, 166, 177
conflict in border regions and in Northern Ireland, 112–3
Conlon, Peadar, 134–5, 137, 141, 153, 155, 178, 185, 190, 196
Connell, William, 73
Connolly, James Brendan, 49
Conroy, James, Jr., 151, 185, 210
conscription, 15
consideration of writing a memoir, 244

Rooney, Andrew, 192
Rose, David, 309, 310, 319
Royal College of Science, 12, 100
Royal Dublin Golf Club, 20, 251
Royal Navy, the, 131, 136, 168
rules of loading an 18 pound artillery gun, 102
rumours about being approached to head the
    British Commandos, 222
rumours about Collins/Lady Lavery relationship, 61
Russell, Charles, 56, 85, 120, 138, 172, 175, 181,
    183, 191, 279
Ryan, Meda, 59, 60, 99, 154, 164, 236, 258
Rynne, Captain Michael, 114

safeguarding of roads and railways during the Civil
    War, 117–8
safety of Collins during the Treaty negotiations,
    55–8, 62
Saggers, Pte. Albert George, 47
Sally's Irish Rogue (film), 246
Salonika campaign, the, 21, 51, 261
Saurin, Frank, 215, 221
Scannell, Rev. Dr. Joseph, 168, 189
School of Musketry on Bull Island, 20
Scott, Paddy, 147
seaborne offensive to capture anti-Treaty
    strongholds in the south, 127–34, 226
Sean Treacy Memorial FUnd, the, 217
searching of civilians, 124
security threat of republicans in Cork and Kerry
    mountains, 128, 149, 176–7, 180
seizure of Blessington, 114
Seltzer, Walter, 248
Senate, the, 201
series of TV films based on Irish folklore, 237
Sévigné, Count, 71–2
Shake Hands With The Devil (film), 247–48, 252
shipping of the remains and burial of soldiers killed
    in action, 140–1
shooting of British officers on Bloody Sunday, 34–5
shooting at Dalton, 90
shootings of RIC officers, 75
Siege of Sidney Street, The (film), 252
signing of the Anglo-Irish Treaty, 226
Singing Flame, The (book), 192
Sinn Féin, 33
Slattery, Jim, 69, 123, 261, 296
Slievenamon (armoured car), 111, 152, 154–6, 159,
    162, 172, 199, 248, 258
Smith, John Joseph, 160–2, 165
smuggling of Thompson sub-machine guns, 49–50
Sniper, The (poem), 28
Snowden, Alec C., 248, 297
SOE (Special Operations Executive), 223
Soldiers Song, The (national anthem), 36
Somerville, Capt. Hugh, 136, 158
Somerville, Edith, 158

Southern Area Command officers, 195–6
southern Unionist community, the, 201
Special Branch, the, 217
Special Operations Executive, the, 101
speech at Woodenbridge by Redmond, 10–11
split in the Irish Volunteers, 10–11
split within the anti-Treaty IRA, 104
Squad, the, 34, 35, 43, 57, 75, 77, 87, 122, 151, 170,
    186, 291
St. Columba's National School, 216
Stack, Austin, 63, 122
Stand To: A Diary of the Trenches, 1915-1918
    (book), 29
Stapleton, Bill, 43, 45, 88, 120, 138, 243
state support for Ardmore film studios, 240, 251,
    253–4
statement by National Army on the use of artillery,
    110–11
status of Ireland during the second World War, 225
Stella Maris convent, Howth, 46, 256
Stuart, Francis, 171
Sturgis, Mark, 66, 68, 69, 74, 75
Sunday Independent, 257–8
supervision of British withdrawal, 79, 82, 94, 224
supply of arms and materiel to the Provisional
    Government, 89–90, 99, 100–1, 103–4, 105,
    107, 110–11, 125
suppression of pro-Treaty pamphlet by the IRA in
    Cork, 77–8
surprise of Royal Navy at Provisional Government
    seaborne operation, 131
suspicions of Dalton by the British, 47–8
Sweetnam, Mathew, 73

t-Óglach, An (publication), 37, 61, 95, 139
takeover of Dublin Castle, 80
talks to restore unity between pro and anti-Treaty
    elements of the IRA, 92–3
Tallon, Joseph, 2
Taubman, Harold, 21, 229–31, 255
Taubman, William, 255
Taylor, Don, 231, 232
tensions on film sets, 246–7
Terrible Beauty, A (film), 252
Third Battle of Gaza, the, 22
This Other Eden (film), 248–50, 252
Thompson sub-machine gun, the, 49, 52, 95, 134
Thornton, Frank, 76, 94, 209, 221
threats to Oireachtas members in reprisal for
    executions of republicans, 202–3
tightening of British security, 47
Times, The, 47, 76, 77, 141, 202
Tipperary arms seizure, the, 67
Tobin, Liam, 34, 36, 58, 104, 130, 132, 140, 146, 148,
    168–9, 179, 190, 203, 208–10, 215, 221; and the
    Army Mutiny, 208, 214, 221
Tobin, Nicholas, 190